Religion
& POLITICS on
the World Stage

Religion
& POLITICS on
the World Stage

An IR Approach

Lynda K. Barrow

LYNNE
RIENNER
PUBLISHERS

BOULDER
LONDON

Published in the United States of America in 2021 by
Lynne Rienner Publishers, Inc.
1800 30th Street, Suite 314, Boulder, Colorado 80301
www.rienner.com

and in the United Kingdom by
Lynne Rienner Publishers, Inc.
Gray's Inn House, 127 Clerkenwell Road, London EC1 5DB
www.eurospanbookstore.com/rienner

Library of Congress Cataloging-in-Publication Data
Names: Barrow, Lynda K., 1961– author.
Title: Religion & Politics on the World Stage : An IR Approach / Lynda K.
  Barrow.
Other titles: Religion and Politics on the World Stage
Description: Boulder, Colorado : Lynne Rienner Publishers, Inc., 2021. |
  Includes bibliographical references and index. | Summary: "Provides the
  information and tools needed to understand the myriad ways that religion
  matters in world politics"— Provided by publisher.
Identifiers: LCCN 2020031869 | ISBN 9781626379084 (hardcover) | ISBN
  9781626379107 (paperback)
Subjects: LCSH: Religion and politics. | Religion and international
  relations.
Classification: LCC BL65.P7 B385 2021 | DDC 327.1—dc23
LC record available at https://lccn.loc.gov/2020031869

British Cataloguing in Publication Data
A Cataloguing in Publication record for this book
is available from the British Library.

Printed and bound in the United States of America

∞ The paper used in this publication meets the requirements
   of the American National Standard for Permanence of
   Paper for Printed Library Materials Z39.48-1992.

5 4 3 2 1

For my parents,
with gratitude for their love and support

Contents

1

Setting the Stage

Religion and Politics on the World Stage is a book about the politics of religion; it is about the ways in which religion is shaping world politics and, to a lesser extent, about how world politics affects religion; and it is also about assumptions, theories, and the ways in which people perceive religion's role in the world. As a book about politics, it concerns collective choices and public policies—laws, treaties, and so on—that affect how people live together. How and by whom those decisions are made usually says something about those who have power. As a book about world politics, it is about actors, actions, institutions, interests, and norms that transcend state borders. As a book about religion and world politics, it is about systems of belief (understandings of the divine and claims about what is true and right) and, in light of those beliefs, how one is to live (what can or must be done—or not done) and the institutions that guide and govern individuals and communities.

The book's argument is straightforward: although often marginalized, religion matters in world politics. As recently as the 1990s, the study of world politics and the practice of statecraft paid little heed to religion's role—and both were impoverished because of it. Religion is influencing politics and power on the world stage and, in various times and settings, is a force to be reckoned with. Therefore, to comprehend the world around us, we need to understand how and why religion matters, to analyze it in a systematic way, and to have a framework in which to fit facts and events that we cannot anticipate today. By the end

1

of this book, readers should know a lot about religion and politics and know how to think about their interactions on the world stage.

Headlines, crises, and a diverse cast of characters—how can we make sense of religion's role on the world political stage? Does religion tend to be the "glue" that binds together societies and alliances or a wedge that drives people and states apart? When is a conflict really about religion? In August 2019, members of the worldwide multireligion organization Religions for Peace gathered to recommit themselves to preventing and transforming violent conflicts, while the United Nations commemorated those who have been victims of violence because of their religion or belief. The following year, the global pandemic (COVID-19) was implicated in inflaming religious tensions. In India, for instance, Hindu nationalists blamed Muslims for the virus. The hashtag #coronajihad began trending, and some members of the Muslim minority became victims of hate crimes. This puts yet another spin on religion, suggesting members of a particular religion can be on the receiving end of violence.

Religion can inspire the construction of breathtaking temples and reconstruction of foreign lands after natural and human-made disasters—and it can inspire the destruction of centuries-old statues, such as the 2001 Taliban bombing of the Bamyan Buddha statues in central Afghanistan. Today, the "hotter bits" of religion often involve one or both of the world's two largest religions, Christianity and Islam, which have fault lines within and between them as well as bridges across them. However, religion is also a hot issue in India, which has a large Hindu majority, and Myanmar (formerly Burma), which is majority Buddhist. These matters affect not only domestic politics but regional and global politics because India is a regional power and the world's largest democracy and, in both cases, what happens at home affects neighbors as well.

Clearly, religion plays diverse roles. How do these glues, wedges, and inspirations interact with politics on the world stage? To frame the answers to such questions, this book explores the trends, theories, assumptions, and actors behind the front-page news. Each chapter begins with two illustrations, discussing specific events that depict key aspects of the nexus between religion and world politics. They range from big, world-rocking events such as the Iranian Revolution to lesser-known events such as the rock musician Bono making Senator Jesse Helms cry.

These illustrations are entryways into the bigger picture, including global trends, such as the waxing of religion's role in politics, ongoing globalization, resurgent nationalism, the rise of populism and identity politics and, perhaps, the waning of liberal democracy.

Politics in the early twenty-first century cannot be understood without taking into account the religious explosion that is occurring. If religion is not taken into account, much that transpires in world politics is unintelligible. It would, for instance, be hard to explain the Iranian Revolution, theological justifications for and attacks on apartheid in South Africa, the events of 9/11, the Lord's Resistance Army in Uganda, the shifting politics of India, and the impact of the Islamic State without some understanding of the religious component. To get beyond the headlines and develop a nuanced understanding of world politics, it is essential to come to grips with how religion affects political leaders, states' foreign policies, and interactions among states and nonstate actors.

Aims

Information is not enough. Informed citizens need a useful and coherent framework for understanding how pieces of information and scraps of analysis fit together. This is the principle aim of *Religion and Politics on the World Stage*.

This book also has some secondary objectives, which go hand-in-hand with its three distinguishing features. First, it explains concepts and situations so as to be accessible to newcomers to the topics. The book is intended as an introductory text in an interdisciplinary area that will help prepare readers for active citizenship in a democratic society. The focus is on religion and world politics, but this requires bringing in elements of domestic politics too, such as the nature of a regime (democratic or authoritarian) and how and by whom public policy is made. The primary audience for this text is the one with which I am most familiar: undergraduate students. In fact, it emerged out of a course on religion and world politics that I have taught since the mid-1990s.

The chapters that follow provide the information necessary to understand and explain significant ways in which religion enters international politics (and vice versa), how this is changing, and why it matters; to fit new events, policies, and pronouncements into a larger framework; and to employ key analytical tools, especially the levels of analysis and major theoretical lenses. These are the central learning objectives.

The illustrations that begin each chapter provide a second distinguishing feature. These are slices of history or extended examples of the intersections of religion and politics, which provide thought-provoking and concrete illustrations of points developed in the chapter. One illustration, for instance, is about Pope John Paul II's impact on the Eastern Bloc and international communism, while another discusses Saddam Hussein's declaration of a holy war. An illustration in Chapter 9 introduces an imam and a pastor in northern Nigeria. The men confronted each other as leaders of rival militias, each believing he was fighting in defense of his faith. Then their relationship was transformed. They joined forces as peacemakers, pursuing a very different kind of faith-inspired work.

Finally, this text applies an international relations framework throughout. It frames the analysis by using the two sets of lenses that are more or less standard in international relations textbooks. One is seeing world politics through the lens of major theoretical perspectives, focusing on realism, liberalism, and constructivism. Theories are important to political scientists' efforts to understand, explain, and predict political phenomena. They are generalizations about how the world works with a set of key factors and central actors and, in the social sciences, assumptions about human nature (how we act when left to our own devices). The levels of analysis are the other set of lenses. This book employs three levels of analysis: individual, state, and systemic (international or global). "Snapping in" a lens "enables us to interpret events or 'facts'" from different vantage points.[1] Zooming in with a macro lens brings small details into focus, while zooming out and taking a panoramic shot provides a very different picture; the small details do not disappear when using a wide-angle lens, but they are no longer in focus. We see different dimensions of religion and world politics, depending on the lens through which we view it. Our perception of reality is altered. Often, we only get a partial or distorted view when we view the world through one and only one lens. Chapter 3 gets at the kinds of distortions and preconceptions that can result from seeing the world through a secularist-tinted lens. Of course, religious-tinted lenses bring their own sets of distortions and predispositions. Purposefully employing analytical lenses also helps us to become more aware of the assumptions and perhaps biases that we bring to our studies.

Each chapter ends with a framework for analysis that demonstrates how particular events can be framed. The bare bones of this framework are as follows:

1. Theoretical Perspectives
   - Realism
   - Liberalism
   - Constructivism
2. Levels of Analysis
   - International/Systemic
   - Domestic/State
   - Individual

Overview

Chapters 2 through 9 follow the same basic structure. As mentioned above, each opens with a description of example events, followed by an explanation of the events' significance, and each closes by placing the material within an analytical framework.

Chapters 2 and 3 provide the historical and theoretical backdrop that informs the rest of the book. They present tools of analysis that facilitate a deeper understanding of the sometimes dramatic and often perplexing events in which religion plays a role. Chapter 2 explains why it is important to understand religion's role in world politics (i.e., it answers the "So what?" question) and why this dimension is so often ignored. It includes an explanation for religion's marginalization in key international relations theories.

The third chapter develops the frameworks of analysis that will be employed throughout the balance of the book. It further builds the historical context, explains the origins and meanings of "secularization," and discusses the need to rethink the legacies of the seventeenth-century European Peace of Westphalia and the assumptions of secularization. It explains the usefulness of the levels of analysis as an analytical tool. It sets out the three major theoretical perspectives employed in the study of world politics. Built into each of the book's chapters, these frameworks serve as a sort of "spine" for the book.

Chapters 4, 5, and 6 explore, in turn, each of the three basic levels of analysis. In other words, they analyze interactions between religion and politics on the systemic, state, and individual levels of analysis.

Chapter 4 digs into the systemic, or global, level of analysis, including transnational religious actors, the relationship between globalization and religion, and religion's impact on foreign policy decisionmaking and national security matters. Religious fundamentalism as well as changing norms and advancing technology all figure into this level of analysis.

Chapter 5 focuses on the state level of analysis, describing and explaining what goes on within states that may affect states' foreign policies and international relations. Often, what happens in one state does not stay there. Events in one country spill into adjacent countries and perhaps beyond. For instance, although the Lord's Resistance Army is based in Uganda, its impacts go well beyond Uganda, affecting three of its neighbors in central Africa: the Central African Republic, the Democratic Republic of Congo, and South Sudan. A state outside of this region, the United States, was also drawn into the Ugandan conflict. In Asia, the government of Myanmar has persecuted Rohingya Muslims, killing thousands and destroying hundreds of villages. This has prompted hundreds of thousands of Rohingya to flee to neighboring Bangladesh. Ideas can spill over, too. During the Arab Spring that began in late 2010, the idea that aging autocrats could lose their jobs began in Tunisia, then spread to Libya, Egypt, Yemen, and elsewhere. The state level is also important in the sense that, despite the well-entrenched international norms of state sovereignty and nonintervention (explained in Chapter 3), states often care about what goes on in other states and seek to affect it. An example here is the US government's criticisms of human rights abuses in China. In short, in the context of the broad trends of globalization and the global resurgence of religion, domestic religious ideas and issues can cross countries' borders, destabilize neighboring states, and become internationalized.

Chapter 6 zeroes in on the individual level of analysis. It includes religion's influence on perceptions, images, worldviews, and actions as well as saints, sinners, and secularists whose actions have affected international relations. Much of the focus here is on exemplars—religiously motivated individuals who, for better or worse, have had an impact on states' foreign policies and, in turn, world politics.

Chapters 7, 8, and 9 pick up important topics. Chapter 7 investigates the ways in which religion is bound up with identity and identity politics, ideologies (especially nationalism), perceptions, grievances, myths, and political action. Identity can link believers to transnational religious communities. A sense of a shared political identity has driven many a conflict in the 2000s. Identity politics contributed to the bloody breakup of Yugoslavia in the 1990s. Pope John Paul II's identity, especially his "Polishness," mattered to Poles living under a communist authoritarian regime in the 1980s.

In 1989, the year the Berlin Wall came down, Francis Fukuyama proclaimed the triumph of Western liberal democracy over two competing ideologies, fascism and communism. Economic and ideological concerns were the focus of twentieth-century politics. Now, he argues, politics pivots on matters of identity, and he opposes this turn to identity politics as contributing to a "crisis of democracy" and challenging liberalism.[2] Group identities, including national identities, are often rooted in ethnicity, language, heritage, attachment to a piece of territory, or religion (or a mix of these). Religion can be an identity marker and it can get wrapped up with ideologies, such as nationalism. Nationalism, the ideology of the nation-state, has been a potent ideology for more than two centuries. We see evidence of Buddhist nationalism in Myanmar and Hindu nationalism in India, each promoting the idea that the majority religion is central to national identity.

The final chapters look at religion's role in conflicts and violence, and then at its role in cooperation and conflict resolution. Conflict and cooperation are central features of international relations, with some contending they are at the very heart of events on the world stage. Hence, these matters warrant special attention. Chapter 8 is about fault lines, conflicts, and violence. The world's two largest religions, Christianity and Islam, are proselytizing and growing and, in some parts of the world, they are colliding. Sometimes, though, religion's contribution to conflict is overdrawn. In addition, the term "holy war" is used rather promiscuously. A tricky but essential task is determining when a conflict is truly a religious conflict—a conflict *about* religion, rather than one that simply *involves* religion. It is one thing to recognize that the parties to a conflict have different religious affiliations, but another thing to say that they are fighting over religion. Making this distinction is all the more important in the early twenty-first century, when many conflicts are wrapped up with matters of identity, including ethnic and religious identities.

Conflict can mean a clash of words, interests, or ideologies, for instance, rather than a clash of armies. It might also mean cyberwarfare, attacks using the internet and other technologies against an adversary's computer systems. When it comes to large-scale political violence, change is afoot. Warfare involving two or more states is not as common as it once was. Armed conflict between or among the world's great powers is even less common. Most armed conflicts are now some variety of war within a state, such as the ongoing conflicts in Afghanistan, Israel-Palestine, Libya, and Syria. Each of these four conflicts has drawn in outside states, internationalizing these conflicts.

In Chapter 9, we see that, while some dismiss religion as irrelevant to world politics in our day, others see religion as inherently divisive and, thus, both a source of conflict and an obstacle to peace and cooperation. Both assumptions need some rethinking. Religion has not gone the way of the passenger pigeon or the saber-toothed tiger, either through the process of modernization or through secularist state policies. On the contrary, it continues to push its nose—and sometimes far more—under the tent of world politics.

As for the second assumption, religion is no more one-dimensional than the texts and histories that inform it and the people who practice it. Religions are not monolithic, nor do their adherents speak with one voice; rather, they contain multiple voices and can be marshaled to support or oppose the nation-state, for instance. Together, Chapters 8 and 9 show that the two-faced nature of religion means it can be a source of conflict or conflict resolution. Religious leaders may call for holy war or for pacifism. Religious organizations can stir up hate and enmity. Conversely, they can work together in transnational organizations in a spirit of cooperation, trying to solve the world's pressing problems, such as poverty and the scourge of war. Chapter 9 focuses on how religion can contribute to peacemaking, reconciliation, and cooperation.

The final chapter of the book steps back to look at the big picture of world politics in this "post" world—post–Soviet Union, post–Cold War, post-9/11 and, as Chapters 2 and 3 suggest, post-secular—to draw conclusions and to spell out some implications for the future. It revisits the idea that, to use Adrian Wooldridge's phrase, "God Is Back."[3] God's "return" to the public and political arena flies in the face of long-held assumptions and theories about the impacts of modernization.

Moreover, religion has come back into a world undergoing some profound changes. States remain the central actors, but are being joined on the world stage by a growing number of nonstate actors, public and private, for-profit and nonprofit, religious and secular. This stage is growing ever more crowded. When it was founded in 1945, the United Nations had fifty-one member states. In 2011, with the addition of the world's newest state, South Sudan, UN membership grew to 193. This number will likely climb given the many peoples, for example the Catalans (in Spain) and the Kurds (in Iran, Iraq, Syria, and Turkey), pushing for independence. Nonstate actors that operate across state borders are likewise growing in numbers. This cast includes intergovernmental organizations (IGOs), nongovernmental organizations (NGOs), multinational corporations (MNCs), terrorist organizations, religious actors, human trafficking rings, drug cartels, and ethnic diasporas. They can wield considerable power and influence. Power is thus shifting slowly away from states, while it is also shifting from the West (especially Western Europe and North America) towards the East (especially China and India).

Chapter 10 also returns to the importance of frameworks for analysis. It explains how religion is woven into the perennial tensions in world politics: conflict and cooperation (or war and peace), centralization and fragmentation (or integration and disintegration), and continuity and change (or "trend and transformation"[4]). We might add the coming and going of democracy along with concerns about the waxing and waning of the liberal world order.

The point of this text is not to suggest that politics on the world stage now revolves around the axis of religion. Far from it. Global climate change, the global economy, and global pandemics are not about religion. However, deciding who "we" are, who is in charge, what to do, whose ideas and values will prevail, whose rights are protected, and whether states cooperate or clash are areas in which religion and politics intersect. The point of this text, then, is to explain how and why ignoring the religious element leads to incomplete or even inaccurate understandings of the world in which we live.

Notes

1. Cohen, *Understanding Environmental Policy*, 13.
2. Fukuyama, "Against Identity Politics: The New Tribalism and the Crisis of Democracy," 91.
3. Wooldridge, "God Is Back," 137–141.
4. Kegley and Blanton, *World Politics*.

2

Religion and World Politics: Why It Matters

Illustration 1: The Iranian Revolution

On December 23, 1978, the Shia Muslim cleric Ayatollah Ruhollah Khomeini called on the world's "freedom-loving Christians" to pray for the deliverance of Iranians living under a "tyrant king" and to advise leaders of powerful countries to end their support of Shah Reza Pahlavi of Iran. Three weeks later, the seventy-eight-year-old religious leader congratulated the Iranian people for having forced the shah to flee the country after a wave of popular demonstrations. In February, Khomeini returned to Iran after fourteen years in exile, receiving a hero's welcome, calling for the creation of a government based on the Quran, and ultimately seizing power. He declared April 1 the "first day of God's government."

During 1978 and 1979, Iran experienced a revolution that was not supposed to happen. The Iranian Revolution wedded religion and politics. It was political in the sense that many Iranians were dissatisfied with the Pahlavi dynasty's domestic policies and foreign policies. Very rapid modernization, including a reduced role for Islamic law and a cozy relationship with the United States, had bred discontent. The shah's politics had managed to antagonize most sectors of society.

It was religion, however, that was the prime mover in the overthrow of the political order. The iconic figure of Ayatollah Khomeini, the center and symbol of the revolt against the shah and *Time* magazine's 1979 "Man of the Year," guided an Islamic revolutionary movement. Khomeini proposed a new kind of state, one founded on Islamic principles and led by the clergy. Islam served as a symbol of resistance against the autocratic shah and his modernizing, Westernizing, and secularizing projects. Khomeini contended that the shah's projects did not push the country in the direction of progress, but toward decadence.[1] In this overwhelmingly Muslim country, many of the revolution's motivations and goals were religious in form and inspiration, Islamic values figured prominently in the revolution's program, and Islam offered a language for critiquing the shah's regime and expressing discontent. Islam brought together diverse sectors of society, including shopkeepers and artisans, the disaffected urban poor, students, professionals, and a grassroots network of clergy who despised Western cultural values. Iran's religious institutions and leaders played a central role, with the country's tens of thousands of mosques and religious leaders providing the most organized social structure.

In short, Iranians rose up against the regime for a variety of reasons—political, economic, cultural, and religious. Organizationally, however, it was Shia Islam that enabled protesters, both secular and devout, to bring down the shah's regime.[2] Religion became a powerful political force. Islam, Islamic ideology, and clergy, while not *sufficient* to overthrow's the shah's regime, were absolutely *necessary* for the revolution to succeed.

For his part, Shah Reza Pahlavi scornfully dismissed the "turban-headed" clerics, supposing that their influence would fade as modernization progressed.[3] Instead, his power and influence came to an abrupt end.

Significance

The shah was overthrown by a theocrat, and the Iranian Revolution brought about a new kind of regime, the world's first "Islamic republic," and introduced political Islam as a modern ideology. Iran remains the only Islamic state established through a popular revolution. This Islamic republic is heavy on Islam and light on republic (or representative democracy). Under an Islamic constitution, religious law largely became civil law. Muslim clerics and Islam play a leading role in shaping public policy, including foreign policy.[4] Although the Iranian Revolution did overthrow the "old order," it was not anticlerical, Marxist, or progressive, nor did it promise to improve people's material well-being, in contrast to the French and Russian revolutions. Instead, in large part it was to restore what had been lost, most notably elements of Islam. Not only is the Iranian regime's identity and legitimacy rooted in a variation of Shia Islam, but religious principles and leaders trump democratic principles and democratically elected leaders, and the state is an instrument of the official religion-based ideology.[5] In addition, Iran remains committed to Ayatollah Khomeini's ideological vision and the foreign policy that sustains it.[6]

Ayatollah Khomeini declared his intent to export this Islamic revolution and, indeed, it has had significant implications beyond its borders. The Iranian government has used religion to rally other Muslims to its side in conflicts. While being distinctly Iranian and Shia, the Islamic revolution's triumph is credited with inspiring Islamist movements and political parties, causing secularists to "tremble,"[7] and raising fears of Islamism (also called *political Islam* and *Islamic fundamentalism*). Iran's revolution demonstrated Islam's mobilizing potential and inspired radical Islamists in various corners of the globe.

The Iranian Revolution also challenged the supremacy of Western-style secular politics and secular ideologies as well as the notion that religion is hostile to social change or altogether irrelevant. This Islamic revolution was not supposed to happen because Iran was a developing, modernizing, and Westernizing country. The shah was "a poster boy for the secularization thesis."[8] His powerful—and increasingly dictatorial and unpopular—regime tolerated Shia Islam so long as it stayed within the home and mosque.[9] However, the very speed and nature of Iranian modernization and Westernization sparked a religious backlash. Mohammad Reza Pahlavi had imposed a form of development that diminished the clergy's power and included the "unveiling" of women. In response, Ayatollah Khomeini and others spoke of "Westoxification"—the West was "toxic," something that "sickened" Iran, or the cause of "inebriation" due to excessive preoccupation with all things Western—and proposed Islamic identity as a response to rapid Westernization.[10]

This revolution has particular relevance for the United States for a number of reasons. First, US foreign policy makers, diplomats, and intelligence services had not thought that religion mattered in world politics. Suffering from a type of "political blindness," analysts had underestimated the political significance of religious identities, institutions, and leadership.[11] Analysts who might have warned the government of the imminent overthrow of the US-backed Pahlavi dynasty were dismissed. The US government was caught off guard by the swift fall of the shah, whom it had praised as a progressive modernizer. Second, the revolution—animated by slogans of "Death to America! Death to Israel!"—overthrew a regime that the US government had supported as a source of stability and anti-communism in the region. The virulently anti-American regime that replaced it has been a source of turmoil and has had difficult relations with the US government and Israel, a close US ally. Third, following the revolution, Islamic student militants held a group of US citizens hostage for 444 days. The hostage crisis was a nightmare for President Carter's administration and marked the start of decades of difficult bilateral relations.

With Iran the dominant Shia power in the Middle East, its revolution has been important for Shia Muslims and Shia-Sunni relations elsewhere. While the vast majority of Muslims are Sunni, Shia Muslims predominate in Iran and neighboring Iraq, where postrevolution Iran has stirred up problems. When Saddam Hussein served as Iraq's secular head of state (1979–2003), Iranian Shia made a "transnational religious appeal" to Iraqi Shia to rise up against the Sunni autocrat and his Baathist party.[12] Feeling threatened by the new Iranian regime, Saddam Hussein invaded Iran. The bloody eight-year war ended in a stalemate. After the United States toppled Hussein's regime and ended Baathist rule in 2003, Iran began aiding Shia militia groups within the country.

The Iranian Revolution was, in many ways, a turning point. Khomeini's vision for the Iranian state included serving as a model for the "Muslim world" and spanning the Sunni-Shia divide. However, Saudi Arabia, the dominant Sunni power in the Middle East, has a competing vision. The two countries vie for primacy in the region. Much as the former Soviet Union sought to export its communist revolution and the United States has sought to entrench a liberal democratic world order, Iran and Saudi Arabia have both endeavored to export their own brands of Islam. Saudi Arabia has funded a wave of Arabization and a reformist type of Sunni Islam called Wahhabism or Salafism, which is increasing religious and political divisions in Asia.[13] Iran, meanwhile, has supported a network of Shia activism; sponsored Hezbollah in Lebanon and Hamas in Palestine, among others; and inspired Shia minorities in some Gulf states.

Finally, the Iranian Revolution was also a turning point because it was at this time that, as Olivier Roy states, "faith made a sudden breakthrough into contemporary global politics."[14] Religious actors began receiving more attention, not just as entities able to affect states' domestic politics, but also able to shape foreign policies and relations among states across the global stage.

Illustration 2: The Arab Spring

The series of demonstrations known collectively as the Arab Spring commenced in the small North African country of Tunisia in the last days of 2010. The precipitating event was an action by a twenty-six-year-old fruit and vegetable vendor, Mohamed Bouazizi. Bouazizi lived in Sidi Bouzid, a small city in Tunisia where many college-educated men could not find jobs. (Bouazizi did not have a university degree.) He sold produce from a street-side cart, but was accused of not having the required permit. Police and market inspectors hassled him, perhaps seeking a bribe. They confiscated some of his wares—pears, bananas, and so on, as well as his electronic scale—and accused him of failing to pay a fine. According to Bouazizi's family members, a policewoman slapped him. Bouazizi went to the headquarters of the provincial government to complain and to ask for the return of his property, but officials did not listen. Apparently, his frustration with Tunisian politics reached a breaking point. On December 17, 2010, standing outside the governor's office, he drenched himself with gasoline and self-immolated, shouting, "How do you expect me to make a living?" This dramatic act severely injured him.

It also generated spontaneous street demonstrations and rioting. Video clips of early protests spread across the internet and social media, and more protests spread as well. Tunisians protested about a host of political issues and injustices, such as corruption and oppression, and economic issues, including high unemployment and rising prices. Confrontations between protesters and government forces turned violent. Many died. Bouazizi himself died, becoming a hero or political martyr of the democratic revolution, though many who knew him described him as an apolitical family man.[15] Just ten days after Bouazizi died, President Ben Ali fled Tunisia, bringing his twenty-three-year reign to a swift conclusion.

Time magazine named "The Protester" as the 2011 "Person of the Year," as Tunisia-inspired uprisings spread across the diverse countries of the Arab world. As in Tunisia, Egyptians revolted against dictatorship, and Hosni Mubarak's decades-long autocratic regime fell quickly. Similarly, rulers were brought down and regimes changed in Libya and Yemen. Major and minor protests spread throughout much of North Africa and the Middle East, with a long and bloody civil war in Syria.

Significance

Two points are especially noteworthy: the role of religion and the attention paid to that role. The Arab Spring uprisings were *not* "Islamic revolutions." It was an Arab, not an Islamic, spring. Protesters had secular grievances and secular agendas; they sought to end harsh dictatorships, rampant corruption, and intolerable socioeconomic conditions. They sought democracy, not theocracy. They did, however, overthrow Arab regimes that had used the "specter of Islamic radicalism" as a rationale for their harsh policies and, ironically, contributed to the political ascendancy of Islamists in various states.[16] In Tunisia, for instance, the Islamist Ennahda party won a majority of seats in the parliament in late 2011, and one of the most controversial issues in drafting a new constitution was the role of Islam in the state.[17] Similarly, in Egypt, the leader of the Muslim Brotherhood, an anti-Western Islamist movement, won the presidential election in 2012, but the following year President Mohamed Morsi was removed by force.

With regard to the second point, when the Arab Spring began some three decades after the Iranian Revolution, religious actors played an important but not pivotal role in the upheaval and removal of autocratic regimes, and it, too, came as a surprise. In the Arab Spring, however, analysts scrutinized Islamist elements from the outset. Although Iran's supreme leader, Ayatollah Ali Khamenei (Khomeini's successor), said the Arab uprisings were inspired by Iran's Revolution, there is little to support that notion.

What had happened during the intervening three decades? Why had so many dismissed religion as a sideshow at the time of the Iranian Revolution, but paid such close attention to it during Tunisia's "Jasmine Revolution"? Had religion (re)claimed a central place in world affairs—or simply in our understanding of it?

The simple answer to the last question—and the reason why it is increasingly important to come to grips with the interrelationships between religion and world politics—is *both*. If it was not already abundantly clear before, the rise, spread, and violence of the Islamic State has demonstrated that religion can be a powerful force in international relations. At the time of the Iranian Revolution, religion was, as the title of a groundbreaking book suggests, the *Missing Dimension of Statecraft*. Virtually all Western intellectuals bought into secularization theory and, much like Iran's shah, assumed that religion was just a dying ember. Most political scientists underestimated religion's role in modern politics.[18] Since religion was not viewed as a vital (let alone world-shaping) force, it did not figure into policy calculations. Now it is clear that it should.

Religion was (and sometimes still is) dismissed as "rhetorical window dressing"[19] or "mere 'sociology,'"[20] neglected or discounted by international relations (IR) scholars, and ignored by those engaged in world politics—states' policymakers, intergovernmental organizations, nongovernmental organizations, and concerned citizens. Such dismissals impoverished understandings of the dynamics of world politics and religion. They downgraded it to the realm of "low politics," reserving serious attention for "high politics" issues at the core of states' national interests, especially matters of war and peace. However, it is evident today that religion is a source of shared identity, offers an alternative to secular ideologies, has prophetic potential that renders it "a political threat to any political order,"[21] "plays a major role in political controversies around the world,"[22] and, by virtue of its potential to foment political instability or foster peace, is an element of national and international security. Events—from the Iranian Revolution to the Syrian civil war—have demonstrated the importance of paying more attention to and better understanding religion's role on the world stage. Given religion's global resurgence, it is apt to become more important in the days and years to come.

The Global Resurgence of Religion

The world has witnessed a global resurgence of religion and, with it, a greater role of the faith factor in the affairs of state. As recently as 1999, *The Economist* magazine published a mock obituary of God, and in 2002 sociologist Steve Bruce's book asserted that "God is dead," echoing a statement Friedrich Nietzsche (1844–1900) had made more than a century before. More recent publications have, however, suggested that rumors of God's death were premature. One book's title proclaims, "God Is Back": God is returning from exile, and religion is coming in from the margins.[23] An article in *Foreign Policy* agrees that God has made a "comeback," but goes a step further by asserting that "God is winning": religion is advancing to the political sphere, where people are choosing the sacred over the secular and "prophetic politics" is becoming increasingly important to global politics.[24] A third publication asserts that the twenty-first century is "God's century": God's partisans are on the world stage, gaining political capacity and setting the political agenda, and they are here to stay.[25]

As this God talk suggests, religion is exploding around the world. Asia, especially East and Southeast Asia, is experiencing an upsurge of religion.[26] Religion is spreading in communist and postcommunist countries such as China and Russia and experiencing a revival or deepening in once-stridently secular countries like Turkey. Religion is growing in salience and persuasiveness. It is gaining political power. In some states, religious actors are challenging secular leaders and politics to determine whose values are inscribed into public policy. Religious belief is providing an alternative to the secular ideologies that prevailed throughout the Cold War. All of this has come as a great surprise—at least to the Western world. And this surprising turn of events is posing challenges to interpretations of the modern world and the principles and rules that guide the Western-based liberal world order.

Religion's resurgence is global in a geographic sense and in the sense that it is occurring in rich as well as poor countries, under democratic and authoritarian regimes, and in countries with different religious traditions. It is influencing people and politics at various levels of analysis. This is not an isolated phenomenon.

This phenomenon is especially evident in two of the world's three great monotheistic and Abrahamic faiths, Islam and Christianity. Other faiths are also part of the larger resurgence of religion, but these two missionary religions warrant more attention for one simple reason: salience. These two, especially, are of "immense importance, informing many domestic and international political issues."[27] Their large and growing numbers of followers and the competition between them lend these two religions a political significance and salience around the world that is unmatched by the other three big, global religions: Judaism, Buddhism, and Hinduism.

First, size: Christianity and Islam are the world's two largest and most universal religions, found in almost every country of the world. Christianity is the single largest faith tradition, encompassing Roman Catholics, Orthodox Christians, Protestants, and Mormons. The largest populations of Christians are located in Europe, the Americas, Africa, and parts of Asia. Islam is the second largest, with some 1.6 billion adherents in the world and large Muslim communities in Africa, Asia, and southeastern Europe. Islam is the dominant religion in about one-quarter of all states, while about half of the world's states have a Christian majority. More than half of the world's population identifies with either Christianity or Islam.

Second, growth: "Explosion" and "resurgence" are the terms most often used to describe the changes afoot since the late 1960s and early 1970s. Muslims and Christians account for much of this resurgence, bolstered by conversions and population trends.[28]

Among Christians, "the most dramatic religious explosion in the world today is the spread of Pentecostalism and evangelical Protestantism."[29] They have been "exploding" in some once solidly Catholic countries in Latin America and spreading in Africa and across the Pacific Rim.[30]

Islam is likewise reviving and spreading around the world. It is resurgent in the Arab world, Southeast Asia, and Central Asia. In sub-Saharan Africa, conversions to Islam are rising[31] (and Christianity is growing apace). Islam is also spreading into the once-mighty strongholds of Christendom, places like England, France, Germany, and Holland.[32] The Pew Research Center has forecast that, in the coming decades, the world's Muslim population will grow twice as fast as the population as a whole and will become the religion with the greatest number of believers.[33] As Islam has surged within and without its heartlands, it has "gained political clout around the world."[34]

Sociologist Peter Berger notes two exceptions to the global trend of religion's resurgence: Western Europe and a particular international subculture.[35] In Western Europe, with the decline of the church-going population, religion has lost most of its former political associations.[36] It has been driven toward "the margins of political and social life."[37] In that region, there is empirical support for secularization theory, though growing Muslim populations may undercut that theory.

The second exception to the global trend is the small but influential international subculture that is imbued with progressive, Enlightenment views. This international intellectual class consists of a secular elite, especially in the West or among people who have received a Western-style education.[38] This group is small, influential, and an exception to the overall trend. Their ideas, ideologies, identities, and outlooks take religion as a more or less irrational vestige of the past.

These exceptions are waning in importance with two shifts under way. One is the rise of the Global South, especially the two Asian giants of China and India. Secular modernity has failed in the developing countries of the Global South. The other is that the masses have become more politically relevant and less willing to follow the lead of the elite.[39]

Marginalizing Religion: Privatizing and Depoliticizing

Religion can be marginalized—and missed or dismissed—in a variety of ways. It can be relegated to the purely private sphere, subjected to state projects of secularization, discounted by policymakers and Western elites, and ignored by the theoretical perspectives applied in the study of world politics.

A chief way to marginalize religion is to narrow its scope of action by relegating it to the private sphere, the realm of hearth and home, as opposed to the public sphere, where politics, the state, and the economy are located. In the two-spheres model (see Figure 2.1), the religious sphere has a set of actors, values, interests, institutions, and items on its agenda that are distinct from those in the public or political sphere. This model leans toward complete separation of these areas.

Religion occupies a distinct, state-free sphere; the state likewise occupies a distinct, religion-free sphere. Affairs of religion and state are tightly interwoven; there is no differentiation between religious and political authority.

Religious privatization means that religious organizations—churches, mosques, synagogues—do not play a role in public life and, in some cases, do not even have the right to do so. They disappear from the public arena. Public space is where commerce and governance take place. It encompasses the state apparatus: houses of parliament, offices that administer and deliver public services, and so on. In privatized religion, faith involves deeply personal matters of propriety, obedience, or ritual observance, matters simply between believers and their God. In effect, then, religious *privatization* means religious *depoliticization*, since it removes religion as a political force.

States often seek to privatize religion precisely because private religion is typically apolitical, merely a matter of personal conscience. Privatized religion is not in a position to engage in a power struggle with state authorities. It does not meddle in politics by "telling society how

Figure 2.1 Two-Spheres Model

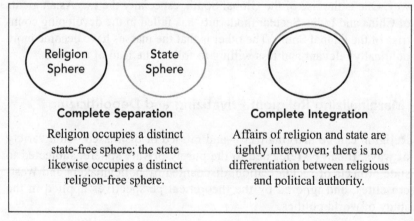

Complete Separation	Complete Integration
Religion occupies a distinct state-free sphere; the state likewise occupies a distinct religion-free sphere.	Affairs of religion and state are tightly interwoven; there is no differentiation between religious and political authority.

it ought to behave."[40] It does not serve as a vehicle for mobilizing protests against injustices. Presumably, privatized religion will neither legitimize nor delegitimize political authority, nor will it challenge the government by being a competing source of public authority.

States that aspire to total control (i.e., totalitarian states) push religious privatization as part of broader efforts to crush all competitors to the state's ideology and institutions. This explains, at least in part, why Nazi totalitarians tried to eradicate one religion, Judaism, and to subordinate others to the state.[41] In a similar vein, the Soviet Union mounted aggressive efforts to rid the state of all public manifestations of religion. Where the state could not eliminate religion, it controlled religion. States in the former Soviet Union and its Eastern European satellites were unable to squelch religion entirely, but they did manage to keep religious organizations out of matters of public concern and to make religious belief a narrowly private concern. During the Cold War, Albania took measures to marginalize religion to an extreme. Communist leader Enver Hoxha, embracing an ideology that rejected religion and facing divisions among Muslims, Orthodox Christians, and Roman Catholics, responded by banning all religions.[42] He declared Albania the first atheist country in the world.[43] Under Hoxha's rule, religion existed only as a private concern.[44]

In the case of liberal democracies, the argument is often made that it is necessary to cordon off and privatize religion to protect the diversity of religious faiths and religious minorities' freedom to worship—or even to protect democracy itself. Creating a religiously neutral public sphere enables liberal democratic polities "to reconcile individual liberty and religious diversity"[45] and to promote tolerance. Some liberal democrats argue that religion is an obstacle to freedom, associating religious influence with the kind of absolutism once prevalent in Europe, or that politicized religion fosters intolerance or even war. The reasoning is that, if religious interests are allowed to shape policies, the tendency will be to "restrict choice in the matter of religion."[46] Some fear that, if religious parties gain office through democratic elections, it will be "one person, one vote," one time only; in other words, they will use democratic processes to get power, but once they have accomplished this, they will subvert these very processes. Further, it is not clear that democracy can accommodate actors who enter the public sphere with uncompromising positions.[47] "Compromise, the mutual accommodation of conflicting claims, is difficult when disputants are the standard-bearers of rival faiths."[48] The logic is that believers do not negotiate matters of religious faith; thus, to forge the compromises that are part and parcel of the democratic process, the public sphere must be "protected" from religion.

Whether religion is marginalized by democrats or authoritarians, the impact on states' foreign policies is roughly the same. Religious ideas, norms, and values will not be as significant as they once were. They will have little influence on foreign policy. But states' foreign policies are not the only factor in world politics; we are living in an age of globalization, advanced telecommunications, and the proliferation of actors on the world stage. Nonstate actors are growing in number and influence. Among these actors, transnational religious associations—the Muslim Brotherhood and World Hindu Council, for instance—are helping to bring religion in from the wings of the world stage.

Coming to Terms

Before digging any deeper, we need a clearer idea of what religion and politics are, respectively. We begin with politics. Generally speaking, politics involves making decisions and choices for a group of people. Two well-known definitions of "politics" come from Harold Lasswell and David Easton. Lasswell said politics is the processes, institutions, and so on, that determine "who gets what, when, and how." This definition is useful in that it suggests that politics concerns the distribution of society's resources. Easton defined politics as the "authoritative allocation of values for society." This definition highlights the question of whose values will prevail in a political community. Making choices for a group, determining who gets what, and having one's values written into public policy—all require power. Power, then, is integral to what politics is all about.

This text focuses on world politics, which reaches beyond states' borders. It includes a variety of actions by state and nonstate actors, including religious actors. It involves conflictual and cooperative interactions, continuities (e.g., anarchy) and changes (e.g., the rising salience of identity politics).

Religion is harder to define. Most definitions include a number of elements. One is a theology, doctrine, or system of beliefs. These beliefs include the belief in God, gods, or some supernatural being and humans' relationship to that being. Theology usually includes truth claims. Second is an ethical code, code of conduct, or rules of what can, should, or should not be done. This is to shape believers' practices and behaviors. Third is the existence of a community or religious group. Steve Bruce sums up these elements as "beliefs, actions and institutions."[49] But there is more to religion. In addition to the universal and transcendent questions associated with belief (What should I believe? What is right and true?) and actions (How should I live?), religion addresses meaning ("Why are we here? What is the purpose of life?"[50]).

In Theory

Explanations for the historic lack of interest in the nexus of religion and world politics can be found in theories that posit a future in which religion is no more than a secondary phenomenon or a by-product. As simplifying devices or conceptual constructs, theories are grounded in patterns among phenomena and make the world around us more intelligible. The purpose of theories is to help us understand, explain, and even predict events in the world. Marxism, modernization theory, and other theories envision a future in which religion becomes mere flotsam in the wake of progress and secularization. Among international relations theories, realism and liberalism have rich intellectual heritages and, at least in Western countries, are the two most influential, though constructivism is increasingly important. Realism and liberalism, like Marxism, "rarely addressed religion at all."[51] Marxism and modernization theory are discussed below, focusing on their conceptions of religion, while IR theories are explained in the next chapter.

Marxism

Marxism or "scientific socialism" analyzes historical processes and socioeconomic change. Writing in the mid-nineteenth century, Karl Marx contended that economics (or people's material conditions) shape politics and that class conflict is the driver of history. He viewed all aspects of capitalist society, including religion, in the context of class conflict. Capitalism, he said, pit urban wage laborers (the proletariat) against industrialists or capitalists (the bourgeoisie).

As an atheist, Marx said little about religion beyond describing it as the "opiate of the masses." Opium creates illusions and serves as a palliative. The biggest illusion religion creates, according to Marx, is the illusion of God. As an opiate, religion also creates illusory happiness among oppressed workers, keeping them from seeing the world as it actually is. Such illusions have the pernicious effect of legitimizing an unjust social, economic, and political order. Religion serves as a palliative or healing salve by appealing to the oppressed masses and providing them with an alternative to despair—or simply a narcotic that intoxicates them. Workers could be consoled by believing that, while things might be tough in this world, their reward would come in the hereafter.

In Marxist theory, religion serves material interests. It is part of what Marx called the "superstructure"; as with other parts of the superstructure, such as politics and law, religion acts as a conservative force that inhibits change and helps to perpetuate a system of class domination. It is one of the ways for the ruling class to dupe urban workers into accepting their lot in life—on the bottom rung of the economic ladder. According to this materialist conception of the world, after the proletariat overthrow the bourgeois capitalist system, this "opiate" would disappear with the oppressive state and its mechanisms of social control, since illusions and palliatives would no longer be needed. Marx offered an alternative to illusory visions of religious paradise: communism would create paradise on earth, a workers' paradise.[52]

In practice, Marxist secular states typically tried to stamp out religion and to *impose* secularization, though Chinese leaders thought religion would die a natural death. Having fought two literal Opium Wars in the mid-nineteenth century, the Chinese were familiar with the horrors of opium addiction. Connecting religion to opium made it fairly easy for Chinese communist leaders to attack and disassemble major religious groups.[53] In the anti-religious, officially atheist polities of the former Soviet bloc, states stifled, controlled, or even abolished religion. Soviet leaders, to use sociologist Paul Froese's words, hatched a "plot to kill God."[54] Despite efforts in China, North Korea, the former Soviet Union, and Eastern Europe, the earthly utopia was not to be.

Marxist-Leninist ideology, as it turned out, had merely created the illusion that communism would yield a religion-free worker's paradise. Revolutions inspired by Marxism never created a worker's paradise. And religious belief did not disappear. Despite decades of forced secularization, belief in God persisted in Albania, the Soviet Union, and elsewhere.[55] In fact, ethno-religious movements in the peripheries were among the forces that brought down the Soviet Union in 1991. Today, Orthodox Christianity is experiencing a revival in post-Soviet Russia. In post-Soviet Latvia, in a highly symbolic move, "a statue of Jesus Christ was installed in the space where a statue of Lenin had once stood."[56] The "opiate of the masses," it turns out, is indeed addictive and a harder habit to break than, say, communism.

Modernization Theory

Like Marxism, modernization theory is a theory of change; it is grounded in Western Europe's experience; and it has been highly influential in shaping assumptions about and views of religion's role on the world stage. Through the lens of this theory, modernization is seen as a process involving total change in societies' structures.[57] It originated with German sociologist Max Weber's observations at the turn of the twentieth century about changes in societies as they urbanized, industrialized, rationalized, secularized, became more literate and technologically advanced, and as institutions became more specialized. The theory posits that, as societies move from "traditional" to "modern," they undergo a transformation at the state/society level of analysis. It takes traditional society as the "problem" and modernization as the "solution."[58] It assumes that modernization is a linear and progressive process of social change; in other words, it continues in one direction (there is no going back) and it produces something new and better. Further, modernization theorists argue that secularization—a shorthand definition is religion's decline or its "steady retreat" from the public sphere[59]—is a central part of it. Following the European pattern, modernizing societies would experience a decline in the influence of religion, which is one of the elements of traditional society, with the end result being highly secular societies in which religion shapes neither the political culture nor the political order. So, if religion remains prominent in a society, it is because of incomplete modernization.[60]

Karl Marx (1818–1883) and leading social scientists such as Max Weber (1864–1920) saw religion as a "premodern relic."[61] Weber anticipated the "disenchantment of the world." Marxism and modernization theory, both of which claimed to be "scientific" and value-neutral, encouraged the idea that as societies progressed they would embrace rational thinking and outgrow religious "superstition." Widespread acceptance of these theories helps to explain the neglect of studies of religion in politics: empirically, the world seemed to be moving inexorably towards "a politics and public life free of substantive religious influence"[62]; normatively this was as it should be. These theories, however, are unable to explain the "re-enchantment of the world" and the "de-secularization of world politics" that has been under way in recent decades.

International Relations Theories

As with Marxist and modernization theorists, international relations theorists have embraced the assumption that religion, mere flotsam in the wake of modernizing forces, was of little or no political significance. International relations paradigms (discussed at length in Chapter 3) have encouraged observers to ignore religion as a political actor. However, although the twenty-first century may not be "God's Century," it is clear that religion is back.[63] Religion has proven to be an "unexpectedly resilient political force that has withstood the onslaughts of modernization."[64] As such, when trying to understand today's politics, we "neglect religion at our peril."[65]

Framing the Analysis

Throughout this text, issues and examples will be framed in terms common to the study of world politics: theoretical lenses and the levels of analysis. Both will be explained in the next chapter. Table 2.1 uses these two analytical tools to provide further insight into the Iranian Revolution, naming some of the revolution's roots and results.

The Cast

Different theoretical scripts highlight different actors. In the Marxist script, classes are the relevant actors within states and within the global capitalist system. For modernization theorists, domestic actors are central for moving from a "traditional" to a "modern" society. Realist scripts are state-centric, meaning they focus on states, especially states' national interests, security concerns, and relative power and position on the global stage. Constructivists' views here—as is often the case with constructivism—are less clear or determinate. Actors might be individuals, subnational groups, states, or transnational groups. Whoever the actors are, for constructivists they have no fixed interests. They are shaped by ideas, ideologies, identities, and norms and reshaped as these identities, norms, and so on change. Liberal IR theorists pay attention to states as well as nonstate actors.

Nonstate actors can be divided into two basic categories: nongovernmental organizations (NGOs) and intergovernmental organizations (IGOs), which are distinguished primarily by their membership. The members of NGOs are private individuals and groups; as the name suggests, they are experts and activists who are independent of governments. Typically, NGOs are nonprofit organizations. As this book's focus is the world stage, we are primarily concerned with intersocietal organizations (sometimes called international nongovernmental organizations [INGOs]), more specifically, transnational religious actors. Examples of such actors include Islamic Relief Worldwide, a humanitarian and development organization; Sant'Egidio, a Catholic organization involved

Table 2.1 Analytical Framework: Roots and Results of the Iranian Revolution

Levels of Analysis	Realism	Liberalism	Constructivism
International/ Systemic	*Roots*: The United States supported the shah's regime as a source of regional stability in a geopolitically important area and as a friendly, oil-rich state that shared a border with the Soviet Union. Under the shah, the US-Iranian alliance served both countries' interests: Iran served as "regional police officer" for the United States, while the United States provided Iran a buffer against potential Soviet incursions. *Results*: Iran became a so-called "backlash state," occasionally aggressive and defiant.	*Roots*: When it is mutually beneficial, states will cooperate, as the United States and Iran did during the shah's reign. *Results*: In 2015, multilateral efforts regarding Iran's nuclear program led to the signing of an agreement, restraining Iran from trying to nuclearize; cooperation trumped conflict.	*Roots*: Rival ideas, ideologies, identities, and norms were constructed in the Cold War context. The East-West ideological divide was joined by another: a Western/secular vs. non-Western/religious divide. *Results*: While distinctly Iranian and Shia, the Islamic revolution's triumph is credited with inspiring Islamist radicals, Islamist political parties, and revolutionary or anti-regime movements elsewhere in the world.
Domestic/State	*Roots*: The shah's regime appeared strong, but was weak and vulnerable. He lost the support of various sectors of Iranian society due to his repressive, Westernizing, and and modernizing rule. The shah's army and police proved ineffective in the face of a mass-based revolutionary movement.	*Roots*: The stability of the shah's regime (as well as the regime's rejection of communism) encouraged the United States to establish a close relationship with Iran. But this relationship and the shah's modernization project contributed to his downfall.	*Roots*: Iran is a Persian, not Arab, country with a Muslim majority. Persian and Islamic influences offered alternative ideas, identity, ideology, and institutions. From the revolutionaries' perspective, the shah embraced failed secular/Western ideologies.

continues

Table 2.1 Continued

Levels of Analysis	Realism	Liberalism	Constructivism
Domestic/State	*Results:* In Iran, religion regained its role as the source of political power and legitimacy. Abroad, the Islamic Republic uses religion to pursue its national interests.	*Results:* Today, Iran's sectarian foreign policy affects relations with the United States, Israel, Iraq, and other states. Iran combines intolerant Islamization at home with support for revolution abroad.	*Results:* Secular/Western ideologies were replaced by distinctly Iranian and Shia revolutionary and absolutist religious ideology—and the Iranian state became the instrument of this ideology. Post-revolution Iran embraces an Islamist and revolutionary identity, and this is reflected in its foreign policy.
Individual (human agents)	*Roots:* The shah (and later the ayatollah) acted as self-interested and power-seeking leaders. *Results:* Ayatollah Khomeini exercised both sacred and secular authority within Iran. He manufactured external crises to stoke revolutionary fires at home to maintain his grip on power. Today his successor, Ayatollah Khamenei, is the single most powerful figure in Iran.	*Roots:* The stability of the shah's regime (as well as the regime's rejection of communism) encouraged the United States to establish a close relationship with Iran. But this relationship and the shah's modernization project contributed to his downfall. *Results:* Today, Iran's sectarian foreign policy affects relations with the United States, Israel, Iraq, and other states. Iran combines intolerant Islamization at home with support for revolution abroad.	*Roots:* The ayatollah and shah had fundamentally different identities and, thus, interests. *Results:* Khomeini enunciated a a particular understanding of Islam and contributed to the creation of a unique regime.

Source: McGlinchey, "How the Shah Entangled America"; Lake, "Confronting Backlash States,"; Skocpol, "Rentier State and Shi'a Islam in the Iranian Revolution," 267; Hunter, *God on Our Side*, 18; Haynes, "Religious Transnational Actors," 7; Juergensmeyer, *Global Rebellion*, 47; Haynes, "Religious Transnational Actors . . . Shia Networks," 135; Esposito, *The Iranian Revolution*, 24; Nafisi, "Shaping a Nation," 43; Haynes, *An Introduction to International Relations*.

in peacemaking (discussed in Chapter 8); the World Council of Churches (WCC), an ecumenical Christian organization; and the Islamic State, a jihadist group led by Abu Bakr al-Baghdadi (discussed in Chapter 5). NGOs now number in the tens of thousands worldwide. They are disproportionately Christian and based in the economically developed countries of the Global North.[66]

Intergovernmental organizations are created by and composed of sovereign states. They are a means for states to organize themselves collectively to pursue common goals. Their scope may be regional (e.g., the African Union and the Arctic Council) or global (e.g., the Organization of Islamic Cooperation [OIC]). IGOs may be specialized organizations or serve many purposes. Of the hundreds of IGOs now in existence, the United Nations is the largest and most inclusive.

As explained in the next chapter, different levels of analysis also bring different actors into focus. The individual level of analysis, as the name suggests, considers the role played by individuals in shaping states' foreign policies and the course of world politics. The state level of analysis looks within states. Political leaders, interest groups, bureaucracies, and various other actors may play the lead or bit parts. Finally, at the global level of analysis, other than central IGOs (the UN, World Bank, and so on), individuals and groups are less actors than acted upon—by the distribution of military power, forces of economic globalization, international law, ideas, and norms.

So What?

So what? What is at stake? Why does religious growth matter to world politics? For starters, religion is not just growing but restructuring. As political scientist Jack Snyder argues, "Religion is taking on new forms, roles and functions in domestic politics and world politics in the 21st century."[67] It is challenging prevailing paradigms. It is reappearing in the public sphere, reengaging in society and politics, reemerging as a political force. It is not just religion, but *politicized* religion, that is resurgent.

At the individual level of analysis, religion can empower people to transform their lives and communities in ways that affect international relations.[68] Consider the role of Ayatollah Khomeini, the central figure behind the Iranian Revolution. Consider, too, those who engaged in risky protests during the Arab Spring. One study found that religion in the form of individual piety was systematically linked to political activism in Tunisia and Egypt at that time. Individuals who read the Quran with some frequency were much more likely to protest.[69] The study's authors determined that reading Islam's holy book motivated pious Muslims to take to the streets.

At the state level, religious institutions can be good vehicles for mobilizing people for political action. Religious parties are gaining power in some places, such as Ennadha in Tunisia, Hamas in the Palestinian territories, Hindu nationalists in India, and various religious parties in Israel. Religion can provide the motive for "world-shaking political movements in international relations."[70] In some settings, domestic religious actors significantly affect the nature of a state's foreign policy.

On the international level, religious organizations and religiously motivated organizations function as transnational actors and affect political outcomes. Religion has proved an important factor in peacemaking, faith-based diplomacy, faith-based development, and civil society.

To sum up, religion matters, first, because it is not simply religion that is resurgent, but religion's political power and its place on the international stage. It is coming in from the margins. It is influencing world politics in several ways: by legitimizing (or delegitimizing) states' foreign policies; because domestic religious issues can "cross borders and become international issues"[71]; through religiously based organizations, including nongovernmental organizations and intergovernmental organizations; through transnational religious networks and organizations; and through other transnational religious phenomena, including religiously motivated terrorism, religion-influenced international norms, and fundamentalist and religious-nationalist movements sparked by modernization.[72]

Second, religion matters in world politics because of religious fault lines and collisions. At the end of the last century, tensions between the two major missionary faiths, Islam and Christianity, "catalyzed interethnic war throughout the world,"[73] though in some instances tensions around religious differences were manipulated by power-hungry politicians or concerned layers of identity of which religion was just one. In the early twenty-first century, religious civil wars are becoming relatively more common in the Middle East and North Africa region.[74] When religion is added to the mix of grievances that lead to civil war, religious identities and core values make them harder to resolve. Moreover, ethno-religious conflicts are sometimes internationalized. For instance, when Yugoslavia was breaking apart along ethno-religious lines in the 1990s, the conflict became internationalized when North Atlantic Treaty Organization (NATO) forces intervened.

The two largest world religions are implicated separately and jointly in conflicts. Separately, Islam and Christianity is each far more likely than any other religion to be involved in religious civil wars. These civil wars can destabilize neighboring countries and become internationalized when outside actors join in the fray. Jointly, Islam and Christianity proffer competing claims about the means to achieve salvation. Although many of their adherents do not aggressively proselytize, Islam and Christianity are proselytizing religions—as opposed, for instance, to Judaism, which lacks an imperative to convert the rest of the world to the one, true faith. Each has a holy book, the Quran and Bible respectively, and an obligation to get it into as many hands as possible. While these faiths usually seek conversions through persuasion, they are clashing in what Micklethwait and Wooldridge call the "battle of the books."[75]

Islam and Christianity are not just near-universal in terms of where adherents are found, but *universalizing*—in some sense, like the two universalizing secular ideologies at the center of the Cold War, each fighting to win "hearts and minds." In the twentieth century, the United States' aim to promote democracy overseas and create a liberal international economic order had messianic overtones. The Soviet Union adopted the "messianic presumption of universality"[76] as its brand of communism, which it actively tried to spread. These secular ideological visions competed for dominance in what each regarded as a zero-sum game. In the language of the Cold War's binary opposition, people may be "nonaligned" (neither Christian nor Muslim), but none embrace both. Christianity and Islam are global rivals for the hearts and souls of millions.

Finally, the global resurgence of religion matters because it challenges our interpretation of the modern world. The world, we have been told, is secularizing. Yet people have not stopped believing, and religion has not lost its influence as a political force; on the contrary, "religion's influence on politics has grown."[77]

The above factors—political power and fault lines—add up to political importance. Christianity and Islam are rising political forces, affecting both domestic politics, states' foreign policies, and global peace and stability. Nevertheless, most international relations textbooks mention religion only in the context of Islamic extremism.

Conclusion

At the outset of this chapter, questions were posed about what had happened during the years between the Iranian Revolution in 1979 and the

Arab Spring in 2011—although the Islamic nature of the Iranian Revolution took scholars and policymakers by surprise, observers were quite attentive to Islamic elements in the Arab Spring. "God's Partisans Are Back" sums up an important shift that occurred during those three decades. In 1979, Western intellectuals (among others) "were in the grip of secularization theory: the belief that religion was a dying supernova, enjoying its final glow before disappearing from history."[78] But religious actors did not act as the theory predicted. Instead, Khomeini conceived of Islam as both a spiritual and a political pursuit. The Iranian Revolution has been followed by decades of "international tensions where faith was a leading factor" (e.g., the Taliban in Afghanistan), the Catholic Church has played a prominent political role, and religious movements are becoming international actors.[79] Hence, in late 2010—when Mohamed Bouazizi set himself ablaze in Tunisia and unleashed uprisings that spread to Egypt, Yemen, Libya, and Bahrain—analysts and media were more attuned to the religious factor.

While the Arab Spring's beginnings were secular in nature, Islamist groups joined in and benefited from elections held after the overthrow of autocratic rulers. In Tunisia, Ennahda ("Renaissance") dominated the political scene and held the post of prime minister for the first couple of years after the overthrow of the previous ruler. In Egypt, led by the Muslim Brotherhood, the Islamist movement that had been growing since the 1970s gained political power in the first elections after the overthrow of Egypt's president, Hosni Mubarak; it won a plurality of parliamentary seats and, later in 2012, the presidency. Both countries also experienced an anti-Islamist backlash, which led to Tunisia's Islamist leader relinquishing power (in January 2014) and the Egyptian military overthrowing President Morsi and banning the Islamist movement to which he belongs, the Muslim Brotherhood.

Expressed in another way, a double movement has taken place: (1) religion has (re)claimed a central place in world affairs itself and (2) our understanding of religion's role in world politics has changed as political scientists and other social scientists have rediscovered religion. Religion is claiming a central place in the post–Cold War international order. Gone are the superpower rivalry and the bipolar system. In fact, faith-based movements and organizations—from the mujahidin in Afghanistan to the Solidarity labor movement in Poland—had a hand in breaking up the Soviet Union and ending the Cold War. However, policymakers' and scholars' attention was focused on ideological clashes, not religious factors. In the early twenty-first century, the processes of globalization have sped up, issues of identity have risen to the fore (sometimes manifested as nationalist-separatist movements or intrastate political violence), and religion has reemerged as a significant factor in world politics.

Religion is resurgent. In the mid-twentieth century the trend was toward the privatization and marginalization of religion. In the early twenty-first century, however, religion has gone public and become a noteworthy force. This empirical trend has political implications on the domestic and international fronts. With this upsurge, religion is stepping out of the private realm of home and mosque, temple, or church. In many parts of the world, it has inspired political leaders and diplomats, given rise to massive political mobilizations and resistance to the state, been mixed up in political conflict, influenced foreign policy and development, and spilled across borders. Polities are grappling with the feasibility and desirability of divorcing spiritual matters from the conduct of the state. An Islamic resurgence was behind the convulsive events in Iran in 1979 and attacks on the United States on September 11, 2001, both of which challenged secular authorities.

The 9/11 attack, a successful attack in the heart of the Western world by a fanatical religious organization, has been instrumental in at least two senses. First, it has created increased awareness of religion's impact on the international stage. Second, it has highlighted the importance of "bringing religion into international relations," as explained in a book by that title.[80] Although religion is not the "black hole" for international relations studies that it once was, a hole remains in IR theorizing.[81]

The answer, then, to the "So what?" question is that the political picture is incomplete when the religious pieces are missing from the puzzle. Viewing world politics with secular blinders risks overlooking the religious dimension, resulting in partial and incorrect understandings of events. The US government's misinterpretation of what was afoot in Iran in 1978–1979—its failure to pay attention to the religious dimension—resulted in an incorrect diagnosis and misguided policy prescriptions. Today, "religion meets IR head on"[82]—not always and everywhere, but often enough to make the case for taking the religious factor into account in both theory and practice.

Three important points made in this chapter are that (1) there is an ongoing upsurge in religious belief, ideas, and movements; (2) religion is growing in salience, persuasiveness, and political power; and (3) all of this has come as a great surprise, at least to much of the Western world.[83] The job of the next chapter is to set out a framework for analyzing religion and politics on the global stage in a systematic way.

Notes

1. "The Speeches of Ayatollah Khomeini," BBC World Service, http://www.bbc.com/persian/revolution/khomeini.shtml.
2. Skocpol, "Rentier State and Shi'a Islam in the Iranian Revolution," 275.
3. Skocpol, "Rentier State and Shi'a Islam in the Iranian Revolution," 274.
4. Handelman, *The Challenge of Third World Development*, 3rd ed., 50.
5. Haynes, *An Introduction to International Relations and Religion*, 356.
6. Takeyh, "All the Ayatollah's Men," 51.
7. Husain, "The Islamic Revolution in Iran," 220.
8. Toft, Philpott, and Shah, *God's Century*, 11.
9. Toft, Philpott, and Shah, *God's Century*, 11.
10. Lee, *Religion and Politics in the Middle East*, 71.
11. Rouleau, "Khomeini's Iran," 1; Hanson, *Religion and Politics in the International System Today*, 296.
12. Nye and Welch, *Understanding Global Conflict and Cooperation*, 220.
13. Kingston, *The Politics of Religion, Nationalism, and Identity in Asia*, 73–74.
14. Roy, "Breakthroughs in Faith," 7–13.
15. de Soto, "The Real Mohamed Bouazizi."
16. Ismael and Ismael, "The Arab Spring and the Uncivil State," 236.
17. Szmolka, "Political Change in North Africa and the Arab Middle East," 133.
18. Fine, *Political Violence in Judaism, Christianity, and Islam*, 3.
19. Bruce, *Politics and Religion*, 4.
20. Luttwak, "The Missing Dimension," 12.
21. Bruce, *Politics and Religion*, 84, 87.
22. Ball and Dagger, *Political Ideologies and the Democratic Ideal*, 254.
23. Micklethwait and Wooldridge, *God Is Back*.
24. Shah and Toft, "Why God Is Winning," 38–43.
25. Toft, Philpott, and Shah, *God's Century*, 207–209.
26. Hefner, "Religious Resurgence in Contemporary Asia," 1031–1032.
27. Haynes, *An Introduction to International Relations and Religion*, 329.
28. Toft, "Religion, Rationality, and Violence," 116–117.
29. Thomas, "A Globalized God."
30. Thomas, "Outwitting the Developed Countries?" 29–30.
31. Juergensmeyer, *Global Rebellion*, 82.
32. Micklethwait and Wooldridge, *God Is Back*, 279, 285.
33. Pew Research Center, "The Future of World Religions."
34. Micklethwait and Wooldridge, *God Is Back*, 279.
35. Berger, "Secularism in Retreat"; Berger, "Secularization Falsified," 24; and Berger, "Faith and Development," 69.
36. Bruce, *Politics and Religion*, 122.
37. Soper and Fetzer, "Religion and Politics in a Secular Europe," 169.
38. Berger, "Secularism in Retreat"; Hertzke, *The Future of Religious Freedom*, 8.
39. Fox, *An Introduction to Religion and Politics*, 2nd ed., 16.
40. Wald and Calhoun-Brown, *Religion and Politics in the United States*, 4.
41. Shah and Philpott, "The Fall and Rise of Religion in International Relations," 43–44.
42. Bruce, *Politics and Religion*, 43, 72.
43. Zuckerman, *Society Without God*, 20–21.
44. Haynes, *Religion in Global Politics*, 11.
45. Bruce, *Politics and Religion*, 126.

46. Bruce, *Politics and Religion*, 245.

47. Tepe, *Beyond Sacred and Secular*, 34.

48. Kegley and Raymond, *The Global Future*, 138.

49. Bruce, *Politics and Religion*, 9.

50. Kingston, *The Politics of Religion, Nationalism, and Identity in Asia*, 71.

51. Fox, *An Introduction to Religion and Politics*, 2nd ed., 59.

52. Micklethwait and Wooldridge, *God Is Back*, 39–40.

53. Zainiddinov, "Religion and the State in Russia and China," 799.

54. Froese, *The Plot to Kill God*, 2.

55. Zuckerman, *Society Without God*, 22.

56. Juergensmeyer, *Global Rebellion*, 157.

57. Leftwich, *States of Development*, 33.

58. Desai, "Theories of Development," 53.

59. Thomas, *The Global Resurgence of Religion and the Transformation of International Relations*, 52.

60. Thomas, *The Global Resurgence of Religion and the Transformation of International Relations*, 7.

61. Bellin, "Faith in Politics," 317.

62. Shah and Philpott, "The Fall and Rise of Religion in International Relations," 46.

63. Toft, Philpott, and Shah, *God's Century*; Bruce, *Politics and Religion*, 2.

64. Handelman, *The Challenge of Third World Development*, 55.

65. Johnston, "We Neglect Religion at Our Peril."

66. Petersen, "International Religious NGOs at the United Nations."

67. Thomas, "Outwitting the Developed Countries?" 39.

68. Thomas, "Outwitting the Developed Countries?" 40.

69. Hoffman and Jamal, "Religion in the Arab Spring," 598.

70. Thomas, *The Global Resurgence of Religion and the Transformation of International Relations*, 12.

71. Fox and Sandler, *Bringing Religion into International Relations*, 164.

72. Fox and Sandler, *Bringing Religion into International Relations*, 163–166.

73. Duncan, Jancar-Webster, and Switky, *World Politics in the 21st Century*, 90.

74. Svensson, "One God, Many Wars," 411.

75. Micklethwait and Wooldridge, *God Is Back*, 267, 271, 272, 278, 296.

76. Von Laue, *Why Lenin? Why Stalin?* 4.

77. Shah and Philpott, "The Fall and Rise of Religion in International Relations," 25.

78. Toft, Philpott, and Shah, "God's Partisans Are Back."

79. Roy, "Breakthroughs in Faith," 7–13.

80. Fox and Sandler, *Bringing Religion into International Relations*, 2004.

81. Cesari, "Religion and Politics," 1330.

82. Clemens, *Dynamics of International Relations*, 278.

83. Thomas, "Outwitting the Developed Countries?" 24; Thomas, *The Global Resurgence of Religion and the Transformation of International Relations*, 26; Tepe, *Beyond Sacred and Secular*, 3.

3

A Framework for
Understanding

Illustration 3: Donald Trump's "Clash of Civilizations"?

Having called for "a total and complete shutdown of Muslims entering the United States" during his campaign, US president Donald Trump initiated a ban on immigration on January 27, 2017, just one week after his inauguration, from seven predominantly Muslim countries: Iran, Iraq, Libya, Somalia, Sudan, Syria, and Yemen. The executive order barred the entry of refugees from these states for 120 days, barred these states' citizens entry into the United States with any kind of visa for 90 days, and barred refugees from war-torn Syria indefinitely.

President Trump's supporters applauded the executive order as a fulfillment of a campaign promise. His action put "America first" and would keep Americans safer, said his base of supporters, by doing everything he could to prevent terrorists from entering the country.

However, the executive order immediately sparked protests. Acting attorney general, Sally Yates, refused to enforce President Trump's executive order, so he fired her. A large number of State Department employees also signaled their disagreement with the order. Then, on February 3, 2017, a week after the Trump administration issued the order, a federal judge in Seattle blocked it with a restraining order, eliciting an angry tweet from the president. Opponents raised concerns about the plight of refugees and violations of the US Constitution's protection of the freedom of religion. Another concern was that the Trump administration was playing right into radical Islamists' assertions that the US "global war on terror" (GWOT), which President George W. Bush declared shortly after the 9/11 attacks in 2001, is really a global war on Muslims. President Trump's top political strategist at the time, Steve Bannon, provided fodder for this view, having said three years earlier that the "Judeo-Christian West" is "in an outright war against jihadist Islamic fascism." For the administration's critics, this smacks of Islamophobia (an intense fear or hatred of Islam and Muslims). Abroad, a number of European allies expressed concerns about the administration's policy.

Trump responded to critics by saying his policy "is not a Muslim ban, as the media is falsely reporting. This is not about religion—this is about terror and keeping our country safe." The executive order, focused as it was on seven states in the Middle East and Africa, did not affect most Muslims in the world. Iran is the only one of the seven countries that makes the list of the ten most populous Muslim countries, and its Muslim population is far smaller than that of Indonesia, India, Pakistan, and Bangladesh.

Significance

New York Times reporters associated the Trump administration's actions and statements with "anti-Islamic theorizing" and referred to Samuel P. Huntington's much-debated "clash of civilizations" thesis.[1] Weeks before President Trump issued the executive order, the CATO Institute, a libertarian think tank, also said that the Trump team seems to have embraced Huntington's ideas of a clash of civilizations.[2]

In the 1990s, Huntington argued that international politics is being redefined and the fundamental source of conflict is changing. With the Cold War's end, conflict no longer revolves around ideological differences or economic and political divisions, but around civilizational differences. Civilizations, he said, have real and basic differences, especially religious differences. In fact, the major civilizations in Huntington's world are largely defined by religion—Buddhist, Hindu, Latin American (predominantly Catholic), Muslim, Orthodox Christian, Sino-centric, sub-Saharan African, and the West—and the fault lines between civilizations have much to do with religion. The biggest gap is between Western civilization and non-Western civilizations. The conflict between the West and Islam is 1300 years old and will likely continue, he argued in the 1990s. He wrote of Islam's "bloody borders," saying there are conflicts to the west, east, north, and south of what he termed the "crescent-shaped Islamic bloc." (This discussion is continued in Chapter 7.) President Trump and many members of his administration, this line of argument suggests, have bought, perhaps unwittingly, into the idea that there is a fundamental clash between the West and the Islamic world.

Others suggest that the Trump administration is playing up a different civilizational conflict: the West versus the Sino-centric (or Confucian) civilization, more specifically the United States versus China. This is seen, for instance, in the trade war between the two countries.

The whole "clash of civilizations" thesis is contested. Yes, argue some, "religions make transnational claims across enormous populations: they are probably the largest unit to which individuals claim loyalty."[3] For many, critiques of Huntington's argument note that it is too deterministic, suggesting that we know what the future of world politics will be like; it can wind up as a self-fulfilling prophecy, sparking hostility and conflict rather than anticipating it; that it overlooks the blurring of civilizational lines that is a by-product of mass communications, mass migrations, and extensive trade relations, among other factors; and that it overrates cohesion within civilizations and downplays struggles within them. The "Muslim world" is not monolithic, and there are good reasons to question the idea of civilizational solidarity among the world's Muslims.

Illustration 4: God and the EU Constitution

In Brussels, Belgium, in February 2002, the Convention on the Future of Europe began and, with it, the drafting of, and debate over, the European Union's constitution. This process brought to the fore questions about Europe's collective values, principles, and identities, and the extent to which they are rooted in Christianity. One of the most controversial issues was whether the constitution would mention the region's common religious (Christian) heritage.

In the "pro-Christianity" camp, which *The Economist* dubbed the "God squad," the Vatican and Poland were the main advocates of including a reference to God or Christianity.[4] Since Poland, which is about 90 percent Catholic, joined the European Union in 2004, the Polish episcopate had said that it wanted to "restore Europe for Christianity."[5] In addition to Poland, predominantly Catholic countries such as Ireland, Italy, Malta, Portugal, and Spain, among others, argued for including a religious reference, as did several Christian Democratic parties across the continent. Germany's delegate to the constitutional convention was also in this camp. Among religious interest groups, a Catholic-Protestant alliance dominated the debate. Pope John Paul II defined European civilization as "Christian." Under John Paul II and then Benedict XVI, the

Vatican (a traditional backer of European integration) worked through-out the constitutional process to get Christianity mentioned in the Pre-amble.[6] Likewise, "Catholic bishops throughout Europe lobbied hard for the constitution to contain a specific reference to Europe's Judeo-Christian roots."[7] They lobbied European institutions and consulted with representatives of other religions.[8]

The pro-inclusion camp argued that mentioning touchstones of European culture and history, such as the Enlightenment, while not also mentioning religion would simply not do justice either to European identity or the course of historical events. After all, before the twentieth century, Europe was often referred to as "'Christendom' because Chris-tianity was officially enshrined and popularly embraced throughout the Continent."[9] Christianity long wielded both spiritual authority and polit-ical influence, serving to legitimize monarchs' "divine right" to rule. In the early twenty-first century, Christianity remains integral to European identity; today, even in highly secularized countries, large numbers of Europeans self-identify as "Christian." Some supporters of this position "contended that Europe's Christian heritage provides it with common cultural underpinnings, and that ignoring religion would rob a unified Europe of its soul."[10]

In the "secularist" or anti-inclusion camp, France was joined by Belgium and Finland, among others. Opponents of mentioning God or Christianity in the EU constitution took various tacks. One argument was that the constitution, the fundamental law applicable to all Europeans, had a secular purpose: to contribute to the integration project, further binding member states together in a federal union. Another line of argument emphasized the secular nature of twenty-first-century Europe, where sec-ularization is deeply woven into the social fabric. The constitutional con-vention's president, Valéry Giscard d'Estaing of France, was reported as saying that "Europeans live in a purely secular political system, where religion does not play an important role."[11] While perhaps acknowledging the historical role of Christianity in the region, some now speak of a "post-Christian" Europe.[12] A third line of argument in the secularist camp was that any religious reference "would undermine the Union's commit-ment to the separation of church and state."[13]

In the end, the "secularist" camp triumphed over the "pro-Christianity" camp, as references to God or Christianity were rejected; in fact, efforts to pass an EU constitution itself failed. The Constitutional Treaty was unveiled in 2003, heads of state and government signed it in November 2004, and it then went to the twenty-five member states for ratification.

(With the addition of Bulgaria and Romania, the European Union has since expanded to twenty-seven members.) The following year, French and Dutch voters nixed it. Since it failed to win the approval of all member states, the treaty did not come into force. The EU now operates, not under a Union-wide constitution, but under a repackaged version of the constitution, known as the Lisbon treaty.

Significance

The process of drafting and attempting to get the EU constitution approved raised larger questions of religion-state relations, religion's place in the European public sphere, the framework of EU governance, and the question of European integration. The constitutional traditions of individual EU member states all "uphold the right to religious freedom, but they offer different interpretations of what this entails in the relationship between public institutions and churches."[14] Some call for clear separations of church and state, but others do not. France's model is one of *laïcité*, with strict separation of religion and state and the privatization of religion; for France, "secularism is sacrosanct." Its policies include enforcing restrictions on religious dress. As such, "the French, in particular, [were] set against mention of religion in the constitution."[15] Spain and Italy have signed concordats (i.e., formal agreements) with the Vatican, "which imply acknowledging a public role for the Catholic Church."[16] The preamble of Germany's basic law (essentially its constitution) references God, while Ireland's fundamental law references the Holy Trinity and the special role of Catholicism in its preamble. Similarly, Poland's 1997 constitution references Poles' Christian heritage and God, while its postcommunist concordat with the Vatican appears to privilege the Catholic Church. Several EU member states have an established church (Denmark, Finland, Greece, Liechtenstein, Malta, and the United Kingdom). As the foregoing suggests, "European societies have markedly different institutional and legal structures regarding religious associations, very diverse policies of state recognition, and of state aid to religious groups, as well as diverse norms concerning when and where one may publicly express religious beliefs and practices."[17] Thus, while religious and political pluralism is a hallmark of every EU state, European states interpret this in very different ways.

Regarding religion's place in the European Union, José Casanova posits that Europe is torn between its "common heritage of Christianity and Western civilization" and "its modern secular values of liberalism, universal human rights, political democracy and tolerant and inclusive multiculturalism."[18] Considered in this light, the controversy about referencing God or Christianity in the EU constitution was centuries in the making.

With regard to religion's place in the European public sphere, the trends are clear. Religion's role is declining. In part, this is due to policy; government restrictions on religious activities have been increasing more in Europe than in any other region of the world.[19] The debate over the EU constitution shows that organized religions and religious sensibilities remain significant, though not necessarily decisive, factors in some public policy debates.

This debate was particularly important—and sensitive—given the arrival of non-Christian immigrants and the efforts of Turkey to join the European Union. In recent years, more than a million people from the war-torn and predominantly Muslim states of Syria, Iraq, and Afghanistan have sought asylum in Europe. Muslims now represent a small but growing part of Europe's population. In Turkey, however, the vast majority is Muslim, and in recent years the country has been ruled by a party steeped in Islam. Critics of Turkey's accession to the EU have been at pains to underscore that the EU is not a Christian club and that the issue is Turkey's failure to satisfy certain economic and political criteria, not that Turkey's population is overwhelmingly Muslim. Nonetheless, any reference to Christianity would likely be perceived as marginalizing other faiths, especially Islam, and perhaps seen as closing the door on Turkey's hopes of accession.

This chapter provides the context for understanding and analyzing the relations between religion and world politics on the world stage. It sketches out the historic backdrop in Europe, with particular attention to the Peace of Westphalia and the march of secularization. It discusses the privatization of religion as well as secularization and modernization theories. Given the course of world events, as this chapter explains, it may well be time to rethink the international norms and assumptions that go along with the "Westphalian synthesis," including the assumption that as goes Europe so goes the rest of the world. The chapter then sets out the two analytical frameworks that are employed throughout the remainder of the book: international relations theory and the levels of analysis.

Westphalian Synthesis:
Old Treaty, Today's International Norms

The distinction between the once-inseparable religious and secular realms was first expounded in medieval Europe, largely in response to the transnational religious wars that raged from 1517 to 1648. Christianity had been the binding force in Europe since the fifth century. Beginning with Martin Luther in 1517, "the Reformation led to the distillation of two separate spheres of influence: the spiritual, led by the church, and the temporal, overseen by the state."[20] Decades of intra-Christian warfare followed the Protestant Reformation, as Christianity was divided among Catholics, Calvinists, and Lutherans, and the idea of a unified Christendom fell apart.

Beginning in the early sixteenth century, the Wars of Religion culminated in the highly destructive Thirty Years' War (1618–1648) and the Treaty (or Peace) of Westphalia. The long and bloody Thirty Years' War was justified by religion, but also prosecuted for a mix of political and economic reasons. During this war, kings and princes fought one another to determine the confessional allegiances of people in their own territories and of their neighbors as well. Realist-style power politics were also a contributing factor in the so-called wars of religion. Civilian populations paid a very heavy price. The Treaty of Westphalia (1648) was signed "by leaders representing two sets of transnational religious belligerents: Catholics and Protestants."[21] It said that "all—princes as well as their subjects—would be free to follow their own religion, as long as they were Catholics, Lutherans, or Reformed."[22]

The bloody and ultimately fruitless nature of the religious wars—so many dead, so little resolved—moved the Continent's rulers to invent "an elaborate set of rules to keep religion out of warfare."[23] It discredited religion in the eyes of many Europeans, making them amenable to secularism.

The Peace of Westphalia led to three important changes in international relations, collectively known as the "Westphalian synthesis." The three elements of the synthesis can be boiled down to sovereignty, nonintervention, and secularization.[24]

The first part was the rise of the system of sovereign states. Territorially defined states became the sole form of legitimate political authority, and secular states alone now wielded what Max Weber called the monopoly on the legitimate use of force. The secular state, so the thinking went, was needed to save us from wars of religion. Given the history of religious strife and violence in Europe, the new arrangement "erected sovereign firewalls of statehood to contain conflict."[25] In foreign affairs, the state acted according to the guiding (secular) principle of national interest. Sovereignty meant states could claim unconditional jurisdiction over domestic matters. Within each state, a single authority was supreme. For this to happen, religious and political authority had to be differentiated across Europe. That is, "for the state to be born, religion had to become privatized and nationalized."[26] People transferred ultimate loyalty from religion to the state, and the sovereign's power trumped the pope's, giving human sovereignty an edge over divine sovereignty (or the sovereignty of the divine's representatives on earth). Religion was transformed in the process, and state sovereignty became a key principle guiding international relations.

The second change, which goes hand-in-hand with the notion of state sovereignty, was the proscription on intervention: henceforth, states were not to intervene to impose religion or change religious-political relations beyond their own borders; each state is sovereign in matters of faith, meaning it can work out religious-political matters on its own and should be able to do so without outside interference. In the context of Europe in 1648, princes were to refrain from trying to convert other princes' subjects. Religion was not to be used to justify intervention in, or war with, another state. This principle developed into a more generalized norm of nonintervention, which became a cornerstone of international relations.

Third, as temporal powers shifted from ecclesiastical to secular rulers, from church to state, religious authorities' temporal prerogatives were sharply curtailed. The triumph of the sovereign state came at the expense of the Holy Roman Empire. European monarchs used the Westphalian settlement to assert their independence from papal authority. The monarchs' legitimacy rested on the divine right to rule. States broke free of Christendom, under which religious authorities both legitimated and constrained kings. Religious authorities, Catholic bishops in particular, had to cede control over vast land holdings, lost the privilege of holding public office, and could no longer raise revenues.[27] No longer able to rule over a united Christian Europe or even to assert temporal prerogatives, the Catholic Church lost transnational authority to the state, and the pope was not pleased by this development. Pope Innocent X (1574–1655) condemned the Westphalian settlement as "null, void, invalid, iniquitous, unjust, damnable, reprobate, inane, and empty of meaning and effect for all time."[28] The secularizing spirit was thus at work reordering authority *within* sovereign states as well as *among* sovereign states.

Two points deserve attention here. One is that the Peace (or Treaty) of Westphalia is generally regarded as a watershed in Western history. Monica Duffy Toft, Daniel Philpott, and Timothy Samuel Shah call it "the founding moment of modern international relations."[29] Westphalia marked the advent of the modern state, the international state system, and the principle of nonintervention; however, it took centuries for the events in Europe to gain traction around the world. (Even in Europe, it was not until the early nineteenth century that the development of the modern state was completed.) In the wake of Westphalia, political authority became increasingly centralized in sovereign states; states grew in power and capacity and in their inclination to exercise authority over religious actors; "states became the chief form of polity in Europe"; and states became the principal actors on the world stage.[30] The other side of the coin is that "God" was squeezed out of foreign policy and off the international stage. The secularizing international states system spread geographically through centuries of European influence and colonization, despite the fact that missionary activity was a central element of European expansion. The cross and sword typically traveled together during the hey-day of European imperialism. Missionaries and colonial administrators as well as foreign capitalists shared the impulse to shape colonial societies into the image of European states. The European system became truly global with the final wave of decolonization after World War II.

The other noteworthy point is that the state system emerged from a "secularizing set of events."[31] The Westphalian system privatized and nationalized religion; it relegated religion to the private sphere and "nationalized it as the basis for organizing modern states."[32] As forms of politics spread from Europe to the rest of the world, they grew increasingly hostile to religion, increasingly subordinating religion to the state. "Secular ideals became the foundation principles of the modern nation-state."[33] Today, with few exceptions, political rule is based on secular, not religious, authority.

Further, as mentioned in the previous chapter and explained below, realism and liberalism—the two most significant traditions of international thought—have secular characters. Looking through the realist lens on world affairs, states pursue security and power, not any specifically religious ends. For realists and liberals alike, states are the primary actors, and states are not swayed by religious actors. Secularism has been pervasive in international relations theory, though there are exceptions to this rule.[34]

Secularization:
Religious Decline, Privatization, Differentiation?

In addition to the factors already discussed, secularization was pushed along by the Enlightenment, rationalism, and the introduction of new sciences and technologies; the French Revolution; and the development of the ideas of Marxism and modernization. The Enlightenment of seventeenth- and eighteenth-century Europe was primarily a movement to apply the rule of reason to various aspects of individual and corporate life, to provide rational explanations for the world, and to eliminate prejudice and superstition. It associated prejudice, superstition, and ignorance with religion, while identifying secularism with reason; thus, Enlightenment thinkers argued for the need to emancipate Western society from theological doctrines and ecclesiastical control. The Enlightenment was prompted by weariness with religious warfare and dogmatism and by the impressive example of the natural sciences. The latter seemed to offer up the secrets of the universe and to contradict certain foundations of religion and the church, while rationalism presumably dislodged the "magical" or "superstitious" thinking associated with religion.

In 1789, the theorists of the French Revolution sought to eliminate bulwarks of the old order (or *ancien regime*), namely the monarchy and the Catholic Church, and to replace them with secular thinking and culture with the nation at the center. Jean-Jacques Rousseau and French revolutionaries identified the church and Christianity as sharply at odds with the kind of republic they sought to establish. For these republicans, church-state separation was not sufficient; establishing a republic required that the state subordinate the church and de-Christianize society. To that end, revolutionaries confiscated church property, required bishops and priests to take an oath of loyalty, and replaced Christianity with a "religion of reason."[35] To solidify loyalty to the republic, they also took education out of the hands of the "reactionary" church.[36] In 1801, on the heels of the revolution, the church was required to relinquish its political authority and to disengage from the state, so as to create a public sphere free of religious interference. In the French model, "religion is both confined to the private sphere and protected by legally enforced freedom of religion."[37] The "radical secularist template" developed in France was imported by radical secularists in other countries, such as Mexico, Atatürk's Turkey, and the shah's Iran.[38]

The Marxist brand of communism, as discussed in the previous chapter, adopted an adversarial stance toward religion. Movements and regimes based on Karl Marx's ideas embraced a radical form of state-imposed secularism.

These philosophies and transnational political movements, and a host of others that emerged in the late eighteenth and nineteenth centuries, "together yielded powerful ideological support for a program of political secularism" that subordinated religion to the state.[39] Secularists sought to ensure religion's political irrelevance. Beginning with the Enlightenment, they denied intellectual respectability to the study of religious actors and preferenced the rational over the religious. Yet all the while, "religion . . . continued to play a large role in the lives of individuals and societies." The result, argues Edward Luttwak, is that the "Enlightenment prejudice" separated the study of politics from the practice of politics.[40]

This trend continued into the twentieth century. In the first three decades of the century, radical political secularism took hold in "Catholic" Mexico, "Orthodox" Russia, and "Muslim" Turkey. In the 1930s and 1940s, the National Socialist (Nazi) party in Germany instituted a harsh "policy of subordinating religious institutions to the state."[41] After World War II, during the final wave of decolonization, the nationalisms associated with such prominent postcolonial leaders as Kemal Atatürk in Turkey, Gamal Nasser in Egypt, and Jawaharlal Nehru in India tended to marginalize religion. For some of these leaders, secularization theory provided a program for action.[42] Toft, Philpott, and Shah assert that, by the late 1960s, "everyone" perceived that secularization would soon be a global reality.[43] It was at this point, however, that the tide began turning. Some of the postcolonial leaders who had been "agents of political secularism" (e.g., Nehru and Nasser) died, while religious movements began a political comeback.[44]

Secularization theory suggests that, as Europe goes, so goes the rest of the world. Europe is the birthplace of the Enlightenment and of many "prophets of secularization": Marx, Durkheim, Weber, Nietzsche, Freud, and Darwin.[45] According to these prophets, the secularization that was part and parcel of Europe's modernization will, in time, occur all over the world. Modernization theory holds that, as societies move from "traditional" to "modern," they undergo a transformation on the state or societal level of analysis. According to the prevailing social science wisdom, "*all* societies would *invariably* secularize as they modernized."[46] In other words, modernization and development theories have had secularist assumptions. Secularization and modernization are thus interrelated processes, with modernization theory being the broader of the two social processes. Modernization would inevitably mean the decline of religion, both on the individual level and as a socio-political force. According to Scott Thomas, despite evidence that undercuts it, secularization theory persists because modernization theory persists.[47]

Secularization comes in three basic flavors: decline, privatization, and differentiation.[48] "Decline" (or the "belief" dimension of secularization) refers to a waning in religious faith and observance. People stop believing, they lose their religious commitment, and religious concerns cast a smaller shadow in everyday life. Religious institutions and belief systems become increasingly irrelevant and marginal to individuals, as seen in declining numbers of self-declared believers. This decline is seen in Denmark and Sweden, which Phil Zuckerman describes as "societies without God"; there, religion has become relatively insignificant, marginal to their culture and daily lives, or simply a nonissue.[49] Another example comes from Japan, where more than 70 percent of the country's citizens say they have no religious faith. Those who claim that God is dead and religion is on life support, sometimes called "declinists,"[50] argue that this is the global trend, that it is not only in Western Europe that religion is experiencing unambiguous decline. Secularists interpret decline as "normal" and "modern."[51] (However, as explained in the previous chapter, decline is not the predominant trend; rather, there is an ongoing global *resurgence* of religion.)

Privatization and marginalization concern the associational or "belonging" dimension of secularization; both entail the loss of the communal element and outward practice. This flavor of secularization means the public demise of religion. People are no longer involved in a religious community, such as a church or mosque, or in any type of religious movement. They become less likely to attend a religious service or donate money to a religious institution. According to the Pew Research Center, a rising percentage of Western Europeans describe themselves as religiously unaffiliated. In France, the overwhelming majority of the population is nominally Catholic, but a smaller percentage of the population believes in a god and even fewer people are regularly practicing Catholics. In Germany, most people no longer attend church, and church buildings are being converted into coffee houses, apartments, or some other secular use.[52] Similarly, church attendance has declined precipitously in Great Britain. In Denmark, most churches were built before 1750; while the population has grown more than six times since then, churches today are "conspicuously under-crowded."[53]

The industrialized democracies of Europe and Japan are the exceptions, not the rule. Elsewhere, many countries are experiencing sweeping political, cultural, and economic changes, such as those that accompany development. Feeling unmoored by these changes, people look for something to hold onto. Religion can provide that anchor. In Asia, outside of Japan, many countries are experiencing a heightened awareness of ethnic and religious identities. Across Asia, it is secularism, not religion, that is eroding.[54]

In some cases, lack of religious affiliation is a matter of "believing without belonging": holding onto one's religious faith but not to a religious affiliation. As a group, however, young adults around the world are less likely either to believe in God or to affiliate with a religion.[55] When modernization leads to a reduction in the *social* significance of religion, such that religion no longer binds people together or forges shared norms and behaviors, this trend supports the secularization thesis.

Religion's reduction to the "sphere of privacy" is important because, according to secularization theory's predictions, religion will become a private matter of no political import. Privatized religion retreats or is excluded from the "public square" and becomes an individual pastime, disconnected from matters of public significance. The values that pervade the secularized public square are not religious values. Religious attachments can affect political party affiliations, voting patterns, political attitudes, and political mobilization, as believers' religious perspectives influence their understanding of "how governments should govern" and religious codes guide their actions.[56] Likewise, religious organizations can be powerful political actors that lobby policymakers on matters of domestic and foreign policy, influence party systems and governing structures, and serve as powerful allies or opponents of the state. However, privatized religion (or "believing without belonging") loses much of its potential for bringing about political or social change. Even if the number of followers is exploding, if religion is simply about reading holy books or praying in private, those making domestic and foreign policies will ask, "So what?"[57]

To reframe this in simpler terms, discussion of religiosity or secularization often refer to the "three B's": belief, belonging, and behavior. Declines in the first two can affect the third, behavior, including political behavior. Citizens with strong religious convictions can be expected to turn to them for guidance on matters of duty to the state and the demands of justice for one's fellow citizens. "One's religion often determines one's values, and hence one's politics. It is natural, then, for citizens to appeal to their religious convictions when deciding how they should act politically."[58]

Social scientists anticipated that modernity would bring the privatization and decline of religion as well as the "institutional differentiation of the religious and secular spheres."[59] With differentiation, religion becomes merely one institution among others. Institutional differentiation means that institutions become more specialized. "Matters of piety" become distinguished from "matters of the polity."[60] Religious institutions that once provided a range of educational, health care, and welfare services cede many of these social functions to other organizations, often organizations associated with the modern welfare state, and the remaining faith-based service providers are state-regulated.

Where differentiation exists, government does not get involved in religious affairs, and religious bodies eschew political privileges and prerogatives.[61] In some states not content to allow secularization to proceed as a gradual historical process, as theory suggests will happen, governments make secularization part of official state policy.[62] They *impose* programs of secularization, including institutional separation, in a top-down fashion. This radical form of secularization, in which the state privatizes religion and tries to repress it, occurred in the former Soviet Union and other communist regimes.

Differentiation can also be part of religion's general decline in the face of the modern state, modern science, and other factors. In this case, "religion's loss of constitutional prerogatives and governmental support in the political sphere" means the loss of religion's public influence.[63] Religion loses its social standing. It is stripped of its traditional educational role and made to compete with more specialized institutions. In terms of the secularization thesis, the independence of religion and politics is a way station en route to eventual extinction.

The opposite of differentiation is *integration*, the intertwining of religious authority and the state, as found, for instance, in Iran and Saudi Arabia and in Afghanistan under the Taliban. When religious authority and political authority are interdependent, or when the institutions are enmeshed, they are "integrated."[64] An example is when the state exercises control over a religion's office and leadership, as the Soviet Union did over the Russian Orthodox Church. Another example is the obverse: when a religion exercises authority in the polity, as found in Iran.[65]

Neither complete independence nor complete enmeshment is found in the real world. Religious organizations cannot be entirely separated from the state because the state exercises sovereign authority. Complete fusion of religious and state organizations has proven to be neither practical nor desirable.[66] However, we can say that the United States is located toward the separation end of the spectrum, and Iran is towards the integration end. Despite French history and ideas, under the secularism and separation of *laïcité* the French state is actually more involved with religious organizations than the American state, placing France to the right of the United States on this spectrum.

The Peace of Westphalia, the creation of the secular state, the Enlightenment—these all happened in *Europe*. These were *Western* phenomena. The norms of sovereignty and nonintervention remained as the colonial powers withdrew, but the disentanglement of religion and government did not. In the Middle East and North Africa, most states name Islam as the state religion.

Rethinking Westphalia and Secularization

We are living in an era often defined by what it no longer is, a "post" era: post–Cold War, post-9/11. The Soviet Union has exited the world stage and taken international communism with it. The ideological conflict that defined the Cold War—basically, liberalism and liberal democracy vs. communism—has ended. East-West divisions have been superseded by a gap between the industrialized democracies of the Global North and the developing countries of the Global South; today, however, there is no face-off between military alliances, and the fear of nuclear annihilation has subsided. Interstate conflict has declined in relative importance as intrastate conflict has risen, often tinged by ethnicity or religion. The multifaceted processes and linkages associated with globalization have grown wider, deeper, and faster and made the world "flatter." The Peace of Westphalia is commonly called a "watershed" event, and some apply the same label to the events of September 11, 2001, when al-Qaeda—a transnational religious actor—sent planes crashing into the Twin Towers of the World Trade Center in New York City and the Pentagon outside Washington, DC. The question here is: Is this "post" era a post-Westphalian and perhaps even a post-secular era?

As stated by columnist Jonah Goldberg, "For decades, students of modernization subscribed to an overriding assumption that . . . more modernity means less religion."[67] In fact, the relationship between religion and modernity is far more complicated than deterministic portrayals of secularization suggest. As societies modernize—that is, urbanize and industrialize—some become more secular, but some do not. Urban areas, rather than proving to be havens of secularization, can be the sites of religious revivals.[68] The world is becoming more religious, not less. Social life in China, for instance, is "religionizing," not secularizing.[69] Industrialization and urbanization have not strengthened secularism in Turkey, as theory predicted, but strengthened certain Islamic tendencies.[70]

Islamic revivalism in "secular" Turkey is seen in the electoral success of the Islamic oriented Justice and Development Party. The Orthodox Church is experiencing a resurgence in postcommunist Russia. Modernization theory—criticized as ethnocentric and just plain wrong—has fallen from grace.

The limits of the secularization thesis should be acknowledged. It may have been useful at one time, when "religion's influence on politics was in global retreat," and it may continue to be right for one part of the world, but today, rather than declining, in much of the world religious faith is "exploding." As such, secularization theory, argue both Peter Berger and Jeff Haynes, is "mistaken."[71] With so many counterexamples to the assumption of worldwide religious decline, secularization theory has simply not "panned out empirically."[72] Certainly, the secularization thesis was wrong about the Islamic world, where Islam has maintained or increased its hold over Muslims. The secularization thesis does hold in one part of the world: Europe is undeniably secularizing. But, the Western European experience, with individualization of religious practices and widespread alienation from church-related religion, is exceptional. The Islamic world has not experienced the secularizing events, such as the Reformation and the Enlightenment, that shaped European history. "Thus, the historical processes that allowed the West to form a concept of separation of religion and state never occurred in Islam."[73] Among highly modernized and developed Western democracies, the US experience is also exceptional. The United States defies the predictions of modernization and secularization theories. In this context, "American exceptionalism" refers to the US status as the most religious of the advanced democracies.[74]

Pippa Norris and Ronald Inglehart, who label the United States an "outlier" and a "deviant case" among highly developed societies, call for moving beyond studies that focus on the United States and Europe to examine broader trends. They argue that secularization needs to be updated to account for divergence in religiosity based on whether people have a feeling of "existential security": those facing risks to themselves, their families, or their communities tend to be much more religious; conversely, those who are less vulnerable to early death or sudden disaster are becoming more secular. The latter tend to be located in richer countries with high levels of human development, such as Britain, Denmark, and France. As countries modernize, their citizens face fewer threats to survival, as things such as potable water are more widely available. Life in poorer, developing countries is more precarious and unpredictable, with less sure access to clean water, sufficient food, decent housing, medicine, employment, and so on. Insecurity with regard to such matters generates greater demand for religion, according to Norris and Inglehart. Typically, poorer countries also have higher rates of population growth, thereby increasing the number of religious people around the globe. Consequently, *"rich societies are becoming more secular but the world as a whole is becoming more religious."*[75]

Barry Rubin flatly rejects the proposition that religion would inevitably decline as the Global South modernized.[76] Similarly, John Micklethwait and Adrian Wooldridge say that "secularization theorists are wrong to claim that modernity and religion are incompatible." Contrary to secularization theorists' expectations, they say, modernizing forces, such as democracy and freedom, are *strengthening* religion in the modernizing world.[77] Toft, Philpott, and Shah agree that democratization is one of the forces that explains religion's global resurgence. The connection is that, as states democratize and their political systems open up, more actors can participate in politics and raise pesky questions about such issues as the proper religion-state relationship.[78] The modernization process, according to Rubin, often strengthens religion's public role by, for instance, making it a necessary ingredient of state-building.[79] Although some associate globalization with secularization, according to Toft, Philpott, and Shah, globalization helps to explain religion's resurgence because so many religious beliefs and communities are transnational. Interestingly enough, another factor they point to is modernization itself. Modernization, rather than leaving religion as mere flotsam in its wake, is contributing to religion's growth. Toft, Philpott, and Shah paint the forces of modernization as including globalization and democratization as well as technological modernization. Modernization contributes to religion's resurgence due to backlash against secular ideologies that have failed to deliver, as discussed in the introductory chapter. Religious actors stand ready to "challenge the state's legitimacy and authority" and to offer alternatives.[80]

More broadly, backlash can be seen in the reaction to a bundle of changes perceived as negative. According to what Sultan Tepe calls the "crisis model," "growing disillusionment with secular nationalism and problems of legitimacy in the existing regimes, along with the differential effects of economic and political liberalization, often initiate social reactions that prompt people to resort to religious doctrines for their expression." [81] In many countries, modern ideas and ideologies have been "perceived as forcibly imposed or imperialistic."[82]

The Islamic revival often manifests as anti-Western because it embodies a reaction against the spread of influential Western ideas, such as secularism and materialism, and the spread of Western power. Islamist groups react "against secularization, enforced modernization and a corresponding decline in Islam's social importance."[83] They want to reverse these trends and recreate Islamic society. And they may perceive modernization, secularization, and Westernization as a package deal. The secularization thesis ignores the fact that "many Muslims feel uncomfortable, if not resentful, when having to work with secular constructs"; instead, they seek "to integrate their political with their religious faith in constructing a community on earth that will be pleasing to Allah."[84] In the late 1970s, Iran's Islamic revolution was a religious reaction to an authoritarian regime's rapid modernization and Westernization. Revolutionaries saw the shah as too close to the (Christian) West.

Secularization has "provoked powerful movements of counter-secularization," a reaction against secularizing forces, the secular elite, and secularized, liberal forms of religion.[85] Counter-secularization is, arguably, as important today as secularization.[86] Evidence of it is found in the role of the Muslim Brotherhood in Egypt and Focus on the Family in the United States. Some speak of the "unsecularization" of the world.

In the process of destroying traditional society, modernization often induces anomie or malaise: feelings of loss of identity and control, uncertainty, dislocations, or disorientation.[87] Modernity "undermines all the old certainties."[88] The difficulty of coping with transformations afoot in the modern world prompts the quest for meaning, identity, a shared set of values, and a sense of moral community. Religion has the ability to provide meaning, purpose, shared values, even community. A return to religion becomes the response to "economic deprivation, social exclusions, and political underrepresentation."[89] It is, in other words, making a comeback as "a solution to many of modernity's problems."[90] Fundamentalist movements—Christian, Muslim, Jewish, and so on—are prompted by the desire to restore and reinforce what is being shaken by modern dislocation and crises, including religious identities and values. Thus, far from taking a unilinear path to secularization, modernizing societies may beat a circuitous path back to religion and religious certainties.

Events have not played out entirely as the closely related modernization and secularization theories had predicted. Certainly, these theories have not held in East Asia. In that region, not only is religion resurfacing, but it has typically been a central concern of the state, used to secure political legitimacy and to promote national unity. In short, in the East Asian countries of China and South Korea, "modernization never led to secularization."[91] In the Muslim world, religion "remains a significant force in many social and political systems,"[92] with Islam experiencing somewhat of a resurgence in the Middle East. In the past half century, Latin America has experienced liberation theology and a surge of Pentecostalism. Born of economic oppression in the late 1960s, liberation theology moved the Catholic faith toward a progressive, grassroots orientation in which the poor and marginalized made their voices heard. This is one example of religion providing a "principle for political consciousness and activism" in the Global South.[93] In the United States, while there is institutional differentiation, religion continues to play a significant role in American public life. However, secularization theory does seem to hold in (parts of) Europe, which is an exception to the broader pattern of global religious resurgence. Scholars appear divided on the question of whether Japan fits the East Asian pattern or the European pattern. Yet even in Europe, which projects a secular image, the politics of religion remains on the public agenda.[94] As it turns out, the world is not experiencing a much-predicted disenchantment, but re-enchantment.

Perhaps it is time to "reconsider Westphalia's legacy."[95] Events and processes have raised questions about both the centrality of the state system and existence or even desirability of a strict separation of religion and politics.

International Relations Paradigms

Like modernization theory and Marxism, international relations theories assume away the importance of religion in world politics. Realism and liberalism have long and rich intellectual heritages, while constructivism is increasingly important.

The predominant paradigm since the end of World War II, particularly regarding "high politics" matters of defense and security, is realism. Realism focuses on national security and power politics, with an emphasis on military power, anarchy, and states, devoting little attention to nonstate actors such as the Roman Catholic Church and the Muslim Brotherhood. From a realist perspective, especially structural or neorealist, the way power is distributed in the international system is important—which states have power, which do not, or, more precisely, which states have power relative to that of other states. States' relative power on the world stage is far more important than, say, their religious orientations. Power determines the role of international institutions (e.g., the International Monetary Fund) and the ideological factors at work in the world.[96]

The international system is anarchic, meaning there is no authority above the sovereign state—nothing like a world government. "Sovereignty" means each state is the highest political and legal authority in the land, exercising exclusive control over its people and territory. The international realm is somewhat like the Wild West, while the domestic realm has authoritative executive, legislative, and judicial bodies, and we expect to find order and security. States have governments, but the world has no established government to dispatch police forces or settle disputes. States must rely on themselves for survival and security, to guarantee agreements among them, and to achieve other goals. Security is never guaranteed.

The "security dilemma" arises when one state's efforts to bolster its own security, typically by building up its military, are seen as threatening to other states, which then bulk up their own military capabilities. The result can be an arms race and perceptions of decreased, rather than enhanced, security.

Seeking power, security, and material well-being, states compete on the world stage. In the absence of built-in checks on states, conflict among them is all but inevitable, though this conflict may or may not turn violent.

In terms of how states relate to one another, "a state is a state is a state," only really differing in terms of their share of global power.[97] States are unitary actors, meaning they speak with one voice and what goes on within states does not really matter. It does not matter whether a state is democratic or autocratic, has an Islamic or Christian orientation, or has a dominant religion or religious pluralism. All states wield power, pursue their national interests, and define their national interests primarily in material terms, power and wealth, which help to guarantee states' sovereignty, security, and their very survival. National interests or *raison d'état* (reason of the state) trump piety, morality, and values. Realist conceptions of power focus on hard power,[98] especially military capabilities (the most temporal of powers), and exclude the kinds of cultural power and the power of moral suasion that are often associated with religion.

The most quoted statement in this regard comes from Joseph Stalin. In 1935, the French foreign minister suggested that Stalin encourage Catholicism as a way to propitiate the pope. Stalin replied, "The Pope? How many divisions has the Pope?" The pope, of course, has no "divisions," just a spiffy looking Swiss guard; however, the pope wields the power of moral suasion and has the ear of about one billion Roman Catholics around the globe. Realists have trouble dealing with the "powerful role of religiousness in most people's lives" and the "power of belief in international relations."[99]

Most realists further assume that states are rational, not moral, actors; their leaders prudently pursue national interests, not moral crusades. As rational actors, states adhere to the "cool calculus of national interest," weighing costs and benefits of potential actions and leaving no room for the "flames of faith" in realist analyses.[100] Such tenets and assumptions led Stanton Burnett to conclude that the realist school is "unflinchingly secular."[101]

The liberal paradigm is also prominent in the West, particularly regarding matters of international political economy. Liberals are more optimistic about human nature and about the possibility of cooperation and progress. Thinkers within this tradition have developed three different emphases. Immanuel Kant (1724–1804) emphasized the importance of establishing stable democracies as a means of ensuring "perpetual peace." Today, the notion of a "democratic peace"—that stable democracies do not go to war with one another—has substantial empirical support. Another emphasis comes from Adam Smith (1723–1790), who promoted free trade as a means to inhibit interstate war. Today, we have Thomas Friedman's "Golden Arches Theory." This theory posits that when countries become economically integrated and meet a certain level of economic development, such that they have a middle class big enough to support a McDonald's chain, they do not go to war with each other.[102] For Smith and Friedman, economic integration raises the cost of going to war and, in so doing, checks the impulse to do so. The third line of emphasis comes from Hugo Grotius (1583–1685), who suggested that sovereign states should follow a body of international laws, and others have advocated creating international institutions. International institutions, laws, and norms serve to regulate competition among actors.

Liberal scholars challenge some of realism's basic assumptions. They "open the box" and analyze the nature of individual states—democratic or autocratic, open or closed, capitalist or communist—and the functioning of domestic political institutions and groups. In contrast to the state-centric realist view, liberals readily acknowledge that states are not the only important actors; states are joined on the world stage by an array of nonstate actors. Liberals downplay the realist focus on competition and the potential for conflict, instead playing up the possibility of state and nonstate actors cooperating to further common interests. Liberal theorists create more space for nonstate actors and ideas in international politics. Ideas come in the form of laws, institutions, norms, and regimes, all of which "limit anarchy and foster cooperation in the international system."[103] Liberals largely accept the modernist presumption that religion will be superseded, and, like Realists, they have "largely ignored the role of religion in international affairs."[104]

Constructivism, while lacking the lineage and development of realism and liberalism, allows much more space for the consideration of factors such as religion in international relations. Constructivists focus on how the social world is constructed by various actors—the words they choose, the information and historical lessons they deem relevant, and the social norms and collective perceptions that shape their thinking. While realism assumes the existence of objective reality, for constructivists realities exist (for instance, some states have nuclear weapons and some do not), but the *implications* of these realities depend on the significance people attach to them.[105]

For constructivists, the keys to understanding international relations are found in ideas, beliefs, identities, values, and norms. Actors gain power when they can persuade others to accept their ideas. The content of prevailing ideas and values determines the global outlook.[106] States are social actors and, in IR, their actions accord with international rules and norms, identities, and institutions. Identity concerns how we see or think of ourselves. Religion, culture, ethnicity, and history are often key signifiers or shapers of collective identity within or across nations. Religions also come with norms of acceptable and unacceptable behavior. Since norms and relationships are constructed, they can also be reconstructed. Former enemies can become friends or allies (or vice versa) and international norms can serve as brakes on once-accepted practices, such as territorial conquest. Religion can be constructed as a key signifier of group identity, serving as a sort of social "glue" or as a source of division, as during the Thirty Years' War and Yugoslavia's dissolution in the 1990s. Another example comes from post-Soviet Russia, where efforts are under way to "re-Christianize" national identity.[107] As discussed in Illustration 4, an important question is whether there is a common European identity and, if so, whether it is grounded in religion or in secularism. Besides religion, the meaning of concepts such as power and anarchy (both are central to realism) depend on their social construction. Even the religious/secular divide so ingrained in Western thinking is a Western construction. The cyberworld's "tabernacle of extremists" can shore up current constructions—prevailing ideas, beliefs, identities, values, and norms—or undermine them.[108]

These three theories, like all theories, purport to explain something. They also have hard cores or assumptions that cannot be proven or disproven; key concepts related to the basic way of thinking about the world; certain kinds of relevant evidence; and internal consistency. The question to be asked of theories is how well they explain what they purport to explain.

Alternative paradigms—whether Marxist, feminist, or world systems models—have been no better than realism or liberalism in terms of injecting religion into the analysis of international relations. Suffering from a secular bias, they have ignored or rejected a role for religion. Grouped together as "conflict," "critical," or "dissident" theories, they focus on historical processes and potential futures, naming inequalities (e.g., gender or class inequalities) as a key source of international tensions.

Levels of Analysis

Although good theories aid in describing, explaining, and perhaps predicting events in the world, the levels of analysis provide an analytical tool or organizational scheme. Together, these levels form a system for organizing the forces and agents on the world stage and focusing on particular aspects of world politics. In explaining international events, they help analysts to "sort out the multiplicity of actors, influences, and processes."[109] The levels of analysis assist by orienting our questions and determining what kinds of data to consider. They have been likened to a camera lens that can zoom in or out, focusing on "wholes" or "parts."[110] Studying events and issues from multiple levels provides insights that might otherwise be missed. Following the lead of a variety of international relations textbooks, this text considers three levels of analysis: the international system, the state, and the individual.

Take the EU example discussed in Illustration 4 in this chapter's opening. The European Union could be analyzed as an incipient supranational entity, an entity that is a major player in international diplomacy and the world economy. The camera lens could move in to examine the dynamics within EU member states on the question of accepting or rejecting the proposed constitution. As Philip Schlesinger and François Foret say, in Europe, "the question of Church-State relations is largely the prerogative of the Member States and significant differences persist at the national level."[111] In other words, the question of church-state (or religion-state) relations is best studied at the state level, rather than the international level. The camera could zoom in still more to focus on key EU, state, and religious leaders.

The levels of analysis can be thought of as an upside-down layer cake, nested boxes, or concentric circles. See Figure 3.1.

Figure 3.1 Depiction of the Levels of Analysis

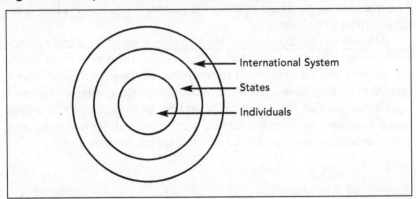

International System

States

Individuals

International, or Systemic Level

The international level of analysis, also known as systemic analysis, is the broadest view of world politics. It considers the "whole" and how the system (or worldwide conditions) affects actors', especially states', foreign policy behaviors. Systemic factors—factors external to state and nonstate actors, most notably the distribution of power—drive or constrain state behavior in somewhat predictable ways. They structure the choices facing decisionmakers. Analysis at this level looks at relations between and among sovereign states as well as nonstate religious actors, such as the Roman Catholic Church and the Muslim Brotherhood, that exercise influence in the international system.

The existence of a "system" suggests two things. One is that the components of the system interact and affect one another. Interconnections among units in the system mean changes in some parts lead to changes in other parts of the system. "Changes in the nature or structure of the international system" lead to changes of states (and nonstate actors) within the system.[112] The system thus functions somewhat like a mobile; however, unlike mobiles, we can find regularities or patterns of interaction among state and nonstate actors. The other point about systemic analysis is that "the collective behavior of the system as a whole differs from the expectations and priorities of the individual units that make it up."[113]

Few leaders would have imagined that the institutional arrangements (the United Nations, World Bank, and so on) cobbled together at the end of World War II would hold into the twenty-first century. Perhaps even fewer anticipated the sudden collapse of the Soviet Union, international communism, and the ideological clash between the super-powers—or that, as Samuel Huntington argued, this ideological clash would be replaced by a civilizational clash. One part of the international system, the institutional arrangements, have remained largely intact since the 1940s, while another part, the structure of power and the source of most international conflict, have undergone profound changes since the early 1990s.

The utility and focus of this level of analysis varies with the theoretical lens that is used. Realists analyze anarchy and how power relationships determine interactions among actors. For them, states are the core units of international relations and the distribution of power is central. "Power—military and economic capabilities—[is] distributed among autonomous, self-interested, and independent states or powers, with each one pursuing its own national interests."[114] This distribution determines outcomes. Rooted in Marxist analysis, radicals focus on the world capitalist system, defined in terms of economic processes and linkages. They draw attention to colonial history and present-day economic domination. Radicals highlight the stratified nature of the system and the uneven distribution of resources. For them, the distribution of wealth is central. Constructivists tend to the global distribution of norms and attitudes and how they can contribute to international order. Human rights, self-defense, and nonproliferation of weapons of mass destruction (WMD) are three international norms that are frequently invoked. For constructivists, ideas, beliefs, values, and identities are socially "constructed," especially by groups to which people belong. Often, religion influences normative values. In contrast to realists' emphasis on anarchy, liberals see international institutions and international regimes as promoting order on the international level.[115] Still, liberals focus much more on state-level institutions and processes than on the international systems as such. By and large, all of these international relations theories have assumed that religion is not an explanatory factor.

Religion is marginalized in all of these approaches. After Westphalia, it became an "illegitimate international actor."[116] It is still recovering from this delegitimization.

State/Comparative Level

The state level of analysis focuses on states as authoritative decision-making units, in the sense that state authorities engage in foreign policy (sign treaties, join alliances, make war, and so on), and "the domestic environment in which policy is shaped."[117] Whereas systems-level analysis takes states as "black boxes" or "billiard balls" (that is, unitary structures that respond to external forces in similar ways), suggesting that foreign policy is shaped more by external structures than by internal factors, state-level analysis "opens the box." Whereas the "systemic level of analysis claims that states are essentially similar" and how they act is largely determined by their roles and influence in the international system,[118] other levels of analysis analyze how states are organized internally and who is in charge.

The state level of analysis considers domestic (subnational) actors and factors, the form of government, the type of economic system (capitalist or socialist), military power, internal dynamics (such as bureaucracies, political parties, interest groups, public opinion, the level of education, and regional or ethnic cleavages), prevailing ideology, political culture, and responsiveness to the public. It considers how the nature of the regime (autocracy or democracy) affects the state's foreign relations. Typically, it looks at how political decisions are made (for instance, the openness of decisionmaking processes) and the state's capacity to carry out its foreign policy decisions. The focus, thus, is "what goes on within states that ultimately has an impact on what goes on between states,"[119] whether it is a religiously based political party pressing a secular state to write religious law into civil law or a state's use of religious symbolism to bolster its legitimacy in the eyes of the people.

The state level of analysis is explored in Chapter 5. This chapter looks within states. It considers why and how religion and politics interact within sovereign states and how these interactions can affect states' foreign policies. The domestic level of analysis is crucial, since "religion's greatest influence on the international system is through its significant influence on domestic politics."[120]

A variety of models, or typologies, of religion-state interaction are available for framing this type of discussion. The simplest, and least useful, is a dichotomy based on the two spheres model.

As explained in the previous chapter, the two spheres model places religious beliefs, actions, and institutions in one sphere and political beliefs, actions, and institutions (including state institutions) in another. The two spheres model often implies empirical and normative claims. The empirical claim, presumably based on evidence, is that religion and politics or the sacred and the secular *can* be separated. The normative claim is that they *should* be separated. The state sphere includes, of course, all the institutions of government. While it has some utility in thinking through issues of religion and the state, in practice this binary is not very useful because neither complete separation nor complete integration exists in the real world.

Individual Level

As Steven Spiegel and Fred Wehling state, the individual level of analysis "puts a human face on world politics."[121] It focuses on human behavior and roles of individual human beings in foreign policy matters. This level of analysis framework points to individual human beings as crucial players in the global drama. It presumes that individuals, especially those with power, can make a difference in world affairs; in other words, it assumes that individuals *matter* and that leaders and leadership matter. It matters, for instance, who occupies the Oval Office or exercises papal authority. The types of data considered include key individuals' leadership styles, personality traits, goals and ambitions, skills, values, ideologies, beliefs, personal relationships, ideological and religious worldviews, and other idiosyncratic factors.

The individual level of analysis typically "focuses on individual decision makers, the roles they play, the perceptions they hold, the ways key decision makers interact in small, top-level groups."[122] These individuals make decisions on behalf of states or key nonstate actors. This level of analysis can also focus on "ordinary citizens whose behavior has important political consequences."[123] In this text, attention will be given, not only to individuals in a position to make foreign policy decisions, but religious actors—operating on their own or on behalf of a religious organization—whose actions have significant consequences in world politics. This includes influential religious leaders—for instance, Ayatollah Khomeini, Pope John Paul II, and Bishop Desmond Tutu—as well as laypeople who play crucial parts in what Charles Kegley and Eugene Wittkopf call "the global drama."[124] As the next chapter will demonstrate, leadership matters. The efforts of faith-based reconcilers, such as Tutu and Carlos Belo, were successful because of their "political savvy and ability to inspire."[125]

On the face of it, the international level of analysis is the logical focus of any study of world politics. However, the individual and state levels come into play because, when it comes right down to it, individuals make foreign policy, and also because so many political matters have an "intermestic" nature: the line between the international and the domestic is often blurred, with some issues (e.g., immigration) clearly straddling the divide. Domestic issues and actors often have an international dimension or international effects. Ethno-religious conflicts, for instance, may have local roots but far-reaching impacts. They may challenge the state's authority and destabilize neighboring states. The actions of Pope John Paul II and the Catholic Church in communist Poland reverberated throughout Eastern Europe. Likewise, issues and actors on the international level can condition politics (and its interactions with religion) within states. Consider how the West's domination has facilitated the spread of democracy and human rights. "Most states (and that includes those such as China that routinely infringe it) now assert the principle of religious freedom."[126] In a more specific example, the actions of external actors, from sovereign investors (e.g., the United Kingdom) to nongovernmental organizations (e.g., the World Council of Churches), helped to weaken the apartheid regime in South Africa. The levels of analysis provide a way to approach the study of world politics, but by no means does it suggest that what happens on one level stays on one level. The next chapter homes in on the individual level of analysis.

Table 3.1 provides an overview of the central analytical and theoretical framework employed in this book. It includes the focus and assumptions of each IR theory at each level of analysis, followed by examples regarding the EU constitution. It demonstrates that the answer to the question of "where" global politics happens is that it occurs on three (or more) levels of analysis and that different IR theories offer different insights into what happens and why. These frameworks enable us to analyze religion's role in a systematic way.

Conclusion

In this text we frame the analysis of religion and politics in three basic ways: historically, analytically, and theoretically. Historically, the West and Western Christianity are framed in terms of the Westphalian synthesis and other secularizing events. Most of the non-Western world, notably the Middle East and the Muslim world, did not experience this same set of events. *Analytically* refers here to the levels of analysis. The levels of analysis are tools or heuristic devices. They help to simplify a complex world so that we can better study our subject. Theoretically, the frames of reference are, first, modernization and secularization theories and, second, the major international relations theories of realism, liberalism, and constructivism. One of the underlying arguments of this text is that the dominant IR theory, realism, misses the boat by ignoring the faith factor and, thus, fails to appreciate how "power relations matter at the intersection of religion and state,"[127] shape states' foreign policies and, thus, shape world politics.

Table 3.1 Analytical Framework: Focus/Assumptions and the EU Constitution

Levels of Analysis	Realism	Liberalism	Constructivism
International/ Systemic	*Focus/Assumptions:* World politics is the realm of power, anarchy, self-help, and the struggle for security and survival. "Anarchy" means that the international system is composed of sovereign states; states are the key actors and there is no higher authority (no world government). Power matters, especially its global distribution among states. States' power and position relative to other states is key. States' vying for power drives international politics. Conflict is more likely than cooperation.	*Focus/Assumptions:* International law, institutions, regimes, processes, and trade reduce anarchy and conflict. Peace, progress, cooperation, and collective gains are possible. The democratic peace theory posits that (stable, consolidated) democracies do not go to war with other democracies.	*Focus/Assumptions:* Global ideas, ideologies, identities, and norms are important, constructed, and sometimes at odds. The international system is itself a social construct, and changes in international norms, ideas, and identities all play a part in what the system means.
	EU Constitution: The Catholic Church may have lobbied for a reference to Europe's common religious heritage to bolster its power and influence in a secularizing region.	*EU Constitution:* Intergovern-mental organizations, such as the European Union, mitigate anarchy and the potential for conflict among member states. In addition, Catholic bishops (leaders in a transnational religious entity) lobbied for reference to the region's religious roots.	*EU Constitution:* The proposed EU constitution raises questions: Might religion serve as a source of legitimation, the basis of social cohesion or a common European identity, or an overarching set of norms? Or might secular identities be privileged such that Christianity is excluded from the public sphere?

continues

Table 3.1 Continued

Levels of Analysis	Realism	Liberalism	Constructivism
Domestic/State	*Focus/Assumptions:* The state is a unitary actor or "black box," meaning internal dynamics are of little import; leaders act in the "national interest" (what is best for the nation-state as a whole) and seek to enhance state power relative to other states.	*Focus/Assumptions:* States' internal attributes, especially regime type and economic system, shape their foreign policies. Pay attention to domestic political dynamics and religious demographics.	*Focus/Assumptions:* Prevailing ideas, ideologies, identities, norms, and values define state interests.
	EU Constitution: Power was a point of contention: how much power the EU would have and how power would be balanced among member states.	*EU Constitution:* EU member states differ in support for further integration and the role of religion in politics. In addition, within states attitudes and party politics (some pro-European integration, others—the "Eurosceptics" were anti-integration) affected the outcome.	*EU Constitution:* States' religious identities affected their stances on the EU constitution, with predominantly Catholic countries (e.g., Italy and Poland) pushing for including religious language and secularist France opposing it.

continues

Table 3.1 Continued

Levels of Analysis	Realism	Liberalism	Constructivism
Individual	*Focus/Assumptions:* Humans want power and are selfish, imperfect, and imperfectible. States' leaders are the most important individuals, since they make foreign policy decisions. Leaders pursue the national interest, especially state power and security; they do so in a world marked by competing states, and their policy options are constrained by the distribution of power within the international system.	*Focus/Assumptions:* Human beings are rational and perfectible. Individuals can learn and cooperate. Individuals, including political leaders, can move beyond the (realist) focus on relative power and gains and consider joint gains.	*Focus/Assumptions:* Human nature is malleable; identity, values, and experiences are key. National leaders' beliefs about the world and foreign policy come from a number of sources.
	EU Constitution: States' leaders took positions on increased integration based on whether or not it would enhance state power and serve their own state's interests.	*EU Constitution:* Europe's leaders often have divergent visions of Europe's future. The leader of the Roman Catholic Church, Pope Benedict XVI, pushed to get Christianity mentioned in the preamble.	*EU Constitution:* Considers how individuals' self-identity as Christian, Muslim, or secular and how that affects their stance on the further integration of European states.

Sources: "Can the Constitution Be Saved?" *The Economist* (April 18, 2005); "Finally, a Constitution. Now the Hard Part," *The Economist* (June 22, 2004); Mingst and Arreguin-Toft, *Essentials of International Relations;* Grieco, Ikenberry, and Mastanduno, *Introduction to International Relations;* Cunningham, *God and Caesar at the Rio Grande;* Casanova, "It's All About Identity, Stupid," 102; Maffettone, "Enlightenment and the European Union Model."

Notes

1. Shane, Rosenberg, and Lipton, "Fringe, Sinister View of Islam Now Steers the White House," *New York Times*, February 2, 2017.

2. Ashford, "Trump's Team Should Ditch the 'Clash of Civilizations,'" *National Interest*, December 7, 2016.

3. Grzymala-Busse, "Why Comparative Politics Should Take Religion (More) Seriously," 423.

4. Schlesinger and Foret, "Political Roof and Sacred Canopy?" 74; "God Meets the Lawyers," *The Economist* 369:8353 (December 6, 2003), 48; Menéndez, "A Christian or a *Laïc* Europe?," 198; "Polish, Belgian Premiers Discuss EU Constitution, Christian Values," BBC Worldwide Monitoring, April 13, 2007.

5. Casanova, "It's All About Identity, Stupid," 89.

6. Schlesinger and Foret, "Political Roof and Sacred Canopy?," 74.

7. "Pope Says European Union Needs Gospel Values," *America* 191:15 (November 15, 2004), 6.

8. Schlesinger and Foret, "Political Roof and Sacred Canopy?," 74.

9. Magstadt, *Nations and Governments*, 19.

10. Goldsmith, "European Union Debates Nod to God," 17.

11. "Unholy Row on God's Place in EU Constitution," *Christian Century* 120:7 (April 5, 2003).

12. Casanova, "It's All About Identity, Stupid."

13. Americans United, "EU Constitution Skips Religious Language," 21.

14. Menéndez, "A Christian or a *Laïc* Europe?" 184.

15. Goldsmith, "European Union Debates Nod to God," 17.

16. Menéndez, "A Christian or a *Laïc* Europe?"180.

17. Casanova, "It's All About Identity, Stupid," 95.

18. Casanova, "It's All About Identity, Stupid," 94.

19. Pew Research Center, "A Closer Look at How Religious Restrictions Have Risen Around the World."

20. Hurd, "Secularism and International Relations Theory," 78.

21. Haynes, *An Introduction to International Relations and Religion*, 107.

22. González, *The Story of Christianity*, 140.

23. Micklethwait and Wooldridge, *God Is Back*, 358.

24. Hanson, *Religion and Politics in the International System Today*, 67; Toft, Philpott, and Shah, *God's Century*, 63.

25. Carlson and Owens, *The Sacred and the Sovereign*, 1.

26. Thomas, *The Global Resurgence of Religion and the Transformation of International Relations*, 25.

27. Shah and Philpott, "The Fall and Rise of Religion in International Relations," 33.

28. Philpott, "The Catholic Wave," 33; Toft, Philpott, and Shah, *God's Century*, 33.

29. Toft, Philpott, and Shah, *God's Century*, 33.

30. Toft, Philpott, and Shah, *God's Century*, 59; Philpott, "The Religious Roots of Modern International Relations," 211.

31. Shah and Philpott, "The Fall and Rise of Religion in International Relations," 34.

32. Thomas, "A Globalized God."

33. Pollis, "Greece," 155.

34. Shah and Philpott, "The Fall and Rise of Religion in International Relations," 34–37.

35. Philpott, "Has the Study of Global Politics Found Religion?" 188; Safran, *The Secular and the Sacred*, 54.

36. Lee, *Religion and Politics in the Middle East*, 21, 29.

37. Berger, "Secularization Falsified," 25.

38. Toft, Philpott, and Shah, *God's Century*, 66.

39. Toft, Philpott, and Shah, *God's Century*, 68.

40. Luttwak, "The Missing Dimension," 9.

41. Toft, Philpott, and Shah, *God's Century*, 71–72.

42. Micklethwait and Wooldridge, *God Is Back*, 50.

43. Toft, Philpott, and Shah, *God's Century*, 74.

44. Toft, Philpott, and Shah, *God's Century*, 75.

45. Micklethwait and Wooldridge, *God Is Back*, 32.

46. Haynes, "Religion and Politics: What Is the Impact of September 11?" 14.

47. Thomas, *The Global Resurgence of Religion and the Transformation of International Relations*, 53.

48. Madeley, "Religion and the State," 177; Lefebvre, "Disestablishment of the Church," 300; Bader, "Religions and States," 56–57.

49. Phil Zuckerman, *Society Without God*, 5, 103, 102.

50. Toft, Philpott, and Shah, *God's Century*, 48.

51. Casanova, "It's All About Identity, Stupid," 89.

52. Zuckerman, *Society Without God*, 110.

53. Paldam and Paldam, "The Political Economy of Churches in Denmark, 1300–2015," 444.

54. Kingston, *The Politics of Religion, Nationalism, and Identity in Asia*, 10.

55. Pew Research Center, "The Age Gap in Religion Around the World," June 13, 2018.

56. Kingston, *The Politics of Religion, Nationalism, and Identity in Asia*, 69.

57. Toft, Philpott, and Shah, *God's Century*, 49.

58. Talisse, "Religion in Politics," 69.

59. Appleby, *The Ambivalence of the Sacred*, 3.

60. Haynes, *Religion in Global Politics*, 9.

61. Shah and Philpott, "The Fall and Rise of Religion in International Relations," 26.

62. Tepe, *Beyond Sacred and Secular*, 42.

63. Shah and Philpott, "The Fall and Rise of Religion in International Relations," 28.

64. Toft, Philpott, and Shah, *God's Century*, 34, 79, 110.

65. Toft, Philpott, and Shah, *God's Century*, 35–36.

66. Lee, *Religion and Politics in the Middle East*, 20–23.

67. Goldberg, "Religion and Politics: Inseparable Through the Ages."

68. Thomas, "A Globalized God."

69. Hefner, "Religious Resurgence in Contemporary Asia," 1033.

70. Szyliowicz, "Religion, Politics and Democracy in Turkey," 200–201.

71. Berger, "Secularism in Retreat"; Haynes, *Religion in Global Politics*, 215.

72. Shelledy, "The Vatican's Role in Global Politics," 150.

73. Fox and Sandler, *Bringing Religion into International Relations*, 90, quoting An-Na'im, "The Islamic Counter-Reformation," 31.

74. Mewes, "Religion and Politics in American Democracy," 14.

75. Norris and Inglehart, *Sacred and Secular*, 217. Emphasis in original.

76. Barnett R. Rubin, "Religion and International Affairs," 21.

77. Micklethwait and Wooldridge, *God Is Back*, 354–355.
78. Toft, Philpott, and Shah, *God's Century*, 172.
79. Barneet R. Rubin, "Religion and International Affairs," 23.
80. Toft, Philpott, and Shah, *God's Century*, 172, 176.
81. Tepe, *Beyond Sacred and Secular*, 43.
82. Barnett R. Rubin, "Religion and International Affairs," 21.
83. Haynes, *Religion in Global Politics*, 126.
84. Johnston, *Faith-Based Diplomacy: Trumping Realpolitik*, 8.
85. Berger, "Secularism in Retreat"; Adogame, "How God Became a Nigerian," 489.
86. Haynes, *Religion in Global Politics*, 218.
87. Juergensmeyer, *Global Rebellion*, 254.
88. Berger, "Secularism in Retreat."
89. Tepe, *Beyond Sacred and Secular*, 43.
90. Micklethwait and Wooldridge, *God Is Back*, 145.
91. Cho and Katzenstein, "In the Service of State and Nation," 170–171, 179.
92. Haynes and Ben-Porat, "Globalisation, Religion and Secularisation," 126.
93. Singh, "Religion and Politics."
94. "Confusing and Confused," *The Economist* 377:8450 (October 29, 2005), 87; Agnew, "Deus Vult," 44.
95. Carlson and Owens, *The Sacred and the Sovereign*.
96. Nau, *Perspectives on International Relations*, 63.
97. Barnett, "Another Great Awakening?" 94.
98. Haynes, *An Introduction to International Relations and Religion*, 430.
99. Hamre, "Religion and International Affairs"; Eliot A. Cohen, "Religion and War," 13.
100. Eliot A. Cohen, "Religion and War," 13.
101. Burnett, "Implications for the Foreign Policy Community," 293.
102. Thomas Friedman, *The Lexus and the Olive Tree*, 248–249, 261.
103. Bellin, "Faith in Politics," 318.
104. Snyder, *Religion and International Relations Theory*, 2; Bellin, "Faith in Politics," 318.
105. Shimko, *International Relations*, 52.
106. Kegley and Raymond, *The Global Future*, 3rd ed., 39.
107. Burgess, "In-Churching Russia," 243.
108. Kingston, *The Politics of Religion, Nationalism, and Identity in Asia*, 11.
109. Thomas, *The Global Resurgence of Religion and the Transformation of International Relations*, 28.
110. Kegley and Wittkopf, *World Politics: Trend and Transformations*, 9th ed., 64; Mansbach and Taylor, *Introduction to Global Politics*, 2nd ed., 7.
111. Schlesinger and Foret, "Political Roof and Sacred Canopy?" 76.
112. Spiegel and Wehling, *World Politics in a New Era*, 2nd ed., 542
113. Gaddis, *The Long Peace*, 218.
114. Thomas, *The Global Resurgence of Religion and the Transformation of International Relations*, 56.
115. Fox and Sandler, *Bringing Religion into International Relations*, 28–29.
116. Thomas, *The Global Resurgence of Religion and the Transformation of International Relations*, 56.
117. McDougall, "Religion in World Affairs."
118. Spiegel and Wehling, *World Politics in a New Era*, 17.

119. Neack, *The New Foreign Policy: U.S. and Comparative Foreign Policy in the 21st Century*, 77.

120. Fox and Sandler, *Bringing Religion into International Relations*, 168.

121. Spiegel and Wehling, *World Politics in a New Era*, 18.

122. Neack, *The New Foreign Policy: U.S. and Comparative Foreign Policy in the 21st Century*, 12.

123. Kegley and Wittkopf, *World Politics: Trends and Transformation*, 9th ed., 17.

124. Kegley and Wittkopf, *World Politics: Trends and Transformation*, 9th ed., 17.

125. Toft, Philpott, and Shah, *God's Century*, 206.

126. Bruce, *Politics and Religion*, 162.

127. Hurd, "What's Wrong with Promoting Religious Freedom?"

4

International Actors: Religion in a Globalizing World

Illustration 5: The Polish Pope

The papal visit to Poland began in June 2, 1979, to the sound of bells pealing throughout the country and to the sight of Poles lining the streets.[1] During his nine days in his native land, perhaps one-third of all Poles came out to see "their pope," hearing his appeals for human dignity, resistance to atheism and authoritarianism, and workers' right to organize. Pope John Paul II never spoke about communism or the Soviet Union directly, but indirectly challenged both.

The pope's impact in Poland and other Eastern bloc countries is perhaps best illustrated by the Soviet Union's reaction. Never before had a pope visited a communist country. In anticipation of the visit, Soviet foreign minister Andrei Gromyko worried that "John Paul's visit to Poland would have 'the same effect on the masses as the Ayatollah Khomeini had in Iran.'"[2] Soviet premier Leonid Brezhnev warned Poland's leader Edward Gierek of the "strategic danger" of such a visit. Brezhnev was apparently alarmed by the pope's active foreign policy and the Catholic Church's "aggressive" actions in the Soviet Union and throughout the communist world, where states greatly restricted religious life. Five months after the visit, the Central Committee of the Soviet Communist Party approved a six-point "Decision to Work Against the Policies of the Vatican in Relation with Socialist States."[3] This was part of the Kremlin's larger efforts to blunt the pope's impact. These efforts ultimately failed.

Within Poland, where state leaders sought to restrict the Catholic Church to moral and spiritual matters, the pope helped unify Polish society; galvanized protesters and political groups; and inspired an unusual alliance of the Catholic Church, intellectuals, and workers, all of whom were in solidarity against the autocratic communist regime. A year after the pope visited Poland, the "Solidarity" movement became a political force. Eastern Europe's first independent (and illegal) trade union grew out of this movement. The movement was rife with "religious symbols and practices,"[4] including "shrines" to Solidarity in many Catholic churches. Led by Lech Walesa, it sought to transform the political system from below.

Solidarity, an independent, nationwide power outside the party-state, mobilized within an alternative sociopolitical space, which churches helped to provide. It threatened to marginalize the Polish communist party, which was the Soviet Union's main lever for exercising influence in Poland. Poles hoped Solidarity would produce favorable political change. They also feared it would prompt armed Soviet intervention. As it turned out, Solidarity was critical to the downfall of Polish communism and helped to undermine communism throughout the Eastern bloc.

So it came to pass in what was supposed to have been a "workers' paradise" that workers' strikes were launched with a Holy Mass. The single greatest catalyst for political change was the election of the Polish pope, the Polish Catholic Church provided leadership for resistance against the regime, and Poles viewed the Catholic Church as the only true guarantor of national sovereignty. In 1981, in response to government efforts to repress Solidarity, the Vatican supported economic sanctions against the Polish government.

John Paul II (born Karol Józef Wojtyla) was the first non-Italian pope in half a millennium and the first Polish pope in the history of the Catholic Church. "Polishness" (that is, his Polish national identity) proved politically significant for the pope as a transnational actor, for the international entity that is the church and, of course, for his native country. He "played a key role in Poland's political transition."[5]

Significance

To put this in perspective, we must distinguish between the underlying, permissive, and proximate causes of the Solidarity movement and Poles' revolt against their Soviet-sponsored regime. The underlying causes or conditions included economic problems, political repression, and the uneasy mix of communist and Catholic identities in Poland, where the Catholic Church is an important symbol of the nation and the transnational church garnered far more respect from Poles than the national government. During my visit to Poland in 1987, two years before the Berlin Wall came down, various Poles told me that their country was 98 percent Catholic, that one cannot be both Catholic and communist, and that I should "do the numbers" and understand that the country was only 2 percent communist. A "permissive cause," meaning something that allowed or failed to prevent Polish mobilization, was the church's autonomy from the state, even under communism. The church occupied a relatively open space in an otherwise closed society, allowing it to become associated with regime opposition. In 1987, in some very old Catholic churches I saw something like shrines to the Solidarity movement, something unimaginable in East Germany at the time. The proximate or immediate cause was the papacy of the Polish pope.

With John Paul's accession to the papacy in 1978, the church joined the struggle against authoritarianism and communism, both of which he had experienced firsthand in Poland. Due to John Paul's support for pro-democratization initiatives, Samuel P. Huntington credits him with spurring the most recent "wave" of democracy, a period in which at least thirty countries made transitions from authoritarianism to democracy. This wave began in the Iberian Peninsula and then washed over Latin America and Eastern Europe. The Pope evinced an abhorrence of all things smacking of communism, including the Marxist theory of class conflict and liberation theology. He advocated a strategy of political change through revolution—in sharp contrast to communist revolutions, this would be a "moral revolution," a revolution of conscience. John Paul himself was called "a revolutionary force," who offered a "moral critique of the Soviet bloc" and affected the course of world events.[6]

The pope was clearly aware of the geopolitical realities of the late 1970s. Consider the situation in Poland at the time he took office. Poland disdained and feared the Soviet Union. In 1939, shortly after Nazis invaded Poland, the Soviets did the same. Then, at the close of World War II, Soviet leaders ensured that Poland would become a communist-dominated state modeled on and constrained by the Soviet Union. The communist regime pressured the Catholic Church. As cardinal in a heavily Catholic country, Karol Józef Wojtyla had likewise pressured the regime. The pope's broader geopolitical concerns cropped up in his statements about the "logic of the blocs," meaning the Cold War division into the Eastern bloc and the Western bloc, and about its fallout in the Global South.

Not only did Pope John Paul II understand the geopolitical realities of his time, but he exerted a profound influence over them. In the

1980s, he worked with US president Ronald Reagan to weaken the Soviet Union's hold on Poland.[7] In 1992, a year after the Soviet Union's implosion, former Soviet premier Mikhail Gorbachev acknowledged that "everything that happened in Eastern Europe in these last few years would have been impossible without this pope."[8] On a visit to Poland nine years later, US president George W. Bush asserted that "the iron purpose and moral vision of a single man, Pope John Paul II, brought communism to its knees."[9] Of course, a number of other factors contributed to the collapse of international communism and the Soviet Union, but these comments by world leaders on both sides of the Cold War divide point to the political significance of papal diplomacy and of this particular Catholic leader.

Illustration 6: Saddam Hussein Plays the Religion Card—or Whose Holy War?

In August 1990, two days after Iraq invaded Kuwait, Saddam Hussein issued a "Call to Arabs and Muslims" for a jihad against Saudi Arabia and its Western allies; then, in July 1991, one day before US-led forces began bombing Iraqi forces, President Saddam Hussein ordered that *Allahu Akbar* (God Is Great) be sewed into the Iraqi flag. The addition of this phrase, originally added in Saddam's own handwriting, was a last-minute attempt to boost the regime's religious credentials and to rally Muslims to Iraq's side of the war. In both instances, he was playing the religion card or, more specifically, the Muslim card. In a surprising move, Saddam Hussein presented himself as the new champion of the Muslim faith.

The backdrop was Iraq's invasion of neighboring Kuwait, swiftly routing the Kuwaiti armed forces, annexing it as Iraq's nineteenth province, and beginning a repressive and brutal occupation. The United Nations immediately condemned the invasion and demanded Iraq's speedy withdrawal. Later in the fall, the UN Security Council drew a "line in the sand": Iraq had to withdraw its forces from Kuwait by January 15, 1991, or face UN-authorized military action. The Arab League also condemned the invasion, but called for a regional "Arab solution." Responding to Saudi Arabia's invitation, the United States committed US troops to shield its ally from a potential invasion by Iraq. For some Islamists, US boots on the ground in Saudi Arabia was a sacrilege, placing troops of "infidels" in the country home to Islam's two most sacred places, Mecca and Medina. Others, viewing it more as a matter of power and sovereignty, were concerned about the assertion of a new form of colonialism. At home, the US-based National Council of Churches (NCC) criticized the build-up of troops in the Persian Gulf, while the National Conference of Catholic Bishops (NCCB) warned that an offensive war would be unjust.

Saddam Hussein's response included calling for the "Muslim masses" to rise up against their rulers (whom he labeled the "emirs of oil") and to defend the holy sites of Mecca and Medina. He also called for a jihad against the Western "invaders" and Saudi Arabia. He said, "Arabs and Muslims and faithful everywhere, this is your day to rise and defend Mecca which is captured by the spears of the Americans and the Zionists. . . . Your brothers in Iraq are determined to (continue) jihad without any hesitation or retreat and without any fear of the foreign power."[10]

On January 9–11, 1991, nearly the UN deadline, Iraq convened a Popular Islamic Conference in Baghdad. Saddam Hussein used the conference to bring Islamists into Iraq's camp, portraying the impending war as between "believers" and "infidels." He "called for Muslims everywhere to declare jihad if Iraq were attacked."[11] In the end, Saddam Hussein did not withdraw Iraqi forces and, immediately after the UN ultimatum expired, the United States led a military action to liberate Kuwait.

Muslims were split regarding Saddam Hussein's invasion of Kuwait and the subsequent US-led war to push Iraq out of Kuwait. Religious leaders in three North African countries (Algeria, Sudan, and Tunisia) sided with Iraq. Ayatollah Ali Khamenei, Iran's spiritual guide and supreme leader, echoed Saddam's call for an anti-American jihad, but probably more as a statement of opposition to the United States than support for Iraq. Osama bin Laden and others who portrayed themselves as representatives of a pure tradition saw the Persian Gulf War as a new "crusade" against Islam. For bin Laden, US troops were not only "infidels," but a modern incarnation of the Christian Crusaders of old, which fueled his anger regarding US encroachment into the "Islamic world."[12] Again, though, it was the Saudi king who chose to bring in foreign troops—despite bin Laden's offer to mobilize fighters to defend the Saudi kingdom. (This stoked bin Laden's anger toward both the US and Saudi governments.) Once the war started, many pro-Iraq Muslims viewed the fight against UN-authorized forces as a jihad. The Arab public opinion opposed the war against Iraq. Some Muslim countries, Jordan and Yemen for instance, were sympathetic to Saddam Hussein.

Although some Muslim leaders and Muslim-majority states supported Saddam Hussein, most Muslim states as well as a good number of Islamic scholars rejected his actions. Following Iraq's aggression against another Muslim state, three hundred Muslim religious scholars declared that Iraq's aggression was "totally un-Islamic," called for the withdrawal of Iraqi forces, and asked the Organization of Islamic Cooperation (OIC) to form a "pan-Islamic" force to replace the foreign soldiers on Saudi soil.[13] The OIC debated the appropriate "Islamic" response. The result: the Saudi-supported OIC condemned Saddam Hussein's invasion and said Iraq should withdraw immediately from Kuwait. Saudi Arabia's highest religious authority called Saddam an enemy of God and issued a decree (fatwa) authorizing a holy war against Saddam Hussein's invading force. Saddam failed to listen to the UN, the OIC, or to the religious scholars who said he lacked the religious authority to declare a jihad.

In the end, a US-led coalition, which counted about a dozen Muslim countries among its ranks, forcibly removed Iraqi forces from Kuwait. Saudi troops, seeing themselves as defenders of Islam, chanted "Allahu Akbar." Saudi and Egyptian clergy called the war against Iraq a holy war,[14] since it was a legitimate defense against an aggressor.

Muslims, again, were split. Which autocratic, Muslim-majority state should they defend: Iraq, Kuwait, or Saudi Arabia? Most Islamists ended up buying into Saddam's narrative,[15] backing Iraq and opposing Saudi Arabia. As a rallying cry against non-Muslims, as this example shows, Islam can be quite effective—and quite complex.[16]

What became known as the Persian Gulf War thus entangled three Muslim-majority Gulf States (Iraq, Kuwait, and Saudi Arabia), a military coalition spearheaded by the only remaining superpower (the United States), pronouncements by the two largest intergovernmental organizations (the UN and OIC), and invocations of "holy war" on both sides of the Persian Gulf War (Iraq and Saudi Arabia). In calling for holy war, each side implicitly claimed that God was on their side. In addition, Saddam Hussein's rhetoric went in an unexpected direction.

Between Iraq's invasion of Kuwait in August 1990 and the commencement of the Persian Gulf War in January 1991, Saddam Hussein "found religion" and championed Islamist causes, such as the Palestinian cause. A couple of years later, Iraq's Baathist regime began a "faith campaign" that entailed adopting Islamic symbols and rhetoric, "building mosques, requiring increased religious education in Iraq, and consistently allying with Islamists abroad."[17] This was a surprising tack for one of the region's most secular regimes. Saddam Hussein, who ruled from 1979 to 2003, was an avowed secularist and governed through the Baath Party (a secular, modernizing socialist movement). Saddam's Iraq had decimated the Shia-Muslim scholars, fought against Islamists and religious dissidents at home, warred against Iran and the Iranian Revolution, and invaded another Muslim state. He would have been expected to use the language of anti-imperialism, not Islam. It was this leader and this regime that suddenly raised the banner of Islam. Few were duped by his "Islamic pretentions."[18]

The Islamic Card

To say that Saddam Hussein "played the religion card" means he used religion as a "tool to achieve policy goals." That is, he "coopted religion,"[19] playing on religious loyalties to serve political ends: rallying Muslims behind him and against the US-led coalition. As Charles Kimball states, "Once Saddam felt strong international pressure after his invasion of Kuwait, he suddenly got religion."[20] Having been considered a "bad Muslim,"[21] he abruptly changed his tune and drew on the rhetoric of jihad. It appears to have been a practical or instrumental move to bolster the regime's legitimacy. Perhaps Saddam had suddenly "found religion"; more likely is that he had found Islam could be politically useful to him. As stated by Saudi Islamic scholar al-Akkas, in framing the Persian Gulf War as a holy war and trying to curry favor with Muslims around the world, Saddam Hussein was "trying to play the so-called Islamic card."[22] In many situations, politicians have the possibility of playing the religion card. In Iraq, as in Nicaragua and Nigeria, some have chosen to do so.

Jihad

The term *jihad* needs some explanation. While often used interchangeably with "holy war," it is more complex than that. It means "striving," "struggle," "effort," or "exertion." The "greater jihad" is a spiritual and moral effort. It is the believer's internal struggle to follow the path of God or to strive in the way of God (or Allah). It is struggle that has nothing to do with armed warfare.

The "lesser jihad" is armed struggle, waged to defend or extend Islam. "Lesser jihad" can be the struggle for independence from European colonial powers. "Jihad, in this sense, provided the motive and the justification for many anticolonial wars and uprisings."[23] Today, it may mean struggling against foreign domination of predominantly Muslim societies. As such, Osama bin Laden's efforts to keep US soldiers off of Saudi Arabian soil were a type of jihad. At various times, bin Laden called for jihad against the United States in response to its assaults on

Muslims. Bin Laden killed and inspired others to kill in the name of religion. He claimed to be a Muslim. In Muslims' holy book, the Quran, he found justification for pursuing jihad as a holy war against infidels. He founded al-Qaeda. Al-Qaeda, Boko Haram, the Islamic State, Islamic Jihad . . . the list goes on. A number of groups that others label "terrorist organizations" invoke Islam and armed conflict.

Calls to this lesser jihad are theologically and politically controversial, as the discussion about Saddam Hussein suggests. There is no "Muslim Vatican" to define what does and does not accord with Islam. In Islam, as in all major religions, things are said and done that co-religionists reject. When abortion clinics are attacked in the name of Christianity, other Christians deny that this is a correct interpretation of Christian texts and traditions. When the Israeli prime minister was killed by a man who believed he was fulfilling God's will, most Jews said he had misconstrued Jewish theology.

For our purposes, suffice it to say that, first, religion is sometimes invoked to justify violence. Second, those who terrorize populations or assassinate political leaders in the name of religion are extremists; their interests and action are outside the mainstream. In the early twenty-first century, the cyberworld is, according to Jeff Kingston, the "tabernacle of extremists."[24] Finally, violence in the name of religion can have repercussions for domestic, regional, and international politics.

This chapter digs deeply into the macro, or global, level of analysis, demonstrating religion's important role in world politics. Events of the past few decades—the Iranian Revolution and Arab Spring, declarations of holy wars, and so on—demonstrate that "religion is a major factor in global affairs."[25]

This wide-angle lens of global/systemic analysis takes in transnational religious actors, ideas, and identities; religion's impact on international conflict and cooperation; and religion's interactions with such factors as power, democratization, and globalization. As globalization increases, it is common to say the world is getter smaller. With twenty-first century telecommunications, we are more aware of political and climatic events in remote corners of the world. Increasingly knit together by internationally traded goods (e.g., coffee and oil), cross-border services (e.g., banking), international organizations (e.g., the United Nations and the International Red Cross and Red Crescent Movement), transnational movements (e.g., the Islamic State), and transnational issues (e.g., communicable diseases), human beings are connected in more numerous and significant ways than ever before.

Shifts at the International Level

The international, or systemic, level of analysis looks at, as the name suggests, the global system as a whole. The many changes in this system may explain why it is currently defined by what preceded it: we are living in the post–Cold War, post-Soviet, post-9/11, and, as Chapters 2 and 3 suggest, post-secular era. This section outlines several major shifts.

First, much of the twentieth-century Cold War was a "tidy bipolar era," with two clear superpowers and their respective "poles" of power, including military alliances.[26] Then, in 1989, the Berlin Wall came down. Today, the Soviet Union and the Warsaw Pact are gone, power is more diffuse, and the distribution of power around the globe is less clear cut. The end of the past century brought the "unipolar moment" in which the United States was the unrivaled superpower. Early in the twenty-first century, the "great wheel of power is turning."[27] Russia is resurgent. China and other states in the Global South are rising.

Second, two major power shifts are afoot, according to Joseph Nye. One is "horizontal"[28]: a shift from the West toward the East, especially the two Asian giants (China and India), and the rise of the "rest" (the non-Western world). The other is a "vertical" shift from states as the locus of power towards nongovernmental actors, including transnational religious actor.

These shifts point to the second major type of change: the proliferation of actors on the world stage. Traditionally, international relations has referred to relations between and among states, especially the most powerful states. The number of states in the United Nations has increased from 159 members in 1990 to 195 in 2020. The Soviet Union splintered into fifteen states, Yugoslavia broke into six separate pieces, Czechoslovakia split in two, South Sudan seceded from Sudan, and other changes occurred. In addition to states, however, the number and significance of nonstate actors is increasing. These actors include multinational corporations and social movements. They include intergovernmental organizations (IGOs), such as the United Nations and the Organization of Islamic Cooperation, and nongovernmental organizations (NGOs) like the Holy See, the World Council of Churches, the Muslim Brotherhood, and al-Qaeda. Transnational communications among such groups are facilitated by social media and increasingly globalized mass media.

Third, driven by information technologies, telecommunications, and transportation, distance is shrinking and territorial borders are becoming more porous and somewhat less important. As the world becomes "smaller," we are witnessing the so-called death of distance. State sovereignty and states' roles are not what they once were. "Domestic" matters such as human rights abuses are now monitored and critiqued by other states and nonstate actors and, under the "responsibility to protect," may elicit foreign intervention. "Problems without passports"—such transnational health scares (e.g., Ebola, COVID-19), environmental concerns (e.g., climate change), crime syndicates, and terrorism—cannot be fixed by one state acting alone. They require coordinated international responses. Certainly, there is no world government—there is no authoritative executive, legislature, or judiciary with the power to compel compliance—but there is a trend toward more *global governance*. *Global governance* refers to international laws, institutions, principles, and processes. These things foster day-to-day cooperation among states and help states work together to solve common problems. In addition, many speak of the emergence of a global or transnational civil society as part of the larger process of globalization. The state is threatened from without by transnational actors, issues, identities, and norms, and from within by ethno-religious movements that threaten to tear it apart.

Fourth, as the world is coming together, it is also being torn apart by nationalist and populist forces. In fact, the prospect of becoming part of a homogenized global society gives impetus to groups to assert their unique identities and, in some cases, the creation of their own states. This explains, in part, the fracturing of multinational states into smaller states. Not wanting to be part of the undifferentiated mass of what Benjamin Barber calls "McWorld" (discussed in Chapter 7), groups construct, reconstruct, or reassert their local identities. When they understand themselves as a unique political community or nation, they push for greater autonomy or self-determination.

Fifth, the nature of large-scale political violence is changing, most notably in the places of the world with weak states and poorly governed societies. *Inter*state warfare (war between two or more states) is less common than it once was. Most armed conflicts are now *intra*state (i.e., some variety of civil war). "New nationalism" is the impetus of much armed conflict in the early twenty-first century. The uptick in nationalism is often associated with the reassertion of local identities, typically associated with ethnicity or religion.

Sixth, it has become common to say that we live in a democratic era. In the last quarter of the twentieth century, democracy swept over

Latin America. With the Cold War's end, democracy swept over much of the former Soviet republics and Eastern Europe. Democracy may still be winning many battles against authoritarianism, but Freedom House proclaimed in 2018 that democracy is in "crisis." Democracy, says Freedom House, is reeling in assaults on freedoms and democratic values.

Finally, religion is claiming (or reclaiming) an important role in the public sphere. "The past half-century has seen a significant increase in the public presence of religion worldwide."[29] As stated by political scientist Brandon Kendhammer, "The secularization thesis promising the decline of religious beliefs and values and the retreat of religious expressions in the private sphere has proven to be spectacularly wrong."[30]

In the context of these shifts, this chapter's focus is on what is variously called the international, systemic, or structural level of analysis—a sort of bird's-eye view of the intersections of religion and politics. We begin with geopolitics, which, like religion, is a way of seeing the world and thinking about the world order.

Geopolitics

Geopolitics views actors on the world stage, especially states, in terms of power and locations on a map. This focus on states and power means geopolitics pays considerable attention to transnational threats but scant attention to transnational religious actors, unless they pose a security threat. Why pay attention to the Catholic Church, which has only Swiss Guards and a postage stamp-sized piece of land? The World Council of Churches, Organization of Islamic Cooperation, and the Muslim Brotherhood lack even these. But they have relationships, ideas, and beliefs that cut across states' borders and affect events on the global stage.

Geopolitics concerns the relationship between geography and politics, especially political power. It is about spatial relations—or, as a realtor might say, it is all about location. Cuba's location goes a long way toward explaining why it was of such value to the Soviet Union and has been such a thorn in the side of the United States. Geography influences regional and global politics. Geopolitics concerns the geographic distribution of political and military power and how states' physical locations, relative sizes, climate, and natural resources affect their power as well as foreign policy decisions and outcomes.

The Cold War involved competing ideologies; probing weak spots in the other sides' sphere of influence; and building up arsenals of tanks, fighter jets, nuclear weapons, and so on to deter any potential aggression. In 1946, Winston Churchill spoke of an "iron curtain" descending across the continent of Europe. On one side of this curtain were Joseph Stalin, the Soviet Union, the capitals of Central and Eastern Europe, and the Communist International (which promoted the spread of communism across the globe). This, said Churchill, was the "Soviet sphere" of influence. On the other side were Churchill's country (the United Kingdom), the United States, and the countries of Western Europe. The UK had been eclipsed by the United States, which he said was at the "pinnacle of world power." Together, these two English-speaking countries needed to push back against the expansive tendencies of the Soviet Union and international communism. These were key points about the geopolitical rivalries that arose just after World War II and endured for four decades.

Today, the Cold War is over, but geopolitics remains. In 1991, the Soviet Union split into fifteen independent countries. Russia is the official successor state of the Soviet Union, getting the USSR's seat in the UN General Assembly and gaining control over all of its nuclear weapons. It has the geopolitical advantage of being in the heartland of a massive continent. Two of the other fourteen states, Georgia and Ukraine, live in Russia's shadow in the sense that they are neighbors of a much larger and far more powerful country. Geography is important here. Georgia and Ukraine share an eastern border with Russia and a western border with countries such as Poland and Romania, which were once part of the Soviet Union's sphere of influence and are now members of both the North Atlantic Treaty Organization (NATO) and the European Union (EU). Russian leaders appear discomfited by the spread of the NATO alliance toward Russia's western border. They want to keep buffer states between themselves and the West. This explains, in part, why Russia briefly invaded Georgia in 2008 and intervened in Ukraine in 2014, taking the Crimean Peninsula.

Spatial disposition matters. The geographic distribution of power matters, too, especially to realists. As these examples suggest, geopolitics frames the world as a great chessboard.

Turning to the Middle East, some states derive power and importance from sitting on huge reserves of oil. An abundance of a natural resource can be a geopolitical advantage and a source of geopolitical competition. Think, for instance, of how the location of big oil reserves affects world politics. Would the United States have so readily committed US troops to defend the Saudi Arabian monarchy if their main export was rutabagas, rather than oil? Some states control crucial strategic trade passages or pipeline routes. Some share a border with a powerful and hostile state—India and Pakistan, for instance—while the United States has the good fortune to be bordered by, as a French diplomat said long ago, weak state, weak state, fish, fish.

Home of the three Abrahamic religions, we see that various great powers have sought to control the Middle East or to tilt this part of the chessboard so as to serve its self-interests—from the Ottoman Empire to the United Kingdom and France to the United States and the Soviet Union—and the same can be said for regional powers.[31] The region was colonized and then, during the Cold War, became the site of strategic intervention by the two superpowers who viewed the region as geopolitically important. Today, we see great power engagement in Syria, with Russia on the side of the Bashar al-Assad regime and the United States focusing much of its efforts on routing the Islamic State, which had seized territory from Syria and Iraq. Within the region, there is an ongoing Sunni-Shia conflict, with fairly distinct geographical divisions. In Syria, this conflict has played out in the contest between the pseudo-Shia leader, Bashar al-Assad, and a Sunni Islamist-led insurgency. Samuel Helfont argues that "sectarian strife" (i.e., Sunni-Shia conflict) "is a hallmark of Middle Eastern geopolitics today.[32] The sectarian divide lines up with the regional power struggle between Shia Iran and Sunni Saudi Arabia.

The idea of a geopolitics of religion is a bit odd because religions have neither hard power nor fixed locations on the global chessboard. However, the Roman Catholic Church, with some 1.2 billion adherents, and Islam, with 1.6 billion believers, have the power to shape global events. The Catholic Church has geographical pillars in Europe, Latin America, and the United States. Muslim-majority societies are located primarily in the arc that goes from West Africa, across northern Africa and the Middle East, to the Central Asian republics of the former Soviet Union. Buddhist-majority societies are scattered across Asia. To say that religions lack hard power suggests they lack the ability to coerce and intimidate, which is based on armed force and economic pressure. Although lacking the hard power that would enable them to command others, religious leaders and institutions may have soft power; that is, they can have intangible resources that enable them to pull others to embrace their agenda. Soft power is attractive or co-optive power, generally based on intangible power resources. A term coined by Joseph Nye, it involves "the ability to get others to want what you want."

Geopolitical circumstances affect states' foreign policies, the pursuit of their national interests, and their international conduct. We now move from an emphasis on geography, power, and states to a far newer analytical perspective with a different set of actors.

Transnational Relations

"Transnational actors" are neither sovereign states nor intergovernmental organizations, whose members are states. They do not represent states. This analytical perspective does not cut states out of the picture, but highlights the role of nonstate actors (or agents). Transnational actors operate across states' borders. They include for-profit, multinational corporations (MNCs), like Nestlé; nonprofit aid and relief groups, like the International Red Cross and Red Crescent Movement; terrorist organizations, like al-Qaeda, which has a network of terrorists; transnational advocacy networks (TANs), which advocate for particular causes (e.g., democracy) and try to influence international norms and standards of behavior; and transnational social movements, among which some count Islamism.

"Transnational" refers to relationships, movements, forces, communication, transactions, and threats that transcend states' borders and affect two or more nations—or, more accurately, two or more *states*— but are not necessarily global. Various types of things cross borders: physical objects (consumer goods, drugs, weapons); people (travelers, migrants, refugees, religious pilgrims, terrorists); services (e.g., banking); money; political movements; challenges and threats (disease, terrorism, human trafficking, acid rain, and so on); and ideas, ideologies, information, norms, culture, and beliefs.

In this era of "post-secular" international relations, faith-based organizations are rising in transnational significance. Part of religion's resurgence is the evolution of religious communities into transnational political actors. This is related to the broader phenomenon of globalization. Religion is rising through transnational organizations, such as the Roman Catholic Church, the World Council of Churches, the Organization of the Islamic Conference (OIC), and the Muslim Brotherhood. To set the stage for the Muslim Brotherhood and the OIC, we turn to Islam and Islamism.

Islam and Islamism

Islam is both the second largest and the fastest-growing major religion in the world, and Islamism, or political Islam, is a fast-moving ideology, entering into the politics of many Muslim-majority countries. Like other major religions, Islam has different branches. (Think, for instance, of

Protestantism and Catholicism within Christianity.) About 85 percent of the world's Muslims adhere to the Sunni branch of Islam and roughly 15 percent to the Shia branch. Islam is the majority religion in one-fourth of the world's states. Of these states, only four—Azerbaijan, Bahrain, Iran, and Iraq—have Shia Muslim majorities. As a religion, Islam teaches believers to pray, fast, give alms, make a pilgrimage, and generally live according to God's will. Followers of Islam are Muslims. Those who embrace Islamism are Islamists. Islamism is bound up with religion's return to the public sphere and the broader resurgence of Islam. While all Muslims may want to influence the government under which they live, to embrace Islamism (i.e., to be an Islamist) generally means to stir a lot more politics into the pot of religion.

To use Daniel Pipes's analogy, the distinction between Islam and Islamism is akin to the distinction between faith and ideology.[33] Islamism (also called "political Islam") is not a religion or a theology, but an ideology. In India, there is a similar distinction between Hinduism and Hindutva; Hinduism is a major religion, while Hindutva (roughly translated as "Hindu-ness") is an ideology. Jeff Kingston calls Islamism an ideology of resistance.[34] It is a collective belief system that can serve as a plumb line against which to measure and critique the current political order. In *Political Ideologies*, Leon Baradat identifies five elements of all ideologies. According to Baradat, ideologies are political statements (they concern the use of power and how decisions are made for a group of people); they assess the present situation (or status quo) and offer an alternative vision of a better future; they are action-oriented (they suggest how to move society from the present situation to the desired future); they are directed at the masses, not the elite, of the population; and they are couched in simple, motivational terms. Islamists' assessment of the political, religious, and social status quo finds it wanting, so they seek change. Hence,

$$Islam + ideology = Islamism.$$

Except it is more complicated than that.

A main source of complication is that Islam, like other religions, is not monolithic, and the term *Islamism* gets applied to a fairly diverse set of actors. The Muslim Brotherhood, political parties like Tunisia's Resistance Party, and al-Qaeda all get lumped together.

Another complicating factor is that the demise of the Soviet Union and international communism initiated a search for a new ideological foe, and some built up Islamism as the new threat. The "red peril" of communism was cut down to size. Now a new threat, the "green menace" arose, green being the color of Islam. Nathan Lean calls Islamism the "new *ism* enemy."[35]

Islamism shares elements with other modern, transnational political ideologies, such as liberalism and nationalism. Islamism is today's ideological vehicle for expressing some Muslims' "grievances, frustrations, anger."[36]

Islamism is a worldview embraced by some Muslims that "situates the religion of Islam at the center of public life. Its principles and values should, in their view, shape political and legal spheres."[37] To the extent that Islam is not shaping politics and the law, change is needed and the masses need to help bring about those changes. Islamism is thus an ideology that encourages political mobilization under the banner of Islam. It is a political project in that it makes claims on political allegiance, mobilizes Muslim identity for political purposes, and seeks to wield state power in order to bring about the vision of the desired future. It posits that "Islam is the solution" to governance issues and society's problems. Islamists see themselves as the "just" pitted against the "unjust," especially rulers at home (dubbed the "near enemy"), but generally against the West, too, which is seen as the root of many injustices and domestic problems (and dubbed the "far enemy").[38]

It also has elements of a transnational movement that is at once religious and political. According to Graham Fuller, Islamism is the "single biggest political movement" across the entire arc of Muslim-majority states.[39]

Intermestic Nature of Islamism

Islamism has both transnational and intermestic features. The term *intermestic* points to the interplay between *inter*national and do*mestic* politics; Islamism arises out of this interplay, which has implications for both international relations and national politics. This interplay developed as a reaction to Western colonization and modernization, on the one hand, and the less-than-stellar governance of many Muslim-majority states, on the other. For Islamists, the problem, and the reason all imported ideologies have failed, is because Islam has been excluded from government, and societies have deviated from the clear and correct path of Islam. Besides being rejected as Western imports, secular governments and worldly "isms" failed to produce the desired results after independence from colonial rule. States tried Arab nationalism, but it failed to unite societies. They tried socialism, but it failed to deliver equality, was associated with "militant atheism," and was discredited by the examples of the Soviet Union and its Eastern European satellites. Other "isms" also failed to deliver on their promises. Hobbled by weak institutions, corruption, misrule, and plain old bad governance, often topped with brutal authoritarianism (as in Sudan and Syria), governments in many Muslim-majority states failed to ensure security and adequately address societal crises. They simply did not deliver the goods. Recall the discussion of the Arab Spring in Chapter 2. Mass protests arose in Tunisia, Libya, Egypt, Syria, Yemen, and Bahrain. "All the protests were driven to some degree by the same set of factors: a large number of unemployed young men, an increase in food prices, and long-standing dissatisfaction with corrupt and repressive governments."[40] Within this economic, political, and ideological context, Islamism became an alternative to the ideologies that were imported and proved wanting. Ideologies and governments failed, according to Islamists, because political leaders and their policies were not sufficiently Islamic. Islam is the solution to such problems.

While Islamists push governments to change their policies and practices, governments in predominantly Muslim states sometimes manipulate Islamist groups at home and abroad to enhance their domestic power and advance their foreign policy interests. This might be Saddam Hussein playing the religion card, Iran supporting Shia Islamists in Iraq and Palestinian Islamists in Israel and Palestine, or Saudi Arabia building mosques and establishing educational programs in other countries to influence their practice of Islam and to build transnational connections.[41]

Islam and Islamism can thus influence states' foreign policies. The foreign policy implications can be militant confrontation or hostile relations with other states and societies, antagonistic relations between Sunni-majority states and Shia-majority states, or Muslim solidarity. Or none of the above. A distinctive "Islamic foreign policy" does not exist.

Over time, Muslim-majority states have gradually bought into the international institutions and norms that govern relations among states. They join the United Nations. They respect other states' borders and sovereignty. Although clashes make the headlines, day-to-day cooperation is the rule.

Islamism's Impacts

Events have shown that, although small in numbers, Islamists can be a highly dedicated and politically influential minority, with big impacts on regional and international relations. Recent decades have seen an upsurge in Islamist movements, politically galvanized by the 1979 Iranian Revolution, the 1980s fight against Soviet troops in Afghanistan, the 1991 Persian Gulf War, the 2003 US invasion of Iraq, the 2011 Arab Spring, and from 2014 to 2016 the advances of the self-proclaimed Islamic State.

If we drill down into Islam, then drill down further into Islamism, we come to militant and exclusionary Islamism. These are extremists. Their actions are often headline news. Their views are not typical of most Muslims or Islamists, and they are uncompromising in their advocacy of their positions. These extremists can be a threat to the Westphalian international system and to international security. They generally reject the global processes of the creation and spread of the Westphalian secular nation-state, the historical forces of Western imperialism and hegemony, and the drumbeat of "Western values and influence."[42] Both the secular nature of the state and the fragmentation of Muslims who should be in one community (the *umma*) violate the unity of Islam—which is associated with the oneness of God—and are, therefore, un-Islamic. Rather than state sovereignty, a bedrock of the international order, or popular sovereignty, a bedrock of democracy, Islamists aver that ultimate sovereignty rests with God alone. For those who want Muslims to be governed by Islamic law, international law is problematic, too, since it is human-made law and does not accommodate Islamic law.[43] Politicizing Islam and adopting an extreme position also poses a risk to international security; some extremists engage in terror in the name of Islam. While Muslims and Islamists as a whole have adapted to the norms, rules, and institutions of the modern international order, extremists tend to buck the system.

As the title of Mohammed Ayoob's book suggests, there are "many faces of political Islam."[44] Islamists differ regarding "'what' to implement and 'how' to implement it."[45] Very different manifestations of Islamism are found in Afghanistan, Egypt, Indonesia, Iran, Pakistan, Saudi Arabia, Sudan, and other states with large Muslim populations.

Muslim Brotherhood

By most accounts, modern Islamism began in Egypt in 1928, when Hasan al-Banna founded the Muslim Brotherhood. This organization represents "one of the Arab world's oldest political movements"[46] and the world's oldest and most influential Islamist organization. In al-Banna's reading, the Quran was a comprehensive life manual and Islam was a "total" system,[47] encompassing religion and politics with no bright line between them.

World events help to explain why the pan-Islamic Muslim Brotherhood arose when it did. It was founded after World War I in the wake of the collapse of the Ottoman Empire (a multinational Islamic empire) and the end of the caliphate system that had long united Muslims. At the time, the Arab-speaking world was a group of colonies. Al-Banna spoke out against the colonizers and "the West" more generally. When Western colonization ended, the Muslim Brotherhood would provide the basis for a new Islamic identity and an Islamic state or global caliphate. Its credo: "Allah is our objective; the Koran is our constitution; the prophet is our leader; Jihad is our way; death for the sake of Allah is our wish."

The Muslim Brotherhood's key ideologue, Sayyid Qutb (1906–1966), was radicalized by the Egyptian government's persecution of the Muslim Brotherhood and the years he spent in prison. He advocated total war against internal and external enemies. On the state level, Qutb denigrated Muslim rulers as unbelievers because they were not trying to Islamicize the state and society. He saw Islam as an alternative to the flawed, human-created systems of capitalism, Marxism, and nationalism.[48] He urged "real" Muslims to emulate the Prophet Muhammad's ways and replace existing (secular) governments and "apostate" rulers (the "near enemy") with Islamic ones. When he was imprisoned and tortured, his writings diverged from al-Banna's. He began calling for active struggle (jihad) against tyranny. On the international level, as he radicalized, Qutb determined that Islam's "far enemy" was "Western civilization." Qutb called for a global struggle against Islam's external enemies.

Qutb's thinking has influenced global terrorists and terrorist organizations, such as al-Qaeda; yet, despite his influence, today's Muslim Brotherhood embraces nonviolent political action and remains inside legal frameworks. Dissatisfied with the Muslim Brotherhood's nonviolent stance, radicalized factions have split off and formed militant organizations. There is a good chance that the Muslim Brotherhood inspired some of the very same leaders of the Islamic State who now reject it.

In Egypt, where it began, the Muslim Brotherhood is "the most cohesive political movement, with an unparalleled ability to mobilize its followers."[49] Initially, the Muslim Brotherhood rose up against the British-backed Egyptian monarchy and, after independence, sought to move Egypt farther from the West and closer to theocracy and the Islamization of society. The secular and repressive Egyptian state alternated between banning and accommodating it.

When the Arab Spring arrived in Egypt in 2011, Egyptians filled Tahrir Square and President Hosni Mubarak stepped down. Despite repression under Mubarak, the Muslim Brotherhood was better organized than non-Islamists, willing to play by the rules of the political game, and poised to acquire power. In the subsequent elections, Islamists won almost three-fourths of the seats in parliament and Egyptians chose the Muslim Brotherhood's candidate, Mohamed Morsi, as president. Politics were becoming Islamized in post-Mubarak Egypt. The Muslim Brotherhood soon signaled its intent to impose its austere, non-egalitarian ideology, including Islamic law, on the entire population.[50] In 2012, Morsi pushed through a controversial Islamist constitution. In addition, having never been in power, the Muslim Brotherhood was not adept at governing and failed to deliver public goods and services. An inept Islamist state was not what Egyptians had bargained for. As in 2011, Egyptians took to the streets. Morsi was toppled by a popularly backed military coup in mid-2013. The coup's leader and country's new president, Abdel-Fattah al-Sisi, then banned the Muslim Brotherhood, branding its Islamist adversaries as terrorists and jailing many of its members.

Although its reach is now global, the Muslim Brotherhood began locally. At the outset, it mostly did charity work among Egypt's urban poor (e.g., building schools and opening health clinics), making up for the government's failure to provide social services, and working to enhance the Muslim community's religiosity. It then added both ballot and bullet political activities, fielding candidates in elections (the ballot part) and engaging in armed struggle (the bullet part). Then it renounced armed struggle.

The Muslim Brotherhood has both national and transnational dimensions. It is national in the sense that there is an Egyptian Muslim Brotherhood, a Jordanian Muslim Brotherhood, a Sudanese Muslim Brotherhood, and so on. Another national dimension is that it is "the parent of many of the Islamist political parties in the region."[51] It is transnational in the sense that, while not global (i.e., it does not have branches everywhere in the world), its ideas and inspiration readily transcend states' boundaries.

The Muslim Brotherhood has spread beyond Egypt's borders and beyond the Arab-speaking Middle East. It now has affiliates in more than seventy countries and has a transnational agenda. The Muslim Brotherhood has become a far-flung collection of groups that, although united in calling for societies under Islamic law, vary widely across the world.

The Muslim Brotherhood and Organization of Islamic Cooperation are both religious transnational actors. Whereas the Muslim Brotherhood is a nongovernmental organization, the OIC is an intergovernmental organization. NGOs are typically nonprofit organizations that are independent from state governments and organized around a specific issue, such as the environment or international development. IGOs, in contrast, are created by a treaty and comprised of and funded by sovereign states to further shared interests. Both are nonstate actors.

Organization of Islamic Cooperation

Like the WCC and the Holy See, the OIC is an important faith-based actor at the United Nations. Founded in 1969 as the Organization of the Islamic Conference, the OIC has attracted more attention and exerted more global influence in the post-9/11 era. Now called the Organization of Islamic Cooperation, the OIC is a geographically, politically, and economically heterogeneous grouping of fifty-seven Muslim countries. It seeks to bring Muslim countries together to support common interests and improve Muslim states' collective position in world politics, as well as to promote peace, security, and Islamic values. It endeavors, for instance, to protect Islam's "true image" and to stop "Islamophobia."[52] Its membership goes well beyond the Arab-speaking world, including countries such as Indonesia, Pakistan, Bangladesh, and Nigeria. Although the OIC charter is vague as to what constitutes a Muslim state, most of the OIC's member-states have Muslim majorities and many have established Islam as the state religion. Islam is the common bond that holds the OIC together. It is the only religiously based intergovernmental organization.

Consider the OIC's response to a controversial US policy announced in January 2017. President Donald Trump issued an executive order that temporarily barred entry to the United States from seven countries (Iran, Iraq, Libya, Somalia, Sudan, Syria, and Yemen). Although Trump insisted this was not a "Muslim ban," all seven are countries with large Muslim majorities. Leaders of major countries that did not make the list of seven, such as Saudi Arabia, were "conspicuously silent" on this issue, prompting a *New York Times* reporter to speculate about a "lack of political solidarity" among Muslim countries.[53] The OIC did, however, find its voice. The world's largest organization of Islamic states issued a statement expressing "grave concern" about the travel ban on seven OIC member states. The organization also said, "Such selective and discriminatory acts will only serve to embolden the radical narratives of extremists."

Some factors impede the OIC's ability to create pan-Islamic identity and unity and to engage in collective political action on behalf of Muslims around the world. First, as with any intergovernmental organization, the OIC can only promote common interests when its member states have common interests. It is tough to coordinate actions among member states when interests diverge. While seeking to further a transnational Islamic identity, the OIC is hobbled by member states' competing national foreign policy concerns and the pursuit of their own narrow national interests. Its member states' tendencies to prioritize national interests over transnational Muslim interests limits the OIC's role as a distinct actor on the world stage.

Collective action is, of course, even more difficult when there are conflicts among the members, including regional power struggles and sectarian differences. Two leading members, Saudi Arabia and Iran, both aspire to be the regional leader. Both make geopolitical calculations. Shia Iran has seen itself as the leader of the Muslim world since its 1979 revolution. Saudi Arabia embraces a particular kind of Sunni Islam, Wahhabism, and is the center of the Wahhabi transnational religious movement. Its claim to leadership rests on being home to Mecca and Medina and having extensive natural resources.

In the Syrian civil war, Iran's Shia authoritarian regime backs Syria's Shia authoritarian regime, which is led by Bashar al-Assad. Saudi Arabia's Sunni monarchy opposes the Syrian regime. (To add to the complicated situation, Russia supports the Syrian regime, and the United States opposes it.) The OIC endeavors to maintain strict neutrality in such conflicts. This stance makes it all the more surprising that the OIC suspended Syria's membership in the organization in 2012, condemning the violence and human suffering in that country.

As such, far from the idea of the Islamic *umma* (community) there are cleavages within the transnational Muslim community. These cleavages became more prominent with the Islamic State, a militant Sunni Muslim group that proved quite willing to kill Shias and moderate Muslims. The sectarian divide dates back to very early Islam when the question of the Prophet Muhammad's successor arose. What has changed of late is that the Sunni-Shia divide has become quite politicized.

The second factor is that the Organization of Islamic Cooperation operates on the basis of conflicting models: the Westphalian nation-state model and the *umma*/Muslim model. While seeking to constitute a new *umma*, a distinct transnational community of all Muslims, the OIC operates within the global nation-state system. It tacitly acknowledges the validity of the Westphalian system by the fact that, as an IGO, its members are sovereign states, by having a seat at the table with other IGOs (e.g., the UN), and by recognizing the authority of international law. Finally, some important groups, such as al-Qaeda, do not see the OIC as sufficiently Islamic and, therefore, do not support its work. So, there are various obstacles to achieving Islamic "one-ness" and the OIC's hoped-for cooperation.[54]

Still, the OIC has spoken as one voice on such matters as Islamo-phobia, socioeconomic development in the Muslim world, combating terrorism, and denouncing the violent acts on 9/11 and Osama bin Laden's claims.[55] Given common threats, such as the Islamic State, forging cooperation among the OIC's member states is as important as ever.

The Roman Catholic Church

The Roman Catholic Church is unique in its role as a geopolitical actor. Active in world affairs for a millennium, it has taken a series of hits in its European home base, but today its role in the world is once again growing. Catholicism has an unusually "internationalist" posture, meaning it encourages peoples and nation-states to pull together, rather than pull in multiple directions in the name of nationalism and national interests. (As mentioned with regard to the EU constitution, the Catholic Church has backed European integration.)

The Catholic Church also has a transnational posture. It has a territorial base; a very large, worldwide flock; and, of late, very well-traveled leaders. In Europe lies the church's traditions, including its historic role as a major political force, and the institution's home base, a small enclave within Italy. Since the mid-twentieth century, however, the Roman Catholic population has become more internationalized as it continues to experience a geographic shift from Europe in the Global North toward the Global South, including Africa, Asia, and Latin America. Today, almost half of the world's Catholics are in the Americas. Latin America provides the bulk of the faithful, so it makes sense that Pope Francis is from Argentina, and the Holy See participates in the Organization of American States (OAS). It engages in a "global struggle for souls."[56] It claims a universal doctrine and has a universal mission. It also has its own transnational communications network.

The Roman Catholic Church has a unique feature: a centralized, hierarchical structure that connects it in a singular way to members of its far-flung flock. At the head of this religious administration is the pope. Globe-trotting popes knit together the Catholic community, make state visits and pronouncements on various issues, and, some contend, contribute to the creation of a global public sphere.[57] Pope John Paul II (1978–2005), who visited more than one hundred countries during his pontificate, "literally became the globe's most visible promoter of religious freedom," which was at the center of his larger promotion of human rights.[58] While popes travel to many states, many state leaders also make a point of visiting the Vatican.

The Roman Catholic Church presents a number of paradoxes. First, the church as an institution and the pope as its leader enjoy political effectiveness without the "normal instruments of political power."[59] It cannot even defend itself and, thus, relies on Italy for protection. Yet the church and the pope have power. A pope's power rests on his leadership roles and styles, the church's geographical bases, and the moral authority to legitimize or delegitimize actions.[60]

This brings us to a second paradox: while popes are transnational actors, men whose pronouncements may have political consequences, they typically deny any political intent. The current pope, Pope Francis, laments the church's politicization. Still, he apologized for church leaders' silence during the 1994 spasm of violence known as the Rwandan genocide. Much to the chagrin of Turkey's leaders, he urged people not to forget the Armenian genocide of 1915. It is hard to be a moral leader without making statements that step on political toes.

Consider his 2017 visit to Myanmar (Burma). The Rohingya are a Muslim ethnic minority in a country with a Buddhist majority. The government slaps the label "Bengalis" on Rohingya, as though they came from Bangladesh, which is located between Myanmar and India. The government does not recognize them as Burmese citizens and asks high-profile international visitors not to use the term *Rohingya*. If the pope used the term during his visit, he risked creating a diplomatic rift and perhaps making life harder for Myanmar's Catholic population. If the pope avoided using the term, then he would appear to be ignoring the plight of this brutalized Muslim population—and would get criticized by international media and human rights groups, which is what happened. The point is, either way—using the term or not using it—could be taken as a political statement by an important figure.

As an individual, the pope is arguably the world's single most important and most powerful religious actor. The pope has been toward the top of *Forbes'* list of "The World's Most Powerful People" each of the past several years. He has spiritual power or the power of moral persuasion as well as the power to legitimize or delegitimize a policy, an act, a leader, or a government.

We arrive at a third paradox: the pope is simultaneously head of a sovereign microstate and of a transnational religious organization; Vatican City State is a state only, while the Roman Catholic Church is a nonstate actor. This points to the pope's and the church's dual character.

Vatican City exercises sovereignty and *temporal* power over a bite-sized territory, while the Holy See embodies *spiritual* sovereignty and power that is not geographically limited.[61]

Like other states, Vatican City is an independent and sovereign territorial entity with fixed borders (the world's tiniest state), a government (a theocracy), a stable population (less than a thousand inhabitants) as well as an independent foreign policy. Its chief foreign policy goals are, beyond survival, defending Catholic communities around the world, promoting peace, and "doing good" or advancing the "good of humanity."[62] The Vatican (technically, the Holy See) is recognized under international law as a member of the community of states. It has Permanent Observer status in the United Nations and is a member of other intergovernmental organizations. It has diplomatic relations with 182 states; it sends diplomats ("papal nuncios") around the globe and receives foreign diplomats; and it has established concordats (formal agreements or treaties) with dozens of states. As such, it can and does enter into international agreements.

As a permanently politically neutral state, the Vatican eschews political alliances and, as a general rule, instead of taking sides, it offers its "good offices" to mediate conflicts. Its global standing enables it to serve as a third party in the peaceful resolution of conflicts, sometimes by creating back channels of communication. For instance, Pope Francis (2013–present) and Vatican diplomats facilitated secret talks between the United States and Cuba, which resulted in the reestablishment of long-suspended diplomatic relations in 2015.

This ties in with the pope's influence as pontiff, a bridge or mediator. The pope carries moral prestige and authority as the "master bridge-builder." Pope John Paul II helped to bridge the divide between his homeland (Poland) and the West. Pope Francis, whose homeland is Argentina, is building bridges between the West and the rest, especially the developing world.

Before Stalin's question about how many military divisions the pope had, Napoleon told his envoy in Rome, "Deal with the pope as if he had 200,000 men at his command." After serving a number of years in Rome, "the envoy said 500,000 was nearer the mark." Today, as then, the pope has no legions of soldiers at his command. What he has is a global flock—legions of Catholics—and a great deal of moral authority, which can "speak truth to power" and persuade or shame other global actors. In the postwar world, Pope John Paul II used his global pulpit to take on communism. In 2015, Pope Francis set out a moral case for protecting the environment.

Popes are not policymakers, but they can influence international agendas. The Catholic Church has no divisions, but at times wields a great deal of political power.

World Council of Churches

Formally begun in 1948, the World Council of Churchs (WCC) is an ecumenical union that represents over three hundred Christian denominations and more than four hundred million Christians in one-hundred-plus countries. As with larger trends in Christianity, while founding churches were largely located in the industrialized countries of the Global North (specifically, Europe and North America), the weight has shifted toward the developing countries of the Global South (Africa, Asia, the Caribbean, Latin America, the Middle East, and the Pacific).

The WCC was created to unify the diverse array of Christians and Christian churches. The desire for unity took a hit when the Roman Catholic Church opted out of membership, but it participates as an observer. This "global fellowship of churches" aims to transcend the interests of national churches and encourage cooperation and the sharing of resources.[63] It holds global assemblies every few years.

The World Council of Churches was founded during the period when the Cold War was just beginning to take shape and the central organizations of the postwar international order were being created, most notably the Bretton Woods system (the International Monetary Fund and the World Bank) and the United Nations. For the WCC's founders, their transnational organization would serve as a check on totalitarian states and Marxist-style collectivism.[64]

In the latter part of the twentieth century, the WCC attacked colonization and South Africa's system of apartheid. The WCC took a stance in opposition to apartheid and in defense of human rights, and it "played an important role" in the downfall of the system of institutionalized racism.[65] It challenged apartheid on theological and moral grounds. It challenged the legitimacy of the white-dominated regime and provided moral, symbolic, and financial support to the people of South Africa.[66] The WCC also supported the international sanctions campaign against the South African government. Such moves gave pause to the regime as well as some South African churches that had provided religious cover for apartheid. The WCC's involvement led Christians on either side of the apartheid debate to begin dialoging. As such, this transnational organization engaged in a pressing international issue.

For some Christian theologians, the WCC became the religious counterpart to the secular United Nations at its founding.[67] Similarly, some call the OIC the "United Nations of Islam."[68] Both are (like the Holy See) nonstate religious actors. However, the WCC is a nongovernmental organization, since its members are private, voluntary organizations; in contrast, the OIC is counted among intergovernmental organizations, meaning its members are sovereign states. The OIC was created by states and can only do what they empower it to do, which limits its ability to forge pan-Islamic unity. The OIC is unique among IGOs in that it has an explicitly religious criterion for membership and that, of IGOs, only the United Nations has more members.

Transnational Religion

After the caliphate was abolished in 1924, Islam had no caliph—no institution or leader comparable to the pope and claiming transnational authority—though ninety years later the Islamic State (ISIS) proclaimed restoration of the caliphate. That is, Islam is a transnational religion, but lacks the Catholic Church's institutional structure, territorial base, diplomatic standing, and centralized hierarchy.

Religious actors that operate transnationally, sometimes called religious nongovernmental organizations (RNGOs or RINGOs) or religious transnational actors (RTAs), connect with "like-minded individuals and groups in different countries" to exchange ideas and engage in collective action.[69]

Transnational religious actors are like their secular counterparts in some ways and distinct in others. Secular and religious NGOs are both increasing in number, encouraged and assisted by the deepening and widening of globalization and the growth of global civil society. Globalization and modern technology, which facilitate the transmission of ideas and information, have had a significant effect, tying the world together in new ways and, as Joseph Nye Jr. and David A. Welch say, lowering "the barriers of entry into world politics."[70] Satellite television stations like Al Jazeera "have greatly increased the speed and volume of information flows to radical groups" in the Muslim world.[71] In 2005, for instance, the news spread quickly about how a Danish publication depicted—and, in the eyes of many Muslims, dishonored—the Prophet Muhammad, eliciting sharp protests from some Muslim governments and the Organization of Islamic Cooperation. The internet and social media facilitate communications within states and transnationally. The ease of travel from one part of the world to another also facilitates the growth of transnational communities. Consider, for instance, the ability of Muslims around the world to hear the Islamic State's call to join in creating a new caliphate and then to travel to the territory held by ISIS.

Religious and nonreligious transnational actors may have similar goals and methods, such as advocacy, but RTAs may also employ distinctly religious methods, such as prayer. As transnational communities of believers, they spread global religious norms. They also engage in missionary activity. The two great monotheistic and universalizing religions, Christianity and Islam, actively seek adherents and, in so doing, foster transnational religious connections. What most clearly distinguish religions and RTAs are their self-definition (they describe themselves as religious) and their membership, which is often defined in religious terms.

To conclude this discussion, transnational interactions, mobilizations, and so on influence international actors, the nation-state foremost among them. RTAs fit within this broader picture.

RTAs are very active in global forums, including the preeminent global forum, the United Nations. An avowedly secular entity, the United Nations nonetheless works with religious actors on a variety of issues, including international development and global climate change, and these actors influence the UN agenda. Such activities embed religious NGOs in global governance. However, the world's second largest religion, Islam, is underrepresented by nongovernmental organizations, while Christianity is probably overrepresented.[72]

In addition, religious movements "may contribute to five types of transnational activities": migration, irredentism, secession, diasporas, and terrorism.[73] The Islamic State certainly contributed to global migration, with thousands joining its efforts in Iraq and Syria and massive numbers of people fleeing the violence and destruction it wrought. Driven by a particular understanding of Islam, the Islamic State's goals and appeal were grounded in religion. In addition, with so many of those refugees being Muslim and going to non-Muslim countries, this wave of migration had a religious dimension.

Irredentism is claiming or actually annexing a region in another state. Examples are Iraq's claims on Kuwait, which led to the Persian Gulf War. Another example is Russia's 2014 absorption of the Ukraine's Crimean Peninsula, which it justified as a means to protect the ethnic Russians living there. Religious-based irredentism occurs when, for instance, Islamic militants seek to reclaim lands where non-Muslim forces or influences have gained a foothold.

Secession or separatism involves people within a state who self-identity as a distinct nation, often because of a shared ethnicity or religion, and aim to carve a new state out of an existing one. Scattered across Iran, Iraq, Syria, and Turkey, the Kurds want a state of their own, but they can only accomplish this by taking territory from existing states.

Diasporas are created when members of a particular group are scattered or dispersed. For instance, when a sizable number of Sudanese refugees are relocated to Grand Rapids, Michigan, they create a diaspora community. Although physically separated, these transnational communities remain connected through ethnic, linguistic, and religious bonds.

To go beyond simply understanding details of particular scenes on the world stage, we need to look for patterns and consider different perspectives. As Nye and Welch say, we need to develop a "conceptual toolkit."[74] As discussed in previous chapters, in world politics this toolkit includes two basic ways of cutting into decisions and events on the global stage. One is the levels of analysis, the other is theoretical perspectives. The first does two things. First, it helps in sorting out and categorizing the multiple factors and agents at work in the highly complex realm of world politics. Each level of analysis explores different factors and actors and raises different questions. Each also "offers different sorts of explanations for international events."[75] Second, being cognizant of the various levels can help us to avoid focusing on one explanation or one set of questions to the exclusion of others.

In Theory

What this text aims to do is to explicate the inclusive nexus of religion and politics on the world stage. Hence, this chapter focuses on the global, or systemic, level of analysis, the next two on the state level, followed by a chapter on the individual level.

Systemic Level of Analysis

While the individual level of analysis focuses on the "trees," this level of analysis focuses on the "forest." Analysis at this level makes some basic assumptions: the international system is a "single whole"; this whole conditions the behaviors of the various parts/actors; and "within this whole, actors interact with and respond to one another in ways that are predictable."[76] That "predictable" part is important insofar as we are trying to understand, explain, and forecast what happens on the world stage.

The system is comprised of a variety of actors (states, intergovernmental organizations, and transnational and multinational nongovernmental organizations), alliances and the distribution of power, and international rules and norms. System-level analysis focuses on the relationships among these actors and factors.

Joseph Nye argues, with a nod to geopolitics, that in the twenty-first century, power is arrayed in a "three-dimensional chess board."[77] The top level is military power, the second level is economic power, and the third level is transnational relations. Military and economic power are elements of "hard power": the ability to command others through coercion (or the credible threat of military force) and economic inducements (the "carrots" of aid or the "sticks" of sanctions). "International political power is largely derived from the world's perception of a nation's independent military and economic resources, and its willingness to invest them—and risk them—in order to change the behavior of others."[78] The United States dominates the top, military level, on which realists focus. "Interstate economic power is distributed in a multipolar manner"—and China's economic rise is shaking up relations on the global chessboard.[79] With regard to the third element on the "three-dimensional chess board," power over transnational matters is much more diffuse.

Transnational religious actors represent one key way that religion affects international relations; the other, discussed in the next chapter, is "domestic religious actors that impact significantly on state foreign-policy formation and execution."[80] This chapter has focused on Catholic and Islamic transnational actors. As Timothy Byrnes states, "Though profoundly dissimilar in numerous ways," Catholicism and Islam are similar in one basic respect: "they are both religious traditions that are fundamentally transnational in nature, and that make universal claims for all persons, at all times, in all places."[81] Both are proselytizing religions. Both claim more than a billion adherents around the globe.

Religion's rise on the geopolitical stage is bound up with religion's resurgence. The global resurgence of religion involves quantitative and qualitative changes: increases in numbers of adherents and in religion's importance to security and politics. Religion has regained significance as a source of faith and as a political force in domestic as well as international politics. In the realm of security, religion may be the source of and the solution to conflicts. Increasingly, too, security involves protecting and defending religious practices and organizations.[82]

Within this context, Islamists and Muslim-majority countries might well share a sense that the deck of the international system is stacked against them. The modern system of secular states is a creature of Western Europe. Other key features were also created by and controlled by the West. This includes the United Nations (no Muslim state has a permanent seat on the powerful UN Security Council) as well as the liberal international economic order and the key institutions that support it, namely the International Monetary Fund, the World Bank, and the General Agreement on Tariffs and Trade (now the World Trade Organization). In addition, their borders were generally drawn by Western colonial powers, and Western interference persists in regions such as the Middle East. This might explain a propensity of Islamists to see "the West" as a threat, much as parts of the West see Islam (or at least Islamism, if such a distinction is made) as a threat.

Constructivism

Much of this chapter is about transnationalism: forces, relations, and transactions that cross state borders and involve more than one nation. Of the theoretical lenses discussed here, constructivism is most useful in gaining a better appreciation of this phenomenon. The proliferation of international religious organizations since the end of World War II is part of the "transnationalization of religions."[83] The theoretical lens of constructivism is well suited to examine this transnationalization as well as nonstate actors such as religious organizations, certainly better than the realist lens. Constructivists are far more attuned than realists to ideas, ideologies, identities, and norms that transcend states' borders.

Religion can play an enormous role in shaping norms and communal identities. In communist Poland, for instance, national identity was wrapped up in Catholicism, frustrating the state's efforts to foster a "communist (secular) identity."[84] As the Cold War was ending, Iraq invaded Kuwait. Once the United States placed troops on Saudi soil and the United Nations authorized a US-led mission to get Iraq out of Kuwait, Iraqi ruler Saddam Hussein called for an anti-American "holy war." Despite the fact that Saddam Hussein was a secular ruler, some responded to his call, which was couched in terms of a shared religious identity and the notion that this identity and religious community were under attack by infidels and outsiders. Referring to Huntington's "clash of civilizations" thesis, this could be seen as civilizational rallying at work.

This "clash" can also be framed as a war of words, ideas, and political ideologies. Lawrence Rubin explains how neighboring states perceived the creation of "Islamic states" in Iran (in 1979) and Sudan (in 1989) as national security threats, not because of their military capabilities, but because of concerns about the projection of Islamism as a transnational political ideology.[85] Ideology and "ideational power," Rubin argues, matter. Ideologies can delegitimize regimes or create "unity of purpose."[86] Ideas and ideologies can become national security threats when they are projected beyond a state's borders and find receptive audiences in other countries. Think of the ideological conflict at the center of the Cold War. What is considered a "threat" can be a matter of perception and can be constructed. This line of thought implies weaknesses in realist takes on states' perceptions of threats and the foreign policies that flow from them.

Realism

The traditional realist framework is rather ill-equipped to deal with what some call the "post-secular" world in which nonstate actors, including religious organizations, and individual leaders are powerful actors on the world stage. First, realists' state-centric worldview, while changing, does not quite know what to do with nonstate actors, such as the OIC and the Roman Catholic Church. For realists, the international system is primarily a system of sovereign states.

Second, realists typically focus on hard-power resources—military and economic power—to the exclusion of the power of persuasion. This worldview makes sense to the realist because the international system is anarchic, meaning there is no authority above the state. In the context of anarchy, "self-help" prevails: states can rely only on themselves to ensure their security, autonomy, and continued existence. For realists, anarchy necessarily leads states to adopt a vigilant foreign policy stance, watching for either encroachments on states' power and security or opportunities to enhance them. So, power matters. States need power, especially military power, to defend themselves and protect their national interests. The UN, OIC, Roman Catholic Church, and other nonstate actors lack military power. The Catholic Church's "military might" consists of the Swiss Guard and, economically, it does not even have independent trade agreements. The church's "expressive power," meaning power associated with articulating, promoting, and representing ideas, is of little consequence to hard-core realists.[87]

Third, realists give little consideration to individuals acting on the world stage. While papal visits and pronouncements are often front-page news in the *New York Times*, the way in which the pope makes the postage stamp–sized Vatican into a stage for pronouncements that are global news has no resonance in the halls of realism. Realism leaves little room to discuss actors such as Pope John Paul II, whose power was grounded in leadership and political savvy, moral authority, and as head of the world's largest, oldest, and most institutionalized transnational religious organization.

Finally, realists follow the signposts of prudence (as in prudent foreign policy), not ethics or religion. States' national interests are what matters. Ethics and religion may or may not be good guides for advancing and defending those interests.

At the international, or systemic, level, realists' focus is on, first, the system's structure and, second, "how a state's position in the international system is related to its foreign policy."[88] To understand a state's foreign policy conduct, look at the global system's structure: states are operating within a framework of anarchy and self-help. A state's position within the international system determines its foreign policy options—bigger, more powerful states have options that others do not. The international system encourages certain foreign policy behaviors, but does not dictate them.

Granted, this is describing realism in quite broad strokes and ignoring the differences among the various strands of realism. However, while realism may have room to accommodate religious influences on states' foreign policies and international relations, it generally has not done so.

Liberalism

The liberal paradigm is less state-centric than realism and readily acknowledges the centrality of nonstate actors, including multinational corporations as well as transnational religious organizations and movements. States are still center stage, but they share the stage with a rising number of nonstate actors and powerful individuals, which can mobilize public pressure and shape the international agenda.

While realists focus on state-to-state interactions, a key liberal proposition is that society-to-society relations also help to explain "patterns of cooperation and conflict within the global system."[89] Thus, liberalism is more attuned to the significance of transnational groups.

Still, liberalism, like realism and constructivism, has largely bought into the social theories that see religion as a private matter of minimal importance.[90] It is not well-attuned to the issues that religion brings to the world political stage, including issues of secularism and foundational assumptions. Also, liberalism tends to focus on secular NGOs to the exclusion of transnational religious actors.[91]

Table 4.1 focuses on the Roman Catholic Church (RCC) as well as Islamists and political Islam, and it demonstrates how they fit into our analytical framework.

Table 4.1   Analytical Framework: Roman Catholic Church (RCC) and Islamism

Levels of Analysis	Realism	Liberalism	Constructivism
International/ Systemic	*RCC:* The Catholic Church is a global actor that has the power of moral suasion, but it lacks coercive power, a distinguishing mark of international politics. Given its lack of economic and military power, it does not affect the global distribution of power. *Islamism:* Islamism is a trans-national force. It may be the only nonstate actor able to resist Westernizing and homogenizing forces on the world stage. Militant Islamists, those willing to resort to political violence to further their objectives, create international security concerns.	*RCC:* The Catholic Church functions both as a high-profile international NGO (or religious transnational actor) and as a sovereign state (Vatican City) that enters into international agreements. *Islamism:* Islamists want to remake the liberal, secular, Western world order. The prevailing world order was created by, and reflects the worldviews and interests of, the United States and the European states that colonized Muslim-majority societies.	*RCC:* The church is an important actor on the battlefield of international ideas and norms. Religious transnational actors like the RCC can shape norms, which states and individuals internalize. *Islamism:* Political Islam is an ideology. The failure of modern secular ideologies contributed to the transformation of the Muslim faith into a political ideology. Like the RCC, it is active on the battlefield of ideas. The global *umma*, a community of all the world's Muslims, is an imagined community. Despite knowing only a small number of its members, Muslims understand or imagine that it exists and identify themselves as part of this transnational Islamic community.

continues

Table 4.1 Continued

Levels of Analysis	Realism	Liberalism	Constructivism
Domestic/State	*RCC:* The Church has a well-institutionalized hierarchical, top-down structure. Power flows from the top down. The global diplomacy of this sovereign state (Vatican City) and NGO (Holy See) furthers the interests of this organization and of its far-flung flock.	*RCC:* Vatican City is a micro-state and a theocracy. Its leader can make decisions without consulting his "constituents" or base.	*RCC:* Diplomats (papal nuncios) and the pope himself try to influence states' policies. State-level gatherings of Catholic leaders can do the same.
		Islamism: With some exceptions, Islamists seek political power in order to create societies in which the state upholds and enforces Islamic law. Islamism grew, in part, because regimes in many Muslim-majority states failed to create national unity, transition to democracy, or deliver economic development and basic public services. Islamists generally want to remake the state by, for instance, replacing Western/secular law with Islamic law.	*Islamism:* Like others, Islamists have multiple touchstones of identity. For them, religious identity is the most important. They seek to reconstruct their governments and societies to better reflect their identities and beliefs.

continues

Table 4.1 Continued

Levels of Analysis	Realism	Liberalism	Constructivism
Individual	*RCC:* Some popes have been powerful figures, even though they have no military power at their disposal.	*RCC:* Popes are transnational actors whose leadership skills, powers of persuasion, and political leanings matter in world politics.	*RCC:* Popes have a global pulpit, enabling them to serve as "norm entrepreneurs."
	Islamism: Some specific militant Islamists (e.g., Osama bin Laden and Abu Bakr al-Baghdadi) wield power and threaten states' interests, especially security.	*Islamism:* Corrupt, aloof, and "insufficiently Muslim" leaders have contributed to the spread of Islamism.	*Islamism:* Individuals key to the evolution of Islamist ideology include the Muslim Brotherhood's founder (Hasan al-Bana) and key ideologue (Sayyid Qutb).

Source: Philpott, "Why Politics Can't Be Freed from Religion."

Conclusion

Religion is an "old/new force in global affairs."[92] The "old" part refers to religion's centrality in pre-Westphalia Europe hundreds of years ago. The "new" part concerns the global resurgence of religion and the "re-emergence of religious actors with political goals."[93] It concerns the "emergent faith-based global political landscape" and the growing strength of transnational forms of organization.[94]

The changing role of the Roman Catholic Church exemplifies this old/new trend. The church cast a very long shadow before the Peace of Westphalia, but afterward its power and influence were greatly diminished. Today, global communications networks provide the pope a global megaphone. Some authors call the Roman Catholic Church "the most influential nonpolitical institution in the world."[95] However, its hierarchical structure makes it atypical as a religious actor. The church also exemplifies the idea of religious transnational actors. RTAs' influence is a key element of the broader resurgence of the faith factor in world politics.

Since the end of the Cold War and on into the twenty-first century, religion has had an important impact on world affairs, as a religious reawakening is occurring on "every inhabited continent."[96] Religion can affect the direction of foreign policy and, in some cases, religious institutions are "just as important as traditional diplomats or the military in the practice of foreign policy."[97] The resurgence of religion's influence is a surprising turn of events—and international relations theory is still trying to catch up.

It is worth reiterating a point made by Toft, Philpott, and Shah: "Religion is far from being the only or even the most decisive factor in global politics. But it [plays] a key role."[98] Liberals might point to religious actors' influence in foreign policy making, while constructivists highlight the transnational beliefs and identities associated with Catholicism and Islamism. Unless religion appears to be a threat to national security, realists might simply yawn. We might add, too, that although more than 100 million emigrants worldwide are Christian (according to the Pew Research Center), Muslim states—Syria, Afghanistan, and Somalia, among others—are major sources of today's refugees, and refugees' religious affiliation sometimes affects their ability to find a new home.

The point of this text is not to suggest that politics on the world stage now revolves around the axis of religion. Far from it. The point is to explain how and why ignoring the religious factors leads to incomplete or even inaccurate understandings of the world in which we live.

Notes

1. Hanson, *The Catholic Church in World Politics*, 198.
2. Hanson, *The Catholic Church in World Politics*, 210.
3. Szulc, "Papal Secrets."
4. Thomas, *The Global Resurgence of Religion and the Transformation of International Relations*, 5.
5. Kingston, *The Politics of Religion, Nationalism, and Identity in Asia*, 47–48.
6. Weigel, "Papacy and Power," 22; Royal, "What Has the Vatican Done Globally?"
7. Carter, *Essentials of US Foreign Policy Making*, 174.
8. Appleby, "Pope John Paul II."
9. Haynes, "Religion and Foreign Policy Making in the USA, India and Iran," 152.
10. O'Brien, "Saddam Comes Out Fighting as Champion of the Fanatics."
11. Helfont, "Saddam and the Islamists," 360.
12. Benjamin and Simon, *The Age of Sacred Terror*, 167, 169.
13. Forbes, "Muslim Scholars Rule Out Saddam's Jihad Calls," 20.
14. Bergen, *Holy War, Inc.*, 230.
15. Helfont, "Saddam and the Islamists," 360–361.
16. Fuller, *A World Without Islam*, 260.
17. al-Rahim, "Inside Iraq's Confessional Politics," 171; Rupert, "Once-Secularist Saddam Discovers Benefits of Moslem Piety"; Helfont, "Saddam and the Islamists," 352.
18. Ajami, "The Summoning."
19. Helfont, "Saddam and the Islamists," 353.
20. Kimball, *When Religion Becomes Lethal*, 152.
21. Roy, *The Failure of Political Islam*, 8.
22. Jenish, "Islam and the Gulf War."
23. Ayoob, *The Many Faces of Political Islam: Religion and Politics in the Muslim World*, 8.
24. Kingston, *The Politics of Religion, Nationalism, and Identity in Asia*, 11.
25. Patterson, *Politics in a Religious World*, 8.
26. Rochester, *Fundamental Principles of International Relations*, 59.
27. Ikenberry, "The Future of the Liberal World Order."
28. Nye, "The Information Revolution and Power," 22.
29. Isaacs, "Sacred Violence or Strategic Faith?" 211.
30. Kendhammer, *Muslims Talking Politics*, 54.
31. Shaker and Bromberger, "Chess Game of Civilizations," 59, 60.
32. Helfont, "The Geopolitics of the Sunni-Shi'i Divide in the Middle East."
33. Pipes, "Islam and Islamism," 22–26; Cagaptay, "Are Muslims Islamists?"
34. Kingston, *The Politics of Religion, Nationalism, and Identity in Asia*, 79.
35. Lean, *Understanding Islam and the West*, Ch. 6.
36. Fuller, "Turkey's Strategic Model," 55.
37. Lean, *Understanding Islam and the West*, 122.
38. Haynes, "Religion and Politics: What Is the Impact of September 11?" 12.
39. Fuller, "Turkey's Strategic Model," 55.
40. Frieden, Lake, and Schulz, *World Politics*, 250.
41. Kingston, *The Politics of Religion, Nationalism, and Identity in Asia*, 73, 77.
42. Haynes, *Religion in Global Politics*, 136.
43. Hill, *Trial of A Thousand Years*, 116.

44. Ayoob, *The Many Faces of Political Islam.*

45. Sellam and Dellal, *Moroccan Culture in the 21st Century,* 78.

46. Arraf, "Muslim Brotherhood, Mainstream in Many Countries, May Be Listed as Terror Group."

47. Soage, "Islam and Modernity," 192.

48. Soage, "Islam and Modernity," 195–196.

49. Trager, "The Unbreakable Muslim Brotherhood."

50. Cagaptay, "Are Muslims Islamists?"

51. Stilt, "'Islam is the Solution,'" 74.

52. Castillo, "The Organization of Islamic Cooperation in Contemporary International Society," 5.

53. Walsh, "Heads of Muslim Nations Not Targeted Are Conspicuously Silent," A1.

54. Bacik, "The Genesis, History, and Functioning of the Organization of Islamic Cooperation," 597.

55. Hossain, "The Organization of Islamic Conference," 304.

56. Agnew, "Deus Vult," 53, 56.

57. Barbato, "A State, a Diplomat, and a Transnational Church," 37.

58. Hertzke, "Roman Catholicism and the Faith-Based Movement for Global Human Rights," 20.

59. Weigel, "Papacy and Power."

60. Kurth, "The Vatican's Foreign Policy," 40–52.

61. Ryngaert, "The Legal Status of the Holy See," 838.

62. Dunn, "Global Reach," 117; "Papal Diplomacy: God's Ambassadors," *The Economist,* July 19, 2007.

63. Haynes, *Faith-Based Organizations at the United Nations,* 14.

64. Mark Thomas Edwards, "Cold War Transgressions," 270.

65. Fox, "State Religious Exclusivity and Human Rights," 931.

66. Warr, "The Normative Promise of Religious Organizations in Global Civil Society," 503, 505.

67. Thomas, *The Global Resurgence of Religion and the Transformation of International Relations,* 161–162.

68. Bianchi, *Islamic Globalization,* 68.

69. Haynes, *An Introduction to International Relations and Religion,* 2nd ed., 98–99.

70. Nye and Welch, *Understanding Global Conflict and Cooperation,* 305.

71. Fealy, "Islam in Southeast Asia," 172.

72. Beittinger-Lee and Miall, "Islam, the OIC and the Defamation of Religions Controversy," 156.

73. Kegley and Raymond, *The Global Future,* 3rd ed., 163–164.

74. Nye and Welch, *Understanding Global Conflict and Cooperation,* 38.

75. Goldstein and Pevehouse, *International Relations,* 19.

76. Duncan, Jancar-Webster, and Switky, *World Politics in the 21st Century,* 77–78.

77. Shaker and Bromberger, "Chess Game of Civilizations," 60; "Cooperation the Key to Winning the Three Dimensional Chess Game of Power," https://stakeholderorgmon.wordpress.com/2016/02/15/cooperation-the-key-to-winning-the-three-dimensional-chess-game-of-power.

78. Bleicher, "China," 2008.

79. Nye, "A Game of Three-Dimensional Chess with China."

80. Haynes, *An Introduction to International Relations and Religion,* 428.

81. Byrnes, "Transnational Religion and Europeanization," 296.

82. Meyer, "Religion and Security in the Post-Modern World," 6–7.

83. Beyer, "Multiculturalism and Religious Pluralism in Canada," 43.

84. Haynes, "Transnational Religious Actors and International Politics," 149.

85. Lawrence Rubin, *Islam in the Balance*, 2–4.

86. Fuller, *The Future of Political Islam*, 42.

87. Hanson, *The Catholic Church in World Politics*, 5.

88. Neack, *The New Foreign Policy*, 126; Neack, *The New Foreign Policy*, 3rd ed., 145.

89. Grieco, Ikenberry, and Mastanduno, *Introduction to International Relations*, 85.

90. Hurd, *The Politics of Secularism in International Relations*, 3, 30–32, 47.

91. Patterson, *Politics in a Religious World*, 57, 59.

92. Appleby, "Globalization, Religious Change and the Common Good."

93. Haynes, "Transnational Religious Actors and International Politics," 147.

94. Hurd, *Beyond Religious Freedom*, xii.

95. Rodden and Rossi, "Not Hitler's Pope," 35.

96. Patterson, *Politics in a Religious World*, 5.

97. Helfont, "Saddam and the Islamists," 353.

98. Toft, Philpott, and Shah, "God's Partisans Are Back," B4–B5.

5

State Actors:
How State-Religion Relations
Affect International Relations

Illustration 7: Daniel Ortega Plays the Religion Card

Daniel Ortega of Nicaragua was a rebel leader, elected president, and then became a "card-carrying Catholic" who "played the religion card."[1] It comes as some surprise that Daniel Ortega would make a religious appeal to the electorate. Ortega first became president in 1979, when the socialist Sandinista National Liberation Front (FSLN) overthrew the US-backed Somoza regime and came to power. During the 1980s, Nicaragua's decade of revolution, the small Central American country was home to a Cold War civil war. The Soviet Union and Cuba aided the Sandinistas, who, in turn, aided leftists in neighboring El Salvador. The United States ultimately backed the "contras," a guerrilla force that fought the Sandinistas for several years and, in 1990, backed a coalition of parties that beat Ortega at the polls.

Although it is unusual for a Marxist to play the religion card, the Sandinistas had managed to bridge the historic gulf between Marxists and Christians. Traditionally, Marxist-Leninist movements had spoken of class warfare, championed the poorer strata of society, and struck an anti-religious posture, while the Catholic Church's hierarchy in Latin America was conservative, anti-communist, and allied with privileged sectors of society. The religious hierarchy generally recommended purely spiritual solutions to the region's problems, addressing spiritual but not physical hunger. In Nicaragua, however, the "popular church" or "people's church," which included laypeople as well as clergy, became identified with the Sandinistas' revolutionary struggle. Some priests, drawn to the Sandinistas because of their shared dedication to the liberation of the poor, took positions at odds with the presiding bishops; in other words, some parish clergy bucked the hierarchy.[2] The Sandinista revolution used specifically Christian imagery and appealed to many devout Christians, such as Ernesto Cardenal. Cardenal, who served in the Sandinista government from 1979 to 1988, was both a Catholic priest and a Marxist. In fact, "several of the movement's key leaders were priests" and, when the Sandinistas set up their new government, five Catholic priests took seats in the cabinet.[3]

At one point, the Sandinistas tried to court Pope John Paul II. In his welcoming speech when the pope visited Nicaragua in 1983, Ortega said, "Our experience shows that one can be both a believer and a revolutionary and that no unsalvageable contradiction exists between the two."[4] However, John Paul was heckled by Sandinistas who were shouting, "Power to the people!"[5] The pope, in turn, berated Father Ernesto Cardenal for his involvement in politics. Wagging his finger, John Paul reproached Cardenal, saying, "You must straighten out your position with the church."[6]

Church opposition to the Sandinistas helped end Ortega's and the FSLN's rule in the 1990 elections. After his party lost the presidency to the standard bearer of the National Opposition Union (UNO), Violeta Barrios de Chamarro, Daniel Ortega embraced Christianity. Ortega's ability to "play the religion card"—in other words, to play up his Catholic credentials in the game of politics—explains, in part, his return to power in 2006. He made overtures to the Catholic Church and was able to mobilize Catholics to support his candidacy, winning the elections of 2006, 2011, and 2016. In this heavily Catholic country, the government and the church are "the country's two most powerful institutions."[7] The institutional church, however, has not always been pleased with how religion and politics have been mixed. According to the *National Catholic Reporter*, the church has taken issue with the Sandinista government's use of piety and religious symbols for political ends.[8]

The "Religion Card"

Politicians are often tempted to "play the religion card"; in other words, they play up their religious beliefs, use their religious credentials or identity to win supporters, or use religion to justify their policy choices. As explained in the previous chapter, like Daniel Ortega, Iraqi president

Saddam Hussein also played this card. Like Ortega, this was a surprise turn for Hussein, who led an authoritarian, secular Baathist regime. Also like Ortega, Hussein was endeavoring to mobilize political support from co-religionists.

In India, which is considered a secular democracy, Prime Minister Narendra Modi and his party, the Bharatiya Janata Party (BJP) have also played this card. In this religiously diverse country, they are pushing the ideas that India is a Hindu nation and that Hindus (who represent about 80 percent of the population) and Hinduism itself are at risk—and only Modi and the BJP can save them. The party's symbolic color is saffron, a color that has long symbolized Hinduism. They are playing the "saffron card" to mobilize political support from Hindus.[9]

Politicians tempted to play the religion card might be warned that religion can be a wild card: religious actors may well have an agenda of their own, and one can never be sure of the direction that believers will go. For instance, religious leaders may support and legitimize the state or they may oppose and undercut it. Others may use the religion card against them. Alternatively, though politicians may be using religion for instrumental reasons—to further their political agenda—religion may become more politically important.

Liberation Theology

Liberation theology, which combines a Christian message or project (saving souls from sin) with the Marxist project (radical action on behalf of the poor), played a role in the 1979 Nicaraguan revolution. This left-leaning theology was born of the economic and political oppression in Latin America in the mid-twentieth century. It moved some priests and parishioners from the conservative and elitist bent—which historically characterized the Roman Catholic Church in the region— toward a progressive, grassroots orientation that privileged the needs of the poor and oppressed. This was the orientation of the liberationist priest Ernesto Cardenal.

In another small Central American country, El Salvador, Arch-bishop Óscar Romero became associated with liberation theology. He spoke on behalf of the poor and condemned the country's oligarchy. Like the Vatican, however, he was ill at ease with the Marxist influences on this theology, especially given Marxism's atheism and materialism. Atheism suggests there is no God, while materialism suggests that humans are worldly beings and that physical and economic factors (not ideas, beliefs, or values) drive history and politics.

Illustration 8: The "Mass" Death of Óscar Romero

On March 24, 1980, less than a year after the Sandinistas came to power in neighboring Nicaragua, Archbishop Óscar Romero was shot dead while saying mass in El Salvador, a heavily Catholic country. (El Salvador means "The Savior.") He was a conservative when appointed to his leadership post in 1977, having criticized priests who bucked state authority for being "politicized."[10] By 1980, perhaps radicalized by the killing of an old friend, Romero had become a defender of social justice and an outspoken critic of the Salvadoran state. The state, in turn, saw him as inciting "leftists" who were a threat to the political order.

As head of the Salvadoran Church, he had a bully pulpit, and he used it. He was popular. He championed the popular cause of social justice, a call for a more just distribution of wealth and privileges within society. Salvadorans who could not hear his homilies in person heard his words through radio broadcasts. During his three years as the top prelate of El Salvador's Roman Catholic Church, Romero's religious discourse grew more radical, concrete, and active.[11] He proclaimed that the face of Jesus Christ is in the poor, and the poor turn to the Church for their voices to be heard.[12] As the "voice of the voiceless" (the oppressed masses), a stance often associated with the progressive church in Latin America, he and many other members of the Catholic Church in El Salvador spoke out against political repression and widespread poverty, calling for reform and democracy. He issued pastoral letters. A 1978 letter, coauthored by one of El Salvador's five bishops and opposed by the other four, spoke of "institutionalized violence" and the church's interest in promoting a more just society. He used his Sunday homilies to condemn atrocities committed by military and paramilitary forces. In one sermon, the archbishop called on soldiers to disobey orders to kill innocent civilians. In a homily the day before his death he appealed to state security forces, saying, "I implore you, I beg you, in God's name I order you: Stop the repression!" He protested state repression through his actions, also. For instance, in 1979, after the military killed a priest and several young people, he ordered that all Catholic churches in the country close for three days. In 1980, he also appealed to US president Jimmy Carter, asking him to halt military aid to the Salvadoran government. Conservatives in both the Salvadoran government and the church labeled Romero's defense of the poor as not just political, but subversive, and labeled him a sympathizer of the left-wing guerrillas.

Significance

Romero's life and death point to some important points about the relationship between religion and politics. First and foremost, Romero's work as archbishop had public and political effects. It was not confined to the private sphere. His high profile and moral legitimacy made him a politically important figure. But the Roman Catholic Church is not a political organization, and "Oscar Romero was not a political leader, although his life and work have had political repercussions."[13] His death had political repercussions, too. His assassination was a "tipping point."[14] The country plunged into civil war and became a Cold War battlefield. Rather than silencing a regime critic, the pro-government forces responsible for Romero's death created a martyr. Romero's martyrdom also drew international attention to the conflict in El Salvador.

Second, given El Salvador's repressive government at the time, Romero and other Salvadorans took great risks by opposing the power structure. The military government and the powerful coffee oligarchs increasingly saw Catholic activists as a big threat. Catholic priests and nuns who were part of the popular resistance found themselves on the receiving end of persecution and state terror. The archbishop's death has been linked to the state's security militia, and he was not the only victim of the state and its supporters. The slogan "Be a patriot, kill a priest" was printed in pamphlets and scrawled on walls.

Another point of significance is that this incident has links to the transnational Roman Catholic Church, discussed in Chapter 4. Pope John Paul II opposed clergy participating directly in politics. The Vatican told Romero to stay out of politics. The papal nuncio, the Vatican's ambassador to El Salvador, stated at one point, "The church is in danger because of the insane behavior of this archbishop."[15]

This raises questions about the church's mission on earth and to what extent it can advance that mission without getting involved in the messy world of politics. Romero's theology appears to have motivated him to speak out on political matters, much like the biblical prophets of old, while his position as a religious leader gave him a platform and audience. Through his sermons and actions, he helped to provide a religious value system and framework for interpreting events. His pronouncements drew devoted followers—and fierce opponents. More than a religious leader, he became a national leader, while the Salvadoran Church became an important political force.[16] One might conclude that

Romero's politics flowed from his religious convictions, whereas Ortega's religion grew out of his political ambitions.

These two scenes from Central America reflect the interplay of religion and politics within states and how these interactions can influence and be influenced by world politics. Nicaragua and El Salvador are small, poor, predominantly Catholic countries. At the time of the 1979 Sandinista revolution and the 1980 slaying of Romero, the Cold War was quite chilly and Central America was in the superpowers' geopolitical crosshairs. In the 1980s, both states were home to Cold War civil wars, meaning civil wars in which each superpower supported the side most closely aligned with its ideology and interests. The Soviet Union backed the Sandinistas in Nicaragua and the anti-government guerrillas in El Salvador. The US government took the other side, supporting bulwarks against international communism. The United States was determined that there would be "no more Cubas" and no "Castro-ized" Central America; that is, no more communist or potentially hostile regimes would come to power in the region. Viewing Central America through a Cold War lens, the US government backed the military regime in El Salvador. In Nicaragua, the United States backed the contras (counterrevolutionaries), a group dedicated to overthrowing the Sandinista regime.

These two scenes also illustrate an important element of the Catholic Church and religions in general. There is a good deal of internal pluralism.

This chapter explores the state level of analysis. It focuses on religion-state interactions and religious influences on states' foreign policies. This level of analysis, like the individual and global levels, is explored to better understand interactions between religion and politics on the world stage, especially as they affect states' foreign policies.

The Domestic-International Nexus

We begin this exploration by returning to the intermestic nature of much of world politics, meaning actors, issues, processes, and so on, that have important domestic dimensions and international dimensions. One international dimension is the system as a whole. Jonathan Fox and Shmuel Sandler say that "religion's greatest influence on the international system is through its significant influence on domestic politics."[17] Another, closely related dimension concerns religion's influence on foreign policy. "Understanding foreign policy is critical because the foreign policy choices that states make have profound implications for relations among states." An "outside-in" approach, most closely associated with realism, analyzes how the international system (forces outside the state) shapes states' foreign policies. An "inside-out" approach focuses on the domestic, rather than external, sources of states' foreign policies.[18]

Like other domestic variables, religion shapes national debates and foreign policy decisions and, thus, affects how states deal with outside actors. With regard to the United States, for instance, Americans' religious sensibilities, religious leaders, and religious organizations go a long way toward explaining why US policy includes regular evaluations of religious freedom abroad.

During the breakup of Yugoslavia in the 1990s (discussed at length in Chapter 7), religious ties help to explain how other states responded to the fierce tug of war over Bosnia. Bosnia declared its independence from the Socialist Federal Republic of Yugoslavia in 1992. Serbs in Bosnia and the Serb-dominated Yugoslav army launched a military response. At this point in time, Serbs were doubling down on their ethnic identity as Serbs and their religious identity as Orthodox Christians. Russia stood by Serbia. In Russia, the Orthodox church wields considerable influence. On the other side, several Muslim-majority countries supported the Bosnian Muslims, making public calls to action and providing arms, ammunition, and financial aid. Many also sent food and medicine—as well as missionaries and mujahidin, militants who engage in the type of struggle called the "lesser jihad" and who see themselves as warriors for the faith. The Organization of Islamic Cooperation (OIC), discussed in Chapter 4, framed the aggression in Bosnia as genocide and as a central concern for the Muslim world. Among other actions, it asked member states to sever diplomatic ties with Serbia.[19] The International Islamic Relief Organization opened an office in Bosnia.[20] With all this attention, Bosnian Muslims gained a sense of being part of the global Muslim community (*umma*).[21] Note, though, that Bosnian Muslims were not particularly religious; after decades under a communist regime, many were self-described atheists. However, during the Yugoslav wars they were identified by religion.

Three years into the bloody conflict in Bosnia, the North Atlantic Treaty Organization (NATO) bombed Serb forces, bringing an end to this civil war. Of NATO's thirty member states all but one is located in North America (Canada and the United States) or Europe, and all but one is historically Christian with a small Muslim population. Turkey is the outlier among NATO countries; in terms of geography, it straddles Europe and the Middle East and, in terms of religion, it is a Muslim-majority country. So, the civil war in Bosnia was internationalized by the involvement of outside countries. NATO's intervention was basically an effort to stop an ongoing humanitarian crisis rather than an effort to support co-religionists. However, ethno-religious ties explain, in part, Russia's allegiance to Serbia. Stephen Saideman makes the broader argument that constituents at home care most about the welfare of "kin" abroad and, as such, shared ties affect foreign policy making.[22]

Another aspect of the domestic-international connection is that states' domestic policies and affairs can be sources of international disputes. An example is China's policies in the region of Tibet. Not long after the Chinese revolution of 1949, the new communist regime sent troops into Tibet and absorbed it into the People's Republic of China (PRC). Since then, Tibetans have pushed to regain their independence, while the officially atheist central government has tried to eliminate Buddhist impacts and to incorporate Tibetans into a unified, multiethnic Chinese nation. The Tibetan resistance has protested, while the central government has encouraged ethnic Han Chinese to move to the region and thereby change its ethnic and religious composition. Tibetan resisters call this "cultural genocide," while Beijing says such moves are necessary to crush separatism. So far, this is a tale of Chinese domestic politics.

Now for the international part. China's acquisition of Tibet created a common border with India. In response to China's attack on Tibet in the mid-twentieth century, Tibetans' spiritual and political leader, the Dalai Lama, appealed to the United Nations. When the Dalai Lama fled China in 1959, India welcomed him as well as other Tibetan refugees. Tibetans established a so-called government-in-exile in India. For the last several decades, this has troubled relations between the world's two most populous countries. As an articulate and influential spokesperson for Tibetans and Buddhism, the Dalai Lama can shape international perceptions.[23] In 2008, *Time* magazine listed him among the world's most influential people. As a global symbol of nonviolence, he won the Nobel Peace Prize. International human rights and religious freedom groups sing his praises. When he visits other countries, he is treated as a political leader. The Dalai Lama tries to garner international support for Tibet; China, however, rejects outside interference in its internal affairs. To the chagrin of the Chinese government, then, events in Tibet affect relations well beyond its borders.

Foreign Policy Implications

In many countries, religion factors into "general foreign policy orientations."[24] By factoring into the foreign policies of individual states, religion reverberates in the international system.[25]

However, the purpose of this chapter is not to suggest that religion determines states' foreign policies or has become the *decisive* factor in either domestic politics or international relations. Arguably, calculations of national interest remain paramount. As such, this chapter makes the more modest claim that religion is often a *significant* factor, especially with regard to legitimizing state policies and actions, so ignoring it means having an incomplete understanding of events. In democracies, especially, we can expect that governments will listen to the demands of religious communities as they would other constituencies. Further, with the global resurgence of religion, religion has (re)gained political influence. To the extent that it exercises influence within states, where foreign policy is hammered out, it affects relations among states and between state and nonstate actors. To come to grips with so many events on the world stage today, secularist blinders must come off.

This chapter addresses central questions about the interaction of religion and politics at the state level of analysis. Why do they interact? (Why do political actors get involved with religion and vice versa?) When are religious actors likely to get involved in politics? (The answer has a lot to do with the benefits and risks of interaction.) How do these interactions affect what happens on the world stage? The balance of the chapter will provide answers to these questions and then couch them in theoretical terms.

Why Religion and Politics Interact

As Mahatma Gandhi wrote, "Those who say religion has nothing to do with politics do not know what religion is."[26] The obverse may also be true. Religion and politics have a lot to say to each other. For our purposes, the emphasis is on domestic religion-politics interactions that also play out on the world stage.

Within the state, religions and religious organizations may get involved in politics and political institutions, and vice versa, for a variety of reasons. Two central reasons are that each has something to gain (or lose) from the other or that they claim authority and jurisdiction over the same areas. Answers to the question of why religion and politics interact concern contested terrains of power, "ideologies of order," values, socialization, religion-state relations, legitimization, and the matter of "who gets what."

Power

Power, the ability to get others to do what you want (or to refrain from doing what you do not want them to do), is so central to politics that it is often included in the very definition. At the heart of politics is acquiring and exercising power to make choices that affect a community of people. Those with political power can make choices that privilege some religions, religious organizations, and religious practices over others. Power can be exercised through coercion or a credible threat to use force, persuasion, or by constructing incentives (e.g., giving financial aid or imposing economic sanctions) to make some options more attractive than others.

Graham Fuller asserts that "power invariably attracts religion, and religion attracts power."[27] While Fuller may overstate the case, religious actors have to consider their relationship to state power, and religion can attract politically powerful actors. Those who wield political power get to make decisions and policies that affect the entire community. Members of the community, naturally hoping that these decisions and policies will improve their lives, try to influence them. Domestic actors try to advance their conceptions of the good life or the good society. Religious actors may themselves seek to gain power to ensure that their religion is the "top dog" in the state.

A case in point is Iraq, which straddles the "Middle East's Shi'a-Sunni fault line."[28] Under Saddam Hussein and the Baath Party, Sunni Muslims dominated and Shia Muslims were repressed, though the population is majority-Shia. After Saddam's overthrow in 2003, the religious tables were turned. The Shia community emerged as the most powerful political force—and, one author argues, Shia politics is politicizing religiosity.[29] Iraq's Shia-ruled neighbor, Iran, also reaped political benefits. An enemy of Iran and perceived enemy of Islam was now out of the picture, an important event in the region's geopolitics. In addition, Iran could now join forces with Shiites in Iraq and meddle in Iraq's domestic affairs.

As this case suggests, religious issues are not just about matters of the spirit, but often wrapped up with power, geopolitics, and states' secular and worldly interests. Religion attracts power to the extent that states use religion, control religion, or magnify and exploit religious differences for political ends. Politicians wanting to gain or retain power turn to religion for its ability to energize politics, confer legitimacy and perhaps moral leverage, and engage religious communities before problems with them erupt.

Consider where Islamism fits within this discussion of power. As explained in the previous chapter, Islamism is both a political ideology and the "single biggest political movement across the entire Muslim world."[30] As an ideology, Islamism offers a critique of the present situation and, finding it wanting, seeks political and social change. Its emergence in recent decades has both domestic and international roots, and its political impacts play out on both domestic and international stages.

Islamists are attracted to power in the sense that they are religious activists who "use Islam as a political force" and often seek to create regimes that rule in accord with the Quran or some version of Islamic law.[31] To affect the nature of a regime, they need political power. Power can be captured through "bullets" or "ballots." The former is a shorthand for political violence; examples include the Iranian Revolution, the Taliban's road to power in Afghanistan, and the Islamic State's endeavor to create a new caliphate. Alternatively, power can be captured through the ballot box or democratic means; examples include Hamas's 2006 electoral victory in the Palestinian parliamentary elections and Islamists' rise to power in Tunisia and Egypt during the Arab Spring. The political system matters. Islamists (and others) have a tough time gaining political power through the ballot box in closed, nonpluralistic political systems.[32]

Religion, noted former Secretary of State Madeleine Albright, is a powerful force, having the capacity to unify or divide and inflame or diminish conflict.[33] Albright also said that religion must have a seat at the table of foreign policy discussions.

Who Gets What?

Political scientist Harold Lasswell provided one of the better-known definitions of "politics," saying it entails the process of determining "who gets what, when, and how." This points us to the notion that politics has to do with the distribution of society's goods and resources. The question of "who gets what" figures into this discussion in two ways: first, the allocation of state resources to religious organizations and, second, social policies and the provision of goods and services. While theologies tend more to matters of ultimate meaning and who wins the big prize of salvation, the day-to-day activities of religious actors may deal with the earthier side of "who gets what." Recall Óscar Romero's call to social justice, a call to change the distribution of wealth and privilege in El Salvador.

To affect the societal allocation of resources, religious actors enter the political realm directly and indirectly. Direct engagement is discussed below under the modes of political action.

Religious actors can enter the political realm indirectly by providing public goods that the state cannot or will not provide. For instance, in Africa under colonialism and in the years after independence, Catholic and Protestant churches provided education, health care, and other types of welfare services. In Papua New Guinea, Christian churches run many schools and health services. On Karkar Island off Papua New Guinea, Lutherans built and maintain the sole hospital, with little government assistance. Likewise, Islamist groups perform charitable works and provide a variety of goods and services, especially in developing countries. In Kenya and Tanzania, for instance, Islamic NGOs have founded and run orphanages. In Egypt, the Muslim Brotherhood's "state within a state" builds clinics and establishes a boys' club, among other things.[34]

As the provision of public goods demonstrates, "Religion can and does serve a variety of public functions."[35] Perhaps religious actors provide goods and services because of a sense of mission. Perhaps, as the title of a book by Nancy Davis and Robert Robinson suggests, they are trying to "claim society for God" by permeating the public space.[36]

Legitimization

Religious actors have a number of things they want out of domestic politics, and states, in turn, have things they want from religious actors. For states, religion can be a source of political support and legitimation. Legitimacy is the widespread sense that political authorities have the right to wield political power, to govern, and to issue certain kinds of commands, such as public laws. States most often solicit religious support or claim divine justification to legitimize the rulers and the regime itself and to legitimize going to war.

With regard to war, it is not unusual for states to justify war by claiming religious guidance or that "God is on our side." Religions' capacity to give (or withhold) "moral sanction to violence" gives them political power and the potential of being powerful political tools. Steve Bruce takes this point a step further by saying, "All states mobilize for war by first enlisting God as their recruiting sergeant."[37]

As for legitimizing rulers, regimes, and their programs, Anthony Gill states, "Throughout most of history—from King David to contemporary Iran—religious authority served to justify political regimes."[38] Three examples illustrate this point. A classic illustration comes from the conquest and colonization of Latin America, otherwise known as the era of Iberian Christendom (1492–1820s), since the states of the Iberian Peninsula (Spain and Portugal) colonized most of the region. The Spanish crown and the Catholic Church both believed that the Spanish empire in the New World derived from God's providential design for bringing the Catholic faith to the indigenous peoples. Conquistadors came bearing crosses and swords. As an instrument of state rule, the church's role was to civilize, Europeanize, and render the indigenous governable and to preach loyalty to the crown of Castile, which coordinated ecclesiastical policy under colonial policy. In return for upholding and legitimizing the colonial system, the Catholic Church had sole access to the region's souls.

The second example comes from South Africa. During the apartheid era in South Africa (1948–1994), whites (Afrikaners) ruled the country, though they were just a small minority of the population. The Dutch Reformed Church (DRC) provided religious justification for the state policy of so-called separate development. Proponents of separate development argued that "each nation has been created by God to fulfill a unique destiny and must be allowed to develop separately from others along its own lines to make its intended contribution to God's plan in the world."[39] Through manipulating biblical references, the Dutch Reformed Church provided both "religious legitimization of Afrikaner nationalism" and a "theological justification for apartheid."[40] It underpinned the National Party, which ruled South Africa from 1910 to 1994, and the government's apartheid policies. Other Christian churches and church leaders (e.g., Archbishop Desmond Tutu) rose in opposition to apartheid, however. Progressive "protest churches" challenged apartheid on religious and moral grounds. By delegitimizing apartheid theology, they cut the support out from under the apartheid system and, with it, undercut the legitimacy of the white-minority government.

This delegitimizing also has international angles. By the early 1990s, religious transnational actors (RTAs) were denouncing the apartheid regime. Other states pressed the regime by applying economic sanctions and trying to isolate it diplomatically.

The South African case, discussed at greater length in Chapter 9, also demonstrates what Scott Appleby calls the "ambivalence of the sacred": religion carries contradictory impulses. Religions can legitimize the state itself, the current government, and extant policies, or delegitimize them.

Turkmenistan provides the third example. An authoritarian country, Turkmenistan is one of five former Soviet republics that are located in

Central Asia and are predominantly Muslim. Constitutionally, it is "a secular state and guarantees equality of all before the law regardless of their religious beliefs."[41] In 1991, the former communist leader Saparmurat Nyýazow became president for life, changed his political identity, and developed a bizarre mix of personality cult, Islam, and nationalism to justify his autocratic rule.[42] He co-opted Muslims, especially regime opponents, by embracing Islam. He used Islamic symbols. He privileged Islam while controlling Islamic institutions.[43] The state-controlled media compared President Nyýazow to the Prophet Muhammad. Nyýazow thus played the religion card, but also stirred in a heavy dose of nationalism. He made a strong connection between Türkmen and Islamic values, describing himself as savior of the former and defender of the latter. Much as Abu Bakr al-Baghdadi proclaimed himself caliph, Nyýazow gave himself the title "Head of the Türkmen." This unusual brew replaced communist ideology as the regime's legitimizer.

Without legitimacy—that is, without the people's buy-in—states lack rightful authority and must rely more on raw power and the threat of violence. States want to ensure citizens' obedience and support at the lowest possible cost. Ideology (or theology) is cheaper than coercion (with heavy reliance on police forces) or patronage (essentially buying people's compliance). So, states may seek ideological or theological support as a relatively inexpensive way to ensure popular support and preserve public order.

Autonomy

Religious actors might turn to the state for privileges or protection—or, conversely, might stiff-arm the state, seeking greater autonomy—and the state, for its part, has to make decisions on protections, privileges, or persecution of religion as well as how separate religion and the state will be. Issues of privileges and autonomy often crop up in constitution writing and rewriting and are especially contentious in religiously divided societies. Such societies grapple with ongoing intra- or inter-religious conflicts regarding the state's religious character. Religious questions are central to constitutional debates in India, Indonesia, Israel, and Turkey.[44]

With regard to autonomy, religious actors seek state protection of religious freedom and from the state's unwarranted meddling in their affairs. Under authoritarian systems, religious organizations may emerge as the only institutional basis of political dissent. For instance, when Lithuania was part of the Soviet Union, the Soviet Republic of Lithuania was the only one of the country's fifteen republics that was predominantly Roman Catholic. The Catholic Church was the only relatively autonomous institution in that republic. It provided the only institutional avenue for citizens to express opposition to the government. Although the church itself was subject to state harassment and restrictions, it became a symbol of resistance to Soviet rule, communism, and forced secularization.[45]

Competing "Ideologies of Public Order"

In a number of his works, sociologist Mark Juergensmeyer discusses religious frameworks and secular-nationalist frameworks as competing "ideologies of public order." Both, he argues, present a coherent worldview, have various levels of meaning, provide a basis of identity and the glue to hold together broad communities, elicit loyalty, offer a basis of nationhood, can sanction violence and killing, claim they can provide justice, and lend authority to the sociopolitical order—all of which makes them potential rivals.[46] Secular nationalism has been called "the most powerful political idea of the past 200 years."[47] It is powerful because it concerns people's group (national) identity, makes claims on their loyalty (with supreme loyalty to the nation-state), ignites political passions, and is durable. Secular nationalism is also a product of the West.

What Juergensmeyer calls "religious nationalism" links religion and the nation-state. Religious nationalists have religious and political interests. Religious nationalists inject religion into public life either by politicizing religion or "religionizing" politics. Religion is politicized when religious identities are used for political ends. This can occur when religious and ethnic identities are tightly linked or when religious identities are employed to serve political purposes. Religion is also politicized when religious causes are taken as the root of political problems or when "religious goals have a political solution."[48] This is most likely to occur during a time of crisis.

Politics is religionized (some say "sacralized") when political issues are couched within a sacred context and religious ideas are the basis of politics. Juergensmeyer cites the Iranian Revolution and the political order it created as an example of religionized politics.[49] In Iran as elsewhere, it is not the content of Islamic traditions and beliefs that matters in international relations, but how Islam facilitates political mobilization and interacts with political belonging and civic identity.[50]

The Chechen movement in Russia provides an example of politicized religion. The Chechens are an ethnic and religious minority within Russia. Since the Soviet Union imploded in 1991, Chechens have been struggling for independence from Russia. Secular nationalism was the initial impulse behind this struggle, framed as Chechens against Russians. After defeats in the 1990s, their largely nonreligious quest for independence took on religious (Islamist) overtones.[51] The separatist conflict morphed into the struggle of a Muslim minority against a non-Muslim majority and religion became politicized.

This conflict within Russia fits into broader discussions of politics. One discussion is about political geography and the number of sovereign states: which groups in the world are granted the right to self-determination? In other words, which nations get to have their own states? And what are the implications elsewhere in the world? If Chechens in southwestern Russia or Tibetans in China gain independence, will that not fan the flames of separatist movements? Another discussion concerns labels and appropriate responses. When are the rights of "repressed minority groups" pushed by international human rights organizations? When are armed separatist movements appropriately called "terrorists" by the states in which they reside and other states around the world?

Questions of religion, politics, and power bring us back to the secularization thesis. Secularization assumes a steady reduction in the "power of religion."[52] However, outside of Europe, religion's power is evident in domestic and foreign politics. In some times and places, religion can help to bring a candidate or regime to power, maintain a regime in power, or undermine a regime's hold on power. Think, for instance, of El Salvador at the time of Bishop Romero's death, when church leaders were associated with popular resistance to the regime. In other contexts, religion is wrapped up with group identity and a desire for self-rule.

When

When do religious actors get involved in the messy business of domestic politics? For the authors of *God in the Tumult of the Global Square*, the time is now. These authors describe a "strident new religiosity" that has fomented conflict between religious activists and secular politics.[53] These "religious activists" have both political and religious interests. They have lost faith in secular nationalism, secular institutions, and secular politicians. They find that the old secular ideologies like Marxism have lost much of their mobilizing power, but religion has not. They are operating within a new framework provided by the advance of globalization.

However, not all religious actors who dip their toes into political waters are activists who are confronting secular politics as a whole. They may simply have religious interests that intersect with politics on certain matters. For such actors, whether and when they choose to become actively engaged in politics depends on one or more of the following factors.

The first factor is political theology, which is a set of ideas about politics that is shared by co-religionists. It includes a religious actor's ideas about what constitutes legitimate political authority; understandings of the right relationship between the state, on the one hand, and religious organizations and authorities, on the other, or between temporal matters and spiritual matters; and determinations of if and when political violence is ever appropriate.

A second reason for engagement is a combination of impetus and political opportunity. The impetus may be frustration or even rage around issues of racism and the opportunity to participate in Black Lives Matter marches. The Arab Spring, also known as the Arab Awakening, provided a political opening in that region. Once it began in Tunisia, citizens in other countries with aging autocrats seized the opportunity to bring about political change.

The third factor is the risks or costs of political involvement, on the one hand, and the potential benefits, on the other. The reasons for and potential benefits of engagement in politics were discussed above, so only the risks or costs will be mentioned here. The otherworldly might be sullied by mucking around in the worldly realm of politics, where subscribers to eternal verities are compelled to make compromises to solve immediate problems. "When religion becomes linked with political forces," says Graham Fuller, "it tends to lose its soul."[54] Religious institutions risk being co-opted by the state and losing their autonomy. Or, if they take up residence in the corridors of state power, they may lose their prophetic voice. They may become caught up in this-world concerns to the neglect of important other-worldly concerns.[55] Political involvement thus entails an assortment of potential dangers.

Interaction creates risks for the political community, too. Intolerance is one risk. A close relationship between religious and political institutions limits a state's capacity to incorporate nonpracticing members of the favored religion, followers of other faiths, as well as agnostics and atheists into full citizenship. These are dangers faced by Israel and Iran, to the extent that Judaism defines the nature of Israel's state and Islam defines Iran's. More generally, any kind of favoritism presents a challenge to pluralism.

How: Modes of Political Action

Religion can affect the temporal world "by what it says and by what it does."[56] According to Toft, Philpott, and Shah, "all of the major religions include organizations of believers who advocate for political causes."[57] Juergensmeyer defines "religious activists" as individuals with religious and political interests.[58]

Many of the world's 7.3 billion people are in some way associated with a religious movement, "a politically active organization based on strong religious convictions."[59] Religion is used to frame such movements. Theology can motivate and mobilize political action, and religious movements have an organizational capacity that enables them to mobilize people, bringing them into the political process. Institutionalized religious bodies, such as Christian churches, offer "mobilization power" in that members share common beliefs and norms.[60] Religions may also be shielded from outside (or state) interference in ways that other civil society organizations are not, sometimes providing the only space to organize and mobilize outside of a repressive regime.[61] Given religion's capacity to foster commitments, it is not surprising that "religious organizations have had long, successful track records in inspiring collective action."[62] Even in highly secular countries, such as Germany, religion can be a source of political mobilization.[63] Mobilization is a crucial element in political action, moving people from inaction to active participation. It is the difference between getting into the game and watching from the sidelines. The question, then, is what form does their advocacy or activism take?

The modes of political action range from inactivity and nonparticipation at one extreme to political violence at the other extreme, as we have seen. In between these extremes are voting; communicating with government officials, fellow citizens, and those in other countries; community, partisan, and government activism; and civil disobedience. For instance, during the 1983 "Euromissile crisis"—when NATO military maneuvers prompted Soviet military responses—some countries' Catholic churches and bishops' conferences wrote letters on peace. In the United States, Catholic bishops published a lengthy pastoral letter entitled *The Challenge of Peace* in which they critiqued US nuclear policies. Today, for the young across Muslim-majority countries, rap music is communicating criticisms of their own autocratic governments and of extremists, such as al-Qaeda, along with demands for political change. Examples of partisan and government activism come from Brazil, an emerging power. There, an evangelical Protestant denomination called the Assemblies of God has put forward candidates for elected office and the "Evangelical Bloc" holds a significant number of seats in the national legislature. Other types of activism include participating in boycotts and protests, attending meetings and rallies, and refusing to obey unjust laws. Activism can take place online, in the streets, or in the courts. Religious groups in the United States often turn to the courts to advance their political agenda or block others' agendas. In some settings, women can declare their activist intent simply by wearing or not wearing an Islamic head covering. Under Tunisia's pre–Arab Spring autocratic regime, the government outlawed the "hijab in government offices, schools, and public facilities to stem the Islamic tide."[64] Wearing the hijab then became an act of defiance and an example of civil disobedience.

Civil disobedience is a form of resistance to state authority that entails breaking an unjust law, doing so without resorting to violence, and being willing to pay the price for the offense. A classic example here comes from Mahatma Gandhi, an Indian spiritual and political leader who took to civil disobedience even before he read Henry David Thoreau's nineteenth-century essay by that name. Unlike Thoreau, Gandhi mobilized the masses. Gandhi used religious rhetoric. He practiced "politically engaged spirituality."[65] He advocated "truth force": the determined but nonviolent resistance to injustice. One of his best-known acts was the 1930 Salt March. Gandhi and his followers protested the British rulers' monopoly on salt production and the imposition of a salt tax. Through the simple act of making salt from seawater without paying the imperial tax, the Salt March was the beginning of India's civil disobedience movement. Like Thoreau, Gandhi was jailed for breaking the law. Gandhi's use of civil disobedience inspired others, such as the Reverend Martin Luther King Jr. and the American civil rights movement of the 1960s.

Political violence, which gets much of the attention, includes riots, assassination, civil war, interstate war, terrorism, and so on. Moving from apolitical quietism to bomb throwing, the potential costs of participation —time, money, reputation, imprisonment, physical harm—rise. The rest of this section looks at partisan activism (political parties) and political violence.

Religious or Confessional Parties

Politico-religious or "confessional" parties deserve special attention, first, because political parties are key actors in democracies and, second, because religiously based parties are associated with so many different religions and have been pivotal actors in so many countries. Religious parties are found in liberal democracies (e.g., Chile and Italy), but also in secular authoritarian regimes that hold elections (e.g., Jordan and Yemen) and theocratic or confessional states that hold elections (e.g., Iran). Jews in Israel and Hindus in India have "formed political parties whose platforms draw from and focus on religious tradition."[66] Israel, a small country with an outsized role in world politics, has a multiparty parliamentary system in which religious parties (e.g., Shas, the National Religious Party, Jewish Home, and United Torah Judaism) are major players. In India, the world's largest democracy, the Bharatiya Janata Party (a Hindu nationalist party) received almost one-third of the vote in the 2014 parliamentary elections. Even Sweden, in the world's most secular region, gave birth to the Christian Values Party in 2014. The bottom line is that religious parties' presence is growing in world politics. The focus here is on two particular sets of political parties: Christian Democratic parties and Islamic parties, both of which have transnational elements.

Christian democracy is an international political movement (or "party family"[67]) that has governed in a number of European and Latin American countries. Roughly speaking, it seeks to unite Christian (especially Catholic) faith and democratic practice, though some argue that the Christian part of these parties is silent. Christian democracy's philosophical roots lie in progressive Catholic social thought and in the political thought of French philosopher Jacques Maritain (1882–1973). It advocates a "third way": communitarianism, which, as developed by Maritain, provides an alternative both to capitalism and to state socialism, to "liberal individualism and socialist collectivism."[68] Usually, these parties are associated with the Roman Catholic Church, Catholic theological doctrine, or church-affiliated civil society organizations, though they may welcome the participation of Protestants and members of other faiths. Their open appeal to observant Christians makes them distinctive.

Philosophically and theologically, Christian democracy began in Europe, though it is now a shadow of the movement it once was in the region. Christian Democratic parties formed transnational networks and were dominant in Western Europe in the immediate postwar era, when European integration began.[69] Catholic political leaders, postwar popes, and Christian Democratic parties strongly supported European integration. For some years, it was the European "continent's leading political party."[70] In Western Europe, where Christian Democratic parties fall on the center-right of the political spectrum, they have governed in several countries, including Belgium (Christian Democratic and Flemish,

CD&V), France (Popular Republican Movement, MRP), Germany (Christian Democratic Union, CDU-CSU), Italy (Christian Democracy, DC), the Netherlands (Christian Democratic Appeal, CDA), and Sweden (Christian Democrats, KD). Christian democracy subsequently spread to Latin America and Eastern Europe. However, as secularization has progressed in advanced industrial (or "postindustrial") countries, religious identities and support for religious parties has weakened, especially in Catholic Europe, and Christian Democratic parties have lost vote share.[71] The exception here is Germany, where the Christian Democratic party remains a force to be reckoned with. In Latin America, Christian Democrats have contested elections in a dozen countries (e.g., Costa Rica, Ecuador, El Salvador, and Guatemala), and became real political forces in two: Chile (Christian Democratic Party, PDC) and Venezuela (COPEI).

Islamic parties are found in a great many countries, including Bangladesh, Egypt, Indonesia, Jordan, Malaysia, Morocco, Pakistan, the Palestinian territories, Sudan, Tajikistan, Tunisia, Turkey, and Yemen. By one count, since 1970, more than 170 Islamic parties have contested parliamentary elections. In the early twenty-first century, such parties have contested elections in some twenty countries—and, typically, have not fared very well. In part, this is because "for years, autocrats in Muslim-majority countries sought to justify their rule by warning that free elections would bring radical Islamic parties to power."[72] Essentially, autocrats' message was "better us than them." With the Arab Spring and "breakthrough" elections after long periods of authoritarian rule, Islamic parties came to power in a small handful of Middle Eastern and North African countries.

Turkey is an important country and an interesting case. It is a member of the NATO military alliance and, decades ago, began the process to join the European Union. A century ago, it established a distinctly secular regime that banned religious parties and prohibited the use of Islam for political ends. Then, in 1995, the Welfare Party (Refah Party, RP) won parliamentary elections and Necmettin Erbakan became the first Turkish prime minister with a "political philosophy based on Islam."[73] Two years later, the military forced the governing coalition to resign. When the government banned the Welfare Party, the Virtue Party (FP) became the standard bearer of Islamism in Turkey. When the Constitutional Court shut down the Virtue Party in 2001, the Justice and Development Party (Adalet ve Kalkınma Partisi, AKP) and Felicity Party (SP) arose in its place. The Islamic and reformist AKP has won and held onto political power. With a string of AKP parliamentary victories, the party's leader, Recep Tayyip Erdoğan, has been in power for many years. After the 2018 elections (in which the AKP, again, did well), constitutional amendments changing Turkey from a parliamentary to a presidential system went into effect. So, despite the prohibition on the political use of Islam, Turkey does have pro-Islamic parties or parties seeking to carve out more space for Islam in the public sphere, and they have done well in the realm of electoral politics. In the past, if such organizations appeared to be endangering Turkish secularism, the military or judiciary would step in. As the AKP has consolidated power, however, it has marginalized the military and judiciary and, thus, their ability to uphold the secular order that Kemal Ataturk established in 1924. During this time, Erdoğan has expanded Turkey's regional and international influence, while at home some Turks fear for the future of their democracy.[74]

Political Violence

A tiny minority of religious actors resort to political violence to increase religion's influence, but they get a great deal of the press. Political violence is a form of high-cost and high-risk activism that contravenes legal and constitutional orders and, often, theological prohibitions. Terrorism gets much of the attention. Political violence, however, also includes rioting, hostage-taking, bombing, throwing rocks or Molotov cocktails, guerrilla warfare, coup d'état, rebellion, revolution, and assassinations of religious and political leaders.

The examples below are of political leaders of several countries—Egypt, India, Algeria, and Israel—who have lost their lives to religious extremists. If you think of a bell-shaped curve, the vast majority of people, whether they are voters or religious believers, fall somewhere near the center or midpoint. Extremists are few in number and fall on the tail ends of a bell curve. In some circumstances, "going to the extreme" means being willing to threaten or inflict physical harm.

In 1981, members of Islamic Jihad assassinated Egyptian president Anwar Sadat, hoping to replace his government with a government better-attuned to Islam. Like the shah of Iran, President Sadat had presided over a secular nation-state and promoted Western-style modernization. A turning point came when Sadat signed the Egypt–Israel Peace Treaty with Israeli prime minister Menachem Begin. This treaty secured the return of the Sinai Peninsula to Egypt (which had lost it to Israel during the Six-Day War of June 1967) and won both leaders a Nobel Peace Prize. However, Egypt's peace with Israel, the so-called Zionist enemy, offended extremists and earned Sadat many adversaries. Opponents called Sadat the "Pharaoh" and portrayed him as an infidel tyrant, though others called him a devoted Muslim. Although "Sadat's murder marked the climax in the political-religious conflict in Egypt," attempts were also made on the life of Sadat's predecessor, Gamal Abdul Nasser (in 1954), as well as Sadat's successor, Hosni Mubarak (in 1995).[75]

In 1984, three years after Sadat's assassination, Indian prime minister Indira Gandhi suffered a similar fate. Two of her Sikh bodyguards assassinated her. Gandhi had infuriated Sikhs by ordering a military raid of their holiest shrine in the Punjab capital of Amritsar.

Another political leader was caught in political violence in 1992. That year, Islamists gunned down Muhammad Boudiaf in Algeria. Boudiaf had recently returned from exile to head the ruling Supreme State Council, following the military's decision to cancel the 1991 election and outlaw the Islamic Salvation Front (FIS). Established just two years earlier, the FIS had seemed poised to win the election. Proclaiming that "Islam is the solution," it wanted to eliminate the secular state and replace it with an Islamic order grounded in Islamic law.[76] It took up arms after the 1991 election was canceled. It was thwarted by the military, which pulled off a successful coup d'état to keep these Islamists from gaining power. The military's move was supported by the United States and France. It sent a signal to other Islamist groups: even if you win popular support at the ballot box, a peaceful route to political power may not be possible.

Three years later, in 1995, Yigal Amir killed Israeli prime minister Yitzhak Rabin, who Eric Hanson calls "the most significant political-religious figure of postwar Israeli politics."[77] In this assassination, a religious Jew (Amir) killed a Jewish leader with secular leanings (Rabin). Some of Israel's religious activists were very unhappy about the Oslo Peace Accords signed by Rabin and Palestinian leader Yasser Arafat. For decades, Arafat led the Palestine Liberation Organization (PLO), so named because it was dedicated to the "liberation of Palestine." In the 1993 Oslo Accords the PLO recognized Israel's right to exist as a state, and the state of Israel recognized the PLO as the representative of the Palestinian people. The peace treaty won its signatories the Nobel Peace Prize, but cost Rabin his life. Amir said he assassinated Rabin to keep the Israeli leader from giving sacred land (parts of the West Bank) to the Palestinians. Amir justified his deed with "Jewish theology, historical precedents, and biblical examples."[78] Note that this assassination has some parallels with Sadat's assassination, including the fact that historic peace accords sparked political violence.

A number of points are notable about the assassinations mentioned. First, like Óscar Romero and Indira Gandhi, some of the state leaders were killed by extremists from within their own faiths. Second, assassinations were by followers of four different faith traditions (Buddhism, Islam, Sikhism, and Judaism). We find, in fact, that political violence is "prosecuted in the name of all of the world's major religions."[79] A sense of religious duty or a need to protect their faith can lead people to get involved in politics, even to political violence carried out in the name of religion. As explained in Chapter 9, roughly the same can be said of peacemaking: elements of all of the world's major religions engage in the quiet work of peacemaking and, often, due so out of a sense of religious duty. Third, while assassins claimed the lives of national leaders, international politics clearly figured into some of these murders. Finally, although these assassinations are examples of violence against state leaders, states have on occasion resorted to heavy-handed crackdowns on religious leaders.

In Theory

In this section, we explore the state level of analysis and look through the lens of the three main international paradigms as well as the "two-level game" model. These lenses and model provide different ways to view state-level religion and politics and their relevance to international politics. Realists, liberals, and constructivists differ markedly as to the utility of the state level of analysis.

State Level of Analysis

States are a natural unit of analysis in world politics. They have sovereignty, governments, well-defined borders, and relatively stable populations. Regional and international intergovernmental organizations (IGOs) are comprised of states and can only do what states allow them to do. It is states that make foreign policy; nonstate actors, whether intergovernmental organizations or nongovernmental organizations, do not.

As expressed by Laura Neack, the focus at the state level of analysis is "what goes on within states that ultimately has an impact on what goes on between states," especially governmental factors and societal factors.[80] In other words, the state level of analysis concerns the leaders, government bureaucracies, interest groups, political parties, and general public. These are the "key domestic actors in foreign policy."[81] They influence states' foreign policy making and states' behavior in the international arena.

Governmental factors refer to the political system (open or closed), the type of regime (democratic or autocratic), the geographic division of powers within a state (unitary or federal), the size of bureaucracies, and state capacity. "State capacity" refers to the ability to administer the state's territory effectively, to use resources to make and enforce rules, maintain order, ensure social peace, and provide other public goods.

It is easier (less costly) for religious groups to mobilize and influence politics in some political contexts than in others. In a closed, autocratic political system, many of the ways that religions or any other nongovernmental actors might enter into the political fray are off-limits. Those doors are closed and opening them can bring very high costs—fines, arrests, exile, jail sentences, disappearances, even death sentences. An example here is North Korea, so closed that it is referred to as the "hermit kingdom." The North Korean government exerts tremendous control over its people's lives, including their political and religious options. Whereas a consolidated or liberal democracy is apt to enshrine religious freedom in the constitution and protect it in practice, an autocratic government may either (a) not guarantee religious or other freedoms or (b) guarantee them on paper but infringe on them in practice. The latter is true of North Korea, which guarantees freedom of religion in its constitution, but violates this freedom in practice. In contrast, in open, pluralistic systems, decisionmaking structures and processes are very accessible to religiously motivated citizens. The United States is a good example of this.

Societal factors include the country's history, economic system and overall wealth, ethnic and religious mix, groups and political parties, media, and so on. The vibrancy of civil society and religious organizations' roles within it figure in as well. A vibrant civil society, often considered integral to a well-established democracy, can be a counterbalance to or check on state power. It can push government leaders to write and implement just and effective foreign policy initiatives.

At the state level of analysis, religious beliefs and structures influence domestic politics, and often the international system, in some basic ways. Individuals' religious beliefs affect their political choices and, as in the example of Daniel Ortega, religious affiliations can play into the acquisition of political power. Religious forces can legitimize or delegitimize government policies or even the government itself. Religiously based organizations, from political parties to terrorist groups, participate in domestic politics—and often spur secular political movements. Finally, as discussed in later chapters, religion influences international relations "when domestic religious issues cross borders and become international issues," sliding from the state into the international level of analysis.[82]

IR Paradigms

For realists, international and systemic factors (or factors external to the state) are more important foreign policy determinants than internal or domestic factors. Realists view states as unitary actors, conceptualized as solid "billiard balls," or closed "black boxes," that pursue national interests. The national interest, meaning the state's self-interest or what serves the interests of the nation as a whole, is a given that does not vary with a state's political, economic, social, or religious makeup. The national interest and, thus, the goal of states' foreign policies, is "to accumulate power and material goods."[83] The head of government (the president, prime minister, or monarch) leads the decisionmaking process, "coordinating, directing, and making final decisions that translate a country's national interests into rational policy decisions."[84] Domestic interest groups, religious institutions, and so on simply do not figure into the essential realist analysis. Likewise, ideologies, cultural factors, and religion may be used by states to justify their actions, but, at the end of the day, do not matter much.[85] From the realist perspective, then, the contents of this chapter can be safely ignored—and the events leading up to, say, the next Iranian Revolution will not figure into the analysis.

Liberals argue that "analysts must open the 'black box' of the foreign policy process" and see how domestic politics works.[86] Whereas realists take the state as a unitary actor, meaning it takes the state as a single entity, liberals look at what is going on within the state that affects foreign policy. In other words, liberals pay much more attention to governmental, societal, and religious factors than realists are wont to do. For liberals, it is important to consider pressure from individuals and interest groups, bargaining among bureaucracies, and the nature of domestic politics. States' "behavior and interactions are shaped by the individuals, groups, organizations, and institutions that make up their country and government" as well as by nonstate actors (intergovernmental and nongovernmental organizations) operating within the international system.[87] Domestic political dynamics vary with the nature of the regime. In closed authoritarian systems, access to policymaking and the ability to affect the government's policies are limited. In open democratic systems, there may be many points of access to policymakers, but religious organizations and leaders must compete with others pushing their own agendas.

The model of foreign policy making as a "two-level game" is relevant here. This is Robert Putnam's idea that, in making foreign policy, state leaders must attend to domestic factors and actors (one level) and to international factors and actors (another level). Depending on the state and the foreign policy issue, religion may figure in at one or both levels, for instance as political parties or as religious transnational actors (RTAs).

Constructivists, as tends to be the case, offer very different insights than realists and liberals. Politics is not so much driven by power, trade, international institutions, and so on, as it is driven by ideas, ideologies, and identities that, in turn, shape states' interests. For constructivists, "'what people believe' shapes what individuals, groups, and states do."[88] Ideas matter. Ideas shape institutions and power. Beliefs matter. Identities matter. State identities are not fixed, but changing. Interactions with other states can affect a state's identity. Norms matter, too, and norms change; changes in social norms "can have tremendous implications for foreign policy."[89] Add "religion" before ideas, beliefs, and identities, and it becomes clear that constructivism is the IR paradigm most able to account for religion's role in world politics.

The analytical framework in Table 5.1 plugs in examples drawn from this chapter.

Conclusion

This book is about the dynamic, dialectical, interactive relationship between religion and politics on the world stage. Analyzing this from the state level of analysis reveals that religion and politics are intertwined in numerous and complex ways, "some cooperative and some conflictual."[90] In many, though not all, states, religion influences national, political movements, parties, and regimes. It can condition political life and shape political loyalties, even as politics shapes religion and religious experiences. Governments influence and often regulate or control religion and religious institutions. They create the political context in which religious actors function. Religion and politics are both potential sources of identity, loyalty, regulation, values, political socialization, and even public goods; hence, they may either reinforce or undercut each other. Each—much like culture, history, and language—can also evoke passionate attachments.

This chapter challenges notions that are often taken for granted. One is that religion matters little as a political player in the modern world. Since the end of the Cold War and the collapse of international communism, "religion has reasserted itself dramatically as a political force."[91]

A second notion is that religion and politics can be neatly separated. For an individual, this seems to suggest that the believer who steps out of a mosque on Friday, a synagogue on Saturday, or a church on Sunday steps into another sphere of life when she or he goes to vote.

Table 5.1 Analytical Framework

Levels of Analysis	Realism	Liberalism	Constructivism
International/ Systemic	States are self-interested actors that seek power and security—but states' pursuit of power is often cloaked by ideals or justified in terms of a set of values. When states spread their political values and ideologies, it can enhance their influence and soft power.	Local or national Islamist parties take cues from the international arena and perhaps the Muslim Brotherhood.	There are rival visions of how the world *ought* to be. There are also rival versions of the ideology of nationalism. Secular nationalism is a Western construct that "religious nationalists" reject.
State/Domestic	Religious organizations act so as to gain state protection and privileges and otherwise further their own interests.	Religious institutions, leaders, ideas, and demographics affect the domestic political context, much as religion's role in society is shaped by the political context. Religion affects foreign policies by justifying and legitimizing or undermining and delegitimizing government policies and behaviors.	States differ regarding their political values and ideologies. States' values affect their perceptions of national interest. These values may or may not be grounded in religious beliefs. Nation-states are built on shared identity, which is politically constructed. What is constructed can be reconstructed/changed.
Individual	Individuals seeking to gain or regain the reins of political power may, like Daniel Ortega, play the religion card. In the foreign policy realm, states' leaders advance national interests.	States' leaders may turn to religion to legitimize their rule and policies.	Powerful individuals can define and redefine states' interests and actions on the world stage.

Source: Hunter, *God on Our Side.*

A third idea that often goes unchallenged is that, like religion and politics, domestic and international politics can be cleanly divided. Sometimes they are separated for simplicity's sake. An introductory course in US politics and a course in world politics may not cover any of the same material. In real life, however, what goes on in US politics and in world politics have a bearing on one another. It can be argued that the international system is "where domestic and international policy processes merge," and that "religion's greatest influence in the international system is through its significant influence on domestic politics."[92] Influence is tough to measure. Also, as explained in the previous chapter, transnational religious actors must be given their due, too.

The fourth perception, which is discussed at various points in this book, is that religion is not of much import at any level of analysis. A counterpoint is that "religion influences international politics in three ways. First, it affects foreign policies through the *individual beliefs of actors*; second, it gives *legitimacy for support or criticism* of government behavior; and third, it can *transform local issues into international issues*."[93] In other words, religion influences international politics at all three levels of analysis. Breaking down neat analytical barriers—public/political and private/religious, domestic and international—makes the study of world politics more complex, but greatly enriches it.

Notes

1. Goldberg, "Religion and Politics."
2. Mulligan, "On the Fifteenth Anniversary of the Sandinista Triumph."
3. Barry Rubin, "Religion and International Affairs," 30; Duffy, *Saints and Sinners*, 372.
4. Hanson, *The Catholic Church in World Politics*, 95.
5. Preston, "Pope Returns in Jubilation and Triumph to Nicaragua"; Barry Rubin, "Religion and International Affairs," 31.
6. Hanson, *The Catholic Church in World Politics*, 95.
7. Kinzer, "Catholic Bishops and Sandinistas Meeting Again."
8. Schmidt, "The 'Not So Cordial' Church-State Relations in Nicaragua," 11.
9. Kingston, *The Politics of Religion, Nationalism, and Identity in Asia*, 34–35.
10. Adams, *Latin American Heroes*, 268.
11. Shortell, "Radicalization of Religious Discourse in El Salvador," 102.
12. Cited in Mang, "Oscar Romero," 283.
13. Brockman, "Oscar Romero," 446, 447.
14. O'Shaughnessy, "God Speaks from Within History," 234.
15. Jordan, "A Man in Dark Times."
16. Prendes, "Political Radicalization and Popular Pastoral Practices in El Salvador, 1969–1985," 129–130.
17. Fox and Sandler, *Bringing Religion into International Relations*, 168.

18. Grieco, Ikenberry, and Mastanduno, *Introduction to International Relations*, 105.

19. Karčić, "In Support of a Non-Member State," *Journal of Muslim Minority Affairs*, 321, 323, 337.

20. Roy, *Globalized Islam*, 313.

21. Karcic, "Globalisation and Islam in Bosnia," 153, 155.

22. Saideman, "Explaining the International Relations of Secessionist Conflicts," 727.

23. Kingston, *The Politics of Religion, Nationalism, and Identity in Asia*, 113.

24. Thomas, "A Globalized God," 99.

25. Fox and Sandler, *Bringing Religion into International Relations*, 168.

26. Shapiro, "Taming Tehran," 147.

27. Fuller, *A World Without Islam*, 23.

28. Ryan, "Imagining Iraq, Defining Its Future," 66.

29. Hazran, "The Rise of Politicized Shi'ite Religiosity and the Territorial State in Iraq and Lebanon," 523.

30. Fuller, "Turkey's Strategic Model," 55.

31. Tamadonfar, "Islamism in Contemporary Politics," 142.

32. Hamid and McCants, "How Likely Is It That an Islamist Group Will Govern in the Middle East Before 2020?"

33. Albright, "Faith and Diplomacy," 3–9.

34. Davis and Robinson, *Claiming Society for God*, 33.

35. Jelen and Wilcox, *Religion and Politics in Comparative Perspective*, 19.

36. Davis and Robinson, *Claiming Society for God*.

37. Bruce, *Politics and Religion*, 4.

38. Gill, *Rendering unto Caesar*, 2.

39. Omer-Cooper, *History of Southern Africa*, 176.

40. Johnston, "The Churches and Apartheid in South Africa," 185, 178.

41. John Anderson, *Religious Liberty in Transitional Societies*, 157.

42. Love, "Taking on Turkmenistan."

43. John Anderson, *Religious Liberty in Transitional Societies*, 157.

44. Lerner, "Permissive Constitutions, Democracy, and Religious Freedom in India, Indonesia, Israel, and Turkey," 611, 614.

45. Froese, *The Plot to Kill God*, 88, 89, 102, 108, 151.

46. Juergensmeyer, *The New Cold War?*; Juergensmeyer, "The Global Rise of Religious Nationalism," 266; Juergensmeyer, *Global Rebellion*, 20–21.

47. Baradat, *Political Ideologies*, 48.

48. Juergensmeyer, "The Worldwide Rise of Religious Nationalism," 11.

49. Juergensmeyer, "The Worldwide Rise of Religious Nationalism," 5–6, 11, 19.

50. Cesari, "Religion and Politics," 1331–1332.

51. Warhola, "The Kremlin's Religion Temptation," 342–343.

52. Martin, *Religion and Power*.

53. Juergensmeyer, Griego, and Sobslai, *God in the Tumult of the Global Square*, 9.

54. Fuller, *A World Without Islam*, 16.

55. Demerath, *Crossing the Gods*, 184, 210.

56. Haynes, *Religion in Global Politics*, 4.

57. Toft, Philpott, and Shah, *God's Century*, 22.

58. Juergensmeyer, *Global Rebellion*, 6.

59. Kegley and Raymond, *The Global Future*, 3rd ed., 161.

60. Gill, *Rendering unto Caesar*, 53.

61. Fox and Sandler, *Bringing Religion into International Relations*, 49.

62. Tepe, *Beyond Sacred and Secular*, 58; Gill in Jelen and Wilcox, *Religion and Politics in Comparative Perspective*, 271.

63. Jelen and Wilcox, *Religion and Politics in Comparative Perspective*, 20.

64. Wright, *Rock the Casbah*, 115, 120, 147.

65. Falk, "Politically Engaged Spiritually in an Emerging Global Civil Society."

66. Ullah, *Vying for Allah's Vote*, 7.

67. Bale and Krouwel, "Down but Not Out," 17, 18.

68. Haynes, *Religion in Global Politics*, 45, 72.

69. Leustean and Madeley, "Religion, Politics and Law in the European Union."

70. Hanson, *Religion and Politics in the International System Today*, 148.

71. Norris and Inglehart, *Sacred and Secular*, 210–211, 228.

72. Kurzman and Türkoğlu, "Do Muslims Vote Islamic Now?" 100–101.

73. Yavuz, "Political Islam and the Welfare (Refah) Party," 63.

74. Barkey, "Turkish Democracy," 75.

75. Ronen, "Radical Islam Versus the Nation-State," 137; Fox and Sandler, *Bringing Religion into International Relations*, 137, 154.

76. Tamadonfar, "Islam in Contemporary Politics," 154–155.

77. Hanson, *Religion and Politics in the International System Today*, 228.

78. Juergensmeyer, *Terror in the Mind of God*, 44.

79. Goldstein and Pevehouse, *International Relations*, 169.

80. Neack, *The New Foreign Policy*, 77.

81. Frieden, Lake, and Schulz, *World Politics*, 145.

82. Fox and Sandler, *Bringing Religion into International Relations*, 164.

83. Fox and Sandler, *Bringing Religion into International Relations*, 167.

84. Duncan, Jancar-Webster, and Switky, *World Politics in the 21st Century*.

85. Goldstein and Pevehouse, *International Relations*, 44.

86. Hook, *U.S. Foreign Policy*, 62.

87. Scott, Carter, and Drury, *IR*, 76.

88. Grieco, Ikenberry, and Mastanduno, *Introduction to International Relations*, 92–93.

89. Goldstein and Pevehouse, *International Relations*, 98.

90. Lee, *Religion and Politics in the Middle East*, 44.

91. Henne, "The Two Swords," 753, 755.

92. Haynes, "Transnational Religious Actors and International Order," 145; Fox and Sandler, *Bringing Religion into International Relations*, 168, quoted in Haynes, *An Introduction to International Relations & Religion*, 55.

93. Sheikh, "How Does Religion Matter?" 374.

6

Individual Actors: Saints, Sinners, and Secularists

Illustration 9: Bono Made Helms Cry

Bono made Jesse Helms cry.[1] He also got Helms to attend his first rock concert—at age seventy-nine.

In 2001, Jesse Helms, an evangelical Christian and conservative Republican senator from North Carolina, was chair of the US Senate Foreign Relations Committee. Helms had no love lost for the US Department of State, the United Nations, foreign aid, or the US Agency for International Development (he wanted to shut it down). He was labeled a staunch unilateralist and dubbed "Senator No" because of his opposition to liberal initiatives.

Bono is U2's lead singer and an ardent social activist with a history of lobbying on liberal initiatives. Much of his political passion focuses on alleviating poverty in Africa. After getting the evangelical leader Billy Graham and Pope John Paul II on board, Bono wanted to get Helms to support international debt relief, especially in heavily indebted African countries. His efforts were associated with the global "Jubilee 2000" initiative, based on the biblical idea of the Jubilee year: every fifty years, debts were to be canceled and slaves freed. The Irish rocker decided that, to advance his agenda of elimininating poverty in the developing world, he would explain the biblical principles to conservative Christian Republicans, like Senator Helms.

Recalled Bono, "'[Helms is] a religious man so I told him that 2,103 verses of scripture pertain to the poor and Jesus speaks of judgment

145

only once—and it's not about being gay or sexual morality, but about poverty. I quoted that verse of Matthew, chapter 25: "I was naked and you clothed me." He was really moved. He was in tears.'"[2]

In fact, Helms *was* moved—moved enough to contact Vice President Dick Cheney, who in turn talked with President George W. Bush. Soon thereafter, with Bono at his side, the president announced an additional $5 billion in aid for the developing world. President Bush also committed to an AIDS initiative.

Thus began an improbable friendship and collaboration to find solutions to African poverty. A Helms spokesperson said, "Sen. Helms thinks very highly of Bono's opinions on public policy issues, and finds him to be a very convincing advocate. It's based on values that they both hold—religious values, Christian values—that reach across the normal lines."[3] The "normal lines" here include the partisan divide, among others. "Helms credited [Bono] with inspiring his new insight into the suffering of others."[4]

Bono has long been a rock activist, whose interest in social causes, like poverty, arises largely from his Christian religious convictions. Bono's activism has included participating in Live Aid (in 1985), supporting such causes as Greenpeace and Amnesty International, and helping to found DATA (Debt, AIDS, Trade in Africa), a nonprofit organization dedicated to increasing awareness of problems in Africa. Religious themes crop up in U2's music, often "blending the political and the spiritual."[5] U2's song titles (for instance, "Yahweh" and "40," a recitation of Psalm 40) suggest the ways in which religious convictions play out in his music.

As a rock star, Bono is known for his onstage performances before sold-out crowds. However, as a social activist, pushing issues such as the cancellation of developing country debt, much of his work goes on behind closed doors.

Significance

The scene depicting the Helms-Bono relationship highlights the importance of key individuals, especially individuals in policymaking positions (such as Helms) or those able to garner broad public attention (such as Bono). In this case, each actor had his own "constituency" or audience. Helms had fellow Republicans, in the Senate and the White House. Bono had his fan base. Each also had the ability to exercise the power of persuasion. The shared touchstones of their Christian faith linked them together in the fight against poverty in the developing world.

Illustration 10: The Self-Declared Caliph

On June 29, 2014, the first day of the Muslim holy month of Ramadan, Abu Bakr al-Baghdadi proclaimed the reestablishment of the caliphate and declared himself caliph. About a week later, during Friday prayers in the Great Mosque in Mosul, Iraq, he proclaimed, "I was chosen to lead you." Baghdadi declared it a "duty" of all Muslims to join him in the project of reviving the caliphate. Baghdadi and his organization thus did what Osama bin Laden and al-Qaeda did not dare aspire to. As the self-styled "commander of the faithful," Baghdadi averred that he was the Prophet Muhammad's rightful successor and ruler of the entire Muslim world—that is, a caliph.

Baghdadi was the leader of ISIS (Islamic State of Iraq and Syria here, Daesh in Arabic, or simply the Islamic State). Integral to Baghdadi's project was seizing territory from Iraq and Syria, governing it, and expanding the amount of lands and people under the Islamic State's command. The Islamic State asserts "that all Muslims—individuals, states and organizations" should obey the caliph.[6] The new caliph (Baghdadi) called on fighters as well as various types of professionals (for example, doctors and engineers) to help build the new "Islamic state." Many heeded his call. Coming from five continents, tens of thousands migrated to land held by the Islamic State to participate in building a new state of and for the faithful. They came from authoritarian countries in the Middle East and from democratic states in Europe and elsewhere. This influx included thousands who pledged allegiance to the black flag of jihadism and the Islamic State. The individual obligation and reward of jihadism (entrance into paradise) is a powerful force for collective action.

Baghdadi wove together an idiosyncratic blend of religion and politics.[7] Baghdadi's authoritarian brand of Muslim politics obliged all faithful Muslims—more specifically, *Sunni* Muslims—to pledge obedience to him as caliph. His exclusivist brand of Islam also labeled Shia Muslims and those unwilling to give full allegiance "apostates" or "heretics," often condemning them to death.

Significance

A caliphate is an expansionist construction that is both a political entity and a religious project, much as the caliph—reflecting the Prophet Muhammad's roles as temporal ruler, religious leader, and holy warrior— is the supreme political, religious, and military authority. As a political entity, a caliphate is a government under a single leader (the caliph) that "represents the unity and the leadership of the 'Islamic world'" (*umma*) under Islamic law.[8] In 1924, when Turkey was being established as a modern secular state, the government abolished the previous caliphate. No caliphate existed from that time until Baghdadi proclaimed its reestablishment ninety years later. Adherents of the Islamic State consider the caliphate "the world's authentic Islamic community."[9] Much as the Sunni faithful are called to join and help build this community, others are excluded, including other Muslims.

Baghdadi's message and means differed greatly from what other Islamists have endorsed. Whereas others saw the caliphate as the end goal of a global struggle, the Islamic State proved impatient for change, ideologically extreme, and known for using heinous and well-publicized acts to expand the caliphate. Its extremist ideology incorporates an apocalyptic vision of a final battle between Islam and the West. These positions and actions made the Islamic State and its project a bridge too far even for al-Qaeda, which severed ties with ISIS before Baghdadi proclaimed the caliphate.

As a theocratic leader, a caliph's duties include forcefully expanding the area controlled by the caliphate through "offensive jihad." Offensive jihad, as the name suggests, goes beyond defending Islam or the geographical boundaries of the Muslim community against acts of aggression; it may, instead, justify physical aggression against non-Muslims. It is associated with radical Islamism. Sayyid Qutb, an important theorist of Islamism, saw it as a means to spread Islam.[10] Offensive jihad ties in with the expansionist nature of a caliphate and the ambition to bring all to Islam or Islamic rule, tightly linking the political and the religious.

The Islamic State wants to be seen as the protector of Sunnis, the leader of global jihadism, and a sort of "state." For a couple of years it ruled an expansionist state or proto-state with the motto "remaining and expanding."[11] It does not recognize the fixed territorial borders that are a hallmark of the Westphalian system, nor have sovereign states recognized it as a state. Rather, the Islamic State claimed chunks of other states' territories. It can be seen as a challenge to the (Western-created) international system of states and the borders drawn by colonial powers. It wants to replace the modern secular state with, as its name suggests, an Islamic state, built on its idiosyncratic version of Islam. Unlike the Taliban in Afghanistan or the Muslim Brotherhood, however, it does not seek power within the existing state system. At odds with the territorially defined borders of the centuries-old Westphalian system, this Islamic state is conceived of as a transnational state. Legitimate states—those recognized by the United Nations and by other states—label the Islamic State not a state but a terrorist organization.

For a short time, the Islamic State seemed almost unstoppable. However, three years after its arrival on the world scene, the tides had turned against the Islamic State. By 2017, it had lost most of the territory it once occupied. By 2019, its leader Abu Bakr al-Baghdadi was dead.

A final note here ties into this chapter's focus. Abu Bakr al-Baghdadi rose or elevated himself to a high position, gained worldwide attention, and convinced many individuals to make the Islamic State's territory their new home. Baghdadi tapped into others' personal convictions and, through the Islamic State's dramatic displays of violence, drew global audiences and attention to their cause. He exploited the sectarian aspects of Syria's civil war and a power vacuum in Iraq and other parts of the region. He acquired hard power and the inclination to use terrorism, guerrilla tactics, and "quasi-conventional" armed forces to achieve his goals.[12] Further, he drew regional and global powers into the fray.

This chapter zeroes in on the individual level of analysis. "The individual level of analysis seeks to understand the motivations of the empowered individual and the context within which they were formed."[13] This level of analysis takes as a given that "individual actors . . . make the real difference."[14] This is true whether the individual heads a government, a political party, a terrorist organization, or a politically engaged religious movement. Social media and the technology of cyberspace facilitate the growth of transnationalism and provide individual and nonstate actors new types of leverage and influence.

Empowered Individuals

The individual level of analysis begins with the understanding that, at the end of the day, it is individuals—politically empowered individuals— who make choices regarding political objectives and the means of pursuing them. These folks tend to be highly dedicated to a cause or belief and often knowledgeable, charismatic, well-connected, and able to leverage resources.

Analysis at the individual level also attends to key people's political skills, values, beliefs, perceptions and misperceptions, images, motivations, worldviews and ideologies, experiences, and actions. For our purposes, the focus is especially on how religion figures into motivations, worldviews, and so on, as well as "saints," "sinners," and "secularists" whose actions, for better or worse, have had an impact on states' foreign policies and world politics.

The Nazi, the Pope, and the Theologian

Some key individuals—a saint, a sinner, and a secularist?—loomed large in the religio-political tug of war in the Nazi era. One, Adolf Hitler (1889–1945), is the more-than-life-sized villain of World War II. Another is the man who was pope at this time. A third is a religious scholar who took on the Nazi regime and its efforts to control Protestant churches in Germany.

Hitler created a totalitarian regime, which gave the National Socialists (Nazis) a monopoly on power and attempted to use the total power of the state to exert total control over society. Nazis bent the institutions and beliefs of Germany's Christians to serve the regime's purposes. The Nazis tried to create a new Germanic religion, the "Reich Church"—a sort of "Nazified Christian Church."[15] This "soulless Christianity," as Madeleine Albright dubbed it, would come under the sway and serve the purposes of the regime and fascism.[16] The Reich Church would be a "racially pure 'people's church,'"[17] excluding Jews who had converted to Christianity and preventing non-Aryans from serving as church ministers. This was in keeping with the anti-Semitism that is a hallmark of German fascism. It was probably also in keeping with Adolf Hitler's personal beliefs.

Ultimately, such beliefs are unknowable; it is fair to say, however, that Hitler had a complex relationship with Christianity and Christian churches. A baptized Catholic, Hitler neither renounced Catholicism nor did the Catholic Church excommunicate him. To rise to power and secure his hold on it, Hitler made tactical alliances with key forces in the state: the army, industrialists, financiers, and the religious establishment. Most Germans were either Catholic or Protestant. Hitler wanted to win their allegiance and that of their churches. He seemed to accept "religious Catholicism," but not "political Catholicism."[18] This makes sense in that, seeking to create a regime that exercised total control over society, a Catholicism that limited itself to preaching, praying, and rituals was okay, while Catholic political parties and Catholic priests involved in politics had to go—after they helped him attain power. The Catholic Center Party and Catholic leaders, including Pope Pius XI, praised Hitler for combating the communist threat, which had arisen after the 1917 Russian Revolution. After becoming chancellor in 1933, and with the promise of signing a concordat (i.e., a formal bilateral agreement) with the Vatican, Hitler got the Vatican and German Catholic parties to support the Enabling Act. This act enabled Hitler to enact laws without the legislature's approval, even if these laws violated the constitution.

Shortly thereafter, Hitler and the Nazis began terrorizing the Catholic Center Party; then, after signing the concordat with the Vatican in 1933, they brought the party down, leaving the National Socialist German Workers Party (i.e., the Nazi Party) as the sole remaining political party. The regime also persecuted, arrested, or exiled Catholic leaders. Hitler and Propaganda Minister Joseph Goebbels tried to undermine support for the church by attacking the clergy's morals.

A second key figure here is Pope Pius XII. The Jewish Virtual Library raises the question of whether Pius XII, who was pope from 1939 to 1958, was a "saint or sinner." Before becoming pope and taking the name Pius XII, he was Cardinal Eugenio Pacelli, and he was the Vatican's secretary of state. Serving in that role, he negotiated an agreement with the Nazi regime. Six years later, the same year World War II began, Pacelli became pope.

In 1933, the Vatican signed a concordat with the German regime. The overall purpose of this "Reich Concordat" was to regulate relations between the signatories. One signatory was Adolf Hitler, who once said the creation of the Third Reich would be a "major defeat for the powers of Jewry, capital, and the Roman Catholic Church."[19] The new Nazi regime hoped to gain a number of things through the concordat: legitimacy and respectability; the allegiance of the country's 20 million Catholics; and the church's complete subordination to the Reich.[20] Under this agreement Catholic bishops had to swear loyalty to the regime, Catholic religious instruction had to inculcate patriotism, and Catholic masses had to offer a prayer "for the welfare of the German Reich and nation." Charging that the church sought to sabotage the government, the Nazi regime got the church to bar clergy's participation in German party politics, a move clearly aimed at undermining the Catholic Church in its political capacity. Through such moves, the regime was trying to restrict the church to purely "religious" matters.

The other signatory was the Vatican's negotiator, who later became Pope Pius XII. Given the stipulations mentioned above, why sign this concordat? As a transnational actor who commanded a great deal of respect, the Catholic Church perceived it could leverage the Nazi regime's desire for respectability and, through the Reich Concordat, it hoped to gain certain protections. The church was especially keen to secure protections of the church's and German Catholics' interests and thus, be able to carry out its spiritual and moral missions. It sought confessional freedom, freedom to publish on spiritual matters and to educate German youth, and freedom to make pastoral visits to public establishments (e.g., penal institutions). According to the concordat's terms, while church leaders would abstain from direct participation in politics, they would not be silenced on matters of basic human rights. The bottom line was that the Reich Concordat would protect the Catholic Church in Germany, but also constrain the political activism of anti-Nazi clergy and lend legitimacy to the regime. In addition, it would unite the two parties in the fight against communism. The Nazis disregarded much of concordat's provisions, but it remained in place.

The third figure here is Lutheran pastor and theologian Dietrich Bonhoeffer, whose writings include the idea of Christian faith as orienting believers to engage in this world and a call to radical discipleship. Bonhoeffer was a leader of the Confessing Church, also known as the German Protestant movement (not to be confused with the pro-Nazi German Christian movement). Emerging in 1934, a year after the signing of the Nazi-Vatican concordat, the Confessing Church resisted the Nazi regime.

Bonhoeffer has been called both a political revolutionary because he conspired to overthrow Hitler and a theological revolutionary because of his repudiation of the dominant "war theology" and the state's image of God. Bucking the state's militarism as well as much of German theology of the time, he adopted a theologically grounded pacifist and antinationalist position. Bonhoeffer was theologically and politically committed to nonviolent resistance to the regime. In an interesting twist, he turned from these convictions to resist Nazism and conspire to assassinate Hitler. Seeing Hitler as the agent, not of God but of the Antichrist, he called for responsible or righteous action. That meant coming to the difficult conclusion that revolution or tyrannicide were necessary steps.[21] Like other anti-Hitler conspiracies, his failed. German authorities arrested Bonhoeffer. They moved him from one concentration camp to another, and in 1945, they hanged him for treason.

Some broader points can be made with regard to this slice of German history. One is that relations between religious institutions and states are always complicated and, in cases like this, bound to conflict. Church and state each claimed that God was on its side. Another point is that, when it gets right down to it, theology is never apolitical. Theology has to do with all of life, including this-worldly aspects that take place within a particular worldly and political context. Theology that "ignores social, political, and economic structures" effectively supports the status quo.[22] Alternatively, theology can assume a prophetic cast, challenging existing political arrangements, repression, and socioeconomic injustices. Third, the causes and consequences of "domestic" matters can and do cross state borders. The actions of some super-empowered individuals do, too. Finally, Bonhoeffer can be counted among "extremists" because his convictions moved him to go to the extreme. He was willing to engage in a costly and controversial move of assassinating a state leader.

Super-Empowered Individuals

A great variety of actors on the world stage exemplify the profound impact one person—historically most often one *man*—can have on politics. These "empowered individuals" may be "religious virtuosi" whose actions are embodied in social protests or whose messages transcend state borders. Think about the opening scene in Chapter 3 about Pope John Paul II, a super-empowered individual who galvanized Poles and contributed to the collapse of communism in Eastern Europe.

Individuals may be some sort of entrepreneur. They may be "norm entrepreneurs," who actively encourage the adoption of certain norms or widely embraced rules for behavior. Like Bono, they use the power of persuasion to get states on board. Over time, as norms are internalized, they shape actors' behaviors. They may be political entrepreneurs, such as Serbian leader Slobodan Milošević, who is discussed in Chapter 7. The term *political entrepreneurs* is used in multiple ways. In this text, they are understood to be "individuals who change the direction and flow of politics."[23] Individuals may also be "idea entrepreneurs," people who influence how others think.[24] They may act like secular leaders until playing the religious card serves a political purpose, as with Daniel Ortega in Nicaragua and Saddam Hussein in Iraq.

Impactful individuals may be influential writers, such as sociologist Peter Berger, who pushed the secularization thesis for years, then reversed course. They may be either "saints" or "sinners," depending on one's perspective. Former archbishop Óscar Romero (discussed in Chapter 5) is actually en route to sainthood. As for the others, whether their actions are righteous, self-serving, heinous, or something else is best left to the reader to decide.

Influential individuals include state leaders (e.g., Mikhail Gorbachev, Angela Merkel, and Vladimir Putin) and individuals in the nonstate arena (e.g., Bono, Abu Bakr al-Baghdadi, actor and UN Special Envoy Angelina Jolie, Bill Gates, and Pakistani activist Malala Yousafzai). They include religious leaders. The current pope, Pope Francis, made *Forbes*'s list of "The World's Most Powerful People 2018," as the spiritual leader of the world's 1.3 billion Catholics as well as an advocate for better management of the global refugee crisis and climate change. Iran's Supreme Leader, Grand Ayatollah Ali Hoseini-Khamenei, also made *Forbes*'s list. Key figures such as these command attention and can influence states' foreign policies and world politics. With the exception of state leaders and Baghdadi, the individuals discussed here do not command armies or economies and, thus, cannot exercise coercive power or offer economic inducements. But sticks and carrots are not the only ways to exercise power. The case of Bono and Helms demonstrates the power of persuasion. The pope, similarly, exercises the power of moral suasion.

Within the super-empowered individuals category, Thomas Friedman adds a subcategory of "super-empowered angry men"—and women, but mostly men.[25] Men like Osama bin Laden are angry at the United States and super-empowered by globalization and the internet. They are super-empowered by new technologies that make it easier to travel and communicate. The *Small Wars Journal* explains, "The basic idea is simple: the individual has much more power to create a difference—negative or positive—than he or she did in the near past."[26] These super-empowered individuals are angry at the sole remaining superpower, which treats them as a serious threat to national security.

Friedman (who won a Pulitzer prize in 2002 for commentary on the worldwide impact of terrorism) named Osama bin Laden among super-empowered angry men even before the 2001 attacks on the United States. Bin Laden despised the United States as the leader of the secular, globalizing West that separates religion and the state. Particular US moves further antagonized him. One was the massive deployment of US troops to Saudi Arabia (the home of two of Islam's most sacred sites) in 1990 to shield the oil-rich country from possible advances by Iraq's army. Another was shortly after 9/11, when President Bush called for a "crusade" against terrorism, which bin Laden took as a crusade against Muslim lands.

Twice bin Laden declared war on the United States. In 1996, he issued a fatwa (a religious ruling or directive) "calling on all devout Muslims to take up arms against Americans in the Middle East."[27] His plan, entitled a "Declaration of War against the Americans Occupying the Land of the two Holy Places," provided a theological justification for waging jihad. Then, in 1998, he issued a second fatwa. This time, he urged Muslims to kill Americans and their allies whenever possible.

As the issuance of religious edicts suggests, bin Laden often framed his and al-Qaeda's mission as religious in nature and his conflict at home and abroad as a religious conflict. He made appeals in the name of Islam and on behalf of aggrieved Arabs.

Bin Laden used twenty-first-century communication tools to spread his message that it was every Muslim's duty to defend the faith. He and the organization he founded proved adept at using the networked world.

He founded al-Qaeda (which means "the base") in 1989. In the next decade, al-Qaeda established cells in twenty countries. It now has global reach and has perpetrated dozens of attacks—in Algeria, Egypt, Indonesia, Iran, Jordan, Kenya, Morocco, Pakistan, the Philippines, Saudi Arabia, Somalia, Spain, Tunisia, Turkey, the United Kingdom, the United States, and Yemen. A decade-long manhunt led to the killing of this super-empowered individual, but the network he created did not die with him. Clearly, Osama bin Laden was a super-empowered individual.

Human Nature vs. Idiosyncrasies

In this chapter, we are studying individuals, especially religiously motivated individuals, as the central movers of what happens in world politics. We have discussed "super-empowered individuals." Are these individuals basically like the rest of us or, are there things about them—their drive, sense of mission, worldview, perceptions, life experiences, and so on—that set them apart? The question raised in this section is whether human beings are all stamped with the same imprint, like sheets of currency rolling off the printing presses, or unique individuals. This is important because it gets at how we as citizens view the world and how foreign policy makers approach it.

Human Nature

A focus on human nature implies that there is something hard-wired into all human beings, regardless of when or where we were born. When the accretions of government laws, cultural understandings, and social mores are stripped away, an unchanging human nature is revealed. And what do we find? Are other people (and states) basically trustworthy and well-intentioned?

"Human nature is built into contemporary IR theory"—with the exception of constructivism, which is largely silent on human nature, since it rejects the assumption that anything is hard-wired or unchanging.[28] A discussion of human nature does, however, elucidate different assumptions underlying realism and liberalism.

The roots of realist assumptions date back to Thucydides, who (in the fifth century BCE) depicted humans as motivated primarily by self-interest, power, and fear, and, in a similar vein, depicted relations among the ancient city-states as driven by rivalry, conflict, and fear, with little hope for justice. Subsequent thinkers in the realist pantheon, among them St. Augustine and Thomas Hobbes, added to realism's views of humanity as egoistic, selfish, or self-serving. Given the chance, people will take advantage of one another. Generally seen as a cold and calculating realist, Niccolò Machiavelli generally found humans to be "ungrateful, dissembling, backstabbing, and untrustworthy."[29]

Such understandings of human nature have profound implications for the nature of world politics. The world, according to an influential twentieth-century realist, Hans Morgenthau, is the result of "forces inherent in human nature," especially an innate drive for power.[30] Stir in state sovereignty and anarchy, meaning there is no power above individual states, and other realist positions follow. Anarchy is to a state what a land with no functioning government is to a human being. Anarchy suggests that world politics is much like the Wild West; with no means to prevent people from acting on their baser instincts, there is an advantage to being well-armed. This leads to the realist principle of self-help: ultimately, each state is responsible for its own security and well-being, as all states will preference their national interests above all others. Human nature means that states had best protect their own interests. Cooperation is difficult; and conflict, though not necessarily violent conflict, is all but inevitable.

Realists want decisionmakers to bear in mind the realities of power and to avoid simply imposing a moral (or religious) answer on a controversial topic. However, some leaders like US president Woodrow Wilson (a theologically liberal Presbyterian) want to bring morality into world politics. He falls into the liberal camp.

Liberalism's views of human nature are often seen as more optimistic. Liberals view humans as by nature rational, essentially good, inherently peaceful, and even altruistic. Whereas realists generally see human nature as a given, liberals are apt to see human beings as perfectible—less hard-wired than realists' humans—through the right kinds of education and creation of the right kinds of institutions. Even if aggression is an ingrained part of human nature, war is learned behavior, and learned behavior can be unlearned. People can learn to look beyond narrow national interests. Peace is possible. Human progress is possible. People form groups and can collaborate and aid one another to build a better world.

Bringing in feminist theory, we find an entirely different take on human nature. Feminists encourage us to ask, Where are the women? They especially take aim at realists' understandings of human nature, arguing that Thomas Hobbes was not theorizing about *human* nature, but about *masculine* nature. Two millennia later, Machiavelli's famous work, *The Prince*, is clearly "about a prince, not a princess."[31] Ann Tickner argues that Hans Morgenthau "paints a gloomy picture of 'political man.'"[32] She contends that realists offer up a partial model of human nature and overemphasize the potential for competition and conflict. The realist model, argues Tickner, is socially constructed and masculinized, but taken as universal and then projected onto states' international behavior. The last part alludes to the tendency to identify certain characteristics of human nature and then to ascribe those same characteristics—self-interested and driven by power, for instance—to states' actions in the world. Feminists make another observation about states: most of the key positions of power and policymaking are occupied by men.

Relying on assumptions about human nature offers a mental short-cut when dealing with the layers of complexity in world politics. It makes it more manageable. It makes it easier to grapple with causes and effects: If we assume X about individuals and states, then Y will follow. Often, though, we do not realize that our perceptions are based on these assumptions, nor do we challenge these assumptions.

Idiosyncratic Behavior

Political psychology provides an alternative to a human nature–based approach to understanding individuals and states. Here, individuals' world-views and motivations are idiosyncratic, not part of a universal human nature. Each individual is, like a snowflake, unique. A leader's or empowered person's perceptions (and misperceptions) of himself or herself, the power and capabilities at his or her disposal, an adversary's character and intentions, an adversary's power and capabilities, and an adversary's signals can be crucial. Leadership and leadership styles matter, too.

Individual-level approaches can also focus on how decisionmakers function in groups or organizations. They may be subject to "groupthink": pressure to conform to a group's norms and expectations. They may engage in analogical reasoning, meaning they use past experiences that seem analogous to shed light on the current situation. In addition, they may (like most of us) prefer cognitive consistency over cognitive dissonance. In other words, they may shy away from information or beliefs that contradict what they know and believe. They may ignore or explain away information that does not fit with their entrenched beliefs and understandings of how the world works.

Focusing on idiosyncrasies gets at the ideas that individuals differ and that their differences affect what goes on in world politics. Leaders' personal experiences and characteristics, personality traits, goals and ambitions, political values and ideologies, personal relationships, ideological and religious worldviews (politically relevant beliefs and ways of seeing the world), leadership skills, powers of persuasion, biases and preferences, and other distinctive factors all matter.

We might, thus, draw a profile of people such as the black-robed Abu Bakr al-Baghdadi, in order to understand the psyche of a man who made a bold, audacious claim to religious authority over some 1.6 billion Muslims. When he rose to international attention in July 2014, his order to all Muslims was as simple as it was extraordinary: "Obey me," he said. What explains his vision and actions? Perhaps personality traits shed some light. Observers have described him as "quiet," "introverted," "paranoid," "ruthless," "charismatic," and a "quiet planner."

We might discuss Baghdadi's life trajectory, though the information available on this shadowy figure is thin and contested. He was born Ibrahim Awwad Ibrahim Al-Badri in Iraq in 1971. He was raised in a lower-middle-class, religiously observant Sunni Muslim family at a time when Iraq was a relatively secular country. He is said to have been quiet, pious, and unexceptional as a child. His piety earned him the nickname "The Believer." His passions were reciting the Quran and playing soccer.[33] He studied the Quran in college and went on to earn a doctorate in Islamic studies, which his supporters believed qualified him to be a caliph and which enabled him to provide religious support for all sorts of actions.

Baghdadi fell in with members of the Muslim Brotherhood and gravitated toward those who advocated jihadism. After the 2003 US invasion of Iraq, the area in which he grew up was heavily bombed. This appears to have been a turning point; this was when he walked onto the path of jihad (the "lesser jihad").[34] US forces labeled Baghdadi a Sunni "foot soldier," picked him up in 2004, and held him in a detention center described as an "al-Qaeda school" for terrorists. His confinement in Camp Bucca seems to have been another pivotal event in his life. In detention, he met like-minded detainees and jihadist commanders. Emerging from Camp Bucca as part of a network of Sunni militants, this man who had been described as introverted and unimpressive quickly rose among the ranks of jihadis.

In 2010, after its top leaders were killed, he became the new leader of the Islamic State of Iraq (ISI) and assumed the name Abu Bakr al-

Baghdadi. (The Islamic State of Iraq was an al-Qaeda affiliate from 2006 to 2012. It merged with another group in 2013 and changed its name to the Islamic State of Iraq and Syria [ISIS]. After Baghdadi proclaimed the caliphate, the name was shortened to the Islamic State.) He claimed his lineage went all the way back to the Prophet Muhammad, and his tribal affiliation bolstered his claim to be in Muhammad's ancestral line, a requirement for a caliph.

Operating at this level of analysis, we might ask, first, whether Baghdadi is a replaceable part in the larger machine of extremist Islamic groups. In other words, would events have unfolded as they had if someone else led the Islamic State? Or did his personal qualities (e.g., his political savvy and ability to forge coalitions[35]) and qualifications (e.g., his lineage and his religious scholarship) uniquely prepare him for the role of commander of the faithful? Second, we might study, for instance, how Baghdadi's unique set of experiences contributed to his political socialization and how his personal history sheds light on the man who declared himself caliph.

We can also bring out how events—the US invasion of Iraq and unrest in Syria—were catalysts or openings for Baghdadi's move and, likewise, how his actions shaped events. Individuals, after all, do not act in a vacuum. They are affected by constraints and opportunities in their country, region, and the world.

At each level of analysis, certain types of questions are raised, certain types of explanations come to the fore, and certain types of variables are studied. At this level, individuals' personalities, preferences, and perceptions are the key variables. As the examples above suggest, faith matters here, too, though clearly the political activism motivated by religious faith plays out in very diverse ways: lobbying, protesting, conspiring to assassinate a political leader, and declaring a caliphate. By "centering our analytical efforts on individuals," the individual level of analysis illuminates the individual, personal "roots of religious politics."[36]

Decisionmaking

Much of world politics centers on states and, at the individual level of analysis, on states' leaders. States' leaders make foreign policy. How they make foreign policy decisions is generally understood to be dependent on idiosyncratic factors and reasoning processes. These have been boiled down to a handful of decisionmaking models.

The first model, the cognitive/emotional approach, ties into the discussion above about psychology and belief sets. It emphasizes the importance of individuals and the subjective nature of decisionmaking. Foreign policy makers look at the world subjectively, through their own psychological lenses. As a good constructivist would say, "We construct the reality in which we operate."[37] Like the rest of us, they have particular psychological mindsets, preconceptions, baggage, and perhaps a reluctance to incorporate new information that does not square with what they already know or think they know.

Another aspect of this model is the tendency to take cognitive shortcuts. One of the most important shortcuts is reasoning by analogy: using past experiences that seem comparable to the current situation in order to shed light on it. As "cognitive misers," decisionmakers also look for information in convenient places. Think of the "drunkard's search." The drunkard searches for his lost house key under the streetlight—not because the key is likely to be there, but because the light is better there than elsewhere.

David Houghton applies this tendency to take shortcuts to the US invasion of Iraq in 2003. In deciding whether to invade Iraq, President George W. Bush and his key advisers drew on the "lessons of 9/11": "rogue states with weapons of mass destruction and ties to terrorist groups were an extreme threat."[38] To call Iraq a "rogue state" is to say it thumbed its nose at international norms; its brutal treatment of its own citizens, its invasion of Kuwait in 1990, and its development of illicit weapons of mass destruction (WMD) all violated these norms. The Bush administration's stated aims for invading were to protect the United States and its partners in the region from WMD and terrorism; to replace a dictatorship with a democratic regime; and to punish Saddam Hussein for his role in the 9/11 terrorist attacks. Impressions, beliefs, and the desire for cognitive consistency can move decisionmakers to ignore or deny any information that does not square with preconceived notions. Bush administration officials dismissed evidence that Saddam Hussein was not in cahoots with al-Qaeda and, thus, had nothing to do with the attacks. Instead, officials looked for evidence that would confirm their beliefs.

Finally, the cognitive/emotional approach points to the possibility of misperceptions and miscalculations. Apparently, Saddam Hussein misperceived the threat of a US invasion, while George W. Bush (thinking Iraq had hidden arsenals of weapons of mass destruction) misperceived the threat Saddam's regime posed. Leaders have certain images of themselves, of their adversaries, and of their adversaries' intentions. These images may or may not be on the mark.

A second model is the rational actor approach. This model takes state leaders as rational actors, meaning they have clear objectives and weigh the costs and benefits concerning how best to achieve their policy objectives. Rational decisionmaking is a process that involves a series of steps taken to arrive at the policy with the best chance of accomplishing the desired goals.

Rational actors make informed, calculated decisions following a set decisionmaking process: First, clearly define the problem. Second, identify objectives and rank them in terms of importance. Third, determine the possible means (or policy options) for achieving the most important objective or goal. Fourth, assess the likely consequences of each policy option, taking into account such factors as internal and external contexts as well as other actors' intentions, capabilities, and likely reactions. Make a choice; carefully weigh the costs and benefits of each option and "select the best option relative to its cost."[39] In other words, policymakers will choose the option that promises to deliver the main policy objective at the lowest cost.

This model assumes that policymakers have complete information, are willing to incorporate new information, and can process a tremendous amount of information. It further assumes they can and will perform complex cost-benefit analyses. These are questionable assumptions.

This model fits with the realist idea of states as unitary actors, "speaking with one voice in international affairs" and pursuing long-term national interests.[40] States' internal political dynamics do not really matter, nor does it matter who leads states. A leader is a leader is a leader.

A third model focuses on "groupthink." This downplays the role of individuals. It suggests that decisions are often made in small groups (e.g., the US National Security Council) and that individuals often act differently within groups than when acting alone. "Groupthink" gets at the social pressures to conform and reach agreement.

Finally, the bureaucratic politics model focuses on the top decisionmakers in government bureaucracies. In this model, foreign policy is the product of "the games bureaucrats play" or bargaining and infighting among government agencies and organizations that operate according to fixed and inflexible routines.[41] Top bureaucrats protect the interests of the bureaucracies they lead, and this can be more important than overarching national interests or solving the problem at hand. An axiom associated with this model is, "where you stand depends on where you sit." That is, a person's vantage point determines their position.

Much as President Bush had a choice among alternative courses of action, so did others discussed in this chapter, including Jesse Helms, Pope Pius XII, and Abu Bakr al-Baghdadi. Their decisionmaking processes may have involved a rational actor approach to achieving goals, group dynamics (of the US Senate, the Vatican, and the Islamic State, respectively), organization structures, or the psychology of each individual.

In Theory

This text incorporates theoretical analyses both because there are links between abstract theory and the real world of policy and because they are useful. International relations theories are useful for filtering out information, revealing weaknesses in arguments, and bringing out assumptions. They can also help us see patterns and form expectations regarding actors' behavior and how these behaviors affect politics on the world stage. Seeing these patterns and expectations enable us to understand and, ideally, predict actions and events.

Individual Level of Analysis

The individual level of analysis points to individual human beings as crucial players in the global drama, bringing out the choices made by key people, especially those making states' foreign policies, or alternatively positing that international politics is an expression of human instincts. It focuses on human behavior and the roles of individuals in affecting foreign policy and world politics. It presumes that individuals, especially those with power, can make a difference in world affairs. It matters, for instance, when particular people speak and act on political issues. For the most part, the "individuals who matter" are "foreign policy elites," meaning those directly involved in making states' foreign policy decisions.[42] However, celebrities like Bono and leaders of nongovernmental organizations, like Abu Bakr al-Baghdadi and Osama bin Laden, do not make foreign policy, but they can *influence* states' foreign policies. How states respond to opportunities and constraints in the world depends on the individuals who determine state policies. States per se do not act; states' leaders do. And leaders are not all cut from the same cloth.

Again, though, state leaders are not the only individuals important on the world stage. "Norm entrepreneurs" (e.g., Pope Francis), "idea entrepreneurs" (e.g., Sayyid Qutb), "political entrepreneurs" (e.g., Slobodan Milošević, discussed in Chapter 7) and leaders of nonstate organizations can also be counted among "individuals who matter." In addition, the behavior of some private, "ordinary" citizens can have important political consequences, especially when they are key players in collective action.

The underlying assumption of the individual level of analysis is that individuals can affect world events in several ways. First, some individuals move world affairs in a direction they might not otherwise have gone. While counterfactuals (asking "what if?") get into dangerous territory, we might ask whether the Iranian Revolution would have happened without the leadership of Ayatollah Khomeini. Would the Soviet Union have reformed and then collapsed if Mikhail Gorbachev had not become the state's leader? Would international communism have collapsed when and how it did without the gritty leadership of Lech Walesa in Poland and a Polish pope (John Paul II) in the Vatican? Would the Islamic State have formed a proto-state and had such a profound impact on politics without the bold claims and leadership of Abu Bakr al-Baghdadi? Typically, too, the focus is on states' leaders. However, Khomeini and John Paul II were religious leaders. Bono is a musician and social activist, though we might count him among Friedman's "super-empowered individuals." Jesse Helms (1921–2008), while having political clout as an influential senator from North Carolina, was not a leader in terms of US foreign policy making. Baghdadi, a self-proclaimed leader of a proto-state, is the exception here. Moreover, as suggested by the actions of Tunisian street vendor Mohamed Bouazizi (discussed in the opening chapter), one need not be a prominent figure—secular or religious—or among the foreign policy elite to influence the course of events on the world stage.

The individual level of analysis can be approached in two basic ways: focusing on fundamental human nature (i.e., analyzing people as a whole) or on key individuals (again, those who make decisions for state and nonstate actors as well as certain "ordinary citizens"). With regard to decisionmakers, their point or location within the government affects how they view an issue or problem.

IR Paradigms

The levels of analysis help us to categorize arguments and sort out the sources of foreign policy. International relations paradigms provide sets of interrelated assumptions and expectations about politics on the world stage. Putting them together, we find that the value of the individual level of analysis varies depending on the IR theory under discussion. According to one text, for constructivists, "individuals are the most important actors in world politics."[43] This makes constructivism the theoretical perspective most attuned to the individual level of analysis.

Recall that, for realists, states are the key actors. Realists are concerned with how states ensure their security and survive in a context of anarchy, uncertainty about others' intentions and capabilities, and self-help. Structural realists or neorealists are especially concerned with the global distribution of power among states (e.g., unipolar, bipolar, or multipolar), relative gains, and changes in balances of power. States compete for power and their national interests may conflict. Conflict between or among states is more likely than cooperation.

Realists give relatively little attention to individuals, seeing policy-makers as more shaped by than shapers of the international system and the imperative to pursue the state's national interests. Realists assume that states' leaders share their state's goals and interests. Leaders, that is, pursue what Hans Morgenthau called "the iron necessities of foreign policy."[44] The approach to and success of these pursuits is primarily explained by the global distribution of power, which affects actors' prospects of survival and of getting others to do what the more power-ful would have them do. The billiard ball metaphor of international rela-tions gets at the idea that states are unitary actors. Power and national interests, not a country's leaders, are what matter. We do not need to crack open the billiard balls (that is, states) and look inside to predict how states will act and react on the green felt of world politics.

To the extent that realists give credence to this level of analysis, they focus much more on the unchanging nature of human beings as a whole than the idiosyncratic factors or decisionmaking processes of par-ticular leaders. Influenced by the likes of Thomas Hobbes (1588–1678) and Hans Morgenthau (1904–1980), realists espouse a pessimistic view of human nature. Realists hold that humans by nature are self-serving, acquisitive, want to dominate, are prone to aggression and struggles for power, imperfect, and imperfectible—or, for Christian theologian Rein-hold Niebuhr (1892–1971), fallen and fallible. Fears and jealousies lead people to be on guard, like gladiators, striking postures of war. Realists project these images onto states. The world, said Morgenthau, is the result of "forces inherent in human nature," especially the innate drive for power and the desire to dominate. As stated by political scientist Joseph Nau, for realists, "the struggle for power goes on at all levels of analysis." At the systemic level, the struggle is between states and other global actors. At the domestic level, groups within states vie for power. At the individual level, individuals who make decisions for states and nonstate actors engage in this struggle.[45] The world is a dangerous place and, as individuals fear violent death, so states fear for their security and survival. Insecurity leads to safeguards: for individuals at home, mace, home security systems, and a bat under the bed; for states, bat-tleships, nuclear weapons, and antiballistic missile systems. For realists, interactions on the world stage are extensions of human nature and con-strained by the global distribution of power.

Liberals have a very different perspective on both human nature and the importance of specific people. Like realists, they take states as key actors, but liberals add nonstate actors: intergovernmental organizations (IGOs), nongovernmental organizations (NGOs), and "individuals who matter."[46] For liberals, then, the individual level of analysis is more appropriate than it is for realists. Tracing their intellectual heritage back to John Locke, liberals see humans as rational and essentially good, with "good" ranging from benign to benevolent. This innate goodness spurred progress and cooperation. Liberals would have it that human beings are perfectible.

In the liberal worldview, international politics includes a variety of actors, including public and private individuals. Like states and nonstate actors, individuals can make a difference. "In the liberal world, a rock star like Bono can have just as much impact as a politician like Russian President Vladimir Putin."[47]

Increasingly influential since the mid-1990s, constructivism focuses on *understandings* of international reality, rather than the search for some objective reality. Constructivism challenges realism's assumptions of objective realities and interests, arguing that both are socially constructed. Likewise, the norms of appropriate behavior on the world stage, where actors interact and develop shared understandings, are socially constructed. Even the international system does not exist in an objective sense; it, too, is socially constructed. Constructivism posits that the keys to understanding international relations are found in the realms of ideas, beliefs, values, identities, and images. Objective realities do exist—for instance, some states have nuclear weapons—but the implications of these realities depend on the significance people give to them.

For constructivists, ideas matter. Organized political violence, whether by the Islamic State or the US government, "must be directed by ideas—ideas about the use of power, about society fallen from grace, about revolutionary upheaval and the promise of a utopian future."[48] Based on his rhetoric, bin Laden justified large-scale violence because of the foreign subjugation of Arab lands and Muslim peoples. He railed against injustices against, and the "fragmentation" of, the Muslim world, largely a result of the West's divide and conquer tactics, and envisioned ending the injustices and fragmentation under a united *umma*. From his perspective, the United States, the leader of the West (the "far enemy"), has long supported the "near enemy." Defeating these enemies and creating a restored, purified, and unified global *umma* required global jihad, using whatever means necessary to advance the struggle.

Consider the different worldviews of Abu Bakr al-Baghdadi and Osama bin Laden, each a leader of a very influential transnational Islamist movement. Their organizations, the Islamic State and al-Qaeda, respectively, officially parted ways in 2014 because of the Islamic State's more extreme and intransigent views. Drawing on elements of religion and modern ideologies, both are appropriately called Islamists. Both advocate the implementation of Islamic law, the reestablishment of the caliphate, and the unity of the *umma*; they looked forward to the coming together of a single global community of Muslims in which political power is exercised in the name of Allah alone. Both also divide the world between "us" and "them," but they differ greatly as to who is "us." Bin Laden appealed to all Muslims, glossing over sectarian differences. Baghdadi appealed to some Muslims and targeted others. Perhaps, these differences can be explained, at least in part, by different perceptions of the march of modernization and threats to their faith.

Of the three major paradigms, constructivism takes individuals most seriously, counting them among the key actors. Constructivists analyze "how state leaders make decisions," how individuals affect discourse (how the world is framed and understood), and how individual beliefs, "character, thinking, and emotion [shape] political choices."[49] Political leaders and activists can, for instance, promote certain ideas and delegitimize others. They can encourage and cajole states to adhere to international norms regarding the use of chemical weapons, for instance, or to do the right thing. States' leaders can also learn; change their understanding of how world politics works, the state's interests, and the best strategy to pursue; and then enact foreign policy changes.

Feminist IR challenges the prevailing paradigms, always asking, Where are the women? For instance, Thucydides' *History of the Peloponnesian War* includes the much-analyzed "Melian Dialogue." The dialogue is between the representatives of Melos (a small, puny, militarily insignificant city-state) and of Athens (one of the superpowers of the time). The Athenians want Melos to submit and be enslaved. The Melian Dialogue is often seen as a sort of morality play for realist-style power politics. The Athenian representatives say, "The strong do what they have the power to do and the weak accept what they have to accept" and, in the end, Athens forces besieged Melos and the Melians who were not killed were enslaved. Feminist IR asks, Where are the women in the "Melian Dialogue"? The representatives were all men. Women are not mentioned until the end, when Thucydides reports that the Athenians killed the adult men and forced the adult women and children into slavery.

As mentioned earlier, feminist IR is especially critical of realism. It is most like constructivism in that both emphasize social constructions.

The analytical framework in Table 6.1 makes some general observations. It also takes as examples two individuals, Abu Bakr al-Baghdadi and Jesse Helms.

Table 6.1 Analytical Framework: Examples from Abu Bakr al-Baghdadi and Jesse Helms

Levels of Analysis	Realism	Liberalism	Constructivism
International/ Systemic	*Abu Bakr al-Baghdadi:* He took advantage of the political instability in the region, in particular the political and military vacuum created by the Syrian civil war, the ongoing conflict in Iraq, and persistent sectarianism in the Middle East. His organization (IS) threatened regional and global security.	*Abu Bakr al-Baghdadi:* Baghdadi and the Islamic State violated the laws of the liberal international system. States need to cooperate to combat them effectively.	*Abu Bakr al-Baghdadi:* His ideology was absolutist, making compromise all but impossible. His vision of a new caliphate was sharply at odds with the long-standing international norm of state sovereignty. Although Baghdadi's attempt to reestablish the caliphate appears to have failed, the idea of accomplishing this may live on.
State/Domestic	*Jesse Helms:* As chair of an important congressional committee, namely the Senate Foreign Relations Committee (1995–2001), Helms wielded power that enabled him to influence US foreign policy.	*Abu Bakr al-Baghdadi:* His organization conquered territory in Iraq and Syria. He proclaimed statehood for the Islamic State and declared the restoration of the caliphate. For a short time, the Islamic State governed a territory and the people within it.	*Abu Bakr al-Baghdadi:* Baghdadi and his followers had a shared identity and framed their actions as restoring the caliphate. (Unlike al-Qaeda, the Islamic State's ideas and beliefs necessitate controlling territory and a population.) Others attacked their ideas and framed the Islamic State's actions as terrorism.

continues

Table 6.1 Continued

Levels of Analysis	Realism	Liberalism	Constructivism
Individual	*Helms:* Helms was a powerful individual and a conservative. He is also called a realist because he strongly defended American national interests; his positions embodied the idea of states as self-interested actors; and he rejected the liberal vision of cooperative multilateralism (e.g., he attacked the United Nations and the International Criminal Court).	*Baghdadi:* Baghdadi sent out a call to Muslims around the world to join him in restoring the caliphate, and many heeded that call. At one time, he proved to be a very effective military commander and ruled a territory.	*Baghdadi:* He self-identified as a caliph and a soldier-imam, though others had very different views of him. The divergent worldviews of Abu Bakr al-Baghdadi and Osama bin Laden help to explain their respective organizations' postures toward fellow Muslims. *Helms:* His Cold War positions were rooted in American ideals and anti-communism.

Sources: Lister, *The Islamic State;* Anderson, "Abu Bakr al-Baghdadi and the Theory and Practice of Jihad."

Conclusion

The individual level of analysis "locates the causes of behavior and out-comes in the nature and characteristics of people."[50] People determine the behavior of nonstate and especially state behavior. In *God on Our Side*, Shireen Hunter argues that internal and external factors—geography, historical experience, resource bases, and the character of their political system—"shape the pattern of states' long-term behavior and the underlying characteristic of their foreign policies."[51] Fair enough. But what about human nature, on the one hand, and the "Trump effect," on the other?

In just the first couple years of his presidency, Donald Trump dramatically changed the United States' short-term behavior and others' perceptions of the country's character. He disparaged long-term allies, abrogating agreements, imposing tariffs, and tweeting comments that altered the tone as well as the content of US foreign relations. At the same time, he seemed to ignore Russia's depredations (such as its military interventions in the neighboring states of Georgia and Ukraine) and held a first-ever summit with the North Korean leader. The wisdom of such moves is not the point here. The point is that individuals, especially those with power, can make a big difference. In the case of President Trump, his personal traits, including his self-perception as the consummate deal maker, have affected the United States' role on the world stage.

In a Ted Talk on "How Great Leaders Inspire Action," Simon Sinek distinguishes between "leaders" and "those who lead." Leaders, he says, have power or authority because of their positions. Serving decades in the US Senate (a state organization), Jesse Helms had power, as did Osama bin Laden as head of al-Qaeda (a nonstate organization). When Ayatollah Ruhollah Khomeini took his place as Iran's Supreme Leader, he stepped into a newly created position that renders tremendous political and religious authority. In the run up to and as a result of the Iranian Revolution, Khomeini was a source of inspiration for many a Muslim.

"Those who lead," according to Sinek, are able to inspire others to action. As a pastor and theologian, Dietrich Bonhoeffer did not occupy a position of power; he did, however, become an inspiration to others. In this respect, he is like Mother Teresa of Calcutta and the Reverend Martin Luther King, Jr. Bin Laden clearly had the ability to inspire, too.

In the next three chapters we see the "two faces of faith" in the world today. This phrase comes from the former prime minister of the United Kingdom, Tony Blair. The first face of faith is "bad religion." It is politicized religion that is associated with intolerance, extremism, and violence and, for those reasons, is a dangerous actor on the world stage. It threatens international peace and security. This face, says Blair, wears "faith as a badge of identity in opposition to those who are different." The second face is "good religion." This is associated with things that "promote the common international good" by contributing to global justice, human well-being, interfaith understanding, and postconflict reconciliation.[52] Rather than divide, this enlightened face of religion is a source of cohesion. Both "faces"—dangerous religion and peaceful religion—make religion relevant to world politics.

The "two faces of faith" offers a "compelling framework."[53] It replaces the old narrative of the secularization thesis and religion's decline as societies modernize. It offers both "structure and simplicity."[54]

Does the "two faces" framework oversimplify a very complex reality? Perhaps. But it also serves as a corrective to the notion that religion itself or religion's intersections with politics are entirely good or bad. Religion has more than one face.

Notes

1. Busby, "Bono Made Jesse Helms Cry," 247–275.
2. Rompalske, "Rock Star to the Rescue," 56.
3. Jacoby, "Singing Bono's Praises," 1A.
4. "Helms' Redemption," *St. Petersburg Times*, February 28, 2002, 12A.
5. Jacoby, "Singing Bono's Praises."
6. Tomé, "The 'Islamic State,'" 123.
7. Esposito, "Islam and Political Violence," 1075.
8. Tomé, "The 'Islamic State,'" 122.
9. Ford, "How Daesh Uses Language in the Domain of Religion," 16.
10. Stahl, "'Offensive Jihad' in Sayyid Qutb's Ideology."
11. Blanchard and Humud, "The Islamic State and U.S. Policy," 5.
12. Hashim, "The Caliphate at War," 52.
13. Megheşan and Dobre, "Political Psychology," 57.
14. Fishel, *American National Security Policy*, 249.
15. Craig, *The Germans*, 97.
16. Albright, "Faith and Diplomacy," 3.
17. Hockenos, "The Church Struggle and the Confessing Church," 4.
18. Cymet, *History vs. Apologetics*.
19. Cited in Rychlak, "The 1933 Concordat Between Germany and the Holy See."
20. John Brown Mason, "The Concordat with the Third Reich," 23–24.
21. Moses, "Dietrich Bonhoeffer's Repudiation of Protestant German War Theology," 122, 354, 361–362, 366–367.
22. Appleby, *The Ambivalence of the Sacred*, 37.
23. Schneider and Teske, "Toward A Theory of the Political Entrepreneur," 737.
24. Hassner, *War on Sacred Grounds*, 96.

25. Thomas Friedman, *The Lexus and the Olive Tree*, 401.

26. Elkus and Burke, "WikiLeaks, Media, and Policy," 3.

27. Carter, *Essentials of U.S. Foreign Policy Making*, 38.

28. Jacobi and Freyberg-Inan, "Human Being(s) in International Relations," 645–665.

29. Elshtain, "Just War, Realism, and Humanitarian Intervention," 91.

30. Morgenthau, *Politics Among Nations*, 3.

31. Pease, *International Organizations*, 92.

32. Tickner, "You Just Don't Understand," 618.

33. McCants, "The Believer."

34. Stern and Berger, *ISIS*, 34.

35. McCants, "The Believer."

36. Tepe, *Beyond Sacred and Secular*, 40.

37. Houghton, *The Decision Point*, 4, 5.

38. Cashman, *What Causes War?*, 73.

39. Houghton, *The Decision Point*, 13.

40. Neack, *The New Foreign Policy*, 3rd ed., 30.

41. Houghton, *The Decision Point*, 11, 18, 57.

42. Mingst and Arreguín-Toft, *Essentials of International Relations*, 7th ed., 182.

43. Grieco, Ikenberry, and Mastanduno, *Introduction to International Relations*, 95.

44. Morgenthau, "Enduring Realities and Foreign Policy," 14.

45. Nau, *Perspectives on International Relations*, 2nd ed., 5.

46. Mingst and Arreguín-Toft, *Essentials of International Relations*, 7th ed., 182.

47. Klarevas, "Political Realism," 20.

48. Khatchadourian, "Behind Enemy Lines," 23–24.

49. Shiraev and Zubok, *International Relations*, 136, 137.

50. Scott, Carter, and Drury, *IR*, 11.

51. Hunter, *God on Our Side*, 63.

52. Hurd, *Beyond Religious Freedom*, 23–24.

53. Hurd, *Beyond Religious Freedom*, 35.

54. Elizabeth Shakman Hurd, "International Politics after Secularism," 952.

7

Identity and Ideology

Illustration 11: Hindu Nationalism in India

On June 21, 2019, the US government released its annual report on international religious freedom and, in the chapter on India, identified limitations on the right to freedom of religion. The report charged that in 2018, Hindu groups had used violence and harassment against Muslims and others to forge a religion-based national identity. It said that the Indian government failed to protect minority religious communities (among others) from attacks and that officials in the ruling Hindu nationalist Bharatiya Janata Party (Indian People's Party, BJP) made inflammatory speeches against the country's Muslim minority. Not surprisingly, the Indian government rejected the report's findings. Prime Minister Narendra Modi's government responded by asserting state sovereignty, saying that no foreign government had the right to criticize its domestic politics. The government also underscored India's credentials as a secular and pluralistic society. The Ministry of External Affairs pointed to the constitution, vibrant democracy, and the rule of law as evidence that India protects fundamental rights, including religious freedoms.[1] For its part, the BJP said the report was an example of "clear bias" and pointed to its country's "deep-rooted democratic institutions."[2] The United States Commission on International Religious Freedom (USCIRF) said, however, that Indian national identity is being conceived in narrower and more religion-based terms and that, in recent years, religious freedom has been on a downward trend as exclusionary

173

and extremist ideas have grown and "conditions for religious minorities in India have deteriorated."[3]

Those responsible for violence against religious minorities appear to enjoy a certain amount of impunity. For example, Hindu nationalists who are pushing a cow-protection bill—which accords with distinctly Hindu views of cows' sacredness—have struck out against Muslims and low-caste Dalits. "Cow vigilantes" are accusing non-Hindus of killing cows and are claiming to be victims. They are also lashing out at Christians who are said to be coercing conversions to Christianity, and several states have adopted anticonversion laws (mostly used against Christians and Muslims) that infringe religious freedom. The 2019 USCIRF report charges that Prime Minister Modi has seldom made public statements condemning mob violence.

Significance

India is a country of 1.3 billion people, making it the world's largest democracy (some 900 million voters!) and second-largest country by population. It is rich in ethnic, religious, and linguistic diversity; however, India (like Nepal) is a Hindu-majority state. India is also a secular state. In the years following independence from the United Kingdom, the first prime minister, Jawaharlal Nehru, and the long-ruling Congress Party advocated for what the Carnegie Endowment for International Peace calls "an Indian brand of secularism" to bind together the country's diverse citizens.[4]

This Indian brand of secularism has eroded with the rising power of "Hindutva" (i.e., "Hindu-ness"), a nationalist political ideology. Hindu nationalists seek a majoritarian nation-state, and Hindu political entrepreneurs promote ethno-religious identities. Hindu nationalists tightly link Hinduism and Indian national identity; the other side of this coin is that they view Muslims and Christians as not being as "Indian." As nationalists, they seek a Hindu nation-state—essentially, a state ruled by and for Hindus. This movement gained significant power in 2014 when, for the first time, the Bharatiya Janata Party won an absolute majority in the lower house of parliament. The danger of majoritarianism is not that the majority rules, but that the majority imposes its views by stifling dissent and trampling on minority rights. In India, it means dominance by the Hindu majority and diminished protections of minority rights.

Nationalism has been a potent political ideology for the past two centuries, driving anticolonial movements in places like the Indian subcontinent in the mid-twentieth century and separatist movements in the early twenty-first century. It can form a bond among all inhabitants of a state or pit some groups against others. While a "state" is a sovereign political structure that governs a particular population and territory, a "nation" is a sizable group of people who are bound together by something deeply shared and fundamental to who they are and who self-identify as members of a nation. Benedict Anderson calls the nation an "imagined community."[5] The basic idea is that, while a nation is too large for members to meet all other community members, all can imagine the existence of this community. The something that binds the nation together can be shared political ideals, such as democracy and individual liberty. This is the basis of a "civic nation" and "civic nationalism." Alternatively, that something can be race, ethnicity, language, a shared history, attachment to a piece of land, or religion. This is the basis of an "ethnic nation" and "ethnic nationalism." How the nation is conceived is important because nations seek self-determination; they want to govern themselves. Nationalism is the ideology of the nation-state. At its core is the principle that nations have a right to determine their own political destiny, to govern themselves; in other words, they have the right to self-determination.

In large countries like India that have a lot of ethnic, religious, and linguistic diversity, the conception of the nation can bind people together or tear them apart. What happens when national identity becomes a political football, as in India today? The Carnegie Endowment asserts that "political entrepreneurs" are promoting ethno-religious identities and that this is "political pandering."[6] Jeff Kingston states that Prime Minister Modi and his party, the BJP, are making national identity a political issue in order to energize their base.[7]

As indicated above, like a shared language and shared history, religion is often a central element of group identity, including national identity. Within religious movements, a belief system of beliefs provides adherents with their main source of identity. As an element of group identity, religion—especially politicized religion—can divide and polarize societies. In the Indian case, *The Economist* says there is a struggle for the country's "soul."[8] Conversely, religion can "create identities and loyalties that transcend national boundaries," beyond the confines of the state.[9] Reinforced by the internet and social media, a religion can be an "imagined community of global believers" with transnational connections and feelings of solidarity.[10] This cropped up in the former Yugoslavia.

Illustration 12: Serbia's "Passion Play"

The event was a massive rally, attended by a million people. The place was Gazimestan in Kosovo, near the field where the epic Battle of Kosovo took place. The key figure was Slobodan Milošević, who was elected president of Serbia that same year. The date was June 28, 1989. On that date in 1914, Gavrilo Princip assassinated Archduke Ferdinand, lighting the long fuse that led to World War I. In this case, however, the rally harkened back to an event that took place a full six hundred years before, the Battle of Kosovo, which over the centuries had become the sacred touchstone of Serbian national consciousness. Serbs, including Orthodox priests, held up posters bearing the likeness of Milošević and Prince Lazar. As a lead-up to the event, the earthly remains of Prince Lazar were paraded around Serbia.

By referring to the Battle of Kosovo and starting his political campaign in Kosovo, Milošević entered the "myth zone."[11] Many myths surround Prince Lazar, the Battle of Kosovo, and "heavenly Serbia."

According to Serbian mythology, in 1389, on the eve of the Battle of Kosovo, the prophet Elijah (or, by some accounts, a grey falcon) appeared before the heroic Serbian prince, Lazar, and offered him a choice: a heavenly kingdom or a military victory over the Ottomans that would give him an earthly kingdom. Lazar chose the former and died in the battle, making him a martyr, "sacrificial victim," or Christ-like figure who lost the armed fight but won a moral victory. The Ottomans defeated the Serbs in the Battle of Kosovo, placing Serbs under Ottoman rule for more than three centuries. This battlefield has been called the "Serbian Golgotha."[12] "In legend, the Battle was also a Serbian sacrifice, which elevated them to the status of a heavenly and chosen people," and elevated Kosovo, "the heartland of the medieval Serbian kingdom" and a foundation of Serbian identity, to the status of the "Serbian Jerusalem."[13]

In the 1989 rally, the myths were revived in what has been called a passion play: a dramatic reenactment of suffering, most closely associated with the betrayal, suffering, and death of Jesus Christ; in this case, though, it evoked the betrayal and suffering of the Serbian people who, according to the Kosovo myths, have been betrayed and victimized throughout the ages. The rally brought together "mythic time" (1389), "sacred space" (Kosovo), "historical memory" (of suffering Serbs living under the Ottomans and killed in World War II), and an "ideology that presented Slavic Muslims as Christ-killers."[14] Milošević used these myths as a lens through which to view the Serbian situation in the late

1980s and to animate Serbian national identity. He appealed to Serb unity, saying, "Words devoted to unity, solidarity, and cooperation among people have no greater significance anywhere on the soil of our motherland than they have here in the field of Kosovo, which is a symbol of disunity and treason. In the memory of the Serbian people, this disunity was decisive in causing the loss of the battle and in bringing about the fate which Serbia suffered for a full six centuries." The "myth of an innocent, suffering Serbia" fed the desire to avenge past wrongs.[15]

The rally also won Milošević—or "Slobo" as some called him—a place in Serbian mythology. He used mythic allusions to present Serbs as the ever-suffering and ever-righteous victims and himself as the new Prince Lazar, the Serbs' "redeemer" or "savior." Further, with the help of Serbian Orthodox Church leaders, Milošević manipulated the Kosovo myth to augment his power and build his nationalist movement.

Myths are stories people tell and retell about themselves, typically in an uncritical way. They may or may not be completely "true" in a factual sense, but these historical narratives are true enough to the people who keep them alive. As Milošević stated during the 1989 rally, "Today, it is difficult to say what is the historical truth about the Battle of Kosovo and what is legend." For Serbian national identity, the historical truth about this battle is less important than how Serbs interpret or construct it. Serbs often interpret their history as one of victimhood. Victimhood myths, like all myths, are important because they help define a community and, functioning as a social glue, they can unite a people. They also articulate a society's or nation's beliefs, values, worldviews, and understanding of its own destiny. They are wrapped up in social identities and understandings of history. The myth of Kosovo is a central pillar of Serbian identity[16] and reflects Serbs' understanding of their place in history. Serbian myths wrap national identity in the mantle of victimhood and the cloak of sacredness.

Significance

In emphasizing the distinctiveness of Serbian identity—and downplaying a shared Yugoslav identity—Milošević's "passion play" set the stage for the violent dissolution of the Yugoslav state in the 1990s. This civil conflict became internationalized with Russia lining up on the Serb/Orthodox Christian side, the UN commitment of blue-helmeted peacekeepers, and ultimately NATO intervention. To be clear, the Yugoslav wars were not about religion—it was not about questions of religious doctrines or religious freedoms, for instance, but religion played a role with regard to identity issues and the involvement of the Serbian Orthodox Church. The involvement of two important intergovernmental organizations (the UN and NATO), an outside state (Russia), and the birth of new states moved this domestic conflict into the realm of world politics.

This chapter explores the ways in which religion is bound up with identity politics, nationalism and other ideologies, perceptions, grievances, myths, and political action. It demonstrates that identity is one of the "critical issues" of the global era in which we live, and religion can be a "locus of identity."[17] Further, religious identities can be politicized.

The chapter unfolds by, first, defining *nationalism* and a variant of it called *religious nationalism* and then describing threats to the state. Next it moves to the phenomenon of identity politics, using the breakup of Yugoslavia as an extended example of how religious identities can be politicized and manipulated. Following the pattern of the other chapters, it wraps up with a theory-based analysis and a table demonstrating how some of the examples discussed fit into the theoretical framework.

Nationalism

Nationalism is the ideology of the nation-state, and it is powerful, resurgent, and contradictory. This ideology posits that the world's peoples are divided up into nations, and each nation deserves its own state. It is contradictory because, while globalization and telecommunications connect us with the world beyond the state that we call home, nationalism pulls in the other direction. As explained by sociologist Mark Juergensmeyer, religion's role here is also contradictory, both supporting nationalist impulses and serving as "windows to a wider world."[18]

Nationalism is powerful because it concerns people's group (or national) identity, stirs people's passions, and makes claims on their loyalty (to the point of extreme sacrifice). It is the belief that each nation should have its own state, its own "place in the sun," so that each nation can determine its own political destiny.

Politically speaking, "a nation is a group of people who regard themselves as a natural political community."[19] This distinguishes nations from other kinds of groups because people regard themselves as part of a particular nation. Students and alumni often identify themselves as part of a college community and this can be a very important form of attachment, but they do not consider themselves a nation. If a group self-identifies as a nation, it will seek self-determination; this can mean autonomy, territory, or secession. The Kurds understand themselves as constituting a unique nation and are seeking to create a new state, Kurdistan.

Psychologically, a nation is a collection of people who feel bound together by something they have in common. This "something" can be loyalty to the state or an ethnic, religious, linguistic, or cultural affinity. Nationalism is a matter of collective identity. People seek their roots. In many countries, religion is one of those roots, and "religion is an integral part of national-identity."[20] For instance, the Philippines was colonized by a Catholic country, Spain, and today Catholicism remains a powerful element of national identity.[21] Other countries, however, have a more inclusive form of nationalism and national identity in which the political community is distinguished by citizenship and shared political values—democracy and equal rights, for instance. A question regarding India is whether it is moving from this more inclusive type of nationalism, born of the movement to achieve independence and the common embrace of democracy, to a more exclusive brand, based on the majority religion.

Religious Nationalism

Chapter 5 touched on sociologist Mark Juergensmeyer's idea of "religious nationalism." As the term suggests, religious nationalism brings together religion and nationalism. Religious nationalists have religious and political interests. "They are political actors striving for new forms of national order based on religious values." They are "nationalists" in the sense that they are concerned with nationalism, the political ideology undergirding the nation-state. Nationalism is a secular ideology. Religious nationalists offer a religious alternative. They offer up religion as a basis of nationhood and the glue to bind the nation together. They are concerned with the ends or purposes of politics and the underlying moral order.[22]

This chapter's opening illustration provides examples of secular and religious nationalists in India. Jawaharlal Nehru was a secular nationalist. When India gained independence in 1947, Nehru proclaimed it a secular state. He embraced secularism and socialism. His successors, Indira Gandhi and her son, Rajiv, had little taste for religion. Hindu nationalists, including those associated with the BJP or the more extreme Rashtriya Swayamsevak Sangh (National Volunteer Organization, RSS), are religious nationalists. Since India is a Hindu-majority society, the BJP has numbers on its side, enabling it to gain political power through the ballot. It is "perhaps the largest religiously based political movement in the world." Hindu nationalists say "Hindutva," or Hindu national culture, is central to Indian nationalism. India is a multinational state; that is, it is a state comprised of multiple nations, with communities that speak different languages, practice different customs, and profess different religious faiths. In India, a secular state is one that treats all religions equally. In a country in which the majority religion, Hinduism, underpins the largest political party (which won the highest office in the land) and has become a political identity, equal treatment by the state is a concern for religious minorities, such as Muslims and Sikhs.

Moving from the world's largest democracy to one of the smallest, we come to Israel. Its territory and population size are about the same as New Jersey's, yet it plays a big role in regional and world politics. Like India, it has a history of religious nationalism. Both Judaism and the land are central to Israeli identity and what it means to be an Israeli citizen.[23] Israel is home to religious nationalist parties, such as the Jewish Home Party and the National Religious Party (NRP). Israel is a binational state, split between those who identify as Israelis and those who identify as Arabs or Palestinians, with the latter seeking a state of their own or at least a greater voice in their political destiny. In fact, the long-standing conflict between Israelis and Palestinians, which is often framed as a religious conflict, can also be framed as a case of conflicting national movements, with each claiming the "collective political right of national self-determination in their own state."[24] In other words, two separate and conflicting nations each want to establish their own state on this small piece of land.

In this context, the so-called nation-state law provoked a lot of controversy. It defines the state of Israel as "the nation-state of the Jewish people." It says that only the Jewish people have the right to self-determination, while the Palestinians have no such right. The controversy, then, concerns what it means for the Palestinian population, which is largely Muslim. However, it also concerns the very nature of the state of Israel, which self-identifies as a democracy and as the national homeland of Jews.

The State

States and their place in the world are being threatened from above and below. "Above" refers to the forces of globalization, centralization, and integration as well as the proliferation of nonstate actors. These nonstate actors include religion. One of the ways in which religion has entered the world stage is through the nonstate actor door as nongovernmental organizations (NGOs), intergovernmental organizations (IGOs), and religious transnational actors (RTAs). When information, ideas, and money readily cross state borders, states lose control over, for instance, their ability to tax corporations and transactions. The counterpart to these forces is the impact of breakdown, decentralization, and disintegration. The latter reflects, in part, a backlash by "those brutalized or left behind" by the new globalized system[25] and those who do not want to be part of a globalized and homogenized world.

This tug of war with the state in the middle can also be framed in terms of transnationalism and nationalism. Transnationalism (discussed in Chapter 4) concerns forces and actors that cut across or transcend states' borders. These include political movements, ideologies, religions, networks, and so on, which may compete with nations and national identities for people's loyalty. Transnational religious communities have existed for centuries, but modern technologies have given them wings.

Still the dear ol' state remains central to domestic and global politics. Only the state has the power to tax us and the responsibility to protect us. States wield types of political power—military and economic—that nonstate actors typically do not possess. States make foreign policy, enter into treaties, and create and control intergovernmental organizations.

Identity Matters

Identity politics is not new, but identity's salience in politics is increasing. It is not new, because it has long been bound up with the central concern of security. For states, security is primarily about protecting borders and ensuring their territorial integrity and freedom to act. Security can also include protecting states' identities. For instance, although the Cold War was driven by conflicting secular ideologies, it sometimes felt more personal. At the time, Americans expressed concerns, not just about the spread of communism, but about the "atheistic" Soviets invading the United States and undermining the American way of life and all those things—freedom, Mom, apple pie, Chevrolets, and so on—that are presumably part and parcel of American identity.

Much post–Cold War conflict is driven by differences in identity. The latter is seen in the numerous twenty-first-century civil wars in which the demarcation between the government and the rebels fighting against it entails ethnic, religious, linguistic, cultural, or other "'identity' issues." Despite secularists' expectations, and perhaps hopes, religion is a "key source of identity for millions of people, especially in the developing world," where so many of today's conflicts occur.[26]

These conflicts are the so-called new wars. This new type of warfare links politics and identities. In these wars, religion often serves as a "public identity marker" and a mobilizing force. New wars involve a mix of state and nonstate actors. These nonstate actors are often stateless communities; another way of saying this is that they are nations without their own state. In contrast, old wars were between states and driven by states' interests, with religion relegated to the private sphere. It is not, then, that new wars are about religion or ethnicity per se, but that "religious and ethnic belonging can be transformed into a resource for political power" and a source of large-scale political violence.[27]

As the name suggests, identity politics is a type of politics that is rooted in people's group identities. As a politics of collective identity, it "stresses strong collective group identities as the basis of political analysis and action."[28] Subnational groups create a self-designated identity or group consciousness. Typically, identity politics arises among marginalized or oppressed groups—Palestinians in Israel, indigenous peoples in Latin America, gays in Africa, Coptic Christians in Egypt, Druze in Israel, Kurds in Turkey, and so on—who believe they are oppressed precisely because of their group membership. Such groups often have shared grievances, have patched together narratives or myths to make sense of their oppression, and engage in political resistance. For instance, the "Kosovo myth" fosters the notion that Serbs have legitimate grievances, having been victimized since 1389. Identity politics increases such groups' self-awareness, facilitates mobilization, and lends them political power. A group with shared demands and grievances is more likely to be heard than an individual. For the marginalized groups, however, ethnic and religious identity are not simply about power or a political calculus; it is who they are. Identity groups often struggle to gain the freedom to practice their religion, exercise political rights, and participate in democratic governance.

Lina Joy

In a case study, Timo Kortteinen presents Lina Joy's experience as a "looking glass into Malaysian society particularly with regards to the construction of ethnic and religious identities."[29] In this multiethnic and multireligious country, Malays and Muslims make up just over half of the population. Ethnic and religious identities are largely conflated.

"Malay" and "Muslim" are interchangeable in terms of both identity and law. All Malays are Muslim by law.[30] And race-based and religion-based politics are familiar parts of the political landscape.

Lina Joy simply wanted to change her Malaysian identity card, but her efforts to do so drew national and international attention. She was born Azlina binte Jailani. She was also born and raised a Muslim, but she renounced Islam, converted to Christianity, and planned to marry a Christian man. This posed a problem, since "Malaysia does not allow interfaith marriages."[31]

Between 1997 and 2000, Lina Joy began the process of changing her name and the religion listed on her identity card. The two were related, as Azlina Jailani is considered a Muslim name. In 1999, Malaysia's National Registration Department (NRD) granted her request to change her name, though her original name appeared on the back of her identity card. According to her national identity card, she remained a Muslim.

In her third attempt to change her identity card, she focused on removing the word "Islam." This time, the National Registration Department said it needed a sharia court (i.e., a court that handles Islamic law) to certify that she had left the Muslim faith before it could make the change on her card; that is, the NRD held that "the renunciation of Islam is a question of Islamic law for Muslim authorities to decide."[32] Lina Joy said that, as a Christian, she did not want to go before a Muslim religious court.[33]

With the National Registration Department's denial, she began proceedings in civil courts. She argued that Article 11 of the Malaysian Constitution, which grants every person "the right to profess and practice his religion," gave her the right to declare her religious status. The High Court said that Article 11 was to guarantee religious *communities* the freedom to manage their affairs without state interference, not to give *individuals* the right to choose their religion.[34] In 2001, she lost her case in the High Court. She proceeded to the Court of Appeal in 2005 and lost again. Her case next came before the Federal Court, the highest appellate court. The Federal Court not only ruled against her, but said one cannot abandon or embrace a religion on a "whim."[35] The Federal Court, much like the NRD, said sharia courts have jurisdiction over such matters. Sharia courts interpret how to apply Muslim law. In other words, the highest civil court in the land said that such matters regarding government-issued identity cards are for Muslim leaders and religious courts to decide. Joy was caught in a classic catch-22: to change her national identity card, she needed a sharia court to legalize her conversion from Islam to Christianity; such courts, however, "consider forsaking Islam a crime. And since she [was] still classified as a Muslim, she could not use the civil-law system."[36]

Identity issues crop up with regard to Lina Joy in particular and Malaysians more generally. What are Lina Joy's key identity markers? What role does or should the state have in determining citizens' identities? Lina Joy was born Malay and Muslim in Malaysia with the name Azlina binte Jailani, which serves as an identity marker. She had no choice in those matters, just as none of us gets to choose the family and country of our birth, but she made the choice to convert to Christianity. In Malaysia, however, to be Malay is to be Muslim. The state appears intent on upholding Malay identity and privileging Islam, effectively refusing Lina Joy's "right to leave Islam."[37] In fact, the law provides means for converting *to* Islam, but not converting *from* it. In the High Court's decision, "according to the judge's reasoning, Islam is part of a constitutionally sanctioned group identity such that religion becomes an immutable trait rather than a consequence of individual choice." After that, when Lina Joy took her case to the Court of Appeal and Federal Court, the judges in both decisions were split 2:1.[38]

Some Takeaways

It is important to note, first, that traits alone do not determine what constitutes an identity group; instead, it is a shared belief that certain traits set a group apart (that group members are alike in some fundamental way) that distinguishes them from other groups. Identity groups are self-defined. Ethnicity, national origin, language, and religion are among the traits that are often seen as crucial in structuring identities, including national identities, but which traits become politically important at a specific time is not a given. Constructivists would remind us that "racial, religious, or other types of identities are constructed and reconstructed constantly."[39] While religion and ethnicity are by no means synonymous, in many settings they go hand-in-hand. In the former Yugoslavia, for instance, "political mobilization took place along the lines of religiously defined ethnic-nationalist parties of Croat, Serb and Muslim orientation."[40] Of course, if certain traits are seen as setting a group apart, they carry the power to include as well as exclude, to divide as well as unite, often creating an "us-them" dynamic.

Second, as the cases of the European Union constitution (discussed in Chapter 3) and Yugoslavia illustrate, identities always have multiple strands and layers. For instance, depending on the context, one might identify as male, feminist, transgender, Muslim, Serbian, Yugoslav, European, middle-class, an Arabic speaker, Western, or an animal rights activist. The context affects which identity is most important in a given time and place.

Third, a sense of solidarity or "groupness," cooperation among identity group members, and common grievances make it easier to organize collective political action on behalf of the group's interests. These interests may arise out of the group itself or be manipulated from above by "entrepreneurial elites" who stand to gain from it politically.[41] Slobodan Milošević is a case in point. In Yugoslavia, political leaders tapped into religious symbols and solidarities to heighten the sense of Serbs as a group, whether they were in the majority as in Serbia or minority populations as in the former Yugoslav republics of Bosnia, Croatia, and Slovenia.

Fourth, while *interests* can be negotiated, *identity* cannot. Interests concern choices—about leaders, issues, policies, and so on. Compromises can be made about who wields political power and how society distributes material goods. One can choose to join an organization such as the National Rifle Association, but cannot choose whether to be born into a Black Muslim family in the United States or into a Catholic Croatian family in Yugoslavia.[42] Although identity can be manipulated, it cannot be negotiated, making identity conflicts especially difficult to resolve. Again, identity is not simply about what people think, but *who they are*. Identity is intensely personal.

Fifth, this brand of politics associates the good of one's group with the common good, though it is one group within a larger society. When such groups seek territory or secession, this hardly serves the country as a whole. Further, since identity politics concerns subnational groups, it "may detract from loyalty to the country or nation as a whole."[43] It can deepen existing rifts, foster disintegration and civil war, and rip a country apart. The former Yugoslavia is a prime example here. Cold War–era leader Josep Broz Tito had vigorously promoted "socialist Yugoslavism" at home, with socialism defining the country's political and economic system and Yugoslavism meaning Yugoslavs were to identify with and be loyal to the state of Yugoslavia. Tito's foreign policy reflected Yugoslavia's geographic position, carefully situated between East and West. Once Tito, the Soviet Union, and the communist East were gone, identity divisions—cultural, ethnic, linguistic, and religious—rose to the surface and were manipulated by politicians like Slobodan Milošević during the post-Tito power struggle. Ethnic and religious identities, both shaped by collective memories, were bound up together.

France can be viewed as a prime example of a country taking active measures to avoid splitting along identity lines. For instance, the French state tries to integrate and assimilate immigrants so that they "leave behind their former nationalities and loyalties" and become fully French.[44] France's efforts to subordinate subnational identities to the state are evident in the national census, which "does not—and by law *cannot*—record a person's religion (or ethnicity)." A controversial law passed in 2004 banned the wearing of "conspicuous religious symbols"—such as Christian crosses, Jewish skullcaps, and the Muslim head scarf—in public places. This means that France's large and growing Muslim population, a population that is marginalized and whose faith is often central to their identity, is expected to place their national identity above their religious identity. This law was passed in the name of national unity.

Finally, "religion provides a particularly potent source of identity, belonging," and communal loyalties.[45] This is due, in part, to the "exclusive" nature of religion: one can be part Serb and part Croat, but not part Christian and part Muslim. This exclusivity may help to explain why "intergroup conflict so frequently falls along religious fault lines."[46]

Today, identity figures prominently in domestic and international politics. It is spurred by externally driven change, namely globalization and high levels of migration. Both sources of change raise fears about the loss of local identities and, in response, leads to a reassertion of those identities. Resistance to externally driven changes comes in the form of the reassertion of ethnic and religious identities, in particular. It is not surprising that religious identities would be reasserted during a religious resurgence. Francis Fukuyama states that "identity politics has become a master concept that explains much of what is going on in global affairs."[47]

Case Study: Breakup of Yugoslavia

Why was Yugoslavia torn apart? One Serb I talked to in 2016 said a "family feud" began with a religious spark. Another spoke of a civil war between people who were relatives and friends. She said their open, mixed, and multicultural society became closed and nationalistic. She added that the 1999 NATO bombing campaign created Serbian victims and strengthened the hand of Serb leader Slobodan Milošević. How are power, identity politics, and religion implicated in the series of conflicts that bloodied this multilingual, multiethnic, and multireligious country in the 1990s? These are the questions this section seeks to answer.

The country of Yugoslavia began unraveling after Josep Broz Tito died in 1980 following thirty-five years in power. Yugoslavia under Tito and communism was an amalgam of peoples and ethnic traditions, languages and alphabets, religions, and multiple interpretations of both history and national origin. Yugoslavia's multiconfessional state included three main religious traditions: Islam, Roman Catholicism, and Serbian Orthodoxy. All three traditions have deep roots in southeastern Europe (known as the Balkans) and for years mixed rather easily in the country's central region, Bosnia and Herzegovina. In this mix, Muslims were a religious minority. In an unusual move, in the 1960s the Yugoslav state recognized "Muslim" as a nation; this meant Yugoslavia now had six officially recognized "constituent nations": Croats, Macedonians, Montenegrins, Serbs, Slovenes, and Muslims. During most of this era, the peoples of these constituent nations lived together in the spirit of cooperation, even harmony. These nations were held together by communist ideology, an authoritarian one-party state, Tito's strong hand, and what one author calls the "civil religion of brotherhood and unity."[48]

Yet, arguably, the "national question" remained: Could Yugoslavia endure as a unified state with a unified nation of Yugoslavs or was it destined to unravel along ethno-religious lines? Were Yugoslavs' primary political identity and loyalty to the federal state or to their constituent nation? As implied by his slogan "brotherhood and unity," Tito attempted to answer the national question by pushing unity, equality, and fraternity among the southern Slavs. This fit neatly with the communist understanding that the key divisions among people are socioeconomic classes, not nations, as captured in Karl Marx's statement that "the workers have no country." Tito shifted the focus from a past of ethnicity and ethnic strife to a communist future. Nationalism was relegated to the dustbin of history, as was religion.[49] The official ideology of socialist internationalism (an interconnected world of socialism) was anti-religious and antinationalist, prohibiting the rise of ethnic/national or religious rivalries. Through the heavy hand of dictatorship, Tito suppressed overt manifestations of nationalism and forced Yugoslavs to put aside ethnic differences. In his "prison-house of nations," Tito contained the threat of breakdown into microstates. In fact, Tito's antinationalist program did bring a degree of unity, some sense of being "Yugoslavs," rather than Bosnians, Croats, Slovenes, and so on. The national question had not, however, been solved.[50]

The years under Tito were "secularizing years."[51] Religiosity declined after the communist takeover in the 1940s. As in other communist states, hypothetically at least, atheistic Marxists held all the reins of political power. To advance in the Yugoslav government, one had to be a member of the Communist Party and, thus, atheist. Under Tito's communist secularism, religious practice lost a great deal of its significance.[52] In fact, there was a relatively high percentage of self-declared atheists and anti-religious attitudes were widespread.[53] Tito tried to delegitimize ethno-religious identity, much as he tried to stifle nationalist impulses. Top-down secularization occurred under the communist government, which limited and strongly discouraged religion. The state, for instance, abolished many traditional Muslim institutions, including charitable organizations and Quranic primary schools, and marginalized the Serbian Orthodox Church, suppressing its press, confiscating its lands, harassing its clergy, and prohibiting the church from nurturing the idea of the Serbian nation.[54] Religion had scant presence in public life.

The upshot was that most Yugoslavs were secular, but religious origin —not language, culture, or basic ethnic stock—is what distinguished Croats, Muslims, and Serbs. Croats were Croats because their religious affiliation, however attenuated, was with the Roman Catholic Church, and Serbs were Serbs because of membership in the Orthodox church. In other words, religion and subnational identification were tightly linked.

Various approaches help to explain the breakup of the Socialist Federal Republic of Yugoslavia into seven small states: Bosnia and Herzegovina, Croatia, Kosovo, Macedonia, Montenegro, Serbia, and Slovenia. Here, the explanations are grouped by levels of analysis.

At the systemic level, the key factor was the end of the Cold War, including the termination of forty-some years of two highly armed and ideologically polarized camps (the Warsaw Pact in the East, the North Atlantic Treaty Organization in the West), each rotating around a superpower; the demise of international communism; and the collapse of the Soviet Union. Each of these changed the international context in which Yugoslavia existed. With the onset of the Cold War in the late 1940s, the Balkan peninsula had taken on importance in the broader East-West conflict, especially after 1948, when Tito broke away from the Stalinist camp and pursued his own brand of communism. Yugoslavia was aligned with neither the Soviet camp nor the US camp, and he deftly exploited Cold War rivalries. In fact, Tito was a leader of the Non-Aligned Movement, a large group of developing countries, most of which had gained independence after World War II. By the end of the 1980s, the ideological glue that had held together Eastern Europe in general, and Yugoslavia in particular, was disintegrating, while (to mix metaphors) the "corset" of East-West tensions that had constrained national aspirations within Yugoslavia was being undone. The Cold

War's end created a rare moment when no external powers were trying to impose their will on the Balkans. Once these external constraints were gone, internal pressures, especially national aspirations, rose to the top of the political agenda. Communists became nationalists. Yugoslavs became Bosnians, Croats, Kosovars, Serbs, and so on. The various peoples of Yugoslavia became preoccupied with independent statehood. Some began itching for power and territory.

Samuel P. Huntington's controversial "clash of civilizations" thesis works at the systemic level, too. Huntington argued that the fundamental source of conflict has changed: with the Cold War's end, conflicts and clashes were no longer along ideological lines, but along civilizational lines. By "civilizations" he means cultural entities and the broadest level of a person's identification. He proposed that the major civilizations are Western, Confucian, Japanese, Islamic, Hindu, Slavic-Orthodox, and Latin American. As the names of many of these "civilizations" suggest, religion is the defining factor of cultural identity. Religion has become more important than national identity and provides a cross-border identity that unites civilizations.

Huntington said that the key dividing line in Europe may be the eastern boundary of Western Christianity, with Roman Catholicism to the west and Orthodox Christianity to the line's east. This line goes through the former Yugoslavia.[55] Geopolitically, Yugoslavia was situated along the Cold War border between East and West. However, in post–Cold War geopolitics, defined by Robert Kaplan as "the battle for space and power," it now occurs not only between and among states but within them.[56] The East-West fault line is gone. But another kind of fault line, according to Huntington's thesis, goes through the former Yugoslavia. The region's "core groups" are divided between Roman Catholicism (Croats and Slovenes, who lived under the rule of Austria-Hungary) and Eastern Orthodoxy (Serbs and Macedonians, most of whom lived under Ottoman rule). Serbs fancied themselves "Christian soldiers" defending Europe against the onslaught of Islamic fundamentalism. Croatia saw itself as a bulwark against the East, Orthodoxy, and Islam.[57]

Unlike ethnic identity, an individual can really only identify with one religion; one can be a Bosnian Serb, but not simultaneously Christian and Muslim. As economic modernization and social change weaken local identities, religion (especially fundamentalist religion) often fills the gap, contributing to the unsecularization of the world. People rally behind co-religionists, as seen in the Persian Gulf War and in the former Yugoslavia.

Moving to the state level of analysis, the Yugoslavia of the late 1980s and early 1990s—with the political vacuum left by Tito's death in 1980 and, eleven years later, the Soviet Union's death—included a volatile mix of competing nationalisms, resurgent religion, and political ambitions. The ethnic, national, and religious identities that intermixed during Tito's reign were politicized and exploited for political purposes after this death. Instead of Tito's focus on communism and common societal elements, rising political leaders *chose* to elevate differences.[58] This interpretation of events posits that the fracturing of the Yugoslav state along ethno-religious lines and the fratricidal bloodshed (including ethnic cleansing) that went along with it were not determined by the hand of fate, but by the calculated choices of political leaders.

A closely related factor was rival nationalisms between Yugoslavia's two largest groups, Croatians and Serbians. Nationalism appeals to a sense of collective grievance against foreigners (and rule by "them") and the desire for self-determination (rule by "us"). After World War II, nationalist movements in sub-Saharan Africa demanded independence and self-rule. Around the world, nationalism with a different flavor— ethnic and religious nationalism—rose to the surface with the Cold War's end, and Yugoslavia was a prime example of this. Croatian leader Franjo Tudjman and Serbian leader Slobodan Milošević both hyped nationalism with a strong ethno-religious component. (See Table 7.1 below.) They spread nationalist propaganda, playing up mythical historical memories and epic poems.

Serbia and Croatia had two major aims: each sought to expand their own group's territory and to augment its national power. Croatians and Serbians had territorial ambitions that put them in direct conflict. One sought to create a Greater Croatia, the other a Greater Serbia. Multiethnic and multireligious Bosnia became the strategic prize that would go to the winner of the two.

Fear was an element here, too. Once the conflict began, Serbs and Croats feared becoming a repressed ethno-religious minority in a state controlled by the other. Serbs claimed they had been victimized by both Croats and Bosnians. Among Muslim Bosnians, fear strengthened their Muslim identity and Islamic ideology.[59]

In addition to gaining territory and power, there was a third aim: creating a homogeneous nation-state with all Croats and only Croats ("Croatia for the Croats") or all Serbs and only Serbs. Such an aim creates what Bruce Jentleson calls "identities of mass destruction" because it can lead to the kind of genocide witnessed in Rwanda or the kind of ethnic cleansing perpetrated in the former Yugoslavia. Homogeneity means getting rid of others. The Holocaust was genocide because of the Nazis' intent to destroy an entire group of people. "Ethnic cleansing" is a closely related concept, but "cleansing" can mean forcibly removing members of a group, rather than killing them.

Table 7.1 Who's Who in the Yugoslav Civil Wars

Republic (federal state)	Key Leader	Religious Association	Aim
Serbia	Slobodan Milošević	Serbian Orthodox	"Greater Serbia" of and for Serbs: He led efforts to "Serbianize" or ethnically cleanse Bosnia-Herzegovina.
Croatia	Franjo Tudjman	Roman Catholic	
Bosnia-Herzegovina	Alija Izetbegović	Izetbegović was Muslim. Bosnia-Herzegovina had a mix of Catholics, Muslims, and Orthodox believers.	"Greater Croatia": In 1990, he campaigned for "a Croatia for Croatians only." In 1991, his aim was to keep Croatia from falling under Serb hegemony. He wanted to take part or all of Bosnia-Herzegovina.
			Keep Bosnia-Herzegovina intact: He embraced Bosnian nationalism and called for Muslim supremacy in Bosnia, but unlike Milošević and Tudjman, he did not pursue territorial aggrandizement.

Source: Kollander, "The Civil War in Former Yugoslavia."

On the state level of analysis, we also encounter the refrain of "age-old antagonisms," "ancient animosities," or "centuries-old hatreds." This refrain suggests violence is inherent to the Balkans, that Slavs are perhaps fated to kill one another. It means that southern Slavs are simply unable to live together peaceably. As stated by one author, the Yugoslav federation "had always been an unnatural amalgamation of hostile groups."[60] In an article entitled "Yugoslavia: New War, Old Hatreds," Dusko Doder states, "The lands of the Yugoslavs have long been haunted by conflict."[61] This comment goes hand in glove with Robert Kaplan's argument that the region's peoples are visited by "Balkan ghosts," "the seething forces of ethnic and religious fear and hatred waiting to be unleashed at the end of the communist era."[62] The communist state under Tito, according to this line of thought, merely suppressed ethnic identities without resolving long-standing grievances. War in Yugoslavia was historically inevitable. In other words, Yugoslavia died a natural death.

However, the "ancient hatreds" thesis (also known as the primordialist theory of ethnic identity) is controversial. Some argue this thesis is historically inaccurate. The hatreds are not ancient. Arguably, the most serious animosity arose out of events that occurred during World War II. In fact, Croats, Muslims, and Serbs had a long history of peaceful coexistence. Others reject the ancient hatreds thesis on the grounds that it assumes that identities and the meanings attached to them never change over time, contradicting the constructivist position that identities and meanings are malleable.

A final state-level factor was Yugoslavia's severe and rapid economic downturn. Industrial production fell. Inflation soared. Workers and state-owned firms struggled. Reforms failed. The country was bankrupt. In part, this downturn was because, with Tito's death and the end of the Cold War, the United States lost all strategic interest in Yugoslavia, so it cut off billions of dollars it had been sending to the government. With the crutch of external aid gone, the economy collapsed and, with it, support for the regime.

At the individual level of analysis, the tale cannot be told without understanding the roles of some key political leaders, most notably Tito and Milošević. First, Josep Broz Tito. Of Croat-Slovene extraction, Tito founded the Socialist Federal Republic of Yugoslavia (SFRY) in 1945. He pushed Yugoslavs to embrace communism. Tito, aided by external pressures associated with superpower confrontation, constrained national ambitions in the multiethnic Slavic country. After he died in 1980, the state's constituent peoples rejected the country he had cobbled together, while the economy went into death throes and politicians manipulated nationalist feelings. People like Milošević sought scapegoats and followers.

Slobodan Milošević was a Yugoslav communist and Titoist who became a Serb nationalist and national hero. In the late 1980s, Milošević embraced the Serb nationalist agenda: "Greater Serbia," incorporating Serb-inhabited lands and gathering all Serbs into one state, and "reclaiming" historic Serbian territory, including most of Bosnia and all of Kosovo. He presented himself as the Serbs' champion. He became a spokesperson for militant religious nationalism in Serbia.[63] He used religion in an instrumental way and found a useful political ally in the Serbian Orthodox Church, which initially supported him and then later backed away from him. In 1989, the year of the rally mentioned at the outset of the chapter, Milošević was the most powerful figure in the Yugoslav federation and sought to follow Tito as the head of all of the Yugoslav government. In fact, Tito's image began disappearing from public spaces, while Milošević's portrait took its place, hanging in offices, stores, and government buildings.

We might say, as in the case of Ortega in Nicaragua (see Chapter 5) that some politicians played the religion card—or in this case, the "ethno-religious card," meaning they played up ethnic and religious identities to galvanize support. Political leaders, most notably Milošević, brought together secular politics and religion to rally co-religionists and create a base of power. He drew on religious myths, as explained above. He resorted to "instrumental pious nationalism," using religion to unite the Serbian population and distinguish Serbs from others—all the while promoting his own political career.[64] Non-Serb religious structures were among the targets; mosques, monasteries, churches, and other sacred places were destroyed. This went along with the de-secularization and de-privatization of religion that occurred in the 1990s.

Although scholars and Serbs are not of one mind with regard to Milošević, some argue that Serbian aggression led by the so-called Black Prince of Balkan politics is primarily to blame for the war that engulfed the former Yugoslavia. He yearned for power and used ethno-nationalism and religion to achieve it. He fanned the flames of nationalism; played up grievances, resentments, and Serbs' sense of victimization; and stoked ethno-religious intolerance. In 1999, the UN's International Criminal Tribunal for the Former Yugoslavia (ICTY) indicted Slobodan Milošević for war crimes. Two years later, he was handed over to the tribunal to stand trial. He died in 2006 before the completion of the trial.

To sum up, identity politics has grown in importance in recent decades. Identity is an element in many of today's conflicts, whether they are violent conflicts, as Yugoslavia experienced, or nonviolent conflicts. Given identity's increasing political salience and religion's resurgence, perhaps it is not surprising that identity and religion often come together. In Yugoslavia's case, they came together in lethal ways.

Religion, then, was certainly an element of the Yugoslavian conflicts of the 1990s. Indeed, argues William Cavanaugh in *The Myth of Religious Violence*, the idea that religion promotes violence is sort of hardwired into Western understandings.[65] As his term "myth" and the discussion in Chapter 8 suggests, however, one would be hard-pressed to argue either that religion *caused* the bloodshed or that the conflicts were *about* religion.

In Theory

Theory and levels of analysis provide insights into the nature and importance of events on the world stage. The first part focuses on identity politics, the second on nationalism.

Levels of Analysis

To illustrate identity issues on multiple levels of analysis, we turn to the Rohingya. The question of Rohingya identity and their quest for recognition are central to this long-simmering conflict.

In Burma (Myanmar), the Rohingya are a Muslim ethnic minority in a country with a Buddhist majority. Most Rohingya live in the Rakhine state, which borders Bangladesh. The state calls them "Bengalis," suggesting they are from the Indian subcontinent and not actually Burmese. The state denies them citizenship, rendering them stateless and vulnerable, since no state is obliged to protect them or provide them public services. Islamophobia enters in here, too. They have long been subject to discrimination. In recent years, Burmese security forces have brutalized them and driven them out because of who they are. Thousands have been killed or subjected to human rights abuses. The Burmese government and military reject these charges. What cannot be denied is that approximately one million Rohingya have left Burma since 2017, when the most recent Rohingya crisis began.

Moving from the state to the regional level of analysis, this crisis has economic and political implications for Southeast Asian countries. The vast majority of the Rohingya have gone to Bangladesh. Many have also gone by boat to Indonesia, Malaysia, and Thailand. As of June 2020, the UN Refugee Agency (UNHCR) had registered more than 740,00 refugees and asylum seekers in Bangladesh and 100,000 in Malaysia. Almost a million Rohingya now live in refugee camps outside of Burma. At times, especially since the onset of the Covid-19 pandemic, states have turned away boatloads of people. A large influx of refugees can affect receiving states in terms of the resources needed to care for displaced people. Another concern is that refugees might become radicalized or have other deleterious effects on domestic politics. Things such as a restive Burma-Bangladesh border could affect the entire region.

The Association of Southeast Asian Nations (ASEAN) is an important regional IGO with ten member states. One ASEAN member, Burma, created the mass exodus of Rohingya. Three others—Indonesia, Malaysia, and Thailand—have been on the receiving end of refugees. (Bangladesh is not an ASEAN member.) ASEAN has stuck to its charter, which says member states will not interfere in the domestic affairs of other member states, so it has not said or done much to help the Rohingya. Going against the organization's Human Rights Declaration, some ASEAN states have denied Rohingyas' right to seek asylum in their countries.[66]

According to Human Rights Watch, ASEAN does not even call them "Rohingya" and, instead, denies the group's self-identity.

On the international level, various arms of the United Nations have responded to the Rohingya crisis. One, mentioned above, is the UNHCR. The UN Human Rights commissioner called the treatment of Rohingya in Rakhine State "a textbook example of ethnic cleansing." The General Assembly is another arm of the United Nations. In early 2020, the General Assembly approved a resolution condemning abuses against Rohingya Muslims and other minority groups in Burma. UN resolutions are not legally binding. However, a third part of the UN system does make legally binding (but not self-enforcing) decisions, the International Court of Justice (ICJ). The ICJ is the top UN court. It ordered Burma's government to take urgent measures to protect the Rohingya. The Organization of Islamic Cooperation (OIC) lauded this effort. The International Criminal Court (ICC), a permanent international tribunal, is investigating alleged crimes against the Rohingya.

The individual level of analysis figures in here, too. Burma's leader, Aung San Suu Kyi, has neither spoken out on behalf of the Rohingya nor criticized the army for treating them harshly. This is especially hard to understand because Aung San Suu Kyi was long known for her valiant struggle against the military regime that ruled Burma, which earned her many years under house arrest. She was awarded the Nobel Peace Prize in 1991 "for her non-violent struggle for democracy and human rights." The Nobel Prize website called her "Burma's Modern Symbol of Freedom." She, much like ASEAN, has been criticized for her lack of leadership. Granted, she is limited in what she can do because, while she is the de facto head of state, she does not control the military.

IR Paradigms

For realists, the Yugoslav conflicts of the 1990s were not about religion, ethnicity, or identity, but matters of security and power. For realists in the US government, the United States had no stake in Yugoslavia's dissolution and the humanitarian tragedy that attended it. Since Yugoslavia was not pulled by the East or the West, as during the Cold War, power relations were not in balance. National interests were not on the line, either, so there was no good reason to intervene.

Liberals embrace internationalism and tend to be leery of nationalism and other obstacles to building global cooperation. Nationalism, as explained above, touches on matters of identity. Identity politics typically divides societies into small groups. It can, however, involve more expansive identities. The creation and expansion of the European Union can be seen as a triumph of liberalism on the regional level, as it has encouraged people to set aside a focus on national identity and national interests and to embrace a European identity and Europe-wide interests. But a Scottish vote on independence (which failed) and Britain's vote to leave the European Union (which succeeded) demonstrate that identity politics is not dead—not by a long shot.

Realists and liberals take identities and interests as "givens," while constructivists see identities as shaped (or constructed) through experience and apt to evolve with changing norms and social contexts; as identities change, according to constructivists, so do perceptions of "reality," interests, and actions. Realists focus on power and high politics—matters of national interests, security, and other matters of critical importance to states—and may relegate identity matters to the realm of low politics. Constructivists do not deny that power and material capabilities are important variables in international relations, but argue that they take on different meanings in different contexts.[67] For instance, countries bordering Russia, but looking westward toward the European Union and NATO, see NATO's and US power as reassuring, while Russia sees it as threatening.

Constructivists bring "a country's values, beliefs, ideology, and culture, and not just anarchic power politics as realists argue, back into international relations."[68] They also bring in identity. States have identities, and these identities move leaders' foreign policy preferences. For constructivists, identity is one of the "foundations of foreign policy and international relations."[69] Groups also have identities. Identity politics involves groups advocating for their interests, which are determined by their group identity.

Constructivists take identity as *constructed*, not given or immutable. Identity is both a political construction and a social construction. Things that are constructed are malleable, not permanent; they can be reconstructed. Identity can change over time. As states' identities shift, "the norms and values of international politics" shift, too.[70] For some, the locus of identity changes. Serbs who had called themselves Yugoslavs began emphasizing their distinctive Serbian identity. The unifying Yugoslav identity began unraveling. While identity is malleable, this does not diminish its political import.

Table 7.2 depicts how the levels of analysis and the central paradigms of international relations apply to the dissolution of Yugoslavia.

Table 7.2 Framing the Analysis

Levels of Analysis	Realism	Liberalism	Constructivism
International/Systemic	As the Cold War structure and the bipolar distribution of power came apart, so did the East-West tensions. These tensions, and Tito's ability to position Yugoslavia between the two sides, had kept a lid on the aspiration of each self-identified nation to have its own state.	The political violence of the 1990s may have justified or even obligated humanitarian intervention by other states. The international community, however, proved unwilling to take meaningful action on behalf of Bosnian Muslims.	When international communism and the ideology that underpinned it began to disintegrate, so did Yugoslavia. Political violence in Yugoslavia and other Balkan states is not inherent, as some argue; it is socially constructed.
Domestic/State	In Tito's Yugoslavia, the Communist party and the army provided the structure and the muscle to hold together disparate peoples, peoples with different histories, religions, languages, and civilizational touchstones. When the state started to collapse after Tito's death, Yugoslavs were no longer sure who would protect them. Insecurity and fear led people to turn toward those who shared their ethnicity and religion.	Tito held Yugoslavs together with a firm hand. His authoritarian, one-party state suppressed ethno-religious rhetoric and identities and used government propaganda to play up the "brotherhood and unity" theme. As the multinational state broke up, it created fears and insecurities as well as conflicts over political boundaries. The search for security explains, in part, the fierce animosities and bloody conflicts among ethno-religious groups.	State and substate identities are not fixed, but constantly being constructed and reconstructed. People who self-identified as Yugoslavs in the 1970s, when Tito endeavored to delegitimize ethno-religious identity, might have emphasized their Serbian-ness in the 1990s (after Tito's death). Also, Tito's socialist internationalist ideology gave way to nationalisms that were linked to religious identity. As the unifying Yugoslav identity weakened and fractured, the state became vulnerable.

continues

Table 7.2 Continued

Levels of Analysis	Realism	Liberalism	Constructivism
Domestic/State	The size of its population and its control over the Yugoslav military meant only Serbia was strong enough to destroy the Yugoslav state.		
Individual	Tito used state power to advance "Brotherhood and Unity" and suppress subnational identities. In the years following Tito's death, Milošević became the most powerful figure in Yugoslavia. His goal was to lead the entire state of Yugoslavia.	Tito developed a personal dictatorship, based on charisma, one-party rule, and his willingness to use force. When he died in 1980, no leader arose to hold together the multireligious and multiethnic state.	Slobodan Milošević, a Yugoslav communist who became a Serb nationalist, sought to Serbianize Yugoslavia, used the Kosovo myth to rally Serbs, and played the ethno-religious identity card.

Sources: Elshtain, "Nationalism and Self-Determination"; Hagen, "The Balkans' Lethal Nationalisms"; Tatari and Shaykhutdinov, "Muslims and Minority Politics in Great Britain"; Steele, "Christianity in Bosnia-Herzegovina & Kosovo"; Perović, "Why Did Yugoslavia Fall Apart?"

Conclusion

In his 1995 book *Jihad vs. McWorld*, Benjamin Barber wrote about the dialectical relationship between the forces of "Jihad" and "McWorld." "Jihad" is his shorthand for the struggle among ethnic, tribal, and religious identities and, in particular, religious fundamentalists' struggle against modernity. These are the bloody, centrifugal forces of fanaticism, exclusion, breakdown, and re-tribalization. Jihad, as Barber conceives of it, is *not* particular to Islam or political Islam, but is related to intolerance, fanaticism, divisiveness, and the "bloody politics of identity." He used the term as a shorthand for the reaction against the imperialism and numbing uniformities of McWorld. "McWorld" is, in essence, globalization (and, to a lesser extent, secularization). It is driven by the centripetal forces of universalizing markets, which knit the world ever closer together through trade. Jihad revolts against and abets McWorld, which imperils and reinforces Jihad. In other words, as secularization is occurring, often accompanied by corrosive materialism, religious identities are being asserted, often in divisive ways.

Four years later, Thomas Friedman published *The Lexus and the Olive Tree*. Like *Jihad vs. McWorld*, it brings out key ways in which globalization is shaping the world today. Friedman's "Lexus" represents the new globalizing system and material conditions—economic development and prosperity—that people want. At the same time, people in some parts of the world want to stay rooted and to hold onto traditions, cultures, and identities, which the olive tree symbolizes.

Globalization, identity, nationalism, and religion are major crosscurrents in early twenty-first-century world politics. In many instances, they are interrelated and, singly or in combination, they feed grievances, myths, and political action.

As the case of Yugoslavia illustrates, religion is often bound up with national identity and nationalism. There, in fact, "one of the few real identity markers was religion, no matter how neglected or repressed it had been."[71] Repressed under communist rule, ethno-religious identities surfaced with the death of Tito and international communism. Catholicism distinguished Croats from Orthodox Serbs. In the 1990s, the Bosnian leader, Alija Izetbegović, essentially linked religion with the nation when he said, "Our motto is to fight and believe."[72] Bosnian, Croat, and Serb leaders all turned to religion to unite and mobilize their people. Paradoxically, once people knew they could be killed because of their religious identity, that identity became all the more important.

The Yugoslavia example also points to the two sides of identity: identity unites (creates and binds "us" together) as it divides (creating "us versus them"). Citizens in the former Yugoslavia could have identified "us" as Yugoslavs and "them" as all others. However, in the 1990s, "us" became Serbs, Croats, and so on, and "them" became all other ethno-religious groups. These, too, are different ways to define who belongs to a particular nation.

Finally, the wars in Yugoslavia point to the increasingly important "new wars" phenomenon. "Old wars" were between states and their clearly identified troops, with the decisive encounter occurring on the battlefield. Think of the two world wars, for instance. New wars came to prominence with the end of the Cold War and the bipolar structure of global power—an end to the United States as one center, or "pole," of power and the Soviet Union the other—and the rising salience of identity politics. Unlike old wars, mobilized ethnic and religious identities are central to new war conflicts. New wars often include massive violations of human rights, such as the ethnic cleansing that occurred in Yugoslavia in the 1990s.

Notes

1. "No Locus Standi: India on US Religious Freedom Report," *Economic Times*, June 23, 2019.

2. "US 'Religious Freedom' Report Biased, Says BJP," *The Times of India*, June 24, 2019.

3. United States Commission on International Religious Freedom, "India."

4. Jaffrelot, "The Fate of Secularism in India."

5. Benedict Anderson, *Imagined Communities*.

6. Jaffrelot, "The Fate of Secularism in India."

7. Kingston, *The Politics of Religion, Nationalism, and Identity in Asia*, 66.

8. "The Struggle for India's Soul," *The Economist*, December 30, 2018; "Narendra Modi and the Struggle for India's Soul," *The Economist*, March 2, 2019.

9. Kegley and Raymond, *The Global Future*, 5th ed., 138.

10. Kingston, *The Politics of Religion, Nationalism, and Identity in Asia*, 77.

11. Cvetkovska-Ocokoljic and Cvetkovski, "The Influence of Religion on the Creation of National Identity in Serbia," 90.

12. Sells, "Kosovo Mythology and the Bosnian Genocide," 181.

13. MacDonald, *Balkan Holocausts?*, 63; Ramet, "Serbia's Slobodan Milosevic."

14. Sells, "Kosovo Mythology and the Bosnian Genocide," 181.

15. Anzulovic, *Heavenly Serbia*, 4.

16. Jason A. Edwards, "Bringing in Earthly Redemption."

17. Juergensmeyer, Griego, and Soboslai, *God in the Tumult of the Global Square*, 20.

18. Juergensmeyer, Griego and Soboslai, *God in the Tumult of the Global Square*, 2.

19. Heywood, *Politics*, 106.

20. Aviad Rubin, "The Status of Religion in Emergent Political Regimes," 496.

21. Kingston, *The Politics of Religion, Nationalism, and Identity in Asia*, 49.

22. Juergensmeyer, *Global Rebellion*, 36; Juergensmeyer, *The New Cold War?*, 6, 178; Juergensmeyer, "The New Religious State," 379.

23. Lee, *Religion and Politics in the Middle East*, 90, 113.

24. Alan Dowty, *Israel/Palestine*, 3rd ed., 9.

25. Thomas Friedman, *The Lexus and the Olive Tree*, 9.

26. Haynes, *Religion, Politics and International Relations*, 107.

27. Schäfer, "The Janus Face of Religion," 414–415.

28. Mandle, "Identity Politics, Feminism and Social Change."

29. Kortteinen, "Islamic Resurgence and the Ethnicization of the Malaysian State," 218.

30. Hamid, "Syariahization of Intra-Muslim Religious Freedom and Human Rights Practice in Malaysia," 28.

31. Deann, "Malay Melee."

32. Joseph, "Unfettered Religious Freedom Hangs by the Thread of Minority Dissent in Malaysia," 221.

33. Guan, "In Defence of the Secular?" 83, 91.

34. Moustafa, "Liberal Rights Versus Islamic Law?"

35. "Religious Conversions: The Moment of Truth," *The Economist*, July 24, 2008); "Malaysia: Lina Joy's Despair," *The Economist*, May 31, 2007.

36. Beech, "Acts of Faith."

37. Kershaw, "The Penalties of Apostasy in Malaysia," 485; Mohamad, "The Ascendance of Bureaucratic Islam and the Secularization of the Sharia in Malaysia," 517.

38. Neo Ling-Chien, "Malay Nationalism, Islamic Supremacy and the Constitutional Bargain in the Multi-Ethnic Composition of Malaysia," 96.

39. Tatari and Shaykhutdinov, "Muslims and Minority Politics in Great Britain," 26.

40. Schäfer, "The Janus Face of Religion," 412.

41. Seymour and Cunningham, "Identity Issues and Civil War," 45.

42. Gergen, "Social Construction and the Transformation of Identity Politics."

43. Wiarda, *Political Culture, Political Science, and Identity Politics*.

44. Wiarda, *Political Culture, Political Science, and Identity Politics*.

45. Kettell, "The Militant Strain," 517.

46. Seul, "'Ours Is the Way of God,'" 553–569.

47. Fukuyama, "Against Identity Politics," The Andrea Mitchell Center for the Study of Democracy.

48. Perica, *Balkan Idols*, 89, 100, 106.

49. Doder, "Yugoslavia," 12.

50. Rieff, *Slaughterhouse*, 48.

51. Francine Friedman, "The Bosnian Muslim National Question," 2.

52. Schäfer, "The Janus Face of Religion," 411, 412.

53. Perica, *Balkan Idols*, 38.

54. Ramet, "The Serbian Church and the Serbian Nation," 305, 310.

55. Huntington, "The Clash of Civilizations?" 30–31.

56. Kaplan, "The Post-Imperial Moment," 75.

57. Sells, "Crosses of Blood," 316.

58. Crnobrnja, *The Yugoslav Drama*, 90, 92.

59. Mojzes, *Balkan Genocides*, 164–165.

60. Kelly, "Surrender and Blame," 44.

61. Doder, "Yugoslavia," 5.

62. Kaplan, *Balkan Ghosts*; Stephenson, Review of *Balkan Ghosts*, 94.

63. Sells, "Kosovo Mythology and the Bosnian Genocide," 184.

64. Drezgić, "Religion, Politics and Gender in the Context of Nation-State Formation," 956; Safran, *The Secular and the Sacred*, 511.

65. Cavanaugh, *The Myth of Religious Violence*, 3.

66. Hoelzl, "As Rohingya Boats Keep Sailing, Southeast Asia Turns a Blind Eye."

67. Uzer, *Identity and Turkish Foreign Policy*, 18.

68. Wiarda, *Political Culture, Political Science, and Identity Politics*.

69. Shiraev and Zubok, *International Relations*, 376.

70. Shiraev and Zubok, *International Relations*, 378.

71. Mojzes, *Balkan Genocides*, 148.

72. Stevanović and Johansson, *Milosevic*, 79.

8

Conflicts:
When Is Religion to Blame?

Illustration 13: Joseph Kony and the Lord's Resistance Army

On July 8, 2005, the International Criminal Court (ICC) issued an arrest warrant for Joseph Kony, the founder and commander-in-chief of the Lord's Resistance Army (LRA). In a move to ensure international accountability, the ICC charged Kony with twelve counts of crimes against humanity and twenty-one counts of war crimes. In a comment on the arrest warrant the ICC prosecutor said the LRA was waging a "criminal campaign."[1] From the ICC's perspective, Kony has established a pattern of "brutalizing" civilians. This pattern includes abducting children and forcing them to be soldiers.

Kony, however, asserts he is fighting a war—a spiritual war—for the Acholi people of northern Uganda and for biblical understandings of justice. He is also fighting against the Ugandan government and army, local defense units, and forces of evil. This, for Kony, is a holy war.

For three decades, Joseph Kony has been both the leader of a Ugandan guerrilla group and a self-styled prophet and spiritual medium who says he was sent by God and is guided (or possessed) by spirits. In northern Uganda, many accept the notion that he has spiritual powers.[2]

Significance

Kony and the LRA are important for several reasons. One is the heavy human toll they have taken on Uganda. Over the course of three decades, they have terrorized northern Ugandans. They have kidnapped, killed, raped, enslaved, or disfigured tens of thousands of people and displaced some two million Ugandans from their homes.

Another reason that the LRA is important is that its impact goes well beyond Uganda, affecting three of its neighbors in central Africa (the Central African Republic, Democratic Republic of Congo, and South Sudan) and moving regional and international actors to respond. Regional actors are concerned about potential threats to regional stability. Regional militaries and an important regional IGO, the African Union, have gotten involved. The conflict also drew in the United Nations, the European Union, and the United States, which deployed US Special Forces. When US forces withdrew in 2017, Kony's forces were said to be far weaker than in previous years and some top commanders faced an ICC tribunal, but Kony remained a fugitive from justice. The UN Security Council condemned the LRA's actions in central Africa and imposed sanctions on Joseph Kony and the Lord's Resistance Army. An unusual twist to this mix of outside actors involves a US-based advocacy group, Invisible Children, Inc. This group posted a YouTube video, *Kony 2012*, that went viral. It brought global attention to events in Uganda, but also oversimplified a complex situation. The involvement of outside states and nonstate actors makes this an example of a civil war that has been internationalized.

Third, on a continent in which religion and spirituality are often linked to social and political life,[3] Kony employs religious language and symbolism to describe himself and his goals. Kony has created an unusual brew of Christian customs, Islamic elements, witchcraft, and terrorism. Before going to fight, Kony's soldiers make a sign of the cross on their chests, foreheads, both shoulders, and their gun. The oil crosses are a kind of anointment. If fighters stick to rules like this, which have been established by spirits, then they will be safe on the battlefield. Spiritual rules and the LRA's belief system also serve very pragmatic purposes: spiritual indoctrination helps to ensure internal cohesion, which is particularly important because so many of this army were abducted and pressed into service, and they create a "pure" in-group and an "impure" out-group. The LRA is thus fighting a spiritual battle on behalf of the "pure" order against the external "impure" order.[4] While his detractors write off Kony and his ongoing armed conflict as irrational at best, there is a sort of internal logic. Kony's stated aim is to replace Uganda's existing government with one based on the Ten Commandments. His vague goals are political in the sense that they entail controlling territory or bringing about regime change in Uganda (i.e., a change in the entire governmental structure) and religious in terms of the nature of that regime (biblically based).

These goals raise the question of whether this conflict is really about religion or about politics or, a third option, about a tight mix of the two. Is "Kony's army a heavily armed religious cult caught in a political struggle, or [is] it a militia with a political agenda carrying a religious banner?"[5] Is religion simply "a cover to disguise a deeper political motive"? Many experts in this area say that, based on the evidence, religion is not just a cover.[6] "The group does not have outwardly fathomable political motives" or a clear political project, besides using the Ten Commandments as a baseline for governance. In other words, the conflict is really *about* religion, while having great political implications and requiring the seizure of the reins of government power in order to fulfill the LRA's religious objectives. Others, however, argue that it is important to understand how grievances against the Ugandan government, ethnic identity politics, and crises within Acholi society contribute to the conflict; yes, this conflict has religious dimensions, but it also has political and economic dimensions. A Congressional Research Service report says that the LRA's grievances concern perceived "political domination and economic neglect . . . yet the group does not have a clear political or economic agenda."[7]

A fifth reason that Kony and the LRA are important is because, as in the conflicts in Yugoslavia in the 1990s, identity politics come into play. The LRA rebellion began in the 1980s. In 1986, Uganda's president Tito Okello was overthrown. The LRA emerged shortly thereafter. The Acholi people—Tito Okello's and Joseph Kony's people—have grievances, not the least of which is persecution by the Ugandan government. Later, however, Kony turned on his own people, conceiving a division between "genuine" and corrupt or "false" Acholi and calling for the latter to be cleansed.[8] Part of the reason for abducting girls and giving them as wives to LRA officers is to create the "nucleus of a new Acholi identity," an identity largely constructed by Kony and the LRA.[9]

Finally, the ICC arrest warrant was the first of its kind. That is, it was the first ICC warrant since the creation of this global institution in 1998. The ICC only steps in when domestic courts are unable or unwilling to investigate and punish alleged perpetrators of war crimes, crimes against humanity, or genocide. In addition to Joseph Kony, the ICC also issued arrest warrants for several high-ranking LRA commanders. Some of these commanders have died, while one has been brought to trial. Joseph Kony remains at large.

Illustration 14: Aum Apocalypse

For riders on Tokyo's subway system on March 20, 1995, the morning commute probably began like most others. They probably did not notice the five men who placed packages, punctured them with sharpened umbrella tips, and then got off the trains. But these packages, placed on five separate trains, released a thick, highly lethal liquid: liquefied sarin. As the sarin vaporized and turned to gas, it quickly circulated among the unsuspecting passengers. This chemical weapon attack occurred where subway lines converged under several government offices. It killed a dozen people and sickened at least 5,000 more, but was intended to kill many, many others.

This coordinated attack was the work of Aum Shinrikyo, led by Master Shoko Asahara. The group's name means Supreme Truth. Considered a "new religious movement" in Japan, the group anticipated Armageddon, the final conflict between good and evil. Asahara prophesied nuclear war that would pit Japan against the United States. (In some interpretations it pit the "Buddhist world" against the "West," sounding a lot like a "clash of civilizations."[10]) This nuclear confrontation would end the world as we know it. The sole survivors would be members of his group.

Some nonreligious events shaped the group's rise in adherents and net worth as well as its turn toward violence. One event was Aum Shinrikyo registering with Tokyo's government as a religious corporation in 1989. This gave it a protected status; under laws to protect religious freedom, registration as a religious corporation protects groups against government monitoring. The following year, 1990, Aum founded Shinri Party as its political arm and fielded two dozen candidates in parliamentary elections, including Asahara himself. The complete failure of its venture into electoral politics was another important event in its violent turn. Their candidates' utter defeat apparently led to a shift from preventing or surviving doomsday to "doomsday initiation" because later that year the group began a string of attacks, with the 1995 sarin gas attack being the most infamous. Their attacks employed chemical and biological agents. Aum had hoped to add nuclear weapons to its arsenal.[11]

With in-house scientists and engineers as well as information and materials coming from Russia and the United States, the group intended to purchase or manufacture biological, chemical, and nuclear weapons of mass destruction (WMD). Armed with WMD and willing to use indiscriminate violence, Aum would bring on the apocalypse or, at the very least, topple the Japanese government. Good would triumph over evil.

Aum Shinrikyo's rivals and enemies were many. They included better-established religions and new religious movements. They also included the Japanese government (because it was too materialistic) and the United States (because it was seeking global domination).

Shoko Asahara, born as Chizuo Matsumoto, founded the group that became Aum Shinrikyo in 1984. He is described as a charismatic, visually impaired, self-anointed guru and prophet, and a yoga teacher. He claimed to possess supernatural powers, such as levitation.

Significance

Aum Shinrikyo began in Japan, but spread overseas in the early 1990s. It established branches in Moscow, New York, and elsewhere, increasing its numbers to about 50,000 worldwide. In Japan, however, it became a "criminal religion" that abducted, assassinated, and attacked, though its followers saw it as a "true religion."[12]

Aum Shinrikyo was armed, not just with WMD, but religious motivation and divine justification, drawing on an array of sources. It saw itself as "a perfect synthesis of all forms of Buddhism."[13] It also mixed in bits of Hinduism, Christianity, and prophecies of the French astrologer Nostradamus (1503–1566). Under Asahara, this mix of influences moved the group from yoga and meditation classes to acts of terrorism. The saffron robes of Buddhist monks are typically associated with meditation, the path to enlightenment, and the renunciation of worldly things. Buddhism, like other global religions, has scriptures and traditions that renounce violence; at the same time, it has adherents who use their religion to justify violence. The existence of groups like Aum Shinrikyo and the Saffron Army point to the "Buddhist ambivalence toward violence."[14]

This "ambivalence toward violence" is an important point here. Sacred texts can call for peace and include violent imagery and rhetoric, enabling people to arrive at very different interpretations and, often, justifications for whatever they are doing in the name of religion.

Another important point comes from Michael Jerryson, who reminds us, "Being Buddhist does not necessarily mean one's actions are 'Buddhist.'"[15] Replace "Buddhist" with Christian, Hindu, Jewish, Muslim, or Sikh, and you get the picture here. Adhering to a particular religion does not mean that one's actions reflect that religion's precepts. Even with the best of intentions, adherents of a religion may not be its best models of living out that religion.

Conflict and cooperation are central features, even the crux, of international relations. Cooperation entails global actors' active, purposeful efforts to work together toward a common goal, such as reducing carbon dioxide emissions, or to realize mutual benefits. Conflict can be between states, between nonstate actors, or between states and nonstate actors. Intrastate conflict is now more common than interstate conflict. Conflict, it should be noted, involves disagreements and disputes, which may or may not entail open hostilities or political violence. Much of international studies concerns how to have more cooperation and less conflict. To achieve this, we must understand the sources of conflict. Our focus is religion's role in conflict.

Religion's Role

Fault lines and conflicts along religious lines are all too often headline news, perhaps creating the perception that religion has bloody hands. Certainly, in this author's experience, when offered the chance to take a course on religion and world politics, some college students are intrigued while just as many express dismay or disgust at religion's role—or what they perceive to be religion's role—on the world stage. But such courses are needed precisely because of the importance of getting beyond such reflexes, assumptions, and misperceptions, for the story is much more complex than that.

We can digest stories about the Islamic State, the Lord's Resistance Army, and Aum Shinrikyo and conclude that religion, whether Islam or Christianity or some faith with elements of Buddhism, is on the whole a negative force in today's world. We can conclude that "religion is a mainspring of conflict" and leave it at that.[16] We *can* do that, yes, but before drawing such conclusions we should make sure we know the whole story. Religion's role in fostering deadly conflict is not the whole story. Religious actors can play positive roles in conflict resolution and peacebuilding in the post–Cold War world, as discussed in Chapter 9. In the LRA's case, religious leaders from Acholi communities (Joseph Kony is an Acholi who set out to protect his people, then turned on them) formed the Acholi Religious Leaders' Peace Initiative (ARLPI) in 1997. The ARLPI is a coalition of Christian, Muslim, and traditional religious leaders. Leaders of this interfaith group see reconciliation, not prosecution and punishment, as the way forward after so many years and so much brutality.[17] They draw on the Quran and the Bible and speak the religious language of forgiveness. Peace in northern Uganda, they say, will come through neither the International Criminal Court nor through a purely military strategy, but through reconciliation.

Note, too, that militant groups like the Lord's Resistance Army are rejected by their co-religionists. Christian leaders not only say that Kony and the LRA violate the very precepts of the Ten Commandments that they claim to promote, most obviously the command not to kill, but many say they are simply not Christian.

Religion's Role

People enunciate very different views on religion's role in the world. Some dismiss religion as irrelevant to political life. Others presuppose that "all religions are violent by nature"; they see religion as inherently divisive and, thus, both a source of conflict and an obstacle to peace.[18] They can back this up with religion's long association with violent conflict, from the Christian Crusades in the Middle Ages, to the seventeenth-century European "wars of religion," centuries of Western imperialists' "civilizing" missions in what we now call the developing world, and even the twentieth-century Cold War against "godless communists."[19] Today, when political leaders yield to the temptation to play the religion card, whether in India, Indonesia, or elsewhere, it can intensify discrimination and violence between religions or between different strands of one religion.[20] A third group takes an entirely different tack, saying so-called religious violence is not really about religion, but a cover for something else. That something else may be political power, a redress of economic grievances, or self-aggrandizement. Yet another group avers that it is not religion, but a "perversion" or distortion of religion or a "false religion" that is to blame.[21] Evidence can be marshaled to support any of these positions, but none of them does justice to the complexity of the matter.

To use Scott Appleby's phrase, we need to understand "the ambivalence of the sacred." Religion, argues Appleby, carries contradictory impulses. The "same texts and practices that have inspired some to extraordinary acts of love and compassion have provoked others to senseless violence."[22] Texts, practices, and traditions are interpreted within certain social, economic, political, and historical contexts. Both wars and peaceful coexistence happen in the name of religion. All "great religions," according to Richard Falk, have both universalistic and tolerant tendencies and tendencies of exclusivism and seeing the world as offering stark black-and-white choices.[23] These contradictory impulses have to do with the relationship between limited human beings and an infinite God, which allows for more than one interpretation of the same sacred texts and histories. Within both Christianity and Islam some groups claim they are returning to the "fundamentals" of their respective religions, but they selectively appropriate traditions, texts, and interpretations of them. Texts and rituals are important, but so are contexts, symbols, meanings, and interpretations. Religious extremists may either see violence as a sacred duty or adopt an unshakable commitment to pacifism. Other adherents of that religion can choose to stand up and dispute that interpretation. While even co-religionists may vehemently disagree with a group's interpretation, this disagreement does not mean that religion is simply being used for political purposes. When, however, religion is implicated in complicated bids for power, they are more likely to occur *within* religions than *between* them.[24]

Ways to Think About Religion and Conflict

In the context of the mega-trends of globalization and the global resurgence of religion, domestic religious issues and religious violence can cross states' borders, destabilize neighboring states, and become internationalized when outside states intervene. The Lord's Resistance Army is a case in point.

The central question in this and the following chapter is, on the whole, what is religion's impact on international life? Is it a *source* of conflict or a *remedy* for it?[25] Religion might seem a natural source of conflict because the three great monotheistic religions (Judaism, Christianity, and Islam) all have a tradition of holy war. However, three other religions (Buddhism, Hinduism, and Sikhism) have traditions of nonviolence. The fact is, millions have been killed in the name of God or religion. Moreover, religious faith may prolong a conflict, making it harder to resolve by transforming conflict over political power, where negotiations and compromise are possible, into a conflict over something that is nonnegotiable: religious faith and practices.

The argument set forth in this text is that religion can be a source of conflict or a resource to transform it. In Uganda, religion is both integral to the LRA's goals in the ongoing conflict and, through the Acholi Religious Leaders' Peace Initiative, a means to foster reconciliation and peace. In Nigeria, where a group called Boko Haram has targeted Christians and those they consider "bad" Muslims, a number of faith-based organizations work to lessen religious tensions and promote peace. Two examples of these faith-based organizations: the Nigeria Inter-Religious

Council (NIREC), which includes Christian and Muslim clerics, and the Interfaith Mediation Centre of Muslim Christian Dialogue Forum (IMCM-CDF). Similarly, Catholics and Protestants have worked to establish a lasting peace in Northern Ireland. Much depends on the time and place.

Tricky and Essential

A tricky—and essential—task is distinguishing between religion's *presence* in conflicts and religion as the best *explanation* for those conflicts.[26] This is tricky because when it comes to violent conflicts, such as wars between or within states, religion "often coexists with, overlays or is partly suppressed by other codes, beliefs, and allegiances."[27] Religion is often fused with ethnicity or nationalism or both, which can be a volatile combination. In addition, religious divides may coincide with other divisions within society (ethnic, geographical, socioeconomic, or political), reinforcing existing cleavages and raising their political salience. As Steve Bruce states, in diverse societies "fault lines are not just vertical but also horizontal"; this can mean that societies are divided not just along economic lines, but along religious or ethnic lines, too.[28] In Sudan, for instance, those who identify as Arab and Muslim tend to live in the north and be better off economically, while those who identify as indigenous Africans and Christian or animist tend to be poorer and live in the south. In such societies, fault lines or cleavages are overlapping. They reinforce each other and heighten the sense of belonging to one group rather than another. This can heighten grievances and provoke conflict if, say, one group believes it is not getting a fair share of the country's economic pie. Alternatively, splits within societies may slice up groups, creating cross-cutting cleavages that pull individuals and groups in different directions. It might be, for instance, that there is no relationship between religious identity, ethnic identity, and positions on political issues. This lessens the likelihood of conflict between or among groups.

Discerning religion's role is also tricky because politicians can and do stir up religious passions to serve their or their group's political objectives. That is, religion can be employed for instrumental reasons—as a means to a political end. Daniel Ortega in Nicaragua and Slobodan Milošević in the former Yugoslavia are examples here.

In addition, religion may be a motive behind, or target of, state-based repression. China's government represses religion in general and religious minorities in particular, such as Buddhists in Tibet, perhaps seeing it as a threat to the government's legitimacy in that region or to national unity, and the mostly Muslim Uighur population in the Xinjiang region.[29] State repression of particular religious groups can also encourage those groups to mobilize against the state. In the past decade, dozens of Tibetans have protested against Chinese rule through the act of self-immolation, setting themselves on fire in a public place to make a political statement.

Another reason this task is tricky is because religion can fuel conflicts that, at their core, are not really about religion. This can happen when religion "shapes the identities and loyalties of warring communities," as in the Yugoslav wars in the 1990s.[30]

This task is difficult because of secularizing assumptions that are prominent in the West. One common assumption or assertion is that conflicts with a religious flavor are really about something else—power, oil, territory, and so on—not about religion or caused by religion. A very different assumption is that "we" in the West are modern, secular, rational, and less prone to violence while "they" in the Muslim world are driven by religious fanaticism and irrationality.[31] The mass media can add to the difficulty by slapping the label "sectarianism" or "religious conflict" on clashes that have a religious element, whether or not religion is the decisive element.

It is essential to understand religion's role in conflict because, to lessen the frequency and severity of conflict, we need to know what causes it. Religion's role is hotly debated. Some dismiss religion as a sideshow in politics or something used for political purposes. Others see religion as inherently irrational and divisive and, thus, both a source of conflict and an obstacle to peace. In *The Myth of Religious Violence*, William Cavanaugh questions the religious-secular divide and the whole idea of religion as the source of violent conflict. He argues that "religious violence is a myth which causes us to exaggerate the religious elements in conflicts and overlook secular causes of violence."[32] Conversely, Jonathan Fox argues that religion's role changes and that, contrary to what modernization theory and secularization theory predict, religion's role in conflict has been increasing. Religion, he demonstrates, "is an important influence on conflict."[33] This chapter sorts out some of the differing claims about religion's role in conflict.

Religious Fault Lines

Paul Marshall has argued that "chronic armed conflict is concentrated on the margins of the traditional religions," where religions intersect.[34] However, while considerable armed conflict occurs along such "fault zones," these conflicts may or may not be about religion.

Two books that focus on conflicts along the Islam-Christianity fault line are *The Clash of Civilizations* and *The Tenth Parallel*. In Samuel Huntington's much-debated book, *The Clash of Civilizations and the Remaking of World Order*, "civilizations" are the broadest cultural entities and the broadest, and increasingly important, level of a person's identification. Most of these "civilizations" are associated with a specific religion. Civilizational differences are now, in this post–Cold War age, the fundamental source of international conflict. Previously, violent conflicts were between states (interstate warfare) and the world's main fault line was the ideological clash between East and West. International conflict is, however, taking on a new pattern. Fault-line wars now occur where the edges of civilizations meet. Civilizations will clash for a number of reasons, with a central one being real and basic differences, especially religious differences. Huntington anticipated clashes between the "Christian" West (Europe and North America) and "Islam" (the bloc of four dozen Muslim-majority countries). In other words, the greatest threat to the West is no longer the Soviet Union and international communism; in Huntington's world, the greatest threat is Islamic civilization, which is experiencing a resurgence. Islamic civilization, he says, has "bloody borders."

Huntington counted the wars in Yugoslavia, especially Bosnia, among fault-line wars and fingered religion as the main source of conflict.[35] The conflicts were largely along religious and ethnic lines: Catholic Croats, Muslim Bosnians, and Orthodox Serbs fought each other. Peter Berger said that these three groups "look alike and . . . speak the same language. They are divided only by religion, which none of them believe in."[36] Religion helped to mobilize members of the three groups and have a distinction on which to focus. In addition, groups appealed to co-religionists: Bosnian Muslims turned for support to Turkey, with which they shared a secular-Muslim identity; Serbs share a Slavic and Orthodox Christian identity with Russia, which extended sympathy and tepid support; and the Croatian leader Franjo Tudjman courted the Vatican, which quickly extended diplomatic recognition to Croatia and Slovenia (both heavily Catholic) when they called for recognition as independent states. But the Vatican was not on board with Franjo Tudjman's strident nationalism, the Croats' use of force against Bosnian Muslims, or what Pope John Paul II called a "bloody fratricidal war." In 1992, leaders of the three main religions in the dispute issued a statement saying it was not a "religious war," but entailed the misuse of religious symbols.[37]

In fact, Yugoslavia's civil war has also been labeled an "ethnic conflict," driven by a narrow, divisive form of nationalism. According to this line of thinking, the crucial difference among Bosnians, Croats, and Serbs was not religion, but a central myth: they were not all part of one nation, but three separate nations. Nationalism, as explained in Chapter 7, can be a unifying force and encourage peoples' demand for self-government or a separatist force. In post-Tito Yugoslavia, it united groups within the state—especially Croats and Serbs—and heightened a sense of difference and defensiveness among them. One result was "ethnic cleansing" in which groups set about systematically removing members of other groups from certain territories, thus "cleansing" the area. Some religious leaders publicly blessed nationalist symbols, while some political leaders played the "religion card."[38] Leaders like Slobodan Milošević and Franjo Tudjman "exploited and manipulated people's nationalist leanings to gain power and prominence."[39]

Nationalism and religion are a lethal combination. "Religious nationalism," which brings together separatism and religion, is a cause of rebellion. Further, argues Jonathan Fox, religious conflicts are more intense and more violent. Nationalism is a primary cause of ethnic conflict, he says, but religion is a very strong "exacerbating factor."[40]

A lesser-known book, *The Tenth Parallel*, also discusses fault lines, but Eliza Griswold focuses on the latitude or "horizontal band that rings the earth 700 miles north of the equator." This band is a geographic, climactic, ethnic, and religious line. It runs through Sudan to the Philippines. In Africa, Islam spread from north to south, driven by trade, force, and conversion.[41] Christianity spread through the European colonial enterprise and Western missionaries' scramble for souls. Islam and Christianity meet along this line, with periods of peaceful coexistence and times of intense competition, the latter often wrapped up with matters of economic and political power. As the book's subtitle, *Dispatches from the Fault Line Between Christianity and Islam*, suggests, this is a faith-based fault line, a place of Christian-Muslim encounter in Africa (e.g., Nigeria and Sudan) and Asia (e.g., Indonesia and the Philippines).[42]

In Nigeria, Islam and Christianity meet along an East-West fault line in the Middle Belt region. In Nigeria as elsewhere along this fault line, the religious encounter includes religious strife as well as shouldering challenges together.

This religious encounter is gaining significance as these two world religions, especially the "hotter bits" (Pentecostalism in Christianity and Islamist elements in Islam) proselytize and experience a resurgence. The increased religious commitment and practice that define this resurgence can, in turn, increase conflict and violence between competing religions. An example comes from Africa, where the numbers of Christians and

Muslims are roughly equal. In terms of the geopolitics of religion, the "great meeting place" runs from Senegal in the west, through Nigeria, and on to Somalia in the east.[43] "Christianity and Islam are transnational and expansion-oriented religions."[44] As their numbers grow, Christianity presses northward, Islam presses southward, and religious tensions simmer. Although tolerance prevails in some areas, in others the exclusivist tendencies within each religion view the other as an adversary with which reconciliation is not possible. In the not-too-distant future, argues Eric Hanson, almost a dozen countries "with large populations will be divided between Muslims and Christians." Indonesia, Egypt, and Sudan will be mainly Muslim. The Democratic Republic of Congo, Germany, the Philippines, and Uganda will be mainly Christian. Three countries, Ethiopia, Nigeria, and Tanzania, will become more evenly divided between the two faiths. This will add to the political significance of these two religions.

In addition to religious resurgence, the political importance of Christian-Muslim fault lines is also bound up with the big trends of globalization and fragmentation. Globalization and fragmentation are in a dialectical relationship in that, as globalization progresses, it makes the world a "smaller" place; increases contact between peoples with different religious, ethnic, or civilizational identities; and has a homogenizing effect. Not wanting to be part of the undifferentiated mass of Benjamin Barber's "McWorld," groups construct or reassert their local identities. Religion is often an integral part of these identities.

When Is It a "Religious Conflict"?

In recent decades, the proportion of armed conflicts involving religion and religious claims has increased dramatically, most notably in the Middle East and North Africa. However, while "religion has increasingly become important in conflicts worldwide," importance and causation are two very different things.[45]

"Religious conflict" means a conflict that is really *about* religion. Such conflicts may pit two or more religions against each other. They may pit different arms of a religion, such as Sunni and Shia, against each other. Faith can also become a battleground when religious and secular powers come into direct conflict on issues regarding religion.[46]

This section aims to explain what it means to call something a religious conflict in the sense that religion is a primary *cause* of conflict. When is religion really at stake? Is it enough that religion is the locus of identity for the communities or states in conflict? When is religion manipulated or exploited for power or to serve other political, economic, or social ends? When is religion's primary function to justify and legitimize groups' actions or to mobilize support for a cause? When does religion simply serve as a handy label? Many violent conflicts have a religious element and bear the label "religious conflict," when they may or may not be *about* religion. Just because religion is *present* in a particular conflict does not mean that religion is the *predominant* factor in the conflict or the best explanation for it. The correlation of religion and conflict does not translate into causation.

Like all forms of political violence, wars and civil wars are political acts. War is organized mass violence between two or more members of the international system (states). Civil war, which has become more common than interstate war, is a protracted and bloody struggle for control of a state that occurs between rival groups (nonstate actors) within a state or between the state and an organized group (nonstate actor). The Correlates of War project sets a threshold of an average of 1,000 battle-related deaths per year for a domestic conflict to be counted among civil wars. While religion is experiencing a global resurgence, interstate conflict (war) is waning, and intrastate conflict (civil war) is waxing.

Since the 1970s, civil wars have become more apt to have a religious element and, more than any other religious tradition, Islam is likely to be involved in civil wars, including intrafaith and interfaith conflicts. Three of the big explanations for Islam's overrepresentation in civil wars are colonization and relatively recent decolonization, globalization, and geography. Globalization makes it easier for ideas to cross borders, including reinterpretations of jihad. Geography is important with regard to the Arab Middle East, which has large Muslim populations, the main Islamic holy sites, and big petroleum reserves that encourage meddling by outsiders.[47]

Direct and Indirect Influences

Eric Patterson provides a good starting point for determining the makings of a "religious conflict." He slices into this topic by naming direct and indirect ways that religion can induce or exacerbate conflict. One direct way is divine revelation, meaning "a religious text or divine revelation directly mandates violence." Patterson names Joseph Kony as an example, since Kony says the Holy Spirit speaks through him. Kony's and the LRA's religious beliefs contribute directly to the conflict in Uganda. Religious authority is a second direct way that religion figures into conflict. This occurs when religious actors, generally those who have legitimacy and authority in the eyes of their group, instruct their followers to kill. In 1095, Pope Urban II launched the Crusades with the words, "God wills it." Almost a millennium later, Osama bin Laden (the al-Qaeda leader) and Abu Bakr al-Baghdadi (Islamic State leader) both claimed authority within Islam, including the authority to prescribe killing. The third way, religious justification, is when religious believers use religion to justify the violence they inflict. Patterson's fourth and final point, sacralization, refers to imbuing a place or tangible thing with an aura of sacredness, making it something holy and worthy of protecting—even at the cost of bloodshed.[48] Often, "religious violence is linked to turf struggles over sacred space."[49] Three religions claim Jerusalem as sacred turf, and two have been willing to fight for it. Another example is Kosovo, which Serbs consider to be sacred space.

Patterson names two indirect ways that religion can inspire or exacerbate violence: identity and symbols. When religious faith becomes central to a group's collective identity, it creates cleavages: divisions that are politically important because they affect political allegiances, competition, and policy preferences. Most so-called religious wars have to do with groups' self-identities. Here, religion serves as an identity marker. Religious symbols can be manipulated by elites and employed to get people off their couches and engaged in collective action; that is, religion can be used to muster people to advance a common objective. Religious symbols then become instrumental, a means to a desired end. Patterson cites the conflict among Bosnians, Croats, and Serbs (discussed in Chapter 7) as an example incorporating both identity and symbols. Serbian nationalists, often with the backing of Orthodox religious leaders, used religious imagery, claims, and symbols to justify aggression against other groups. After years of secularizing communism, there were low levels of religiosity among Yugoslavs. Still, with Christians waving the Jerusalem Cross and Muslims the battle flag with a crescent, religion was an important factor in the group versus group violence that tore the state apart.

Having looked at direct and indirect ways in which religion can be important to a conflict, the next step is to consider when a conflict is truly a religious conflict. A religiously sanctioned conflict could be fought with goals—territory, oil, power, revenge, and so on—that have nothing to do with religion and from which the legitimizing religion will reap no religious dividends. Often, conflicts that are labeled religious or ethno-religious are less about religion and more about political power, land and the citizenship of those living on it, resources (e.g., oil or water), or historical memories of glory or injustice. Alternatively, actors use religious rhetoric to gather the resources and the recruits needed to carry out violence. In conflicts that are not about religion, religion may be used as a means to an end, rather than as the driving force. So when is a conflict truly a religious conflict?

Religious Conflict

We can meaningfully circumscribe the category of "religious conflict" by limiting it to instances when "at least one side has raised explicit demands from the onset of the conflict relating to religious issues."[50] Sudan is an example here. Beginning in 1983 and continuing for two decades, two sides clashed. On one side: the central government in the North, dominated by Arab Muslims, which tried to homogenize and unify the country by bringing the peripheries under Islamic and Arab influence. On the other side: those who pushed back. In the western part of Sudan, a conflict began in Darfur in 2003. In the South, where the conflict began twenty years earlier, they were mostly indigenous Africans and practitioners of either Christianity or traditional African religions.

The causes of the civil war between the North and South are complex. Overlapping ethnic, religious, and geographic differences reinforced one another, creating a kind of fault line. But this was not a case of primordial differences making conflict all but inevitable. It was, rather, the politics of Sudan's authoritarian regime, which marginalized and neglected the South, that led to conflict. The North dominated politics and allocated resources so as to disproportionately favor that region at the expense of other regions. The South had plenty of grievances. Southerners sought greater political freedom, economic opportunity, and access to the oil resources in the South.[51] Clearly, part of what fueled this conflict was Southern resentment for getting the short end of the economic and political sticks.

Yet, Francis M. Deng stated in the *Middle East Quarterly*, "Religion is the pivotal factor in the conflict," and indeed an argument can be made that this was a religious conflict.[52] One piece of evidence is that the South appealed for "Western support by portraying the struggle as one between a Christian South and an Arab Islamic North seeking to dominate the nation."[53] A more important piece of evidence has to do with the timing of the South's rebellion. It began when the central government declared sharia the foundation of Sudan's legal system. When this occurred in 1983, it provoked resentment and unease among Christians and animists in the South. That same year, the Sudan People's Liberation Army (SPLA), the main rebel force, took up the South's cause.

It was not the religious divide as such, but the regime's intent to disregard this divide and impose religious conformity and to "Islamify" the country, perhaps with the intent of consolidating the power of the ruling elite in the capital. It was the question of whether or not all Sudanese would be subject to Islamic law that made this a religious conflict.

A conflict is a religious conflict when it is really about or caused by religion. It is a religious conflict when religion defines the political goals or ends to be achieved through violence, or when religion is a primary (or central) issue. It may be that the conflict concerns whose religion (or interpretation of a religious tradition) will prevail in the state. Will one be privileged? Will one, a few, or all religions be suppressed? In Sudan, privileging Islam over other religions was not the only issue, but a central one. It seems to explain why the civil war began when it did.

In religious conflict, the issues at stake between conflicting states or conflicting groups are "religious in nature." These might be issues regarding control over holy sites, whether the state will be governed by religious law, or which religious team will rule particular lands. The Crusades and the Thirty Years' War (which led to the Peace of Westphalia) are examples here; the former sought to reclaim the Holy Lands for Christianity, while the latter was about confessional allegiances mixed in with power politics. However, by this measure the Serbian-Bosnian conflict was not a religious conflict. While religious identity entered in, there were no religious demands or issues.[54] The same can be said of the contested island of Cyprus. Greeks in Cyprus identify with the Christian Orthodox Church, while Turks in Cyprus are Muslim. Ethno-religious differences are, however, just one layer of a multilayer problem. The "Cyprus problem," which has involved many global actors over the years, "operates on local, regional and international levels."[55] It is not enough to say that it is a religious conflict simply because the battle lines are drawn between two groups with different religious affiliations. In and of themselves, differences in religious identity do not mean conflict.

To dig deeper into this complex matter, we have a couple of additional ways for distinguishing "religious conflicts" from others. First, a clear sign that a given conflict is really about or caused by religion is when it centers on orthodoxy or orthopraxy. Orthodoxy concerns getting theologies and religious doctrines "right," while orthopraxy has to do with doing the "right" things. Orthopraxy has to do with performing the "right" rites and rituals and doing what religion requires while refraining from doing what is forbidden. Orthodoxy and orthopraxy are in play when a conflict is fought over doctrinal differences and religious

Truth—"truth" with a capital "T" because there is only one, our group espouses it, and "we" insist that "they" buy into it, too. Conflict may arise when one group brands another's religious practices heretical and forbids them. Conflict can turn violent when interpretations of texts and traditions lead religious actors to seek a state that favors their religion and suppresses others or when laws and institutions suppress their religious practices.[56] In and of themselves, differences in religious beliefs and practices do not mean conflict, let alone violent conflict.

A second way to discern if a conflict is a "religious conflict" is by determining whether religion is central or peripheral. Especially with regard to civil wars, to say that religion is "peripheral" means that the conflict is really about politics, or that some other factor (e.g., competition for scarce resources) is far more important than the religious factor. It is not enough to say that religion influences actors' identities and loyalties, that combatants identify with different faith traditions, or that religion fuels a conflict. In Yugoslavia in the 1990s, religion provided a collective identifier, a way to distinguish friend from foe. That alone did not make it a religious conflict.

In contrast, when religion is central, combatants differ regarding religion's role in state and society. Parties in the war want a different relationship between their religion and the state, typically fighting for the imposition of their religious tradition throughout the state. In Afghanistan, for instance, when the Taliban ruled in the 1990s, they claimed to rule in accordance with the Quran. They sought to apply a legal code that adhered closely to Islam and to require orthopraxy, including how men and women dressed.[57] Similar things could be said about the Islamic State (or ISIS) that, like the Taliban, wanted to impose its particular interpretation of Islam. As part of its effort to establish an Islamic state, ISIS engaged in religious cleansing in Iraq, trying to rid the country of its non-Muslim citizens. In 2014, the year it proclaimed the establishment of an Islamic state, ISIS gave Christians in the city of Mosul two bleak options, "convert or die."[58] The Islamic State's victims also included large numbers of Shia Muslims. In addition, the Islamic State also fought to expand its territorial reach. These projects and the violence associated with them are, clearly, about religion.

The "I's" Have It

India, Indonesia, Iran, Iraq, Israel, and (Northern) Ireland—all have had violent conflicts with a religious dimension. Some of these conflicts are domestic, others between states, and some a mix of the two. This section briefly examines two examples—Israel-Palestine and Northern Ireland—with the purpose of determining whether the religious dimension is peripheral or central. The brevity of this examination necessitates focusing on a few features of each complex conflict to discuss whether it ought to bear the label of a sectarian or religious conflict.

Northern Ireland

A joke about Northern Ireland goes like this: A gunman appears and confronts a passerby. Holding a gun to a man's head, he asks, "Are you Catholic or Protestant?" Nervously, the man says, "I'm an atheist," to which the gunman replies, "Yes, but are you a Catholic or a Protestant atheist?"[59] As this joke suggests, in Northern Ireland religious identity is a ready means for distinguishing friend from foe. Religious identities are bound up with conflicting national identities, creating a dangerous combination. In Northern Ireland, "one is born a Protestant or a Catholic"; group membership is not a matter of choice, so even atheists bear a religious label.[60]

From the 1960s to 1998, a low-intensity conflict of killings and reprisals resulted in about 3,500 deaths and many more injuries. Known as "the Troubles," this era of conflict formally ended in 1998, with the Good Friday Agreement. It is often called a "sectarian" conflict, meaning it was primarily about religious differences between two Christian sects. As expressed in a piece by the Council on Foreign Relations, it "largely pitted the historically dominant Protestants against the Catholic minority."[61]

Some argue that religion was central to the conflict in Northern Ireland, sometimes pointing to the baleful, pernicious effects of divisive brands of religion. They say that, if a true religious conflict is to be found, this is it. However, others say this is not it, arguing that religion was peripheral or simply resisting the idea of religion's importance to the conflict.[62] In what sense did rival versions of Christianity contribute to the political violence than spanned three decades? Is religion simply a "marker of conflicting national identities" or a convenient, but misleading, way to speak of the two sides of a political divide?[63]

Religious conflict? Yes. We begin with the argument that religion was a central factor in the conflict. This was sectarian violence—an "unholy war of religion"—because religious issues were very important, especially since they were wrapped up with history and with issues of sovereignty, discrimination, and political and economic power.

For Michael Burleigh this point is clear: "the long-term origins of the problem are obviously religious," and "reminders of ethnoreligious battle lines" remain.[64] The conflict's historical roots go back centuries and have much to do with religion. This historical sketch offers just the bare bones.

In the late seventeenth century the Plantation of Ulster began. England "planted" English and Scottish Protestants in the northern part of Ireland, known as Ulster, while uprooting Catholics. This provoked settler-native problems and Protestant-Catholic problems. In 1685, King James, a Catholic, came to power as king of England and Ireland and king of Scotland. He favored his co-religionists. Five years later, the Battle of the Boyne pit King James against William of Orange, a Protestant. William's victory ensured British Protestant supremacy over the Catholic Irish.

Fast forward to the twentieth century (1920–1921), when the Government of Ireland Act divided Ireland into thirty-two counties. Six northern counties became Northern Ireland, and the other twenty-six counties became Ireland. The northern and heavily Protestant counties, also called "Ulster," remained in the United Kingdom. The twenty-six predominantly Catholic counties achieved independence and became the Irish Free State, which later became the Republic of Ireland. In both places, the religious minority said they faced discrimination.

The conflict known as the Troubles began in the late 1960s. Facing religious-based discrimination in employment and housing, the Catholic minority in Northern Ireland launched a campaign to end their marginalization and gain expanded civil rights from the Protestant majority.[65] This campaign—whether interpreted in the positive light of a civil rights movement or more negatively as a "campaign of terror"—sparked a Protestant backlash and prompted the United Kingdom to dispatch thousands of troops in a failed effort to keep the peace.[66]

Religious politics are integral to the politics of Northern Ireland, and this was a religious conflict. There were real religious differences on a number of matters, including rival versions of Christian theology and religious authority. Religion was *the* symbol of what divided the two communities. Communal identities were defined in *exclusive* terms. Religious affiliation shaped identity and was interwoven with national identity, and some religious leaders promoted this association. "People were killed in the name of religion and those killed were identified by their killers as belonging to the 'rival' religion."[67]

Even if this conflict was not *about* religion, religion mattered in indirect or peripheral ways. Religion mattered because it provided symbols and shaped political allegiances, objectives, and identity. In Northern Ireland, religious identity incorporated all other identities, except sex.[68] Historically, Catholicism was central to an Irish identity and, if Northern Ireland was politically united with Ireland, the result would be a predominantly Irish and Catholic state. Religious differences coincided with other differences, especially political differences. In majority-Catholic Ireland, Protestants were on the receiving end of religiously inspired discrimination; in the majority-Protestant area of Northern Ireland, the situation was reversed.[69] Religious leaders allowed and sometimes promoted a religious-nationalist mythology, some using religion to legitimize violence, and some sectarian propagandists manipulated religious symbols. "Symbols of religious affiliation" marked public identities.[70]

Religion also mattered because it is hard to disentangle religious divisions from political and national divisions. This division shows up during elections, when Catholics overwhelmingly vote for nationalist parties and Protestants do the same for the parties that want to keep Northern Ireland in the United Kingdom.[71]

Religious conflict? No. The conflict in Northern Ireland was not a religious struggle, though this is a common misperception. Politics and national identity were at least as important as religion.

The central point on this side of the argument is that the main conflict of the Troubles was really political, not religious. It was a problem of access to political power. It was a conflict between two groups with different and irreconcilable political aspirations, combined with Ireland's and the United Kingdom's incompatible assertions of national sovereignty over Northern Ireland. On one side of the struggle were those who wanted to see Northern Ireland remain part of the United Kingdom. On the other side were those who wanted Northern Ireland to be part of the Republic of Ireland—or, at least, to enjoy "Home Rule," meaning considerable autonomy from the government in London. These nationalists, or republicans, who happened to be born Catholic, wanted Northern Ireland to unite with the rest of the emerald isle. Unionists, or loyalists (those loyal to the British Crown), who happened to be born Protestant, wanted Northern Ireland to remain part of the United Kingdom of Great Britain and Northern Ireland. The shorthand given to each side was, respectively, Catholics and Protestants. These religious labels, however, mask pivotal socioeconomic issues, political stances, and national identities. Labeling it a "Catholic-Protestant" conflict is too simplistic. (See Table 8.1.)

A second point is that, while religious divisions coincide with political divisions, ultimately the conflict was about political divisions. In the seventeenth century it was settler against native. In the twentieth century it was unionist against nationalist; alternatively, it was an ethno-religious

Table 8.1   The Two Sides

	Nationalists/Republicans	Unionists/Loyalists
Political emphasis	Nationalism: Irish republicanism	Unionism: British loyalism
Identity	Catholicism and "Irishness"	Protestantism and "Britishness"
Political aim	Unified Ireland—unite Northern Ireland with the Republic of Ireland; become Irish citizens (i.e., unify the Irish nation in one state); Get British out	Keep Northern Ireland in United Kingdom; retain British citizenship
Political parties	Sinn Fein ("We Ourselves"); Social Democratic and Labour Party (SDLP)	Ulster Unionist Party (UUP), largest pro-British party; Democratic Unionist Party (DUP)
Paramilitary	Irish Republican Army	Ulster Volunteer Force

majority that wanted to remain dominant versus an ethno-religious minority that saw itself as exploited and oppressed.[72] In Northern Ireland, Protestants/unionists have tended to enjoy power and privileges that Catholics/nationalists have not.[73]

A third point concerns identity. In Northern Ireland, argues James Kurth, "ethnic identity is religious identity."[74] "Protestants" embrace British national identity. Protestants' group identity is grounded in shared historical experiences, traditions, values, and beliefs and in the expectation of having certain privileges. They are also called "unionists" because they support continued political union with the country formally known as the United Kingdom of Great Britain and Northern Ireland. "Catholics" embrace "Irishness," rather than "Britishness," and Irish national identity. They wanted to fold Northern Ireland into the Republic of Ireland. Religious identity mostly exacerbated or compounded what was essentially a nationalist conflict. As stated by D. E. Benson, "The intergroup conflict in Northern Ireland is fundamentally a conflict based on identities sustained by religious symbols and rituals," not by religion itself.[75]

As in the violence in Bosnia—which pit Bosnian Muslims against Catholic Croats and Orthodox Serbs—religion was not central to the conflict. Nonetheless, the two sides in Northern Ireland identified with two different faith traditions, and religion created group identities and loyalties.[76] The conflict, however, was really about power, politics, and political allegiances. Religion is an identity marker, which some politicians used to further a political agenda.

Fourth, this was "not a battle of churches" or about establishing one religion or the other. Although religious symbols and legitimation were part of the Troubles, there was not a push to ensure a particular type of Christian beliefs and practices. Major actors did not make religious demands. Some church leaders were quite outspoken, but most clergy and active parishioners were not violent extremists.[77] On the contrary, for the most part Protestant leaders and the Catholic hierarchy condemned violent political activism.

Violence was perpetrated by British forces and nationalist and unionist paramilitaries. Militants were not inspired by Christian beliefs. It was not about religious doctrine or rival understandings of religious Truth. Neither side said a mandate for violence came from scripture.[78] It was also not "about whether one religion and its institutions, practices, and moral laws [would] be established by law or otherwise favored over other religious groups."[79] The Troubles began when church attendance was dropping and relations between the two main branches of Christianity were improving.[80] "Protestant" and "Catholic" objectives, then, were not religious in nature. In short, it was not a religious war.

Finally, if it was truly a religious conflict, then the Good Friday Agreement either would not have happened or it would have entailed very different elements. This agreement reshaped political institutions and created power-sharing arrangements, suggesting it was essentially an agreement to end a *political* conflict.[81] As a rule, political settlements can be reached only when conflicts are amenable to compromise, which is not true of most religious conflicts nor of most identity conflicts. It is hard to compromise on matters of religion or identity.[82]

Israel-Palestine

The conflict in Israel-Palestine has a lot of moving pieces. It has drawn in regional actors (Arab states), big powers (e.g., the United States), intergovernmental organizations (e.g., the United Nations and the European Union), and transnational actors. It has historical, ethnic, national, religious, and purely political factors at play. Moderates and hard-liners exist on both sides.

The conflict commenced after Israel declared itself an independent state in 1948. The violence has included three wars with neighboring states, Palestinian uprisings, crackdowns by Israeli security forces, and violent skirmishes. The situation in Israel-Palestine is further complicated by the region's economic and strategic importance, such that there are multiple levels of conflict and important actors on multiple levels of analysis. This conflict goes beyond Palestinians and Israelis; it is part of the broader Arab-Israeli conflict. Many Arab states support the Palestinians, while the United States is a staunch supporter of Israel.

Much like Northern Ireland, the conflict in Israel-Palestine is often viewed as example of a "religious war." Others, however, argue that the conflict in Israel-Palestine is not a "clash of religions."[83] Which side is right? Is this a clash between Muslims and Jews or is it about other matters that have been "religicized"? To say it has been religicized is to say that, at root, the conflict is *not* based on religious prejudices or practices, creedal differences, or whose religion will prevail in society; it is really about something else, but has been framed as a religious controversy.[84]

Religious Conflict? Yes. Most Jews call the land "Israel" and most Muslims call it "Palestine," and this is a case of "religions in collision."[85] Followers of various religions "struggle over religion's place in society and over sacred land," with "competing religious claims to the same piece of territory."[86] On each side (Israelis and Palestinians) are people claiming "God is on their side."[87]

Jews and Muslims assert competing, mutually exclusive religious claims to the small territory the state of Israel governs. Both sides assert their right to all of this land, with Jerusalem as the grand prize for the winning side. Jerusalem is holy to all three monotheistic, Abrahamic faiths: Judaism, Christianity, and Islam. Two of the three are fighting over the Holy Land. (Christianity is not central to the fray.) This is a high-stakes, zero-sum game: any inch of territory that one side gains is a loss for the other. The "two-state" solution entails ending the conflict by dividing Israel between the rival claimants. This has not worked. Jerusalem is hard to divide, and the Temple Mount is hotly contested. The Western, or Wailing, wall is the holiest site in Judaism; on the other side of the wall, the Dome of the Rock is the third holiest site in Islam. Both sides have centuries-old claims to this small area. Disputes have erupted over who can pray where. This is a conflict over "divine real estate."[88] Since this sacred space is religiously important and unique, competition over it can result in an intractable conflict.[89]

The above includes two points in favor of the religious conflict argument. One is the sacred nature of the disputed land, creating a struggle over "sacred space." Jews (and some Christians) believe God/Yahweh promised this land to the Hebrews and their descendants. Israel's significance and right to exist comes from Judaism.[90] Contemporary Islamists designate Palestine as a "religious trust for all Muslims."[91] The other argument is that, despite many efforts, no political settlement has borne fruit because it is not, at its core, a political conflict. It is a religious conflict, and such conflicts include nonnegotiable absolutes.

A third point is that the conflict involves not only which religion prevails in society and in public law but also the existence and nature of the state of Israel. The Jewish and democratic state of Israel shows preference toward Jews by excluding some from military service, for instance. After considering the move for a number of years, in mid-2018 the Israeli government passed legislation proclaiming Israel "the nation-state of the Jewish people." While formally a secular state, the Israeli state privileges Jewish people with regard to language, immigration, citizenship, land ownership, and now the right to self-determination.

Finally, although religious frames of reference were secondary during the early stages of conflict, they have grown. Increasingly, in this "religious war," Judaism has assumed an enlarged public role. Some Israelis who have endorsed a "religious vision of Israel" wield influence in the political parties that have seats in the national parliament.[92] They want the Jewish state to reflect and support Jewish law, though other Israelis resist the expansion of the "public scope of religious law."[93] Among Arabs there is growing Judeophobia, with Muslim leaders calling for holy war against Jews and Israel; among Israelis there is growing Islamophobia, with some Jewish leaders calling for Muslims to be killed and the Al-Aqsa mosque destroyed.[94]

On the Palestinian side, too, religious frames of reference have grown in significance. A contributing factor was Hamas's 2006 electoral victory. Hamas—the Islamic Resistance Movement—resists what it sees as Israeli occupation. Like so many other Islamist groups, Hamas seeks a system of "rule based on religious law."[95] Its stated purpose is to establish an Islamic state throughout Palestine. Hamas has a military wing and has called for armed struggle against the Israeli state. It has also provided social services and participated in the Palestinian political process in the Gaza Strip. Its 2006 win in Palestinian elections may signify that the religious camp is trumping the nationalist camp.[96]

Two final notes on this side of the argument. First, both sides have factions, with the religious elements among them tending to fan the flames of discord, making a peace agreement that much harder. Second, in Israel-Palestine and in the region, conflict is increasingly *religious* conflict.[97]

Religious conflict? No. The other side of the argument is that, while it involves religion, this conflict is really about something else. Like Northern Ireland's Troubles, it is about how lines are drawn on the world map and who rules.

The conflict can be described as a "real-estate dispute," a disagreement over "sovereign control of territory" or, to use Thomas Friedman's words, a fight over "who owns which olive tree."[98] Both sides claim the right to control a scarce resource, land. Since both want all of the same piece of land, their claims are mutually exclusive—and the "loser faces the threat of being left stateless."[99]

Both sides have developed emotionally and politically loaded— and conflicting—narratives around this conflict. They tell very different stories, but have the same punch line: Israel-Palestine is their rightful homeland.

The Jewish story goes something like this: For 3,500 years they were a distinct people, but without a territorial base. During their long history of exile and statelessness, the Jewish diaspora spread to Russia, Europe, and elsewhere. They were often subject to persecution or threatened by assimilation and, thus, loss of their unique identity. This exile, along with God's promise, fed the longing for a common homeland. For Jews, the Holocaust cemented the basic tenet of Zionism (Jewish nationalism): Jews need a state of their own. After World War II, they got it.

The Arab/Palestinian story is equally compelling: After Islam emerged in the seventh century, its adherents began developing a collective identity as Arabs, Muslims, and subjects of the Ottoman Empire. In the late nineteenth and early twentieth centuries, non-Muslim foreigners began entering in large waves. As the number of Jewish immigrants rose, so did Arab alarm. At about the same time that the Ottoman Empire crumbled, the Balfour Declaration (1917) pledged the creation of a Jewish "national home" in Palestine. For Palestinians and the wider Arab community, this was the manifestation of old-fashioned imperialism and colonialism.[100] When waves of Jewish immigrants arrived in Palestine, a distinct Palestinian identity developed, defined by attachment to a particular piece of land and ethnic descent as well as a reaction to the Zionist threat and a sense of having been wronged.[101] Creation of the state of Israel and, the other side of this coin, Palestinian dispossession, was a calamity. Palestinians became a stateless nation. Granting Zionists the right of self-determination meant denying Palestinians that same right, which was cemented by the 2018 nation-state law.

So, at the heart of the decades-long conflict between Palestinians and the state of Israel are political issues: self-determination and sovereign control over land. The conflict can be framed as a case of competing nationalisms: Jewish nationalism and Palestinian nationalism.

Breaking this down further underscores the political nature of this conflict. Persecution of Jews as a people was a main driver for establishing Israel as a safe haven. Although it is the world's only Jewish state, "the 1948 Declaration of Independence did not mention God or Jerusalem, and the founders were all essentially secular."[102] Today, Jews are not of one mind with regard to the religious nature of the state. Similarly, the Palestinian struggle for statehood began as a secular nationalist project. Today one of the Palestinians' key political groups, Fatah, remains secular and nationalist and is often at odds with the Islamist group Hamas. The Palestinian banner is thus carried by secularists and Islamists, and the Israeli flag is carried by some with a secular vision of their state and others with a religious vision.

This evidence points to religion as an "intervening," not pivotal, factor in this dispute.[103] This conflict is not about religion.

These two examples demonstrate the importance of going beyond facile statements about so-called religious conflicts and distinguishing between religion's *presence* in conflicts and religion as the best *explanation* for those conflicts.[104] Religion can be present and even important in a conflict, while not getting at the root causes of it. Correlation does not mean causation.

In Theory

In addition to using international relations paradigms and levels of analysis to provide a framework of understanding, as done in previous chapters, this chapter also sets out social science approaches. These theories represent alternative ways of understanding and explaining the focus of this chapter, the religion-conflict nexus.

Levels of Analysis

The usefulness of the levels of analysis becomes evident with regard to conflict. Conflicts are generally complex matters, involving a mix of actors and motives. To understand the rise of nonstate actors that engage in conflict against the state or other nonstate actors requires looking at all three levels. In the case of a nonstate actor such as Boko Haram in Nigeria, we look at the surge of Islam and modern religious terrorism on the international level, the "deficiencies and failures" of the fragile

Nigerian state and the animosity between the group and the state, and the individuals who lead the organization.[105]

In explaining war, Kenneth Waltz argues that to understand why war occurs we have to understand that there are multiple interrelated causes of war. He uses the term *image*, rather than level of analysis. Focusing on a single image—humans, the state, or the state system—results in incomplete analysis. Men and women and states are proximate (or immediate) causes of war, while the international environment is the "permissive cause" in the sense that it permits (does not prevent) war. Thus, he posits the importance of finding the inclusive nexus of the causes of war.[106] That is to say that he questions single-cause explanations for a given conflict and, instead, looks for connections among multiple causes.

Certainly, this inclusive nexus must be considered with regard to Israel-Palestine. There, the important actors include individuals, especially the Palestinian and Israeli leaders; groups, including Israeli and Palestinian political parties as well as Fatah and Hamas; the state of Israel and the Palestinian-controlled Gaza Strip and West Bank; regional actors, including Iran and Arab states; and international actors, such as the United Nations and the European Union.

Stepping back to look at the big picture, a couple of points can be made about the global or systemic level of analysis. One point is that contextual factors figure into religious actors' choices to embrace or eschew violence. In the West since the Peace of Westphalia, religious justifications for war have largely gone the way of the dodo bird. Outside the West, transnational networks and the global dynamics of colonialism, imperialism, and interventionism—almost entirely driven by the West—figure prominently into many states' histories. Factors at this level of analysis are, in Kenneth Waltz's words, "permissive causes" of warfare: they allow war to happen (and may explain why war in general happens), but they fall short of explaining why a conflict erupts in a particular time and place.

We can, for instance, say that the nature of Western colonialism and decolonization left the states of sub-Saharan Africa more conflict-prone than regions that decolonized much earlier. We can also accept Eliza Griswold's argument that a religious fault line runs through the northern part of this region. However, unless we study what is going on at the state and individual levels of analysis, we cannot explain why Sudan's civil war erupted when it did.

Another point is that the resurgence of Islam is the "boat" on which Islamism (i.e., political Islam) rides—and some Islamist groups are riding the modern wave of religious terrorism. The Taliban in Afghanistan and the Islamic State are prime examples of Islamist movements. Such movements are important to global politics because some have demonstrated the power to dramatically reshape a country's domestic politics (as the Taliban did in Afghanistan in the 1990s), challenge state sovereignty (as the Islamic state is doing in the Middle East), and shape countries' foreign policies (as seen in Iran). Some of them have become transnational actors that challenge the existing world order in which territorially defined states are central actors. To be clear, Islamist groups may have nothing to do with religious conflict, but some do.

Moving to the state level, the question is: how do domestic political and societal factors affect the decision to engage in political violence? Political factors include regime type (democratic or authoritarian), division of powers, interest groups, political parties, and decisionmaking processes. Societal factors are historical, cultural, economic, religious, and demographic (the percentage of adherents of different religions) matters. Together, these are key contextual factors.

Nigeria serves as an example. First, demographics: Nigeria's population is roughly divided between Christians and Muslims, with the south being predominantly Christian, the north predominantly Muslim, and the two meeting in the Middle Belt. Second, two important things are happening with regard to the intersection of religion and politics: the rejection of the "two spheres" model and the introduction of sharia. Both Christians and Muslims generally reject the idea of separating life into distinct religious and secular spheres.[107] Instead, they would like religious values to play a greater role in the country's politics. This touches on the desired nature of the state. After transitioning to democracy with a federal structure, a dozen of Nigeria's northern states with Muslim majorities implemented Islamic law. In addition to religious motives for this change, this move advanced the objectives of improving governance and reducing corruption and inequality. Conflict over the sharia issue led to violence between Muslims and Christians. The perception that Islamic law failed to produce the desired changes also opened the door for increasingly radical and violent religious challengers to enter.[108] It is not surprising then that, contrary to the assumptions of modernization and secularization theory, religion and religious cleavages remain important when it comes to political parties, political mobilization, political legitimacy, political debates, conflicts, and representation in government (or the distribution of power and privileges). Even the national census is sometimes politicized on religious grounds, regarding whether Christianity or Islam is numerically superior and more widespread. This is the domestic context in which, according to

Freedom House, "sectarian violence in the restive Middle Belt region" is a security challenge.[109]

Social Science Approaches

Jonathan Fine sets out three theories that predominate in the analysis of religion, conflict, and international politics: instrumentalism, primordialism, and constructivism. Of the three approaches, the instrumentalist approach is most likely to write off religion or religious differences as central to conflicts. Instead, where a religious element is part of a conflict, it is used in an instrumental way; in other words, it is a tool used by self-interested elites to serve political goals. Religion is the most potent and least expensive way to persuade the masses and mobilize them for conflict, provide a unifying mission, and justify the use of force.[110] But conflict itself is about "who gets what, when, and how."[111]

Primordialists are most likely to see religion as the main cause of armed conflict, religious conflicts as unsolvable, and such conflicts as a persistent feature of world politics.[112] Primordialists tend to raise the refrain of "ancient" or "primordial" hatreds, which implies that conflict is almost inevitable. Memories of long-past conflicts and grievances never die. The "age-old antagonisms" thesis is often invoked to explain the conflicts that tore apart Yugoslavia after the fall of communism. This is the specter of "Balkan ghosts": ancient and unchanging hatreds in the Balkan region—despite "evidence of five hundred years of shared inheritance and civilization."[113] The past is never really past.

Constructivists, according to Fine's analysis, take religion seriously while asserting that "purely religious conflicts are relatively rare." Other factors muddy the waters, such as competition over power, raw materials, or land. These may be the root causes of a given conflict, but when religion is added to the mix, it "sustains, prolongs, and intensifies conflict." Religion can also play a very different role, setting in motion conflict resolution or transformation.[114] Conflict transformation means that religion can alter attitudes and the relationships between the parties to a conflict and bring about "religious peacebuilding."[115] Given the ambiguity of religious traditions and doctrines, religious actors might either escalate or de-escalate conflict.

IR Paradigms

As we continue looking through the constructivist lens, we see that events on the world stage including political violence are historically and socially conditioned, not inevitable or due to human nature.[116] Historical grievances might be one of the factors that explain conflict. Social forces may condition actors to see other groups or states a certain way—as friends, enemies, or frenemies. Prevailing norms, values, ideas, ideologies, and identities affect actors' inclination toward conflict or cooperation. Political scientist John Mueller has conjectured that war may be just an idea, and a really bad one at that. Or perhaps war is an institution, like slavery once was, and like slavery it can become discredited and obsolete—all without changing human nature, the nature of nation-states, or the international system.[117] During the Cold War, mutually exclusive political ideologies were at the heart of the superpower conflict. As we have seen, assertions of exclusive identities may lead to conflict. In the case of Israel-Palestine, historical narratives have been constructed and hardened in ways that make it more difficult to arrive at a peace settlement. These accounts of what happened or who did what to whom are not written in stone. It would not be easy, but such accounts can potentially be changed or reconstructed in ways that would lower the barriers to an agreement. An upshot of the constructivist view is that war and other forms of political violence might end without far-reaching changes at any level of analysis.

In contrast, for realists, conflict and political violence are rooted in human nature, and religion can be used or misused to further interests. Thomas Hobbes, whose views of human nature inform realists' views, described humans as being driven by fears (especially of violent death) and drives (especially the drive for power and self-preservation). Conflict, for Hobbes, was all but inevitable, with the possibility of war of all against all. In the Hobbesian tradition, realists see humans (and states) as power-hungry, self-interested, and acquisitive by nature. Writing in 1991, on the eve of the Soviet Union's dissolution, William Lind asserted that human nature made it unlikely that a new era of the "peaceful exchange of ideas and commerce" was dawning.[118] Cooperation is often difficult, even if actors share the same basic goals, because in a world of anarchy there are no guarantees.

In a realist take on the Yugoslav conflicts (1991–1995) discussed in Chapter 7, fear became a motivating factor, rising as the state was failing.[119] As the state's central institutions collapsed and the state lost its monopoly on the use of force, conditions began to look a lot like the anarchy that prevails in world politics. Different ethnic groups—Bosnians, Croats, Serbs—were left in a "self-help" situation; each had to provide for its own security because the collapsing state could not or would not do it. Fear drove the security dilemma. Each group, wary of the others' intentions, took actions to protect itself. Other groups perceived these moves as offensive, not defensive, and thus threatening; hence, they took measures to protect themselves. When legitimate authority disintegrates, fear fosters hatred of the ethnic or religious other.

Liberals study domestic factors and international institutions to understand cooperation and conflict. They are also more optimistic than realists, insisting that cooperation is possible and violent conflict is not inevitable. For liberals, a world of democracies connected by trade and international institutions would be a more peaceful world. The "democratic peace" is the idea that well-established democracies will not fight each other. Within democracies, disagreements are resolved through peaceful means: compromise, legislation, courts, and elections. Democratic states likewise learn to resolve disagreements with each other through nonviolent means. When states have vibrant trade relations, it is more prudent to resolve disputes rather than go to war and damage both states' domestic economies. International law and organizations can also help to keep the peace. They help to keep international interactions orderly and predictable.

Table 8.2 frames the analysis of topics discussed in this chapter using Joseph Kony and the Lord's Resistance Army (LRA) as an example.

Conclusion

"Faith matters."[120] Despite the march of modernity and secularization, "religion is shaping the world."[121] Despite the predictions of the "death of faith," we are seeing people "dying for faith."[122] The world is desecularizing, while the nature of conflict is changing, and there is often a link between the two, "with contemporary globalization conflicts between religions and between religion and politics are set to become more, rather than less, problematic."[123]

The statements above may underscore an impression that religious resurgence has been accompanied by a rise in wars with religious dimensions. In fact, the *number* of wars with a religious element has remained fairly flat since the 1980s; however, the *proportion* of conflicts with a religious dimension is greater now because interstate war has become so rare and because civil wars with a religious element tend to be more intractable and, thus, last longer.[124] This is because religion can convert conflicts into value conflicts, disputes over right and wrong, and be tied to other aspects of identity. In addition, firm religious convictions can lend strength, purpose, and righteous anger to a cause and can render some points nonnegotiable.

Table 8.2   Framing the Analysis: Lord's Resistance Army and Joseph Kony

Levels of Analysis	Realism	Liberalism	Constructivism
International/ Systemic	The Lord's Resistance Army, though not particularly powerful, poses a threat to regional security.	The LRA's campaign has drawn in the international community, including regional governments, nongovernmental organizations (e.g., Invisible Children), the United Nations, and the International Criminal Court (ICC).	The Lord's Resistance Army bucks international norms.
Domestic/State	Under British colonial rule, which ended in 1962, many of the Acholi people occupied positions of power in the police and military forces. In independent Uganda, Tito Okello, an ethnic Acholi and high-ranking military officer, served briefly as president. This was the first time that an Acholi held the reins of state power in Uganda. When Okello was overthrown in 1986, many Acholi feared the loss of their group's power.	Joseph Kony seeks, through an armed insurgency, to change the fundamental nature of Uganda's government. The government's ability to bring the group to heel is hobbled by military incompetence and a lack of political will.	LRA members are bound together by grievances and a common identity. They construct themselves as an in-group, while Acholi people who are not in the LRA become the out-group.

continues

Table 8.2 Continued

Levels of Analysis	Realism	Liberalism	Constructivism
Individual	Perhaps Joseph Kony simply seeks recognition and power, and attacks and abductions bolster his political capital.	Two key individuals are behind the rise of the Lord's Resistance Army, Joseph Kony and Alice Auma, who led a predecessor movement in the 1980s.	Very different identity factors come into play here. One is that the intragroup conflict (Acholi vs. Acholi) means the dividing line is between individual Ugandans who are LRA members and nonmembers. Another is that Joseph Kony seeks to construct a new, "genuine" Acholi identity.

Sources: Jeffrey, "Hope for Uganda"; Bevan, "The Myth of Madness"; Bailey, "The Quest for Justice"; Jo-Ansie van Wyk, "Joseph Kony and the Lord's Resistance Army"; Thompson, *Armed Groups*.

However, as explained in this chapter, a conflict with a religious element is not necessarily *about* religion. Religion can be used as a means to an end. Religion can also serve as a "convenient marker" to differentiate opponents who are primarily driven by other interests, such as gaining power, redressing economic grievances, or claiming territory.[125] We need to distinguish between real religiosity and identity politics to understand what is going on around the globe, especially with regard to violent conflicts.[126]

To the extent that religion is addressed in international relations texts or considered a causal variable in world politics, it is often linked to strife and bloodshed. This makes sense, given the rise in the proportion of violent conflicts that have a religious element and the ways in which even local conflicts can have international impacts. However, this view also makes religion sort of a one-dimensional cardboard cutout: when, rather than being a purely private matter, it enters the public realm, bad things happen. Religion is relevant on the world stage when dangerous forms of it cause international problems and necessitate international solutions. Religion also becomes relevant on the world stage "when it can be put to use to promote the common public international good. This is accomplished through humanitarian and development projects, human rights campaigns, transitional justice efforts, and so on. These two 'sides' of religion—dangerous religion and peaceful religion—are what Tony Blair refers to as the 'two faces of faith.'"[127] This is the subject of the next chapter.

Notes

1. Stigen, *The Relationship Between the International Criminal Court and National Jurisdictions*, 369.
2. Titeca, "The Spiritual Order of the LRA."
3. Titeca, "The Spiritual Order of the LRA."
4. Titeca, "The Spiritual Order of the LRA."
5. Eichstaedt. *First Kill Your Family*, 98.
6. Jackson, "Negotiating with Ghosts," 323.
7. Congressional Research Service, *The Lord's Resistance Army*, 6.
8. Branch, "Exploring the Roots of LRA Violence."
9. Bailey, "The Quest for Justice," 252.
10. Metraux, "Religious Terrorism in Japan," 152.
11. Nehorayoff, Ash, and Smith, "Aum Shinrikyo's Nuclear and Chemical Weapons Development Efforts," 35–36.
12. Metraux, "Religious Terrorism in Japan," 1142, 1154.
13. Juergensmeyer, *Terror in the Mind of God*, 38.
14. Jerryson, "Buddhist Traditions and Violence," 37.

15. Jerryson, "Buddhist Traditions and Violence," 59.

16. Eliot A. Cohen, "Religion and War," 15.

17. Jeffrey, "Hope for Uganda," 12.

18. Aden, *Religion Today*, 253.

19. Hopmann, "Groupthink."

20. Kingston, *The Politics of Religion, Nationalism, and Identity in Asia*, 210.

21. Aden, *Religion Today*, 252–253.

22. Stephen Healey, review of *When Religion Becomes Evil*, 58.

23. Falk, "Religion and Global Governance," 7.

24. Griswold, *The Tenth Parallel*, 282.

25. Weigel, "Religion and Peace," 172–192.

26. Kurth, "Religion and Ethnic Conflict."

27. Eliot A. Cohen, "Religion and War," 14.

28. Bruce, *Politics and Religion*, 111.

29. Cimmino, "Threat from Tibet?" 6

30. Philpott, "Explaining the Political Ambivalence of Religion," 505–525.

31. "Religious Violence as Modern Myth," 487.

32. Bruce, review of *The Myth of Religious Violence*, 110–111.

33. Fox, "The Rise of Religious Nationalism and Conflict," 727.

34. Marshall, "Keeping the Faith," 52.

35. Bieber, "The Conflict in Former Yugoslavia as a 'Fault Line War'?"

36. Berger, "Secularization Falsified," 25.

37. Powers, "Religion, Conflict and Prospects for Reconciliation in Bosnia, Croatia and Yugoslavia," 221–222.

38. Ivekovic, "The Political Use and Abuse of Religion in Transcaucasia and Yugoslavia," 30.

39. "War and Ethnic Cleansing in Yugoslavia," GlobalSecurity.org, https://www.globalsecurity.org/military/world/war/yugo-hist4.html.

40. Fox, "The Rise of Religious Nationalism and Conflict," 726, 728.

41. Haynes, *An Introduction to International Relations and Religion*, 303–304.

42. Griswold, *The Tenth Parallel*, 3, 11, 82, 178.

43. Pew Research Center, "Tolerance and Tension."

44. Dowd, "Religious Diversity and Violent Conflict," 157.

45. Basedau and Koos, "When Do Religious Leaders Support Faith-Based Violence?" 760.

46. Candia, Chryssavgis, and Lee, "Faiths' Fault Lines," 20.

47. Toft, Philpott, and Shah, *God's Century*, 153–157.

48. Patterson, *Politics in a Religious World*, 77–79.

49. Demerath, *Crossing the Gods*, 173.

50. Svensson, "One God, Many Wars," 412.

51. "Sudan: Race and Religion in Civil War," Berkley Center for Religion, Peace, and World Affairs, Georgetown University, August 2013, 4.

52. Deng, "Sudan – Civil War and Genocide," 13–21.

53. Grieco, Ikenberry, and Mastanduno, *Introduction to International Relations*, 369.

54. Isaacs, "Sacred Violence or Strategic Faith?" 212–213.

55. İlke Dağlı, "The Cyprus Problem."

56. Philpott, "Explaining the Political Ambivalence of Religion," 518.

57. Toft, "Religion, Rationality, and Violence," 118, 120; Toft, "Getting Religion?" 97.

58. Shea, "Barbarism 2014," 34, 39.

59. Berger, "Secularization Falsified," 25.

60. Guelke, "Religion, National Identity and the Conflict in Northern Ireland," 102–103.

61. Landow and Sergie, "The Northern Ireland Peace Process."

62. Demerath, *Crossing the Gods*, 47.

63. Guelke, "Religion, National Identity and the Conflict in Northern Ireland," 104.

64. Burleigh, *Sacred Causes*, 379.

65. Burleigh, *Sacred Causes*, 388.

66. Bruce, *Politics and Religion*, 211.

67. Philip Barnes, "Religion, Education and Conflict in Northern Ireland," 132.

68. Easthope, "Religious War in Northern Ireland," 431.

69. Burleigh, *Sacred Causes*, 382.

70. Benson, "Religious Orthodoxy in Northern Ireland," 219, 220.

71. Bruce, *Politics and Religion*, 117.

72. Appleby, *The Ambivalence of the Sacred*, 109.

73. Benson, "Religious Orthodoxy in Northern Ireland," 227.

74. Kurth, "Religion and Ethnic Conflict," 284.

75. Benson, "Religious Orthodoxy in Northern Ireland," 227.

76. Toft, "Religion, Rationality, and Violence," 118, 120; Barnes, "Religion, Education and Conflict in Northern Ireland," 132.

77. Alan Dowty, *Israel/Palestine*, 3rd ed., 48.

78. Pauletta Otis, in Seiple and Hoover, *Religion and Security*, 20.

79. Appleby, *The Ambivalence of the Sacred*, 174.

80. Guelke, "Religion, National Identity and the Conflict in Northern Ireland," 110–111.

81. Hoge, "An Irish Accord."

82. Steve Bruce in Guelke, "Religion, National Identity and the Conflict in Northern Ireland," 110.

83. Dowty, *Israel/Palestine*, 3rd ed., 48.

84. Milton-Edwards, "Political Islam and the Palestinian–Israeli Conflict," 68.

85. Haynes, *Religion in Global Politics*.

86. Johnston, *Faith-Based Diplomacy*, 4.

87. Micklethwait and Wooldridge, *God Is Back*, 315.

88. Magid, "Sacred Real Estate," 27.

89. Fox, *An Introduction to Religion and Politic*, 2nd ed., 50–51.

90. Halbertal, "Religion and State, One and the Same."

91. Fox and Sandler, *Bringing Religion into International Relations*, 139.

92. Toft, Philpott, and Shah, *God's Century*, 4.

93. Wald and Shye, "Interreligious Conflict in Israel," 160.

94. Ma'oz, "A National or Religious Conflict?"

95. Juergensmeyer, *Terror in the Mind of God*, 213.

96. Malki, "Beyond Hamas and Fatah," 134.

97. Schenker, "Religion and the Conflict."

98. Snow, *Cases in International Relations*, 4th ed., 61, 62; Thomas Friedman, *The Lexus and the Olive Tree*, 31.

99. Dowty, *Israel/Palestine*, 3rd ed., 5.

100. Dajani Daoudi and Barakat, "Israelis and Palestinians," 57.

101. Israeli, "State and Religion in the Emerging Palestinian Entity," 232–233.

102. Schenker, "Religion and the Conflict," 129.

103. Fox and Sandler, "The Palestinian-Israeli Conflict," 137.

104. Kurth, "Religion and Ethnic Conflict."

105. Onapajo and Uzodike, "Boko Haram Terrorism in Nigeria," 26, 29.

106. Waltz, "Explaining War."

107. Campbell, *Nigeria*, 43.

108. Kendhanmer, *Muslims Talking Politics*, 2, 11, 17–23.

109. "Nigeria," in *Freedom in the World 2020*, Freedom House, www.freedom house.org/country/nigeria/freedom-world/2020.

110. Fine, *Political Violence in Judaism, Christianity, and Islam*, 39–40; Stein, "Competing Political Science Perspectives on the Role of Religion in Conflict," 23.

111. Stein, "Competing Political Science Perspectives on the Role of Religion in Conflict," 23.

112. Fine, *Political Violence in Judaism, Christianity, and Islam*, 39.

113. Sells, "Religion, History, and Genocide in Bosnia-Herzegovina," 41.

114. Fine, *Political Violence in Judaism, Christianity, and Islam*, 39.

115. Appleby, *The Ambivalence of the Sacred*, 7.

116. Faseke, "The Battle for Hearts and Minds," 45.

117. Mueller, "War Has Almost Ceased to Exist," 320.

118. Lind, "Defending Western Culture," 44.

119. Kissane, *Nations Torn Asunder*, 109–110, 160.

120. Campbell, *Nigeria*, 41.

121. Wooldridge, "God Is Back," 137.

122. Al-Rasheed and Shterin, *Dying for Faith*, xix, xvii.

123. Turner, *War and Peace*, 1.

124. Mason and Mitchell, *What Do We Know About Civil Wars?* 25.

125. Lounsbery and Pearson, *Civil Wars*, 45.

126. Fukuyama, "Religion as Identity Politics," 20.

127. Hurd, "International Politics After Secularism," 947.

9

Fostering Peace: Can Religion Help?

Illustration 15: Fighting Apartheid in South Africa

In 1984, Desmond Tutu was awarded the Nobel Peace Prize for his steadfast opposition to South Africa's apartheid regime. Tutu saw social justice as a spiritual and theological matter, and he saw prayer as one of the ways to struggle against the injustices of apartheid. "People of faith," he said, have a "religious duty" to stand up to injustice and oppression and to stand against the "evil of apartheid."[1] He found in his religious tradition "a theology of reconciliation."[2] As a church leader and a civil rights leader, he expressed his commitment to a nonviolent approach to ending apartheid and condemned all violence, whether committed by the government or by its opponents. He rejected both the government's imposition of apartheid by brute force and the opposition's resort to military struggle. The Nobel committee commended his "nonviolent path to liberation" and saluted "his clear views and his fearless stance, characteristics which had made him a unifying symbol for all African freedom fighters."[3] Winning the Nobel Prize helped to draw the world's attention to apartheid and to the struggle of the African National Congress (ANC) and others to overturn the system.

Later, however, Archbishop Tutu reluctantly accepted that the repressive nature of the South African state meant Christians might have to resort to a selective use of force. In a 1988 *New York Times* editorial, he wrote of the state's incitement and use of violence and he said he sympathized with South Africans who turned to violence, though he was sticking to a nonviolent approach. Regarding religion's role in violence, he once said, "I don't know any religion that promotes violence. It is the adherents of whatever religion."

Significance

As explained in Chapter 4, during the apartheid era in South Africa (1948–1994), whites, though in the minority, ruled the country. "Apartheid" has been loosely translated as meaning "apartness" or "separateness." It was a system of legalized segregation that split South Africa into races and tribes. Apartheid privileged the white minority while it denied social, political, and economic equality to the black majority. To ensure its hold on power, the government banned opposition groups (e.g., the African National Congress), forcing them underground, and jailed opposition leaders (e.g., Nelson Mandela and Steve Biko). Through conflicting interpretations of the Bible and Christian imperatives as well as through action and inaction, Christianity was bound up with apartheid.

Christian theology and churches were on both sides of the apartheid issue. On the side upholding the system, the ideology of Afrikaner nationalism provided the theoretical basis for apartheid, while the Dutch Reformed Church (DRC), the established church, provided the theological basis. The dominant church of Afrikaners, it was a powerful "influence in shaping the values, norms, and institutions of the Afrikaner Community." Whatever the source of Afrikaners' prejudices with regard to skin color and intermarriage, the church reinforced their ideas about group exclusiveness and apartness. The DRC developed an elaborate scriptural justification for maintaining strict racial separation, including the idea that God willed ethnic groups to retain their distinctiveness. Politically, the upshot was that the DRC delivered ethical and religious legitimization of Afrikaner nationalism. It propped up the National Party, which ruled South Africa from 1910 to 1994, and the government's apartheid policies. The DRC supplied the theological justification for the state's policy of apartheid. The Dutch Reformed Church began turning away from this stance in 1986.

Other Christian churches and church leaders rose in clear opposition to apartheid well before the DRC shifted its stance, with many launching a religious critique of state policy and judging the system irredeemably evil. Progressive "protest churches" became a central point of opposition to apartheid and in defense of equal human rights for all South Africans. They challenged apartheid on religious and moral grounds. With clear parallels to liberation theology in Latin America, "prophetic" or "black" theology identified salvation with liberation and called for an end of exploitation and oppression.[4] Christian theologians and church leaders produced the 1985 *Kairos* document, which provided a theological critique of the situation in South Africa at the time; critically analyzed churches' roles and challenged churches to take action against injustice and oppression; and rejected any theology that suggested there could be reconciliation without justice. The *Kairos* document also condemned so-called state theology, which lent religious legitimacy to the apartheid state. As one of the writers of the *Kairos* document said, the theology of the state buttressed the "repressive legal order" and legitimated it in the eyes of the Christian community.[5] The Christians who declared apartheid a heresy "were thinking politically about religion and religiously about politics," as though the two occupied one sphere of human activity, not two.[6]

By delegitimizing apartheid theology, apartheid's Christian opponents undermined support for the apartheid system and, with it, undercut the legitimacy of the white-minority government. The churches played another key role, too: since the government banned most black political organizations and exiled or imprisoned most secular antiapartheid leaders, churches were the only institutions in a position to confront the system that long prevailed in South Africa.

Illustration 16: The Pastor and the Imam

The violence that hit the Nigerian state of Kaduna in the 1980s reached a peak in 1992, when rioting led to the deaths of hundreds, both Muslims and Christians. Several churches were burned to the ground. The Zangon Kataf riot was precipitated by the relocation of a market. A key issue was which group had the right to regulate the market, the Kataf or the Hausas. The Kataf are a predominantly Christian ethnic group. The Hausas are mostly Muslim. In a country in which religion and ethnicity tend to coincide, the conflict acquired the character of a religious war, though it was more about politics and economics than religion (or ethnicity). This violence swept up two men, one a Christian leader and the other a Muslim leader.

The Christian leader was Pastor James Movel Wuye. In his earlier years, Pastor James was a feared Christian militia leader in Kaduna. Looking back, he said, "We carried pictures of those [of us] who'd been killed. We were martyrs: we felt that we were dying in defense of the Church."[7] The war, like the faith itself, became a struggle for liberation. He incited violence and, in 1992, lost an arm to a machete blow.

The Muslim leader was Imam Muhammad Nurayn Ashafa. In his earlier years, Imam Ashafa led a militia. His followers wielded machetes—including the one that lopped off Pastor James's arm—and Christians killed his uncle. Reflecting on this time, Ashafa said, "We planted the seed of genocide, and we used the scripture to do that."[8] When Christian militiamen killed his mentor in 1992, he wanted to avenge his death by killing Pastor James.

This story does not end there. Instead, after being moved by an imam's Friday sermon, Imam Ashafa forgave James. He approached the wary pastor and suggested they stop fighting. Like Ashafa, Pastor James was moved by words from a fellow cleric. In the mid-1990s, he shifted from a militia leader to a peace activist, becoming "one of the most prominent peace activists in Nigeria."[9] Imam Ashafa likewise became an outspoken peace activist. Years later, he stated, "Any religious group that kills in the name of religion is a fake—no religion that is divinely inspired sanctions or approves of the shedding of blood."[10] These two leaders pivoted from advocating fighting on behalf of their respective religions to fostering amity, from inciting violence to working for peace and tolerance, from killing in God's name to faith-inspired peacemaking.

Together, they founded and direct the Interfaith Mediation Centre, located in Kaduna. They try to quell disputes. They set up an early warning system so that, when there are rumors of violence, they can defuse the conflict before blood is shed. They train "religious youth leaders to be peacemakers," rather than conflict mongers. In 1999, they coauthored a book titled *The Pastor and the Imam: Responding to Conflict*. In 2003, the two faith leaders brought their respective religious communities together. When the workshop began, participants on each side blamed the other for the religious violence in Nigeria. The pastor and the imam employed both conflict resolution techniques and religious exhortations. They turned the tables, with the Christian leader making references to the Quran and the Muslim leader making reference to the Bible. Thus, they employed two key features of peacemaking: building mutual respect and finding or creating common ground. At the conclusion of the gathering, participants issued a joint statement that included seventeen recommendations, among them calls to pray for each other, love each other, and "shun religious bigotry in politics."[11]

Their faith-based work is important not only to Kaduna state or Nigeria. They have taken their call for interreligious dialogue and peacemaking on the road, traveling to other parts of Africa and beyond the continent. Their mediation efforts have received international support.

The two men share conservative moral values as well as exclusive understandings of salvation and considerable missionary zeal. Ashafa admits to proselytizing among Christians, saying, "I want James to die as a Muslim, and he wants me to die as a Christian. My Islam is proselytizing, it's about bringing the whole world to Islam."[12]

Significance

This illustration is significant for various reasons. First, as discussed in the previous chapter, a religious fault line runs through Nigeria—and many other states (Indonesia, Malaysia, the Philippines, Somalia, and Sudan) are similarly bisected by a geographic, ethnic, and religious divide along the tenth parallel. The northern half of Kaduna state is mostly Muslim, the southern half mostly Christian. Religious competition between adherents of these two religions is a highly significant political issue. In the north, Christians say they are discriminated against, while in the south Muslims say they are treated as second-class citizens. Competition between Muslims and Christians sometimes degenerates into political violence. In the 1990s, interreligious violence claimed more than 10,000 lives, with many of these deaths occurring in Kaduna.

Second, in northern Nigeria, religion is a "powerful source of identity," friction, and reconciliation.[13] Religion is not the only cause of conflict; ethnic differences, political and economic grievances, competition for power and territory, and issues of weak government and impunity figure in, too. However, it is often hard to disentangle the religious element from the others, since ethnic identity so often corresponds with religious affiliation that, in turn, overlaps with political and economic grievances. In addition, some militia groups play up religious divisions to mobilize followers. Following the 1992 riots, a Christian trader said, "It began as an ethnic dispute, but they turned it into a religious fight."[14]

This leads to a third point: there are differing interpretations of the 1992 riots and subsequent conflicts in Kaduna. Are they *religious* conflicts? The *New York Times* and other US newspapers labeled these events "religious riots." Supporting this position is the fact that, whatever the root causes of the conflict, Christians were on one side and Muslims on the other. Others say such conflicts are "ethno-political" and that "religion is only an incidental factor."[15]

A fourth point is that Imam Ashafa and Pastor James each remained committed to his own religion from the time he urged followers to raise up weapons to the time he called on to them to raise up prayers. What changed was each man's interpretation of what his religion required of him.

Two-Faced Religion

What are we to make of the examples discussed above? Regarding South Africa, the Center for Systemic Peace characterizes the political violence that occurred from 1983 to 1996 as an "ethnic/civil war" in which some 20,000 people died. According to the same source, in 2003, the year the pastor and the imam were bringing together their faith communities in northern Nigeria, the country was in the midst of ethnic violence (Christian-Muslim).

Looking beyond these cases, what is religion's impact on international life—a source of conflict or remedy for it? Douglas Johnston and Brian Cox make the case for both. They argue that religion is a powerful "double-edged sword": "It can cause conflict or it can abate it."[16] Religion can be a source of violent conflict or a source of social tolerance, democratic pluralism, and nonviolent conflict resolution.[17] It can feed conflict or, conversely, cooperation.

Chapter 8 discussed Northern Ireland's Troubles, which pit Catholics/ nationalists against Protestants/unionists. The picture is incomplete if it focuses only on the belligerence and violence of the two sides. Although churches have been criticized for inaction and complicity in the conflict, top religious leaders on both sides condemned sectarian violence. Scott Appleby states, "Having acknowledged that they were part of the problem, most of the churches of Northern Ireland gradually came to see themselves as part of the solution. The end of sectarianism begins with the 'sects.'"[18] The picture becomes more complete—and more complex—when religion's role in sowing and hardening divisions, on the one hand, and pushing forgiveness and reconciliation, on the other, are brought into view.

George Weigel writes that the *un*secularization of the world (i.e., the religious resurgence) has "complexified" the matters of religion, peace, and conflict. Two pieces offer good insights into this complex matter: *The Ambivalence of the Sacred* by Scott Appleby and "The Janus Face of Religion: On the Religious Factor in 'New Wars'" by Heinrich Schäfer. The fact that co-religionists may disagree as to whether they should embrace pacifism, militarism, or just war is further evidence of the ambiguous relationship between religion and violence.

Ambivalent, Janus-Faced Religion

Appleby writes about the ambivalence, or flexibility, of the sacred. Religion, he says, carries contradictory impulses. Religion has the ability to convey the seeds of peace as well as violence; in fact, within the same religion, some bear ploughshares and others the sword. This ambivalence has to do with the relationship between an infinite God and "contingent" (or limited) human beings, who struggle to comprehend the holy and to put "the 'mind of God' into human action."[19] Human beings study religious texts and traditions and come up with multiple, even contradictory, interpretations of what to believe and what to do.

Appleby emphasizes the tension within what he calls "militant religion." Militant religion is manifested in very different ways. On the one hand are religious peacemakers—that is, "militants for peace." Religious peacemakers renounce violence and try to limit its frequency and scope. They preach forgiveness. They may engage in "religiously inspired healing" and express inclusivist and pluralist understandings of religion. This impulse inspires pacifists. They can "channel militant energies into coalition building and peacemaking."[20] On the other hand are what Appleby calls religious "extremists." Extremists exalt violence, especially as a means to purify the community or to vanquish the enemy. They may be "holy warriors," who engage in acts of ritualized hatred or who preach revenge, retaliation, and an intolerant brand of faith. These self-styled true believers may see violence as a sacred duty. Appleby offers the Taliban and their exclusivist understanding of Islam as an example. Today we could point to the Islamic State as well. The problem, according to Appleby, is not religion, but extremism. Both peacemakers and extremists are passionate and claim they are seeking justice. Both are also "radicals" in the original sense of this word; they are going back to the fundamentals, or roots, of their religion.

Authentic responses to the sacred take very different forms, in part due to the complexity and internal pluralism of religious traditions. Thus, the "same texts and practices that have inspired some to extraordinary acts of love and compassion have provoked others to senseless violence."[21] Much as the Christian Bible is open to interpretation, so is Islamic law. What believers take as hallowed religious traditions in fact interact with other traditions, outsiders, and the external environment. Religions are not unchanging, ahistorical entities. Moreover, a religious tradition can inspire very different political agendas and quite different views of the right social order. Consider the South African case. It demonstrates that religion can uphold a conservative agenda or support a progressive take on the social order—and interpretations of a religion such as Christianity can change.

Given the "ambivalence of the sacred," much depends on religious leaders, again reminding us of the importance of the individual. In a given time and place, prophets, priests, pastors, rabbis, and imams deem certain things as permitted or forbidden. For instance, most Israeli rabbis do not condone violence, but a small group of extremists does. Certainly, the example of the imam and the pastor in Nigeria fit here, too. Those two religious leaders shifted from participating in violence to working together to end it.

A variation on Appleby's theme is Heinrich Schäfer's notion of the "Janus Face of Religion." The Roman god Janus is represented as a god with two faces, one looking one direction and the other looking in the opposite direction. Religion is "Janus-faced" in that "every religion can be a base for respect *and* for violence."[22] Religion has the ability "to solve problems as well as create them," to spark conflict as well as to transform it.[23] The three monotheistic "cousins"—Christianity, Islam, and Judaism—all have "sacred scriptures, histories and traditions [that] include both peace and violence."[24]

We see these two sides in the former Yugoslavia. The conflicts of the 1990s have been called religious wars, though, as explained in Chapter 7, religion was just one of the elements that contributed to the violence. Belligerents had different religious identities. It was not a religious conflict, but the religionization of politics; it was not fought over territory and political power, but politics and political issues were couched within a religious context. Serb and Croatian leaders had nationalist agendas. Serbia was "the architect of the Yugoslav breakup and the biggest perpetrator of wartime atrocities."[25] The Serbian Orthodox Church abetted Slobodan Milošević's manipulation of religious symbols and the Kosovo myth to augment his power and build his nationalist movement. It also helped spread an exclusionary Serbian identity, an identity steeped in the conviction that Serbs are victims. In 1993, while the conflict was still raging, the United Nations established an ad hoc court called the International Criminal Tribunal for the former Yugoslavia (ICTY). Serbia was obligated to arrest war crimes suspects and turn them over to the ICTY. Putting Serbs on trial suggests that Serbs were perpetrators, not victims, of atrocities. Some Orthodox clergy have defended those accused of war crimes. (After the conflict, the Serbian government did comply with the court, handing over Milošević and other suspects, including Radovan Karadzic.) "In comparison to the other two major religious communities," Catholic and

Muslim, the Serbian Orthodox Church has been deemed the most damaging.[26] The other two religious communities are also implicated, however. Some Catholic, Orthodox, and Muslim clerics played into extremists' hands, by remaining silent or actively supporting the use of religion and religious symbolism to further political projects.

Some clerics reversed course and others resisted extremism from the beginning, showing the potential for religion to serve as a check on violence. In 2012, the Sant'Egidio movement (discussed below) brought together Catholic, Orthodox, and Muslim leaders, who "reaffirmed their belief in peace and reconciliation."[27]

A Global Face

The United Nations is the preeminent global forum, and both secular and faith-based nongovernmental organizations have been active in the UN since its founding. Religious organizations are among the thousands of nongovernmental organizations with consultative status in the UN system, most of which (more than 5,000) are registered with the UN Economic and Social Council (ECOSOC). Representing many of the world's religions, they include B'nai B'rith International, the Consultative Council of Jewish Organizations, Religions for Peace, the World Council of Churches (WCC), the World Fellowship of Buddhists, the World Jewish Congress, the World Muslim Congress, the World Muslim League, and the Quaker United Nations Office. The Committee of Religious NGOs at the United Nations describes itself as "a coalition of representatives of religious, spiritual and ethical nongovernmental organizations who exchange varying points of view and are dedicated to the pursuit of peace, understanding and mutual respect."[28]

The UN Economic and Social Council is one of the UN's six main organs. Its purview includes economic, social, environmental, and health issues. The NGOs that have been granted consultative status in ECOSOC are engaged in activities related to development and humanitarian aid. Religion motivates and inspires their work.[29]

Religion also inspires many religious communities and religious leaders to address contemporary global challenges, such as alleviating poverty and avoiding violent conflict. Three initiatives for a new millennium are discussed below. All addressed important global challenges at the start of the twenty-first century.

The Jubilee 2000 campaign combined secular and religious appeals to further its goal of alleviating the debt burden of countries that were both poor and heavily indebted. The campaign's name refers to an exhortation in the Hebrew bible (i.e., the Old Testament, a sacred text for Judaism and Christianity) to wipe the slate clean during the "jubilee year." Every fifty years came a time to rest, cancel debts, and free slaves. The Jubilee 2000 movement called for canceling the external debts of the world's poorest countries by the year 2000, the start of the new millennium. The idea was that big creditors, such as the United States and the World Bank, would write off the debts of highly indebted poor countries (HIPC). Many considered these onerous, unpayable, and a hindrance to economic development and poverty reduction. This initiative was championed by an informal transnational network of progressive religious organizations, political leaders, civic groups, development NGOs, student activists, and rock stars. (Recall Chapter 6, where one rock star, Bono, made Senator Helms cry.) The network, which arose to solve a particular global issue, achieved its goal and then dissolved, as planned. It has been hailed as an unusually successful global campaign. In 1996, the World Bank, the International Monetary Fund, and creditor governments created the HIPC Initiative to provide debt relief.

Not only does the Jubilee 2000 campaign point to the importance of religion in world politics, but it is indicative of why religious organizations have become recognized as "legitimate actors in the field of development and humanitarian aid."[30] Another big reason for such recognition is that religious organizations do not simply advocate for development and humanitarian aid, but in many instances they also provide it. This aid comes directly from religious organizations or, alternatively, it comes from IGOs like the World Bank or from state members of the Organization for Economic Cooperation and Development (OECD), which includes some of the world's wealthiest states. In the latter case, religious (and secular) nongovernmental organizations serve as conduits of aid where they are already on the ground or established in local communities.

Like Jubilee 2000, the Millennium Development Goals (MDGs) bring together development themes and the start of a new millennium. In 2000, nearly all independent states agreed to eight Millennium Development Goals with the promise that each and every goal would be met by 2015. The secretary general of the World Conference of Religions for Peace called cooperation among the world's religions crucial to this effort. Religions for Peace developed an "action toolkit" entitled "Faith in Action" for advancing multi-religious action and for ending poverty.[31]

In 2016, the Sustainable Development Goals (SDGs) came into effect, picking up where the MDGs left off. Some see faith-based organizations as crucial to the attainment of this new and expanded set of goals.

The Millennium World Peace Summit also played off the idea of the start of the twenty-first century as a pivotal time. In 2000, a thousand religious and spiritual leaders from around the world gathered at the United Nations headquarters in New York to consider ways that religion can help prevent wars. These leaders also sought to increase cooperation among religions. One of the summit's stated goals was to create the World Council of Religious Leaders to work with the United Nations to foster peace and work toward the resolution of global problems. This council remains active.

Peacemaking and Reconciliation

Religion and faith-based peacemaking and reconciliation are clearly important when a conflict is about religion or when religious elements of a conflict are hard to disentangle from other elements (as in many conflicts in sub-Saharan Africa), but they can also play an important role when a conflict has nothing to do with religion. Religion and faith-based diplomacy had a hand in bringing reconciliation to post-apartheid South Africa. They could help to bring about a "peaceful solution to Iran's nuclear challenge." Religious scholars from different religions could join with ethicists, government officials, and so on "to discuss ethical constraints on nuclear weapons."[32] Here, the focus is on efforts by individuals and faith-based organizations to end conflicts by mediating between parties and to nurture postconflict reconciliation.

Faith-Based Diplomacy

Diplomacy, the conduct of official relations between or among states, can follow one of two basic tracks. "Track I" is traditional diplomacy through official channels, such as states' leaders, foreign ministers, and ambassadors, who talk and engage in formal political negotiations—dialogue, bargaining, and defending states' national interests. This track is grounded in the Westphalian idea that states have "legitimate and authoritative control over war and violence in international relations" and, thus, states are the "key to war or peace."[33] Track I diplomacy is a game of states and intergovernmental organizations (IGOs), such as the United Nations. "Track One Diplomacy is usually considered to be the primary peacemaking tool of a state's foreign policy."[34] Former US secretary of state Madeleine Albright explained that "diplomats use everything from reason and logic to the threat of military force to achieve their ends" and, typically, religion is not a consideration.[35] This track thus has a history of discounting religious factors and actors, even when taking them into account may be crucial to bringing in all the relevant players and finding lasting solutions to problems. Hence, Douglas Johnston and Cynthia Sampson's book is entitled *Religion, the Missing Dimension of Statecraft.*

Faith-based diplomacy enters through the gate of multitrack diplomacy. These other tracks typically complement official, state-based Track I efforts. "Track II" is informal, unofficial, behind the scenes diplomacy, involving people other than states' diplomats (i.e., people who are not states' formal representatives), including a variety of non-state actors: nongovernmental organizations, the business community, activists, religious organizations, and so on. Papal diplomacy is but one example. Track II diplomacy happens outside of official, state channels. Such diplomacy is informal in that an integral part is off-the-record and behind-the-scenes interactions. "'Track II' diplomacy grew out of the observation that private individuals, meeting unofficially, can find their way to common ground that official negotiators can't."[36]

Religion-inspired peacemaking expands the role of faith and religion into the existing tools of statecraft. Faith-based diplomacy (or "soulcraft") not only brings religious actors into the process, but draws on the unique factors and virtues that they bring to the table.

The first factor is motives. Faith-based diplomats are propelled by faith, ethics, and religious norms, rather than interests. "Religion . . . has the power to make people do things that transcend self-interest."[37] This holds for faith-based diplomats and, because of this, they may be accepted as good, "neutral" mediators or apolitical forces for change. In the case of South Africa, for instance, religious institutions and leaders served as ethical brokers.[38] Faith-based diplomats act beyond the confines of their own interests, but they are also well-positioned to bring warring parties to do things that transcend their immediate self-interests.

Second, faith-inspired diplomats and peacemakers have contacts and forms of influence that states' official diplomats do not. They might bring "familiarity with local situations and close contacts with grass roots movements" as well as local governments.[39] With this comes an understanding of the social, cultural, and religious traditions of the communities involved. They know about local needs, histories, and grievances. Often, they have grassroots ties and are well-established in the community. Certainly, local religious leaders, such as the pastor and the imam discussed early in the chapter, bring familiarity and influence to the table.

Third, they bring authority, legitimacy, and leadership to the table. Religious peacemakers may have unique authority and leverage to reconcile conflicting parties. In many communities around the world, religious actors have unmatched authority, including spiritual and moral authority, which gives them a unique capacity to garner support for a peace process.. This authority can also legitimize or delegitimize violence in contexts as different as those in Nigeria and Yugoslavia. Faith-inspired peacemakers are either indigenous to the community or have been there a fairly long time, so they seem committed to the community's well-being. Religious identities give religious peacemakers unique stature in communities and the credibility to lead.[40]

Fourth, they have religious resources. Although faith-based diplomats can use "secular" peacemaking methods, they can also call on religion, religious concepts, and religious identity for motivation and as practical tools. Faith-based diplomacy brings in the faith of the diplomats as well as the parties to a conflict. Since "moral warrants for peacemaking exist in the theologies of all major world religions," this type of diplomacy brings in theologies as well as sacred texts and religious traditions.[41] In addition to drawing on religious symbols and practices, prayer may be an element of a diplomatic initiative.

Fifth, forgiveness and transformation may be incorporated. Transformation includes changing negative attitudes and moving away from negative images of the other. For Scott Thomas, it refers to "the way people in conflict can be transformed by their relationships with God and so transform their relationships with others in their community."[42] Forgiveness is closely associated with some religious traditions, but not usually part of political vocabularies. It was, however, part of Archbishop Desmond Tutu's vocabulary at a time when apartheid was ending in South Africa and people were looking for a way forward. He wrote a book entitled *No Future Without Forgiveness*. Tutu later wrote that forgiveness and reconciliation are not "namby-pamby," but the "stuff of *realpolitik*" (i.e., based on realistic, practical politics and closely associated with the realist paradigm).[43] Two religious leaders in Nigeria, the pastor and the imam, found justification within their respective religious traditions for fighting each other and, later, felt called by their faith to forgive each other. Transformation, forgiveness, healing—these elements are alien to Track I diplomacy.

Religion played a beneficial role in twentieth-century conflicts in the Balkans, Northern Ireland, and South Africa by encouraging reconciliation between former enemies and helping them arrive at political solutions.[44] As these examples suggest, religion can be utilized either to stir up old hatreds and deepen divisions or to get people to forgive and, perhaps, forget.

A growing number of organizations are turning to faith-based, Track II diplomacy. Some are not explicitly tied to a particular religion. An example is the US-based International Center for Religion and Diplomacy (ICRD), which has helped to broker deals in Afghanistan, Kashmir, Sudan, and elsewhere. Some are interfaith, such as the Interfaith Mediation Centre in Nigeria, discussed above. Some are tied to one particular religion, such as the Sant'Egidio community, discussed below, and a number of Muslim organizations. Muslim peacebuilding actors are active on the local, national, regional, and international levels, but are generally not well institutionalized.

Sant'Egidio

The Sant'Egidio community is a transnational Roman Catholic fellowship (an association of laypeople, as opposed to clergy) encompassing over 50,000 members and operating in some seventy countries. Sant'Egidio brings to the table neutrality, impartiality, and grassroots knowledge of situations.[45] Most of its efforts focus on "non-religious" conflicts.[46] The authors of *God's Century* identify it as a key example of the "global outbreak of religious initiatives for peace." This nongovernmental organization established an international outreach in the 1970s and, since then, it has played a "direct and crucial role" in various peace efforts around the world.[47] It helps bring warring parties together and broker deals in places like Algeria, Kosovo, Guatemala, and Sierra Leone.

In the African country of Mozambique, Sant'Egidio was important to forging a peace agreement in 1992. What did Sant'Egidio do? It engaged in Track II "citizen" diplomacy and brought the parties together in almost a dozen rounds of peace negotiations over many months' time. The result: the General Peace Accord signed on October 4, 1992, ending sixteen years of civil war (1977–1992) that had left some 1 million people dead. The civil war arose shortly after colonial rule ended in 1974. The new government of Mozambique supported black guerrillas that opposed white-minority rule in South Africa and Rhodesia (now Zimbabwe). The South African and Rhodesian governments, in turn, sponsored the Mozambican National Resistance (RENAMO), an insurgency that fought the Mozambican government.

Sant'Egidio's keys to success in places like Mozambique tie in with the main arguments of the book *God's Century*, which proclaims the twenty-first century is "God's Century." One line of argument in *God's Century* concerns the relationship between religious and political authority, in particular whether these authorities are integrated or independent of one and other. Broadly speaking, independence is a crucial ingredient of moral authority and in turn, of gaining trust and prestige. An independent actor is not perceived as connected to state authority or holding a partisan position. Sant'Egidio is an "institutionally independent actor"; it has "no formal ties to a state," few formal ties with the disputing parties, and no stake in political and economic power or the issues at hand. In Mozambique, Sant'Egidio's efforts succeeded because both sides perceived it as impartial with no agenda or interest except to end the violent conflict and promote peace. According to the authors of *God's Century*, it was Sant'Egidio's lack of official state or UN authority that made Mozambique's government more willing to sit down with the militant organization RENAMO, which it considered "rogue bandits." The NGO did, however, work with the United Nations and the governments of ten states. And it continued working after the peace accord was signed.[48]

The other line of argument in *God's Century* concerns political theology, which is a religious community's ideas about political authority and justice. It comes out of reflections on religious texts and traditions as well as changing circumstances. Sant'Egidio's political theology is rooted in the Second Vatican Council and the community's interpretation of the New Testament. Sant'Egidio's political theology promotes dialogue, peace, and social justice through outreach to the poor, reconciliation, and building relationships.

According to *God's Century*, "Religious actors mediate best when they keep a distance from both state authority and armed opposition groups, and when they carry a political theology that stresses peace and social justice."[49] That describes Sant'Egidio.

Religious actors can promote peace and cooperation. Conversely, as explained in the previous chapter, they can promote conflicts and violence. This, in a nutshell, is the ambivalence of the sacred. The next section shines a different light on this discussion. Depending on the context and the religion itself, religious organizations, leaders, and believers may invoke pacifism, holy war, or the just war tradition.

Pacifism, Holy War, Just War

On August 2, 1990, Iraq invaded the neighboring state of Kuwait. Within four days the United Nations Security Council approved worldwide economic sanctions against Iraq. Later that month, the Security Council authorized the use of force to carry out the sanctions it had approved. Between that time and January 16, 1991, when a US-led coalition initiated military action to drive Iraq out of Kuwait, Americans had an unusual debate. The debate centered on the question of whether the United States should take decisive military action against Iraq in early 1991 or wait for sanctions and diplomacy to work. The national debate was peppered with questions about the nature of the US approach. Would it be militarist or pacifist? Could this war against Iraq be a "just war"?

The just war tradition is a long-standing moral framework for appraising the use of large-scale lethal force. It injects moral decisionmaking and accountability into the larger decisionmaking process. The central purpose of the just war framework is to limit and restrain entry into, and the conduct of, war. It shares with international law and the UN charter a strong presumption against military intervention in other states, but acknowledges that moral imperatives may trump the norm of nonintervention. It is not a peace-at-any-cost stance—war is sometimes necessary, especially to defend people under attack. War may be justified as a necessary evil, but to do so it must meet certain criteria.

These criteria fall into two groups, known by the Latin terms *jus ad bellum* and *jus in bello*, referring to the right or the laws governing going to war and conducting a war. The first set of criteria (*jus ad bellum*) are used to determine whether recourse to war is justified. To be justified, a war must be fought for a just cause, the clearest of which is as a response to unjust aggression or an attack. In addition, just, peaceful ends must be sought. The intention must be to promote the good, such as rolling back aggressors and deterring future aggression. A third criterion is "last resort." All alternatives to armed force—diplomatic negotiations, economic sanctions, and so on—must be tried before going to war. The war must be declared by a political authority, someone with responsibility for the public good. The idea is to protect against the arbitrary use of force by limiting those who can call for it. Finally, there must be a reasonable hope of success in war. This is a "counsel of prudence."[50] If there is not a good chance of success, it is a suicide mission, not a prudent action.

The second set of criteria (*jus in bello*) concern right, or just, conduct during a war. A just war cannot be pursued by unjust means. Two rules apply here: proportionality and discrimination. The former is the idea that, to be just, an armed response must be proportional to the evil that has been inflicted and to the goals sought. War always involves suffering and destruction, but these bad effects cannot outweigh the good to be achieved from engaging in war. "Discrimination" is about noncombatant immunity. A distinction must be drawn between combatants and noncombatants. Combatants are fair game in war. Noncombatants, however, are considered "innocents" who do not pose a threat and should not be harmed—or, at least, they should not be targeted or hurt intentionally.

In their struggle against apartheid in South Africa, two prestigious church leaders disagreed on methods. Alan Boesak, president of the World Alliance of Reformed Churches (WARC), advocated a "prophetic—and selectively violent"—approach, loosely along the lines of just war theory.[51] Desmond Tutu, an Anglican bishop and president of the South African Council of Churches (SACC), embraced a pacifist stance.

Pacifism is an approach that relies on nonviolence and diplomacy to resolve conflicts. For pacifists, nonviolence is a matter of principle; they have a strong presumption against the use of force on human beings and, therefore, may be troubled by the monopoly on the use of force that is part and parcel of the modern state. Pacifism presumes that the costs of force are always too high, and war, by definition, is unjust. Mahatma Gandhi once said, "I oppose all violence because the good it does is always temporary but the harm it does is permanent." "Absolute" or hardline pacifists say violence is always wrong, irrational, inhumane, and illegitimate. "Pragmatic" pacifists are "willing to accept some limited use of force for self-defense or to uphold justice and protect the innocent."[52] In general, pacifists advocate nonviolent means to resist, resolve conflicts, advance political aims, and address the underlying causes of conflict. These means include diplomacy and economic sanctions—and perhaps loving one's enemy.

The pacifist stance is closely associated with Buddhism and Christian "peace churches" (e.g., Quakers) as well as twentieth-century movements to disarm or denuclearize the world. In fact, though, all major religions encourage reverence for life and discourage taking a human life.

In some ways, the third approach, militarism, is the antithesis of pacifism. Unlike pacifism, there is no moral presumption against military force.

Militarism can refer to a few different things. One is an excessive reliance on the military in pursuing a state's political and economic goals. A second is seeing war as a goal in and of itself, not merely the means to an end. A third concerns the militarization of civil society, with the military exercising excessive influence and offering the best model for how to mobilize and organize society. Fascist Germany's use of its military to pursue its goals aggressively, combined with glorification of war and the martial spirit, make it a clear example of militarism. In the African and Latin American contexts, militarism is used to describe military intervention in domestic politics and excessive reliance on the military to solve political problems, perhaps acquiring the reins of states power through a coup d'etat.

The religious brand of militarism is found in holy wars, crusades, and jihad. It "marries religion and the military,"[53] as one author phrases it, and glorifies unrestrained war against the enemy. Judaism, Christianity, and Islam all have a holy war or crusading element. Holy war is prosecuted as a religious duty, encouraging the unrestricted use of force in God's service. When people believe that God is not only on their side, but on the side of using lethal force to fulfill some divine purpose, they respond to the battle cry with zealous devotion. Although most of the West now rejects the kind of tight interweaving of religion and politics that gives rise to a crusading mentality, after the 9/11 attacks President Bush called for a "crusade" against a new kind of evil, terrorism. For some Muslims, this evoked the history of the crusading Christian knights of the Middle Ages who repeatedly attacked Muslims to wrest control of Jerusalem from them; from this perspective, President Bush's "crusade" was not really against terrorism, but a war of Christians and the West against Islam. It appears that this was a poor choice of words on President Bush's part, rather than a call to holy war. Others have, however, called for holy war. When Iraqi tanks drove into Kuwait in 1990, "Saddam declared the invasion of Kuwait a great jihad or holy war."[54] In a 1998 manifesto, Osama bin Laden declared war against the "Jews and the Crusaders." Ayatollah Ali Khamenei, Iran's spiritual guide, has called for an anti-American jihad. This concerns a narrow definition of jihad.

Jihad means struggle, effort, striving, or "fighting in the path of God"—which generally does not involve the use of force. The "lesser jihad" involves armed struggle or striving in the path of God via the "sword," perhaps fighting against Islam's enemies. So, while many in the West equate jihad with holy war, that is at best a partial understanding of the term.

As explained in Chapter 6, Abu Bakr al-Baghdadi was the leader of the Islamic State and a self-proclaimed caliph; as caliph, his duties included forcefully expanding the area controlled by the caliphate through "offensive jihad." Offensive jihad is a form of lesser jihad that, as the name suggests, goes beyond defending Islam or the geographical boundaries of the Muslim community against acts of aggression. It is a "jihad of conquest" that may be used to justify physical aggression against non-Muslims. The Islamic State goes beyond this, engaging in acts that seem to glorify violence. Offensive jihad is associated with extremist elements within Islamism. Sayyid Qutb, an important theorist of Islamism, saw it as a means to spread Islam. Offensive jihad ties in with the expansionist nature of a caliphate and the ambition to bring all to Islam or Islamic rule, tightly linking the political and the religious.

Together, pacifism, just war, and militarism are three traditional Christian approaches to war. However, Christian and secular tenets of just war are the same. Further, pacifist and militarist views are found in other religious traditions as well. Most major religious traditions have developed what is known as "principled nonviolence." Buddhism, while strong on pacifism, has neither a holy war nor a just war tradition. In recent years, Buddhist monks in Asia have turned militant, playing a role in intercommunal conflicts. Religion is thus a "double-edged sword"; it can inspire calls to the most unforgiving forms of armed conflict or it can encourage peaceful resolution of conflict.[55]

In Theory

Theories of international relations help us to make sense of the blizzard of information and events in the world around us. They can help us to raise the right kinds of questions, tease out the implications of the answers we find, uncover weaknesses in arguments, and bring underlying assumptions out into the light of day.

IR Paradigms

Despite the news headlines, world politics is much more than problems, threats, and conflicts. It is also about advances, conciliatory gestures, peacemaking, and reconciliation.

Realists would be a bit skeptical of this proposition. Going back to Thomas Hobbes, from his book *Leviathan*, we come away with the idea that jealousies lead individuals to be on guard, like gladiators, striking postures of war. The picture is an ongoing state of war because, with humans governed by their passions and power struggles, conflict is always possible. Coercive power—exercised by a great Leviathan-like monster (Hobbes's vision of a powerful state)—must be employed to restrain people, so they have to keep promises of peaceful coexistence, rather than acting on their baser instincts. Now move from the individual to the international level. No Leviathan exists in world politics. "There is no government standing above nation-states to guarantee their safety, their security, or their survival."[56] States are sovereign. States' national interests diverge. States compete for power and security. The result is that, with no supranational authority, each state pursues its national interests in ways that lead to competition and, quite possibly, conflict. Cooperation is possible, but hindered by anarchy and the competitive nature of world politics. So states strike the postures of gladiators, and conflict is more likely than cooperation and peaceful coexistence.

From the liberal standpoint, however, compromise and cooperation can be the hallmarks of the international order. Indeed, when it comes to matters of peacemaking and reconciliation, this is largely a liberal game. Critics label liberals "idealists" or even "utopians" because of their optimism with regard to human nature and the potential for peace and harmony among individuals, within states, and on the international level. The liberal idea of a "democratic peace," however, has good evidence to support it. Well-established democracies (not newly formed states or states transitioning from an authoritarian regime to a democratic one) do not go to war with one another. These consolidated democracies do not always agree, but they resolve their disputes with words, not guns.

At the core of liberalism is the promise that progress is possible and that democracy, global trade, and international institutions will strengthen peace. Immanuel Kant's ideas inform liberal notions that a community of democratic states would make for a more peaceful world. In his eighteenth-century treatise, *Perpetual Peace*, he said that "peace among nation-states is best maintained through an informal federation of republican regimes." Today's liberals thus hope that more states will move from the "authoritarian" to the "democratic" column and that democratic norms will spread. With regard to global trade, the argument is that global economic ties will tamp conflictive impulses because states will hurt themselves if they fight their trade partners. International institutions take the edge off anarchy and provide forums for ongoing discussions, curbing conflict, and encouraging peace and reconciliation. Democracy, interdependence, and internationalism—these will go a long way toward tipping the balance toward peace.

For constructivists, the keys to understanding international relations are ideas, beliefs, values, identities, and images, all of which are constructed and inform states' interests. Whether states' relationships are cooperative and peaceful or conflictive depends on their values, views, ideas, elite beliefs, and images of each other. Prevailing beliefs about norms—how states should behave—are very significant, too. These factors shape international political realities.

US-China relations serve as an example here. The United States is the world's most powerful state. China is quickly climbing the rungs of world power. How US foreign policy makers view China's rise is not a given. The image of China as competitor can evoke very different policy responses than seeing China as an enemy.

It is worth bringing in two "critical" or "dissident" perspectives on world politics: Marxism and feminism. These approaches to international relations have a couple of elements in common. One is the understanding that there are well-entrenched hierarchies in place and this needs to change. Another is that both are self-consciously emancipatory, meaning they seek to end inequalities and injustices.[57] These inequalities and injustices, which reflect the prevailing hierarchies, provoke tensions and conflict in the world.

Marxism (as discussed earlier in the book) uses class as its primary lens, focusing on the struggle between the "haves" and "have-nots." State policies are made by and for the "haves," the ruling classes, and come at the expense of the "have-nots." On the international level, the former colonial powers more or less function as a ruling class (the "haves"), while the former colonial states in Africa, Asia, and Latin America are held down (the "have-nots"). International institutions like the United Nations and the World Bank serve the interests of the rich and powerful states. For Marxists, the "world's distribution of resources is fundamentally unfair" and exploitative.[58] For enduring peace, there must be social justice and emancipation.

Feminism uses gender as the primary lens for viewing relations at all three levels of analysis. For feminists, gender matters. "Gender" refers to the social and cultural meanings attached to biological differences. Feminists take gender as constructed. The state is an expression of patriarchal power; there are entrenched patterns of male dominance. World politics is likewise marked by patriarchy, which results in a bias toward masculine behaviors and values. World politics is conflictual. This conflict is due to the "superior-subordinate nature of gender relationships" (i.e., gendered hierarchies).[59] Feminism reveals the masculine biases of realism, liberalism, and Marxism, all of which are silent on issues of gender. For feminists, a key question is: where are the women? Any photograph of world leaders certainly gives the impression that world politics is a man's world.

Levels of Analysis

Peacemaking and reconciliation involve actors at all three levels of analysis. Consider once again the example of South Africa, which is now counted among the world's most important emerging countries, known collectively as the BRICS (Brazil, Russia, India, China, and South Africa).

During the apartheid era, it occupied a different place on the world stage, especially once the concerted effort to end apartheid began.

At the international level, state and nonstate actors were involved in this effort, censuring the South African regime and trying to isolate it. However, state involvement goes back to well before apartheid began; it goes back to the imposition of foreign rule centuries ago and, with it, the importation of a new religion, Christianity.

Intergovernmental organizations got involved in the anti-apartheid effort by condemning apartheid and excluding the regime from engagement in important IGOs. The United Nations, for instance, condemned the regime's racist system repeatedly. The General Assembly's first anti-apartheid resolution dates back to 1962, when it called apartheid a threat to international peace and security. A 1973 resolution labeled apartheid a "crime against humanity." In 1974, South Africa's membership in the UN General Assembly was suspended. In 1977, the UN Security Council imposed a total arms embargo on South Africa to encourage political reform. The European Community (precursor to the European Union) imposed limited trade and financial sanctions. Intergovernmental and nongovernmental organizations also endeavored to isolate South Africa in other areas of international life. As early as the 1950s, a "sports boycott" began, international sports associations—most notably, the Federation of International Football Associations (FIFA), and the International Olympic Committee (IOC)—began suspending South African teams from membership and excluding them from participation.

In the latter part of the twentieth century, as apartheid became an increasingly contentious issue, various states imposed punitive sanctions in an effort to force the South African government to change its domestic policies. The logic behind economic sanctions is that they inflict economic hardships, which hurt the regime directly and also increases citizen pressure on the regime, leading to changes in the regime's policy or conduct. (Sanctions' ability to achieve this goal remains an open question.) Pressure from the United States and the United Kingdom was particularly important. In the 1980s, the US government enacted the Comprehensive Anti-Apartheid Act, while shareholders pressured US-based transnational corporations to withdraw from their operations in South Africa. Many US universities and colleges had endowment funds invested in South Africa, and students on some campuses pushed them to divest with the idea that pulling out investments would hurt the South African government and move it to end apartheid. "By 1988, a total of 155 colleges had at least partially divested."[60] The United Kingdom also took steps to force the South African government to negotiate with its opponents, though Prime Minister Margaret Thatcher—much like President Ronald Reagan in the United States—was reluctant to impose sanctions. The South African government was highly reliant on foreign capital; as such, the ultimate success of the British anti-apartheid campaign in getting British banks out of South Africa dealt a financial blow to the apartheid regime. Front-line states (Angola, Botswana, Mozambique, Tanzania, Zambia, and Zimbabwe) called for comprehensive sanctions by Western countries.

Other states expressed disapproval and sought to isolate the South African regime politically, by severing diplomatic ties. Most newly independent African states refused to establish diplomatic ties with the regime.

Nongovernmental organizations in the form of transnational religious actors (TRAs) were also involved in the anti-apartheid campaign. Since some 80 percent of South Africans are Christians, Christian organizations are particularly relevant here. The broadest Christian body, the World Council of Churches, determined that apartheid had to be confronted, and it funded black liberation movements in South Africa and the neighboring state of Rhodesia, now Zimbabwe.[61] In 1982, the World Alliance of Reformed Churches declared apartheid a sin and "heresy" and severed ties with the churches that upheld apartheid. The Roman Catholic Church also condemned apartheid. However, the Christian League of Southern Africa, which included the Dutch Reformed Church among its members, supported apartheid and used religious grounds to justify it.

On the state level, factors internal to South Africa also played a pivotal role. These include political organizations, most importantly the ruling National Party and the two main organizations trying to end apartheid, the African National Congress (ANC) and the Pan-African Congress (PAC). Religious organizations, as has been discussed, were likewise on both sides of the issue. The DRC supported the regime. On the other side, many credit the South African Council of Churches, led by Desmond Tutu, with bringing a prophetic voice to the apartheid issue.

On the individual level, Desmond Tutu, Nelson Mandela, Steve Biko, and Frederik Willem de Klerk (the last leader of the apartheid regime) are among the most important figures in South Africa. However, other individuals—such as leaders of some states, IGOs, and NGOs—were important, too.

The analytical framework in Table 9.1 takes as examples the illustrations from Nigeria and South Africa discussed in the chapter's first pages.

Table 9.1 Analytical Framework: Examples from South Africa and Nigeria

Levels of Analysis	Realism	Liberalism	Constructivism
International/ Systemic	*South Africa:* South Africa's strategic location and rich resources make it geopolitically important. Under President Reagan, the US government saw the South African regime as anti-communist, pro-West, and a vital Cold War ally. Friendly relations with the South African government thus served US economic and security interests.	*South Africa:* Economic inter-dependence, including substantial investments by the United Kingdom and the United States, help explain why the United States and United Kingdom wanted to avoid conflictual relations with South Africa.	*South Africa:* This example demonstrates how international norms and understandings of what is acceptable state behavior can change over time. Segregating races and subjugating one to another, while long a part of human history, violates today's norms.
Domestic/State	*South Africa:* As all sovereign states tend to do, the South African state pushed back against outside interference in its domestic politics. States often reassert their sovereignty in such situations.	*South Africa:* This example demonstrates how what goes on within states can affect states' external relations. The domestic politics of the United Kingdom and the United States drove those states to try to change the domestic politics of the South African state.	*South Africa:* The apartheid regime constructed race as a fixed identity. It used theology to justify its policies, but theological interpretations changed. These and other changes undercut the regime's legitimacy.
Individual	*Nigeria:* Their initial clashes between the pastor and the imam fit with realist understandings of human nature, including the passions and drives that lead to conflict.	*Nigeria:* The compelling story of the pastor and the imam is a tale of good leadership and reconciliation. It provides support for a positive view of human nature in which people work together for the common good.	*Nigeria:* The pastor and the imam changed their interpretations of their respective holy scriptures and what it means to be a religious leader. Each also changed his image of the other.

Source: Martha van Wyk, "Sunset over Atomic Apartheid."

Conclusion

Religion's relationship to conflict and peacemaking is quite complex and becoming more so with religion's resurgence. In *The Global Future*, authors Charles Kegley and Gregory Raymond point out that, "in theory, religion would seem a natural force for global harmony. Yet millions have died in the name of religion."[62] There is no straightforward relationship or correlation between religion and conflict, on the one hand, or religion and cooperation or peacemaking, on the other. Religion is not simply a creative or destructive force. Religion has the ability to carry the seeds of peace as well as violence; even within the same religion, some bear ploughshares and others the sword. Religion can be a source of violent conflict or a source of social tolerance, democratic pluralism, and nonviolent conflict resolution. Religious scriptures do not "promote a singular coherent view of matters of temporal authority and political life," though fundamentalists would argue they do. They "contain a diversity of political ideas."[63] The complexity and internal pluralism of religious texts and traditions explains, at least in part, why authentic responses to the sacred can take very different forms. Another "complexifier" is that religion can be a "force multiplier," enabling it to have an outsized role in gathering support for war or peace.[64]

Certainly, religion has been deeply implicated in violence around the world, and this is often headline news. Less well known are religion's roles in peacemaking, reconciliation, and good works. This is the seldom-told story both because of the nature of much that is deemed newsworthy—"If it bleeds, it leads"—and the quiet, behind-the-scenes nature of peacemaking and reconciliation efforts. This is the story that this chapter aims to tell in order to provide a more nuanced understanding of religion's role in the world today.

Notes

1. Appleby, *The Ambivalence of the Sacred*, 12–13.
2. Toft, Philpott, and Shah, "God's Partisans Are Back," B4–B5.
3. "Desmond Tutu," Nobelprize.org.
4. Haynes, *An Introduction to International Relations and Religion*, 307, 309.
5. Goba, "The Kairos Document and Its Implications for Liberation in South Africa," 317.
6. Magaziner, "Christ in Context," 82.
7. Quoted in Griswold, "God's Country," 53.
8. Quoted in Griswold, "God's Country," 54.

9. "Life and Death in the Middle Belt: A Clash of Civilizations in Nigeria," *Der Spiegel*, March 18, 2014, http://www.spiegel.de/international/world/life-and-death -in-the-middle-belt-a-clash-of-civilizations-in-nigeria-a-670178.html.

10. Taylor, "Ex-Foes Unite in Pursuit of Peace," B1.

11. Smock, *Religious Contributions to Peacemaking*, 18, 21, 27.

12. Quoted in Griswold, "God's Country," 55.

13. Griswold, "God's Country," 42.

14. "Nigeria Quells Religious Riots," *New York Times*, May 20, 1992.

15. Opeloye, "The Socio-Political Factor in the Christian-Muslim Conflict in Nigeria," 234.

16. Johnston and Cox, "Faith-Based Diplomacy and Preventive Engagement," 14.

17. Weigel, "Religion and Peace," 173.

18. Appleby, *The Ambivalence of the Sacred*, 180, 192, 236.

19. Appleby, *The Ambivalence of the Sacred*, 29.

20. Appleby, *The Ambivalence of the Sacred*, 13, 27; Appleby, "Retrieving the Missing Dimension of Statecraft," 240, 243.

21. Healey, review of *When Religion Becomes Evil*, 58.

22. Schäfer, "The Janus Face of Religion," 407.

23. Micklethwait and Wooldridge, *God Is Back*, 363, 364.

24. Esposito, "Islam and Political Violence," 1068.

25. Subotic, "Europe Is a State of Mind," 311.

26. Velikonja, "In Hoc Signo Vinces," 25–40.

27. "Religion, Conflict and the Balkans: An Unholy Powderkeg," *The Economist*, June 25, 2014.

28. Committee of Religious NGOs at the United Nations, https://rngos.wordpress .com.

29. Petersen, "International Religious NGOs at the United Nations."

30. Petersen, "International Religious NGOs at the United Nations."

31. "Faith in Action: Working Toward the Millennium Development Goals," Religions for Peace, http://vivatinternational.org/wp-content/uploads/2009/12/English -MDG-toolkit.pdf.

32. Tannenwald, "Using Religion to Restrain Iran's Nuclear Program."

33. Thomas, *The Global Resurgence of Religion and the Transformation of International Relations*, 174–175.

34. Mapendere, "Track One and a Half Diplomacy and the Complementarity of Tracks," 67.

35. Rob Moll, "The Father of Faith-Based Diplomacy," 54.

36. Homans, "Track II Diplomacy."

37. Anft, "Man in the Middle," 30.

38. Hanson, *Religion and Politics in the International System Today*, 52.

39. Thomas, *The Global Resurgence of Religion and the Transformation of International Relations*, 185.

40. Little, *Peacemakers in Action*, 4–5.

41. Johnston and Cox, "Faith-Based Diplomacy and Preventive Engagement," 15.

42. Thomas, *The Global Resurgence of Religion and the Transformation of International Relations*, 183.

43. Tutu, "The Struggle for Social Justice in Post-Apartheid South Africa," 110.

44. Hanson, *Religion and Politics in the International System Today*, 316.

45. "Not a Sword, But Peace," *The Economist* 388:8587, July 5, 2008.

46. Haynes, *Religion, Politics and International Relations: Selected Essays*, 118.

47. Toft, Philpott, and Shah, *God's Century*, 176, 188.

48. Toft, Philpott, and Shah, *God's Century*, 175–177, 188.
49. Toft, Philpott, and Shah, *God's Century*, 196.
50. Little, "Introduction," xxix.
51. Hanson, *Religion and Politics in the International System Today*, 64.
52. Cortright, *Peace*, 14.
53. Turshen, "Militarism and Islamism in Algeria," 1–2.
54. Kimball, *When Religion Becomes Lethal*, 150.
55. Johnston and Cox, "Faith-Based Diplomacy and Preventive Engagement," 14.
56. Michalak, *A Primer in Power Politics*, 1.
57. Shimko, *International Relations*, 47.
58. Shiraev and Zubok, *International Relations*, 125.
59. Pease, *International Organizations*, 95.
60. Gethard, "Protest Divestment and the End of Apartheid."
61. Macqueen, "Ecumenism and the Global Anti-Apartheid Struggle."
62. Kegley and Raymond, *The Global Future*, 5th ed., 138.
63. Rees, "'Really Existing' Scriptures," 20.
64. Seiple and Hoover, *Religion and Security*, 21.

10

Concluding Thoughts

Illustration 17: New Religious Regulations in China

On February 1, 2018, new Regulations on Religious Affairs (RRA) went into effect in China. The government's stated goals of these regulations was "ensuring citizens' freedom of religious belief, maintaining religious and social harmony, and regulating the administration of religious affairs."[1] Whatever their stated purpose, these regulations further restrict religious practice in China. They restrict venues for religious activity. They require that all online religious activity, such as proselytizing, be reported to local authorities. They essentially ban "unauthorized" religious teachings by severely limiting who is allowed to establish religious schools. They even restrict citizens' religious behavior when traveling outside the country.

This regulation is part of President Xi Jinping's initiative to make religions in China more "Chinese" and to respond to "challenges in the religious sphere that he perceives to be detrimental to his ruling objectives."[2] Among these challenges, Xi and the Chinese Communist Party (CCP) seem particularly concerned about religious "extremism" as well as "foreign" influences on, or infiltration of, religion in China; with them comes the possibility of religious subversion of the Chinese system. Given its historic connection to the West, Christianity is considered an avenue for Westernizing and dividing China and, thus, destroying social harmony and undermining regime stability. Seeing the Vatican as competing with the state for people's loyalties, the Chinese government severed diplomatic relations with it in 1951, just two years after the Chinese Communist Party came to power.

The broader context is that, as a communist country, communist party members are strongly discouraged from holding religious beliefs, and China is officially atheist with extremely high government restrictions on religion. Although the constitution guarantees religious freedom, such freedom is controlled and restricted, especially for religious minorities. The Chinese government officially recognizes only five religions, and only those five are allowed to practice their religion freely. Even these, though, are not protected from government interference. All religious groups must register with the government; often, officials deny registration requests from groups that are not affiliated with the state-recognized patriotic religious associations. A dozen groups have been labeled "evil" or "heterodox" cults and banned altogether.

The United States Commission on International Religious Freedom (USCIRF) reports that the Chinese government persecutes members of all religious faiths. Religious freedom is especially shaky for Tibetan Buddhists, Turkic Muslims (including Uighurs), and Falun Gong practitioners. The government has incarcerated perhaps a million Uighurs, partly so Uighurs can be socialized into a homogenous Han-Chinese identity. Repression, the government's default response to faith-based organizations, may have the wholly unintended effect of heightening religious identities among the persecuted. At the end of the day, as Jeff Kingston says, the "CCP trumps God."[3] The state acts to serve its perceived interests.

Significance

China is an extremely important actor on the world stage and its international influence has been increasing. Like India, China is an Asian giant by almost every measure. Demographically, it has the world's largest population, though India is gaining on it. Geographically, it has the fourth largest territory on earth, just a bit smaller than the United States' landmass. Economically, years of rapid growth lifted hundreds of millions of Chinese out of poverty and into the middle class. Its national economy continues to outpace the US economy in terms of growth and now rivals the US economy in size. Militarily, it has the largest standing army in the world and is expanding its naval capabilities. It centers its military energies on the South China Sea. Politically, it is the largest remaining communist, party-run state. The political system is locked down and, by most accounts, increasingly authoritarian. Internationally, it is counted among the BRICS—Brazil, Russia, India, China, and South Africa—which are the world's key emerging countries. This grouping has evolved into an intergovernmental organization (IGO) that is seeking a larger role for emerging powers in global governance. As one of the five permanent, veto-wielding countries on the UN Security Council (P5), China participates in global security governance.

Its improving position on the world stage has led to a great deal of discussion about the implications of a rising China. Some see the "China model" (or "Beijing consensus") as an alternative to the prevailing Western model of development and the liberal international order that was established after World War II. A potential ideological competitor of the West, the China model is more reliant on state control of politics and the economy. Realists would note that China's growing power affects the distribution of power in the international system. Back in the fifth century BCE, Thucydides warned that rising powers challenge established powers. A rising China may emerge either as a global threat or a global partner, and there is considerable concern around the question of whether China's rise will continue to be peaceful.

But China's global image and the attractiveness of the China model are limited by the government's track record on human rights issues like religious freedom. International criticism, including from various United Nations organs, increased with the new Regulations on Religious Affairs. Two watchdogs, Human Rights Watch and Freedom House, have also criticized China's increasingly tight restrictions on religion since Xi Jinping became leader of the Chinese Communist Party in 2012. A Freedom House report details the "religious revival, repression, and resistance in China today."[4] As the Chinese government's discrimination against and persecution of religious groups has intensified, the US government has condemned China's track record on human rights in general and freedoms of speech, association, and religion in particular. In March 2019, US Ambassador at Large for International Religious Freedom Sam Brownback accused the Chinese party-state of being "at war with faith."

The new Regulations on Religious Affairs are also significant because the Chinese state is tightening the reins on religion at a time when religious observance is increasing.[5] Amid China's rapid modernization and rise in living standards, people are turning to religion. Across this "radically secular society . . . hundreds of temples, churches, and mosques open every year, attracting millions of new worshippers."[6] Perhaps the state is tightening restrictions, not because religious doctrine threatens to undermine communist ideology, but because religious groups' organizational capabilities might enable them to challenge the CCP's legitimacy and control.[7] Regardless of the state's motives, events in China appear to be at odds with the assumptions of modernization theory and the secularization thesis.

We thus see, first, that religious resurgence can elicit domestic policy changes and, second, that how states treat religion at home can affect relations with other states. The Westphalian norms of sovereignty and nonintervention are being challenged by new norms, especially the responsibility to protect, and religious believers are among those needing protection from their own governments.

Takeaways

My hope is that the reader will take away from this text an understanding of what it means to say that "God is back" and, with it, why religion matters on the world stage. Analytical frameworks will, I expect, help you to make sense of this and facilitate your understanding of religion and world politics.

"God Is Back"

In the early twenty-first century, if religion—once the missing dimension of statecraft—is not taken into account, much that transpires on the world stage is unintelligible. Most obviously, this includes the terrorist attacks of 9/11, the subsequent US declaration of the "war on terror," the long and ultimately successful hunt for Osama bin Laden, and the deaths in Afghanistan of some 3,500 coalition members and countless Afghanis. But other events, too, would be hard to understand. For instance, the religious element is central to the conflict over Kashmir, which is claimed by two nuclear-armed adversaries, India and Pakistan, one predominantly Hindu, the other largely Muslim. Similarly, while Northern Ireland's Troubles and the conflict over Israel/Palestine are not at their core about religion, the religious element is important to these conflicts. In Israel/Palestine, a major stumbling block to a lasting agreement between the two sides is the status of Jerusalem, which is home to major holy sites of Judaism, Christianity, and Islam. With regard to Iran, the radical religious nature of the regime goes a long way in explaining the rhetoric that continues to poison that country's relations with Israel and the United States. In the Middle East, the Iraq–Saudi Arabia competition is more about power politics than religion.

However, religion matters. Iran has backed so-called proxy militias in Iraq, Saudi Arabia, and Yemen; that is, it engages in conflicts indirectly, through nonstate alliances in order to support other Shia Muslims, garner influence, and export its revolutionary ideology. Meanwhile, oil-rich Saudi Arabia has been funding mosques and schools in Asia and spreading its Salafi-Wahhabi brand of Islam. Certainly, to grasp the nature and impact of the Arab Spring (explained in Chapter 2), it is necessary to know a bit about how Islam developed as a religio-political movement and about the role of Islamists, especially the Muslim Brotherhood, from Tunisia to Egypt.

Religion's role on the world stage today flies in the face of presumptions about our modernizing world. As stated by columnist Jonah Goldberg, "For decades, students of modernization subscribed to an overriding assumption that . . . more modernity means less religion."[8] The modern world was—social scientists long argued—to be characterized by a division between politics and religion, with nationalism and national identities built on secular beliefs and values. Contrary to such long-held assumptions, in many respects the world is becoming more religious, not less.

Religion Matters

Given that "God is back," a second takeaway is that *religion matters on the world stage*. In the early twenty-first century, world politics cannot be fully understood without attention to the role of religious actors and beliefs. As recently as the 1990s, religion was largely ignored in the study of world politics and the practice of statecraft, despite the 1979 Iranian Revolution. Since then, real-world events have pushed scholars of international relations to examine the global resurgence of religion.

A line from *Death of a Salesman* is apt: "Attention must be paid." Attention must be paid to power, geography, international law and institutions, and the global economy—all topics explained in textbooks on world politics. To get the full picture, however, attention must also be paid to religion, something to which textbooks often give scant attention.

Religion matters in world politics—but the religious resurgence can be a blessing or a bane or, most likely, both. It can contribute to peace and cooperation and it can drive conflict and division.

Religion matters in world politics—but some issues have nothing to do with religion. Some issues may have a religion angle, but not the angle presented in the media. One of the things this text is designed to do is to give some guidance as to when and why religion matters.

Frameworks for Analysis

The third takeaway, which ties into a central goal of this book, is to provide frameworks for analysis. These include theoretical, analytical, historical, and political frameworks. Theoretical frameworks include Marxism and modernization theory, but the book focuses on the three main international relations theories: realism, liberalism, and constructivism.

The levels of analysis—individual, state, and global—offer an analytical "spine" that runs through the book. It provides the organizational structure for Chapters 4, 5, and 6, which analyze interactions between religion and politics on the systemic, state, and individual levels of analysis, respectively. In other words, this text takes "different points of entry into the world of religion and politics," at three levels of political-religious interaction.[9] Chapter 4 digs into the international setting or the global level of analysis, including transnational religious actors, the relationship between globalization and religion, and religion's impact on foreign policy decisionmaking and national security matters. Chapter 5 focuses on the state level of analysis, describing and explaining what goes on within states that can affect states' foreign policies as well as interactions with state and nonstate actors. Chapter 6 zeroes in on the individual level of analysis. It includes religion's influence on perceptions, images, worldviews, and actions, as well as religious "heroes" and "villains" whose actions have affected international relations. Much of the focus is on exemplars—religiously motivated individuals who, for better or worse, have had an impact on states' foreign policies and the world in which they are played out.

The book is structured around analytical frameworks for two good reasons. First, in the highly complex real world in which we live, offering a "silver bullet" or a single explanation for why events occur makes things simpler, but often at the risk of oversimplification. Each theoretical and analytical perspective—each "way in" to a topic—provides insights into what transpires on the world stage, but also has blind spots. The best way to deal with these blind spots and to get the full picture is to study religion and world politics through various lenses and inquire into what is going on at various levels of analysis. These frameworks shine a spotlight on different answers to the "so what?" and "how?" questions. So what? Why does religion matter in world politics? How does religion matter? Second, although these analytical frameworks are employed in virtually all textbooks on international relations or world politics, this text shows how the religious factor fits within these broader understandings.

Equipped with these frameworks, an informed student of world politics is better prepared to analyze other events, events we cannot yet imagine, and to place them within a web of interconnections.

Constants and Changes

Politics on the world stage include a number of constants and changes. Constants enable us to note patterns, develop theories, and hazard informed predictions about the future. Changes and unexpected events keep things interesting, especially since they can catch even keen observers by surprise. Exhibit A is the sudden and unanticipated end of the Cold War, with the destruction of the Berlin Wall and the collapse of both the Soviet Union and international communism.

The constants center around two tensions at the heart of world politics. One is conflict and cooperation. The other is globalization and fragmentation.

World politics is a lively mix of disharmony/conflict and harmony/cooperation. Of the two, it is easier to point to examples of conflict. The United States is sharply at odds with China over trade and with Iran over the development of its nuclear capabilities, and it has been involved in armed conflict in Afghanistan since 2001. Since Russia's 2014 annexation of Crimea, separatists have taken up arms against the Ukrainian government. Civil war in Syria has led to a great deal of death, destruction, and displacement. The Islamic State took advantage of the unrest in Syria and Iraq, using force to carve out its own space. Iran and Saudi Arabia vie for supremacy in the Middle East. Civil war continues to roil South Sudan. Christians and Muslims clash in northern Nigeria. China cracks down on religious groups at home and flexes its military muscle in the South China Sea. Shadowy groups engage in terrorism and cyberwarfare. The list goes on.

Conflict, especially violent conflict, garners much more attention than cooperation and peacemaking. Before reading this text, you were probably familiar with, for instance, some of the conflicts that seem to implicate religion in one way or the other. Were you equally familiar with religion's role in peacemaking and reconciliation? Efforts to keep the body politic healthy and functioning simply do not get as much press as actors and actions that threaten to tear it limb from limb.

In fact, though, cooperation in the world is "constant and ongoing."[10] It serves as a sort of backdrop of what is playing out on the world stage. Cooperation entails working together to achieve a desired outcome, making at least one actor better off than it would have been and having the potential for mutual gain. Actors may cooperate on some issues and be at odds on others, but they rarely resort to the use of force. In a world of anarchy, there are no guarantees of cooperation. Still, though, every day sovereign states work together to achieve shared objectives. Planes land in foreign airports, snail mail reaches Peace Corps volunteers in Sierra Leone, and most states quietly heed the dictates of international law.

The second central tension in world politics involves integrative and disintegrative trends. Francis Fukuyama frames it in rather stark terms: "Our present world is simultaneously moving toward the opposing dystopias of hypercentralization and endless fragmentation."[11] (Benjamin Barber framed it as the forces of "McWorld" and "Jihad.") The world's becoming "smaller," more integrated, even hypercentralized because of various forces associated with globalization and the idea of a global village: international trade, global communications and transportation networks, information technology, and so on. Consequently, events and decisions in one part of the world increasingly affect people in other parts. The Islamic State, for instance, posted videotapes of its brutal actions as well as its reclusive leader, Abu Bakr al-Baghdadi, to prove that he had not died during the fight to crush ISIS. (He did die in 2019.) Such videos serve as propaganda and recruitment tools. Globalization can also, as constructivists would note, carry shared norms with it. Regionalization is also bringing states and peoples together, especially the European Union, which is moving people to identify as European, rather than as French, Germans, Italians, and so on.

While all this integration is happening, disintegration and breakdown—seemingly "endless fragmentation," in Fukuyama's words—are also occurring. The early twentieth century witnessed the breakdown of old empires (Austro-Hungarian, Ottoman, and Russian), followed by independence movements in the Indian subcontinent and Africa. Nationalist movements in peripheral parts of the Soviet Union were one of the factors that contributed to its collapse and disintegration in 1991. Shortly thereafter, two other communist states, Czechoslovakia and Yugoslavia, fell apart, with Kosovo declaring its independence in 2008. In 2011, Sudan split into two pieces. Separatist parties and movements are active in many parts of the world, including liberal democracies like Belgium, Canada, Italy, and the United Kingdom.

Identity politics figure in here. Local and regional identities (e.g., Scottish) as well as religious and ethnic identities (e.g., Kurdish and

Palestinian) are profoundly important in the early twenty-first century. Economic and ideological concerns were the focus of twentieth-century politics, but, Francis Fukuyama argues, politics now pivots on matters of identity.[12] Good constructivists would remind us that identities—religious or otherwise—are not fixed. Identity may be fluid. Those who identify as Yugoslavs one day may identify as Croats the next.

Another dynamic at the heart of world politics is continuity and change, long-term trends and transformations. Some aspects of world politics are resistant to change. First, while the state is challenged by integrative and disintegrative trends and many obituaries have been written for the dear old state, the system of sovereign states endures. Second, power politics, as all good realists would remind us, still matters. Third, anarchy remains. There is no world government or authority that can exercise authority over states, especially powerful states. Something of the "Wild West" endures in world politics. Fourth, in the context of anarchy and power politics, state competition casts the shadow of potential conflict (though not necessarily violent conflict) over world affairs. If religious discourse and identities enter in, it can make conflicts less tractable, harder to resolve.

At the same time, the world is ever-changing. First, while states remain the world system's basic units, they now share the world stage with a greater number and variety of actors, intergovernmental organizations such as the United Nations, and nongovernmental organizations such as the one founded by the pastor and imam in Nigeria. Second, power remains important, but power is shifting and dispersing. Gone is the simplicity of the Cold War rivalry. The United States is clearly the top dog today, as it has been since the Soviet Union collapsed in 1991. However, the two Asian giants (China and India) are rising along with other states in the Global South. The sizes of their populations and economies, along with their possession of nuclear weapons, make them powers to be reckoned with. In fact, while the twentieth century is called the "American century," the twenty-first century may be the "Asian century." Third, anarchy remains, but it is not what it used to be. Ending anarchy would mean creating a world government, and there does not seem to be much appetite for that. However, along with economic integration and a variety of international institutions has come greatly increased interdependence among states.

A fourth trend, the shift toward open markets and a global economy, links states together economically. Although this might mean more trade conflicts, it makes violent conflict between states somewhat less likely— as good liberals would tell us—because states are reluctant to fight their trade partners. Those looking through the liberal lens would also remind us that the growth of international institutions and the development of international law mitigate the effects of anarchy. No global *government* exists, but global *governance* continues to develop. That is, international "rules, norms, and organizational structures" help states deal with common problems while not undermining state sovereignty.[13]

The fifth trend concerns states and the form of states' governments. Throughout most of human history, humans have lived under some form of authoritarianism. Democratic practices did not reach much beyond ancient Athens until after the US and French revolutions. In the mid-twentieth century, democracy found its footing. From the mid-1970s through the decline of the Soviet Union and on into this century, the number of electoral democracies continued to increase and it appeared that an open and liberal world order was here to stay. Just a few years ago democracy seemed triumphant. In recent years, however, democracy has experienced setbacks in all regions of the world. Freedom House is sounding the alarm that democracy is in "crisis" and in "retreat" across all continents. While military coups have become relatively rare, states are moving from democracy to authoritarianism via elected autocrats. Democratic systems are being challenged from within by leaders who come to power through democratic means (elections) and then subvert democracy by muzzling the media, arresting political opponents, and tinkering with the constitution, as is happening in Russia.

States, too, are changing. As the world stage becomes more crowded with other actors—nongovernmental organizations like Doctors Without Borders and intergovernmental organizations like the United Nations—states, borders, and sovereignty matter less. Global challenges, from climate change to Covid-19, do not respect states' borders or sovereignty. Sovereignty is diluted as the realist focus on national security is met by new attention to human security; while the former is about the protection of the state, the latter is about protecting individuals. The Westphalian norms of state sovereignty and nonintervention now run up against the idea that states have the responsibility to protect people.

Sixth, the nature of warfare is changing. War is shifting from interstate to intrastate, meaning from war between states to war within states in which nonstate actors are involved. These civil wars tend to occur in the Global South and have elements of nationalism or identity politics and, often, a religious angle of some sort. Jeff Kingston says that a "toxic tide" of nationalism and religion has swept across Asia.[14] Yet, "ethnic or religious differences alone do not cause the interest conflicts that underlie civil wars."[15] When these differences mean groups face discrimination or political exclusion because of their ethnicity or religion, then grievances or the desire to control the levers of government power may give rise to internal violence.

The final change is, of course, the religious resurgence on the world stage. This resurgence is occurring in the world's most populous countries, China and India, and across Asia. Religious belief and practice are spreading in Africa. In fact, the only region where religion is losing ground rather than gaining it is Western Europe. This religious resurgence has an impact on the world. It affects states' domestic politics, including elections, as well as states' foreign relations. It affects conflict and cooperation. Ongoing globalization increases cultural interaction and facilitates the spread of beliefs, while technological advancements facilitate the spread of transnational religious organizations. All this is happening despite ongoing modernization and the efforts of secularizing regimes.

The bottom line is that various oppositions and divergent impulses are at work in world politics. Interactions are complex, often contradictory, and almost always interesting to note.

Some Projections

Given the contradictory impulses discussed above, what are realist, liberal, and constructivist projections for world politics in the not-too-distant future? Hailing back to Thucydides' work in the fifth century BCE, realists emphasize constants. Hence, they "expect more of the same." Human nature remains the same, states remain the core units of international relations, states pursue national interests defined in terms of power, the international system remains largely anarchic, the security dilemma continues, and the potential for conflict endures. Power and the distribution of power among independent, self-interested states remain central. This distribution determines outcomes. In short, most of the changes under way in the international arena, including religion's resurgence, do not have much effect on the future of world politics. But, changes in the distribution of power—from the bipolar Cold War era, to the unipolar era of the 1990s, to the rise of "the rest"—do matter. The United States is in *relative* decline; its power is not diminishing, but others, especially China, are closing the gap.

Liberals see changes and are optimistic about many of them. Each of the three strands of liberalism is important here. Economically, interdependence is increasing, and this is reducing the likelihood of interstate war. Politically, the general trend is toward democracy, though there have been some setbacks of late. Ongoing democratization bodes well for a future "democratic peace." Since well-established democracies do not fight one another, the more such democracies exist, the greater the prospects for peace. Internationally, anarchy is being chipped away, global civil society is emerging, and states are learning the benefits of peace and cooperation. This encourages sovereign states to come together to resolve shared problems like Ebola and resource depletion.

For constructivists, the future may be radically different from today. Interests and political interactions may change dramatically. Or not. Much depends on "decision-making elites' identities, assumptions, and interpretations" of what's going on in world.[16] For constructivists, identities, ideas, beliefs, and values are socially "constructed," especially by the various groups to which people belong. Constructions are important. States can construct foreign enemies. If, for instance, political leaders assume or perceive an "Islam versus the West" clash of civilizations, then foreign policies will reflect or even encourage antagonistic relationships. What is constructed can change. Or stay the same. As Nils Bohr, a Nobel laureate in physics, said, "Prediction is very difficult, especially if it's about the future."

What of religion's role in world politics? An article published by the World Economic Forum declared that "the impact of religion is on the rise on a global scale."[17] Will this impact continue to rise? The clear shortcomings of twentieth-century secularization theory might encourage a bit of humility in reading the tea leaves of the future. As expressed by Jonathan Fox, "the social sciences prematurely predicted religion's demise as a significant social, political, and economic factor." Clearly, organized religion has not gone the way of the woolly mammoth, nor have religious influences been confined to the private spaces of home and temple. Much of religion's role in the future will depend on changing demographics and religious conversions, and these two factors suggest that in the world of 2050 more people will be affiliated with a religion (rather than identifying as a nonbeliever) and the world's Muslim population will be much larger. For the most part, the Muslim world, unlike the West, has "never accepted the Westphalian concept of religion being irrelevant to world politics."[18]

Religion's impact on world politics is highly complex. There are, and will likely continue to be, elements of change and continuity and of cooperation and conflict.

Revisiting the Analytical Framework

The framework in Table 10.1 below returns to the central elements of the theoretical framework used throughout this text. It also demonstrates, first, how all of the levels of analysis contribute both to foreign policy making and to the interaction between religion and politics on the world stage and, second, how the analysis of religion might be incorporated into the main international relations paradigms of realism, liberalism, and constructivism. These three paradigms differ regarding the main forces driving international relations. Henry Nau boils them down to a focus on power, institutions, and ideas, respectively.[19] None of these theories had predicted religion's demise; they simply ignored it. Finally, it suggests how the religious factor can be incorporated, to varying degrees, into this framework. That is, it makes inferences about where religion and world politics fit within the overall scheme. Since IR theory is largely silent on religion, these inferences are based on reasoning and extrapolation.

With this framework in mind, my hope is that you will have a better, richer understanding of world politics and especially the religious factor. Then, when the next religious revolution happens, the next power-seeker uses religious rhetoric and symbols for political ends, or the next conflict is labeled a "religious" conflict, you will have the tools to judge matters for yourself.

The global resurgence of religion—and with it the "resurgence of religion in 21st century world affairs"—means that, if we are to understand events on the world political stage today, we must be attentive to and knowledgeable about the religious factor.[20] Without regard for this factor, we get only a partial picture of the drivers of Iran's foreign policy, the timing of communism's end in Eastern Europe, the conflict that tore apart Yugoslavia, the impetus behind the rise of the Islamic State and the declaration of a caliphate, or the rocky road to democracy in countries that experienced the Arab Spring. We need to consider whether leaders' religious rhetoric is born of religious conviction or whether they are playing the "religion card" for political purposes. We also need to look closely when a conflict is labeled a "religious" or "sectarian" conflict to determine if, on the one hand, the conflict is really about religion or, on the other, religion is simply part of the mix.

Informed public opinion is crucial to functioning democracies. It rests on having a good grasp of how domestic and international politics work and a good analytical framework for making up one's own mind about the meaning of statements, policies, and events.

Table 10.1 Analytical Framework and Religion and World Politics (R&WP)

Levels of Analysis	Realism	Liberalism	Constructivism
International/ Systemic	States are the central actors. They have the greatest economic and military capabilities. States' foreign policies and actions shape and are shaped by the international context, especially the distribution of power. Since states' power relative to other states is what matters, international politics becomes a zero-sum game in which one state's gain is another's loss. "Anarchy" is a better descriptor than "system," since few international rules or norms constrain states' actions. Since all states want power and there is no central power to check states and their ambitions, conflict is more likely than cooperation.	States are key actors, but they share the world stage with NGOs and IGOs. International institutions, economic interdependence, and stable democracies all help to make for a more peaceful world. Liberalism holds that progress is possible. Anarchy can be mitigated through international institutions, international law, and collective action. Through collective security, states can deter and counter aggression by other states. World politics can be a positive-sum game with states cooperating to serve mutual interests and achieve mutual gains.	The power of ideas, ideologies, identities, and norms is important because these factors affect or "construct" international politics and the international system. At the same time, international relationships shape identities. Actors' identities are constructed (i.e., actors define who "we" are and who "they" are), and these identities affect their behavior.

continues

Table 10.1 Continued

Levels of Analysis	Realism	Liberalism	Constructivism
International/ Systemic	*R&WP:* Religious actors (except for the Holy See) are not state actors nor, as a rule, do they have hard power. As such, they are simply on the wings of the world stage.	*R&WP:* Since World War II, religions have become transnationalized. Religious transnational actors, like other nonstate actors, are rising in influence. Religious freedom is on the international agenda, with international declarations calling for states to protect them.	*R&WP:* Ideas, ideologies, identities, and norms may be grounded in religious beliefs, values, and understandings. Interpretations of religious histories and texts can change, and identities and understandings can change with them.
Domestic/State	The state is a unitary actor (like a solid billiard ball) that is driven by the imperatives of national interest, especially security and survival. Like a billiard ball, what goes on inside does not really matter. States' internal dynamics, including links between politics and religion, are of little consequence.	Regime type and states' domestic institutions, policymaking processes, and internal dynamics matter. First, open, pluralistic regimes create more access points and allow more actors to influence the foreign policy-making process. Second, consolidated and stable democracies do not go to war with each other. Third, several factors (how constitutions are drafted, leaders are chosen, decisions are made, and who weighs in on these matters) affect foreign policy making.	States' identities and interests are constructed, not given. Collective identities can be based on, for instance, secular nationalism or ethnicity and religion. States' interests can change.

continues

Table 10.1 Continued

Levels of Analysis	Realism	Liberalism	Constructivism
Domestic/State	*R&WP*: Neither morality nor religious imperatives are sound or prudent bases for foreign policy.	*R&WP*: The constitutions of numerous sovereign states protect religious freedom, though such protection may not be guaranteed in practice. Religion and religious actors (e.g., religiously based political parties and interest groups) may play a role in shaping states' policies, including foreign policies.	*R&WP*: Secularism and the separation of religion and politics are social constructs. They are neither givens nor unalterable facts, but notions constructed in the West. In the early twenty-first century, religious ideas have gained increased potency in politics. Public actors, including religious actors, present rival visions of what constitutes an ideal society.

continues

Table 10.1 Continued

Levels of Analysis	Realism	Liberalism	Constructivism
Individual	Humanity is flawed, egoistic, and power-seeking.	Humans are essentially good and able to cooperate. Liberalism shares the Enlightenment belief that humans are rational and can chart a path to progress.	Individual decisionmakers typically reflect and support their society's norms, values, and ideologies.
	Like states' internal workings, it is not necessary to analyze individual decisionmakers because all states and all states' leaders try to bolster state power, security, and well-being.	The individual decisionmaker is an important unit of analysis. Individuals, alone or with others, define national goals, weigh policy alternatives, and make states' foreign policies. It is individuals who perceive and misperceive rhetoric and actions in world politics. Individuals are, however, constrained by the domestic context.	However, leaders can foster changes in ideas, ideologies, and identities. How they conceive of the world affects how the groups and states they lead act on the world stage.
	R&WP: Individual religious actors play only bit parts.	*R&WP*: Religious leaders, like their counterparts in the state, can affect how world politics is framed and understood.	*R&WP*: Religion influences states' foreign policies through the individual beliefs of key actors. Elites' beliefs matter.

Sources: Mingst, *Essentials of International Relations*; Nau, *Perspectives in IR*, 2nd ed.; Snyder, "One World, Rival Theories."

Notes

1. Zhang, "China."
2. Chang, "New Wine in Old Bottles," 37–38.
3. Kingston, *The Politics of Religion, Nationalism, and Identity in Asia*, 68–70.
4. Cook, "The Battle for China's Spirit."
5. Albert, "Religion in China."
6. Johnson, "China's Great Awakening."
7. Albert, "Religion in China."
8. Goldberg, "Religion and Politics."
9. Tepe, *Beyond Sacred and Secular*, 40.
10. Spiegel, Matthews, Taw, and Williams, *World Politics in a New Era*, 6th ed., 4.
11. Fukuyama, "Against Identity Politics," Andrea Mitchell Center for the Study of Democracy.
12. Fukuyama, "Against Identity Politics: The New Tribalism and the Crisis of Democracy," 91.
13. Mingst and Karns, *The United Nations in the Post-Cold War Era*, 4.
14. Kingston, *The Politics of Religion, Nationalism, and Identity in Asia*, 1.
15. Frieden, Lake, and Schulz, *World Politics: Interests, Interactions, Institutions*, 4th ed., 247.
16. Spiegel, Matthews, Taw, and Williams, *World Politics in a New Era*, 6th ed., 500.
17. Grim, "How Religious Will the World Be in 2050?" https://www.weforum.org/agenda/2015/10/how-religious-will-the-world-be-in-2050/.
18. Fox, *An Introduction to Religion and Politics*, 2nd ed., 195–196.
19. Nau, *Perspectives on International Relations*, 2nd ed., 63.
20. Kubálková, "A 'Turn to Religion' in International Relations?" 19.

Bibliography

Abaigar, Victor Urrutia. "Church and State After Transition to Democracy: The Case of Spain," in William Safran, ed., *The Secular and the Sacred: Nation, Religion and Politics.* Portland, OR: Frank Cass, 2003.

Abdo, Geneive, and Anna L. Jacobs. "Are COVID-19 Restrictions Inflaming Religious Tensions?" Brookings Institution. April 13, 2020. https://www.brookings.edu/blog/order-from-chaos/2020/04/13/are-covid-19-restrictions-inflaming-religious-tensions.

Abram, Marco. "Building the Capital City of the Peoples of Yugoslavia: Representations of Socialist Yugoslavism in Belgrade's Public Space 1944–1961." *Croatian Political Science Review* 51:5 (2014), 36–57.

Abu-Nimer, Mohammed. Review of *Peacemakers in Action: Profiles of Religion in Conflict Resolution*, edited by David Little. *Journal of Law and Religion* 24:1 (2008/2009), 177–181.

Abu-Nimer, Mohammed, and S. Ayse Kadayifci-Orellana. "Muslim Peace-Building Actors in Africa and the Balkan Context: Challenges and Needs." *Peace and Change: A Journal of Peace Research* 3:4 (October 2008).

Adams, Jerome R. *Latin American Heroes: Liberators and Patriots from 1500 to the Present.* New York: Ballantine, 1991.

Aden, Ross. *Religion Today: A Critical Thinking Approach to Religious Studies.* Lanham, MD: Rowman & Littlefield, 2013.

Adesoji, Abimbola O. "Between Maitatsine and Boko Haram: Islamic Fundamentalism and the Response of the Nigerian State." *Africa Today* 57:4 (Summer 2011), 99–119.

Adogame, Afe. "How God Became a Nigerian: Religious Impulse and the Unfolding of a Nation." *Journal of Contemporary African Studies* 28:4 (October 2010), 479–498.

Agnew, John. "Deus Vult: The Geopolitics of the Catholic Church." *Geopolitics* 15 (2010): 39–61.

Aikman, David. "The Great Revival: Understanding Religious Fundamentalism." *Foreign Affairs* 82:4 (July/August 2003), 188–193.

Ajami, Fouad. "The Summoning." *Foreign Affairs* 72:4 (September/October 1993).

Albert, Eleanor. "Religion in China." Council on Foreign Relations, October 11, 2018. https://www.cfr.org/backgrounder/religion-china.

Albright, Madeleine. "Faith and Diplomacy." *The Review of Faith and International Affairs* 4:2 (Fall 2006).

Alford, Deann. "Malay Melee." *Christianity Today* 50:11 (November 2006).

Americans United. "EU Constitution Skips Religious Language." *Church & State Magazine* 57:7 (July/August 2004).

Amstutz, Mark. *International Ethics: Concepts, Theories, and Cases in Global Politics.* Lanham, MD: Rowman & Littlefield, 2005.

An-Na'im, Abdullah A. "The Islamic Counter-Reformation." *New Perspectives Quarterly* 19:1 (2002), 31.

An-Na'im, Abdullah A. "Political Islam in National Politics and International Relations," in Peter L. Berger, ed. *The Desecularization of the World: Resurgent Religion and World Politics.* Grand Rapids, MI: William B. Eerdmans, 1999.

Anderson, Benedict. *Imagined Communities: Reflections on the Origin and Spread of Nationalism.* New York: Verso, 1991.

Anderson, Gary. "Abu Bakr al-Baghdadi and the Theory and Practice of Jihad." *Small Wars Journal,* August 12, 2014.

Anderson, John. *Religious Liberty in Transitional Societies: The Politics of Religion.* New York: Cambridge University Press, 2003.

Anderson, Roy R., Robert F. Seibert, and Jon G. Wagner. *Politics and Change in the Middle East,* 8th ed. Upper Saddle River, NJ: Pearson Prentice Hall, 2007.

Anft, Michael. "Man in the Middle." *Johns Hopkins Magazine,* Summer 2011.

Anzulovic, Branimir. *Heavenly Serbia: From Myth to Genocide.* New York: New York University Press, 1999.

Appleby, R. Scott. *The Ambivalence of the Sacred: Religion, Violence, and Reconciliation.* Lanham, MD: Rowman & Littlefield, 2000.

Appleby, R. Scott. "Globalization, Religious Change and the Common Good." *Journal of Religion, Conflict and Peace* 3:2 (March 2010 Supplement).

Appleby, R. Scott. "Pope John Paul II." *Foreign Policy* 119 (Summer 2000), 12–24.

Appleby, R. Scott. "Retrieving the Missing Dimension of Statecraft: Religious Faith in the Service of Peacebuilding," in Douglas Johnston, ed., *Faith-Based Diplomacy: Trumping Realpolitik.* New York: Oxford University Press, 2003.

Arraf, Jane. "Muslim Brotherhood, Mainstream in Many Countries, May Be Listed as Terror Group." National Public Radio, February 22, 2017.

Ashford, Emma. "Trump's Team Should Ditch the 'Clash of Civilizations.'" *The National Interest,* December 7, 2016.

Atman, Abdel Bari. *The Secret History of al Qaeda.* Berkeley: University of California Press, 2008.

Ayoob, Mohammed. *The Many Faces of Political Islam: Religion and Politics in the Muslim World.* Ann Arbor: University of Michigan Press, 2007.

Ayres, Alyssa. "How the BRICS Got Here." Council on Foreign Relations, August 31, 2017. https://www.cfr.org/expert-brief/how-brics-got-here.

Bacik, Gokhan. "The Genesis, History, and Functioning of the Organization of Islamic Cooperation (OIC): A Formal-Institutional Analysis." *Journal of Muslim Minority Affairs* 31:4 (December 2011), 594–614.

Bader, Veit. "Religions and States. A New Typology and a Plea for Non-Constitutional Pluralism." *Ethical Theory and Moral Practice* 6:1 (March 2003), 55–91.

Bailey, Christopher E. "The Quest for Justice: Joseph Kony and the Lord's Resistance Army." *Fordham International Law Journal* 40:247 (February 2017), 246–328.

Baker, Raymond W. "The Paradox of Islam's Future." *Political Science Quarterly* 127:4 (Winter 2012/2013), 519–566.

Bale, Tim, and André Krouwel. "Down but Not Out: A Comparison of Germany's CDU/CSU with Christian Democratic Parties in Austria, Belgium, Italy and the Netherlands." *German Politics* 22:1/2 (June 2013), 16–45.

Ball, Terence, and Richard Dagger. *Political Ideologies and the Democratic Ideal*, 5ᵗʰ ed. New York: Pearson Longman, 2004.

Baradat, Leon P. *Political Ideologies: Their Origins and Impact*, 11ᵗʰ ed. Upper Saddle River, NJ: Pearson Prentice Hall, 2012.

Barbato, Mariano. "A State, a Diplomat, and a Transnational Church: The Multi-layered Actorness of the Holy See." *Perspectives: Central European Review of International Affairs* 21:2 (2013), 27–48.

Barkey, Henri. "Turkish Democracy: Two Steps Forward, Two Steps Backward." *Harvard International Review* (Spring 2014), 75–78.

Barnes, L. Philip. "Religion, Education and Conflict in Northern Ireland." *Journal of Beliefs and Values* 26:2 (August 2005), 123–138.

Barnett, Michael. "Another Great Awakening? International Relations Theory and Religion," in Jack Snyder, ed., *Religion and International Relations Theory*. New York: Columbia University Press, 2011.

Basedau, Matthias, and Carlo Koos. "When Do Religious Leaders Support Faith-Based Violence? Evidence from a Survey Poll in South Sudan." *Political Research Quarterly* 68:4 (December 2015), 830–842.

Bashar, Iftekharul. "Impact of the Rohingya Crisis on the Threat Landscape at the Myanmar-Bangladesh Border." *Combatting Violent Extremism and Terrorism in Asia and Europe* (2018), 29–42.

Beech, Hannah. "Acts of Faith." *Time International*, South Pacific Edition, June 11, 2007.

Beittinger-Lee, Verena. "Catholicism at the United Nations in New York," in Jeremy Carrette and Hugh Miall, eds., *Religion, NGOs and the United Nations: Visible and Invisible Actors in Power*. New York: Bloomsbury Academic, 2017.

Beittinger-Lee, Verena, and Hugh Miall. "Islam, the OIC and the Defamation of Religions Controversy," in Jeremy Carrette and Hugh Miall, eds., *Religion, NGOs and the United Nations: Visible and Invisible Actors in Power*. New York: Bloomsbury Academic, 2017.

Bellin, Eva. "Faith in Politics: New Trends in the Study of Religion and Politics." *World Politics* 60:2 (January 2008), 315–347.

Benjamin, Daniel, and Steven Simon. *The Age of Sacred Terror: Radical Islam's War Against America*. New York: Random House, 2003.

Benson, D. E. "Religious Orthodoxy in Northern Ireland: The Validation of Identities." *Sociological Analysis* 53:2 (1992), 219–228.

Bergen, Peter L. "Excerpts from *Holy War, Inc.*" *Phi Kappa Phi Forum* 82:1 (Spring 2002).

Bergen, Peter L. *Holy War, Inc.: Inside the Secret World of Osama bin Laden*. New York: Free Press (1ˢᵗ Touchstone Edition), 2002.

Berger, Peter L., ed. *The Desecularization of the World: Resurgent Religion and World Politics*. Grand Rapids, MI: William B. Eerdmans, 1999.

Berger, Peter L. "Faith and Development." *Society* 46:1 (January 2009), 69–75.

Berger, Peter L. "Secularization Falsified." *First Things: A Monthly Journal of Religion and Public Life*, February 2008.

Berger, Peter L. "Secularism in Retreat." *The National Interest* 46:3 (Winter 1996), 3–12.

Bevan, James. "The Myth of Madness: Cold Rationality and 'Resource' Plunder by the Lord's Resistance Army." *Civil War* 9:4 (December 2007), 343–358.

Beyer, Peter. "Multiculturalism and Religious Pluralism in Canada: Intimations of a 'Post-Westphalian' Condition," in Sonia Sikka and Lori G. Beaman, eds., *Multiculturalism and Religious Identity: Canada and India*. Montreal and Kingston: McGill–Queen's University Press, 2014.

Bianchi, Robert. *Islamic Globalization: Pilgrimage, Capitalism, Democracy, and Diplomacy*. Hackensack, NJ: World Scientific, 2013.

Bieber, Florian. "The Conflict in former Yugoslavia as a 'Fault Line War'? Testing the Validity of Samuel Huntington's 'Clash of Civilizations.'" *Balkanologie* 3:1 (July 1999), 34–48.

Blanchard, Christopher M., and Carla E. Humud. "The Islamic State and U.S. Policy." Congressional Research Service, February 2, 2017.

Bleicher, Samuel A. "China: Superpower or Basket Case?" Foreign Policy in Focus, May 8, 2008. http://www.fpif.org/reports/china_superpower_or_basket_case.

Boari, Vasile, and Natalia Vlas, eds. *Religion and Politics in the 21st Century: Global and Local Reflections*. Newcastle upon Tyne: Cambridge Scholars, 2013.

Boehle, Josef. "The UN System and Religious Actors in the Context of Global Change." *Crosscurrents* 60:3 (September 2010), 383–401.

Branch, Adam. "Exploring the Roots of LRA Violence: Political Crisis and Ethnic Politics in Acholiland," in Tim Allen and Koen Vlassenroot, eds., *The Lord's Resistance Army: Myth and Reality*. London: Zed, 2010.

Brett, Edward T. "Archbishop Arturo Rivera Damas and the Struggle for Social Justice in El Salvador." *Catholic Historical Review* 94:4 (October 2008), 717–739.

Brewer, Paul R., and Marco R. Steenbergen, "All Against All: How Beliefs About Human Nature Shape Foreign Policy Opinions." *Political Psychology* 23:1 (March, 2002), 39–58.

Brockman, James R. "Oscar Romero: Shepherd of the Poor." *Third World Quarterly* 6:2 (April 1984), 446–457.

Bruce, Steve. Review of *The Myth of Religious Violence: Secular Ideology and the Roots of Modern Conflict*, by William T. Cavenaugh. *Scottish Journal of Theology* 65:1 (February 2012), 110–111.

Bruce, Steve. *Politics and Religion*. Malden, MA: Polity, 2003.

Bueno de Mesquita, Bruce. *Principles of International Politics*, 4th ed. Washington: CQ Press, 2010.

Burgess, John P. "In-Churching Russia." *First Things: A Monthly Journal of Religious and Public Life*, May 2014.

Burgess, John P. "Orthodox Resurgence: Civil Religion in Russia." *Religion in Eastern Europe* 29:2 (May 2009), 1–14.

Burleigh, Michael. *Sacred Causes: The Clash of Religion and Politics, from the Great War to the War on Terror*. New York: HarperCollins, 2007.

Burnett, Stanton. "Implications for the Foreign Policy Community," in Douglas M. Johnston and Cynthia Sampson, eds., *Religion, the Missing Dimension of Statecraft*. New York: Oxford University Press, 1994.

Busby, Joshua William. "Bono Made Jesse Helms Cry: Jubilee 2000, Debt Relief, and Moral Action in International Politics." *International Studies Quarterly* 51:2 (2007), 247–275.

Byrnes, Rita M., ed. "Religion and Apartheid," in *South Africa: A Country Study*. Washington: GPO for the Library of Congress, 1996.

Byrnes, Timothy A. "Transnational Religion and Europeanization," in Timothy A. Byrnes and Peter J. Katzenstein, eds., *Religion in an Expanding Europe*. New York: Cambridge University Press, 2006.

Byrnes, Timothy A., and Peter J. Katzenstein, eds. *Religion in an Expanding Europe*. New York: Cambridge University Press, 2006.

Cagaptay, Soner. "Are Muslims Islamists?" The Washington Institute, May 18, 2015. http://www.washingtoninstitute.org/policy-analysis/view/are-muslims-islamists.

Campbell, John. *Nigeria: Dancing on the Brink*. Lanham, MD: Rowman & Littlefield, 2011.

"Can the Constitution Be Saved?" *The Economist*, April 18, 2005.

Candia, Carla, John Chryssavgis, and Brook Lee. "Faiths' Fault Lines." *World Policy Journal* 28:4 (Winter 2011/2012), 20–33.

Carlson, John D., and Erik C. Owens, eds. *The Sacred and the Sovereign: Religion and International Politics*. Washington DC: Georgetown University Press, 2003.

Carrette, Jeremy, and Hugh Miall, eds. *Religion, NGOs and the United Nations: Visible and Invisible Actors in Power*. New York: Bloomsbury Academic, 2017.

Carter, Ralph G. *Essentials of U.S. Foreign Policy Making*. Indianapolis: Pearson, 2015.

Casanova, José. "It's All about Identity, Stupid." *Index on Censorship* 33:4 (2004), 88–103.

Cashman, Greg. *What Causes War? An Introduction to Theories of International Conflict*. Lanham, MD: Rowman & Littlefield, 2014.

Castillo, Víctor Luis Gutiérrez. "The Organization of Islamic Cooperation in Contemporary International Society." *Revista Electrónica de Estudios Internacionales* 27 (June 2014).

Castles, Stephen. "Globalization, Ethnic Identity and the Integration Crisis." *Ethnicities* 11:1 (March 2011), 23–26.

Cavanaugh, William. *The Myth of Religious Violence: Secular Ideology and the Roots of Modern Conflict*. New York: Oxford University Press, 2009.

Cavanaugh, William T. "Religious Violence as Modern Myth." *Political Theology* 15:6 (November 2014), 456–502.

Cesari, Jocelyne. "Religion and Politics: What Does God Have To Do with It?" *Religions* 6:4 (2015), 1330–1344.

Cesari, Jocelyne. *What Is Political Islam?* Boulder: Lynne Rienner, 2017.

Chang, Kuei-Min. "New Wine in Old Bottles." *China Perspectives* 1/2 (2018), 37–44.

Cho, Il Hyun, and Peter J. Katzenstein. "In the Service of State and Nation: Religion in East Asia," in Jack Snyder, ed., *Religion and International Relations Theory*. New York: Columbia University Press, 2011.

Cimmino, Ryan. "Threat from Tibet? Systematic Repression of Tibetan Buddhism in China." *Harvard International Review* 39:4 (Fall 2018), 6–7.

Clemens, Walter C., Jr. *Dynamics of International Relations: Conflict and Mutual Gain in an Era of Global Interdependence*, 2nd ed. Lanham, MD: Rowman & Littlefield, 2004.

Clements, Kevin P. "Principled Nonviolence: An Imperative, Not an Optional Extra." *Asian Journal of Peacebuilding* 3:1 (May 2015), 1–17.

Cohen, Eliot A. "Religion and War." *SAISPHERE*, 2009.

Cohen, Steven. *Understanding Environmental Policy*, 2nd ed. New York: Columbia University Press, 2014.

Congressional Research Service. "The Lord's Resistance Army: The U.S. Response." September 28, 2015.

Conteh-Morgan, Earl. *Collective Political Violence: An Introduction to Theories and Cases of Violent Conflicts*. New York: Routledge, 2004.

Cook, Sara. "The Battle for China's Spirit: Religious Revival, Repression, and Resistance Under Xi Jinping." Freedom House. February 2017. https://freedomhouse.org/report/china-religious-freedom.

Cortright, David. *Peace: A History of Movements and Ideas*. New York: Cambridge University Press, 2008.

Craig, Gordon A. *The Germans*. New York: New American Library, 1982.

Crnobrnja, Mihailo. *The Yugoslav Drama*, 2nd ed. Montreal and Kingston: McGill-Queen's University Press, 1996.

Cucchiara, Martina. Review of *Hitler's Religion: The Twisted Beliefs That Drove the Third Reich*, by Richard Weikart. *The Catholic Historical Review* 103:3 (Summer 2017).

Cunningham, Hilary. *God and Caesar at the Rio Grande: Sanctuary and the Politics of Religion*. Minneapolis: University of Minnesota Press, 1995.

Cvetkovska-Ocokoljic, Violeta, and Tatjana Cvetkovski. "The Influence of Religion on the Creation of National Identity in Serbia." *Journal of Identity and Migration Studies* 4:2 (2010).

Cviic, Christopher. *Remaking the Balkans*. New York: Council on Foreign Relations, 1991.

Cymet, David. *History vs. Apologetics: The Holocaust, the Third Reich, and the Catholic Church*. Lanham, MD: Lexington, 2010.

Dağlı, İlke. "The Cyprus Problem: Why Solve a Comfortable Conflict?" Oxford Research Group, April 5, 2017. https://www.oxfordresearchgroup.org.uk/blog/the -cyprus-problem-why-solve-a-comfortable-conflict.

Danziger, James N. *Understanding the Political World: A Comparative Introduction to Political Science*, 5th ed. Boston: Longman, 2000.

Dajani Daoudi, Mohammed S., and Zeina M. Barakat. "Israelis and Palestinians: Contested Narratives." *Israel Studies* 18:2 (Summer 2013), 53–69.

Davis, Nancy J., and Robert V. Robinson. *Claiming Society for God: Religious Movements and Social Welfare*. Bloomington: Indiana University Press, 2012.

Deacon, James, and Diane Brady. "The Will to Fight—and Die." *Maclean's* 104:6 (February 11, 1991).

Demerath, III, N. J. *Crossing the Gods: World Religions and Worldly Politics*. New Brunswick, NJ: Rutgers University Press, 2003.

Deng, Francis M. "Sudan-Civil War and Genocide: Disappearing Christians of the Middle East." *Middle East Quarterly* (Winter 2001), 13–21.

Desai, Radhika. "Theories of Development," in Paul Haslam, Jessica Schafer, and Pierre Beaudet, eds., *Introduction to International Development: Approaches, Actors, and Issues*. New York: Oxford University Press, 2009.

de Soto, Hernando. "The Real Mohamed Bouazizi." *Foreign Policy*, December 16, 2011.

Diamantopoulou, Elisabeth A. "Religious Freedom in the Light of the Relationship Between the Orthodox Church and the Nation in Contemporary Greece." *International Journal for the Study of the Christian Church* 12:2 (May 2012), 164–175.

Dizboni, A. G. *Islam and War: The Disparity Between the Technological-Normative Evolution of Modern War and the Doctrine of Jihad*. Lewiston, NY: Edwin Mellen Press, 2011.

Doder, Dusko. "Yugoslavia: New War, Old Hatreds." *Foreign Policy* 91 (Summer 1993), 3–23.

Dowd, Robert. "Religious Diversity and Violent Conflict: Lessons from Nigeria." *The Fletcher Forum of World Affairs* 38:1 (Winter 2014), 153–168.

Dowty, Alan. *Israel/Palestine*, 2nd ed. Malden, MA: Polity, 2008.

Dowty, Alan. *Israel/Palestine*, 3rd ed. Malden, MA: Polity, 2012.

Drezgić, Rada. "Religion, Politics and Gender in the Context of Nation-State Formation: The Case of Serbia." *Third World Quarterly* 31:6 (2010), 955–970.

Duffy, Eamon. *Saints and Sinners: A History of The Popes*, 2nd ed. New Haven: Yale University Press, 2006.

Duncan, W. Raymond, Barbara Jancar-Webster, and Bob Switky. *World Politics in the 21st Century*, 3rd ed. New York: Pearson Longman, 2006.

Dunn, Dennis J. "Global Reach." *The Wilson Quarterly*, Autumn 1982, 113–123.

Dunn, Kevin C. "Killing for Christ? The Lord's Resistance Army of Uganda." *Current History* 103:673 (May 2004), 206–210.

Easterbrook, Gregg. "The End of War." *The New Republic*, May 30, 2005.

Easthope, Gary. "Religious War in Northern Ireland." *Sociology* 10:3 (September 1976), 427–450.

Edwards, Jason A. "Bringing in Earthly Redemption: Slobodan Milosevic and the National Myth of Kosovo." *Advances in the History of Rhetoric* 18 (2015), S187–S204.

Edwards, Mark Thomas. "Cold War Transgressions: Christian Realism, Conservative Socialism, and the Longer 1960s." *Religions* 6:1 (2015), 266–285.

Eichstaedt, Peter. *First Kill Your Family: Child Soldiers of Uganda and the Lord's Resistance Army*. Chicago: Lawrence Hill, 2013.

Eickelman, Dale F., and James Piscatori. *Muslim Politics*. Princeton: Princeton University Press, 1996.

Elkus, Adam, and Crispin Burke. "WikiLeaks, Media, and Policy: A Question of Super-Empowerment." *Small Wars Journal*, 2010, 4–10.

Elshtain, Jean Bethke. "Just War, Realism, and Humanitarian Intervention," in John D. Carlson and Erik C. Owens, eds., *The Sacred and the Sovereign: Religion and International Politics*. Washington: Georgetown University Press, 2003.

Elshtain, Jean Bethke. "Nationalism and Self-Determination: The Bosnian Tragedy," in G. Scott Davis, ed., *Religion and Justice in the War over Bosnia*. New York: Routledge, 1996.

Esposito, John L., ed. *The Iranian Revolution: Its Global Impact*. Miami: Florida International University Press, 1990.

Esposito, John L. "Islam and Political Violence." *Religions* 6:3 (2015), 1067–1081.

Esposito, John L. *The Islamic Threat: Myth or Reality?* New York: Oxford University Press, 1992.

Evans, Ernest. "Observations: The Vatican and Castro's Cuba." *World Affairs* 161:2 (Fall 1998), 112–115.

Falk, Richard. "The Christian Resurgence and World Order." *Brown Journal of World Affairs* 12:2 (Winter 2005/Spring 2006), 129–137.

Falk, Richard. "Politically Engaged Spiritually in an Emerging Global Civil Society." *ReVision* 15:3 (Winter 1993).

Falk, Richard. "Religion and Global Governance: Harmony or Clash?" *International Journal on World Peace* 19:1 (March 2002), 3–35.

Faseke, Babajimi Oladipo. "The Battle for Hearts and Minds: Religious Peacebuilding as an Alternative Solution to Boko Haram Terrorist Threat." *IUP Journal of International Relations* 7:4 (October 2013), 41–58.

Fazili, Yousra Y. "Between Mullahs' Robes and Absolutism: Conservatism in Iran." *SAIS Review* 30:1 (Winter-Spring 2010), 39–55.

Fealy, Greg. "Islam in Southeast Asia," in Mark Beeson, ed., *Contemporary Southeast Asia*, 2nd ed. New York: Palgrave Macmillan, 2009.

Fine, Jonathan. *Political Violence in Judaism, Christianity, and Islam: From Holy War to Modern Terror*. Lanham, MD: Rowman & Littlefield, 2015.

Fishel, John T. *American National Security Policy: Authorities, Institutions, and Cases*. Lanham, MD: Rowman & Littlefield, 2017.

Fleron, Frederic J., and Erik P. Hoffman, eds. *Post-Communist Studies and Political Science*. Boulder: Westview Press, 1993.

Forbes, Cameron. "Muslim Scholars Rule Out Saddam's Jihad Calls." *Sydney Morning Herald*, September 15, 1990.

Ford, Theresa. "How Daesh Uses Language in the Domain of Religion." *Military Review* (March–April 2016), 16–27.

Fox, Jonathan. *Ethnoreligious Conflict in the Late Twentieth Century: A General Theory*. Lanham, MD: Lexington, 2002.

Fox, Jonathan. *An Introduction to Religion and Politics: Theory and Practice*. New York: Routledge, 2013.

Fox, Jonathan. *An Introduction to Religion and Politics: Theory and Practice*, 2nd ed. New York: Routledge, 2018.

Fox, Jonathan. "The Rise of Religious Nationalism and Conflict: Ethnic Conflict and Revolutionary Wars, 1945–2001." *Journal of Peace Research* 41:6 (November 2004), 715–731.

Fox, Jonathan. "State Religious Exclusivity and Human Rights." *Political Studies* 56 (2008).

Fox, Jonathan, and Shmuel Sandler. *Bringing Religion into International Relations*. New York: Palgrave MacMillan, 2004.

Fox, Jonathan, and Shmuel Sandler. "The Palestinian-Israeli Conflict: A Case Study of Religion and International Politics," in Jonathan Fox and Shmuel Sandler, *Bringing Religion into International Relations*. New York: Palgrave MacMillan, 2004.

Frieden, Jeffrey A., David A. Lake, and Kenneth A. Schulz. *World Politics: Interests, Interactions, Institutions*, 4th ed. New York: Norton, 2019.

Friedman, Francine. "The Bosnian Muslim National Question," in Paul Mojzes, ed., *Religion and the War in Bosnia*. Atlanta: Scholars' Press, 1998.

Friedman, Thomas. *The Lexus and the Olive Tree*. New York: Anchor, 2000.

Froese, Paul. *The Plot to Kill God: Findings from the Soviet Experiment in Secularization*. Berkeley: University of California Press, 2008.

Frucht, Richard. Review of *Religion and War in Bosnia*, in *Journal of Church and State*, Winter 2000.

Fukuyama, Francis. "Against Identity Politics." Andrea Mitchell Center for the Study of Democracy. https://www.sas.upenn.edu/andrea-mitchell-center/francis-fukuyama-against-identity-politics.

Fukuyama, Francis. "Against Identity Politics: The New Tribalism and the Crisis of Democracy." *Foreign Affairs* 97:5 (September/October 2018), 90–114.

Fukuyama, Francis. "Religion as Identity Politics." *SAISPHERE*, 2009.

Fukuyama, Francis, and Michael McFaul. "Should Democracy Be Promoted or Demoted?" *Washington Quarterly* 31:1 (Winter 2007/2008), 23–45.

Fuller, Graham E. *The Future of Political Islam*. New York: Palgrave Macmillan, 2003.

Fuller, Graham E. "Turkey's Strategic Model: Myths and Realities." *Washington Quarterly* 27:3 (2004), 51–64.

Fuller, Graham E. *A World Without Islam*. New York: Back Bay, 2010.

Gaddis, John Lewis. *The Long Peace: Inquiries into the History of the Cold War*. New York: Oxford University Press, 1987.

Gelot, Ludwig Mikael. "Thomas Hobbes's Leviathan and the Theological Origins of Secular International Politics." *Political Theology* 12:4 (October 2011).

Genest, Marc. *Conflict and Cooperation: Evolving Theories of International Relations*. Belmont, CA: Cengage Learning, 2004.

Gergen, Kenneth J. "Social Construction and the Transformation of Identity Politics." Swarthmore College. http://www.swarthmore.edu/SocSci/kgergen1/text8.html.

Gerges, Fawaz A. *The Far Enemy: Why Jihad Went Global*. New York: Cambridge University Press, 2005.

Gerges, Fawaz A. *ISIS: A History*. Princeton: Princeton University Press, 2016.

Gerner, Deborah. *One Land, Two Peoples*. Boulder: Westview Press, 1994.

Gethard, Gregory. "Protest Divestment and the End of Apartheid." *Investopedia*, June 25, 2019.

Ghobadzdeh, Naser, and Shahram Akbarzadeh. "Sectarianism and the Prevalence of 'Othering' in Islamic Thought." *Third World Quarterly* 36:4 (2015).

Gill, Anthony. *Rendering unto Caesar: The Catholic Church and the State in Latin America*. Chicago: University of Chicago Press, 1998.

Gleditsch, Nils Petter, Erik Melander, and Henrik Urdal. "Introduction: Patterns of Armed Conflict Since 1945," in T. David Mason and Sara McLaughlin Mitchell, *What Do We Know About Civil Wars?* Lanham, MD: Rowman & Littlefield, 2016.

Goba, Bonganjalo. "The Kairos Document and Its Implications for Liberation in South Africa." *Journal of Law and Religion* 5:2 (1987).

Goldberg, Jonah. *Liberal Fascism*. New York: Random House, 2007.

Goldberg, Jonah. "Religion and Politics: Inseparable Through the Ages." *Cedar Rapids Gazette*, November 12, 2006.

Goldsmith, Rebecca. "European Union Debates Nod to God." *Christian Century* 121:5 (March 9, 2004), 17.

Goldstein, Joshua S., and Jon C. Pevehouse. *International Relations*, 10th ed. New York: Pearson, 2013.

González, Justo L. *The Story of Christianity*, Vol. 2. New York: HarperCollins, 1985.

Grieco, Joseph, G. John Ikenberry, and Michael Mastanduno. *Introduction to International Relations: Enduring Questions and Contemporary Perspectives*. New York: Palgrave Macmillan, 2015.

Griffin, Michael. *Islamic State: Rewriting History*. London: Pluto, 2016.

Grim, Brian J. "How Religious Will the World Be in 2050?" World Economic Forum. https://www.weforum.org/agenda/2015/10/how-religious-will-the-world-be-in-2050.

Grim, Brian J. "Restrictions on Religion in the World: Measures and Implications," in Allen D. Hertzke, ed., *The Future of Religious Freedom: Global Challenges*. New York: Oxford University Press, 2013.

Griswold, Eliza. "God's Country." *Atlantic Monthly* 301:2 (March 2008).

Griswold, Eliza. *The Tenth Parallel: Dispatches from the Fault Line Between Christianity and Islam*. New York: Farrar, Straus and Giroux, 2010.

Grung, Anne Hege. "The Two Pluralisms in Norway." *Society* 54:5 (October 2017), 432–438.

Grzymala-Busse, Anna. "Why Comparative Politics Should Take Religion (More) Seriously." *Annual Review of Political Science* 15 (2012).

Guan, Yeoh Seng. "In Defence of the Secular? Islamisation, Christians and (New) Politics in Urbane Malaysia." *Asian Studies Review* 35:1 (2011).

Guelke, Adrian. "Religion, National Identity and the Conflict in Northern Ireland," in William Safran, ed., *The Secular and the Sacred: Nation, Religion and Politics*. Portland, OR: Frank Cass, 2003.

Gurian, Waldemar. "Hitler's Undeclared War on the Catholic Church." *Foreign Affairs* 16:2 (January 1938).

Hagen, William W. "The Balkans' Lethal Nationalisms." *Foreign Affairs* 78:4 (1999), 52–64.

Hague, Rod, and Martin Harrop. *Political Science: A Comparative Introduction*, 7th ed. New York: Palgrave Macmillan, 2013.

Hague, Rod, Martin Harrop, and John McCormick. *Political Science: A Comparative Introduction*, 8th ed. New York: Palgrave Macmillan, 2016.

Halbertal, Dov. "Religion and State, One and the Same," in Eliezer Ben Rafael et al., eds., *Handbook of Israel: Major Debates*. Berlin: De Gruyter Oldenbourg, 2016.

Hale, Christopher W. "Religious Institutions and Civic Engagement." *Comparative Politics* 47:2 (January 2015).

Hale, William. "Christian Democracy and the AKP: Parallels and Contrasts." *Turkish Studies* 6:2 (Summer 2005), 293–310.

Halliday, Fred. "The Iranian Revolution." *Political Studies* 30:3 (September 1982).

Hamid, Ahmad Fauzi Abdul. "Syariahization of Intra-Muslim Religious Freedom and Human Rights Practice in Malaysia: The Case of Darul Arqam." *Contemporary Southeast Asia* 38:1 (2016).

Hamid, Shadi, and William McCants. "How Likely Is It That an Islamist Group Will Govern in the Middle East Before 2020?" Brookings Institution, August 2, 2017.

Hamre, John. "Religion and International Affairs." *SAISPHERE*, 2009.

Hampson, Michael Edward. *Rationalizing the Profane: Explaining the Violence of the Lord's Resistance Army*. PhD dissertation, University of California, Irvine, 2013.

Handelman, Howard. *The Challenge of Third World Development*, 3rd ed. Upper Saddle River, NJ: Prentice Hall, 2003.

Handelman, Howard. *The Challenge of Third World Development*, 5th ed. Upper Saddle River, NJ: Pearson Prentice Hall, 2009.

Hanson, Eric O. *The Catholic Church in World Politics*. Princeton: Princeton University Press, 2014.

Hanson, Eric O. *Religion and Politics in the International System Today*. New York: Cambridge University Press, 2006.

Hashim, Ahmed S. "The Caliphate at War: Ideology, War Fighting and State Formation." *Middle East Policy* 23:1 (Spring 2016).

Hashmi, Sohail H. *State Sovereignty: Change and Persistence in International Relations.* University Park: Pennsylvania State University Press, 1997.

Hassner, Ron E. *War on Sacred Grounds.* Ithaca: Cornell University Press, 2009.

Hastedt, Glenn, Donna L. Lybecker, and Vaughn P. Shannon. *Cases in International Relations: Pathways to Conflict and Cooperation.* Washington DC: CQ Press, 2015.

Haynes, Jeffrey. *Faith-Based Organizations at the United Nations.* New York: Palgrave Macmillan, 2014.

Haynes, Jeffrey. *An Introduction to International Relations and Religion.* New York: Pearson Longman, 2007.

Haynes, Jeffrey. *An Introduction to International Relations and Religion*, 2nd ed. New York: Pearson, 2013.

Haynes, Jeffrey. "Religion and Foreign Policy Making in the USA, India and Iran." *Third World Quarterly* 29:1 (February 2008).

Haynes, Jeff. "Religion and Politics: What Is the Impact of September 11?" *Contemporary Politics* 9:1 (March 2003).

Haynes, Jeffrey. *Religion in Global Politics.* New York: Longman, 1998.

Haynes, Jeffrey. *Religion, Politics and International Relations: Selected Essays.* New York: Routledge, 2011.

Haynes, Jeffrey. *Religious Transnational Actors and Soft Power.* Burlington, VT: Ashgate, 2012.

Haynes, Jeffrey. "Transnational Religious Actors and International Order." *Perspectives* 17: 2 (2009), 43–69.

Haynes, Jeffrey. "Transnational Religious Actors and International Politics." *Third World Quarterly* 22:2 (2010), 143–158.

Haynes, Jeffrey, and Guy Ben-Porat. "Globalisation, Religion and Secularisation – Different States, Same Trajectories?" *Totalitarian Movements and Political Religions* 11:2 (June 2010).

Hazran, Yusri. "The Rise of Politicized Shi'ite Religiosity and the Territorial State in Iraq and Lebanon." *Middle East Journal* 64:4 (Autumn 2010).

Healey, Stephen. Review of *When Religion Becomes Evil* by Charles Kimball. *Christian Century*, October 9, 2002.

Hefner, Robert W. "Religious Resurgence in Contemporary Asia: Southeast Asian Perspectives on Capitalism, the State, and the New Piety." *Journal of Asian Studies* 69:4 (November 2010), 1031–1047.

Hehir, J. Bryan. "The Moral Measurement of War: A Tradition of Change and Continuity," in John D. Carlson and Erik C. Owens, eds., *The Sacred and the Sovereign.* Washington DC: Georgetown University Press, 2003.

Helfont, Samuel. "The Geopolitics of the Sunni-Shi'i Divide in the Middle East." Foreign Policy Research Institute, December 12, 2013. https://www.fpri.org/article /2013/12/the-geopolitics-of-the-sunni-shii-divide-in-the-middle-east.

Helfont, Samuel. "Saddam and the Islamists: The Ba'thist Regime's Instrumentalization of Religion in Foreign Affairs." *Middle East Journal* 68:3 (Summer 2014), 360.

Henne, Peter S. "The Two Swords: Religion-State Connections and Interstate Disputes." *Journal of Peace Research* 49:6 (November 2012).

Hertzke, Allen D., ed. *The Future of Religious Freedom: Global Challenges.* New York: Oxford University Press, 2013.

Hertzke, Allen H. "Roman Catholicism and the Faith-Based Movement for Global Human Rights." *The Review of Faith and International Affairs* 3:3 (Winter 2005–2006), 20.

Heywood, Andrew. *Politics.* London: Palgrave, 2002.

Hill, Charles. *Trial of A Thousand Years: World Order and Islamism.* Stanford: Hoover Institution Press, 2011.

Hockenos, Matthew D. "The Church Struggle and the Confessing Church: An Introduction to Bonhoeffer's Context." *Studies in Christian-Jewish Relations* 2:1 (2007), 4.

Hoelzl, Verena. "As Rohingya Boats Keep Sailing, Southeast Asia Turns a Blind Eye." *Foreign Policy*, May 14, 2020.

Hoffman, Bruce. *Inside Terrorism*, 3rd ed. New York: Columbia University Press, 2017.

Hoffman, Michael, and Amaney Jamal. "Religion in the Arab Spring: Between Two Competing Narratives." *The Journal of Politics* 76:3 (July 2014).

Hoge, Warren. "An Irish Accord: The Overview; Irish Talks Produce an Accord To Stop Decades of Bloodshed with Sharing of Ulster Power." *New York Times*, April 11, 1998.

Homans, Charles. "Track II Diplomacy: A Short History." *Foreign Policy*, June 20, 2011.

Hook, Steven W. *U.S. Foreign Policy: The Paradox of World Power*. Washington DC: CQ Press, 2005.

Hook, Steven W. *U.S. Foreign Policy: The Paradox of World Power*, 2nd ed. Washington DC: CQ Press, 2008.

Hopmann, P. Terrence. "Groupthink: Religion, Identity, and Violent Conflict." *SAISPHERE*, 2009.

Hossain, Ishtiaq. "The Organization of Islamic Conference (OIC): Nature, Role, and the Issues." *Journal of Third World Studies* 29:1 (Spring 2012).

Houghton, David Patrick. *The Decision Point: Six Cases in U.S. Foreign Policy Decision Making*. New York: Oxford University Press, 2013.

Howard, Lise Morjé. "Sources of Change in United States–United Nations Relations." *Global Governance* 16 (2010).

Hunter, Shireen T. *God on Our Side: Religion in International Affairs*. Lanham, MD: Rowman & Littlefield, 2017.

Huntington, Samuel P. "The Clash of Civilizations?" *Foreign Affairs* 72:3 (Summer 1993), 22–49.

Huntington, Samuel P. *The Third Wave: Democratization in the Late Twentieth Century*. Norman: University of Oklahoma Press, 1991.

Hurd, Elizabeth Shakman. *Beyond Religious Freedom: The New Global Politics of Religion*. Princeton: Princeton University Press, 2015.

Hurd, Elizabeth Shakman. "International Politics After Secularism." *Review of International Studies* 38:5 (December 2012), 943–961.

Hurd, Elizabeth Shakman. *The Politics of Secularism in International Relations*. Princeton: Princeton University Press, 2008.

Hurd, Elizabeth Shakman. "Secularism and International Relations Theory," in Jack Snyder, ed., *Religion and International Relations Theory*. New York: Columbia University Press, 2011.

Hurd, Elizabeth Shakman. "What's Wrong with Promoting Religious Freedom?" *Foreign Policy*, June 12, 2013.

Husain, Mir Zohair. "The Islamic Revolution in Iran," in Mir Zohair Husain, ed., *Global Islamic Politics*, 2nd ed. New York: Longman, 2003.

Ikenberry, John G. "The Future of the Liberal World Order." *Foreign Affairs* 90:3 (May/June 2011).

Ilishev, Ildus G. "The Iran-Saudi Arabia Conflict and Its Impact on the Organization of Islamic Cooperation." Wilson Center, June 2016. https://www.wilsoncenter.org/publication/the-iran-saudi-arabia-conflict-and-its-impact-the-organization-islamic-cooperation.

Isaacs, Matthew. "Sacred Violence or Strategic Faith? Disentangling the Relationship Between Religion and Violence in Armed Conflict." *Journal of Peace Research* 53:2 (2016), 211–225.

Ismael, Jacqueline S., and Shereen T. Ismael. "The Arab Spring and the Uncivil State." *Arab Studies Quarterly* 35:3 (Summer 2013).

Israeli, Raphael. "State and Religion in the Emerging Palestinian Entity." *Journal of Church and State* 44:2 (Spring 2002).

Ivekovic, Ivan. "The Political Use and Abuse of Religion in Transcaucasia and Yugoslavia." *Comparative Studies of South Asia, Africa, and the Middle East* 17:1 (1997).

Jackson, Paul. "'Negotiating with Ghosts': Religion, Conflict and Peace in Northern Uganda." *The Round Table* 98:402 (June 2009), 323.

Jacobi, Daniel, and Annette Freyberg-Ina. "Human Being(s) in International Relations." *International Studies Review* 14:4 (December 2012), 645–665.

Jacoby, Mary. "Singing Bono's Praises." *St. Petersburg Times*, June 2, 2002.

Jafari, Sheherazade. "Local Religious Peacemakers: An Untapped Resource in U.S. Foreign Policy." *Journal of International Affairs* 61:1 (Fall/Winter 2007).

Jaffrelot, Christophe. "The Fate of Secularism in India." Carnegie Endowment for International Peace, April 4, 2019.

James, Jonathan D. *Transnational Religious Movements: Faith's Flows*. Thousand Oaks, CA: Sage, 2017.

Jeffrey, Paul. "Hope for Uganda." *America*, August 18–25, 2008.

Jelen, Ted G., and Clyde Wilcox. *Religion and Politics in Comparative Perspective: The One, the Few, and the Many*. New York: Cambridge University Press, 2002.

Jenish, D'Arcy. "Islam and the Gulf War." *Maclean's* 104:6 (February 11, 1991).

Jentleson, Bruce W. *American Foreign Policy: The Dynamics of Choice in the Twenty-First Century*, 4th ed. New York: Norton, 2010.

Jerryson, Michael. "Buddhist Traditions and Violence," in Mark Juergensmeyer, Margo Kitts, and Michael Jerryson, eds., *Violence and the World's Religious Traditions: An Introduction*. New York: Oxford University Press, 2017.

Jervis, Robert. "Hans Morgenthau, Realism, and the Scientific Study of International Politics." *Social Research* 61:4 (Winter 1994).

Johnson, Ian. "China's Great Awakening: How the People's Republic Got Religion." *Foreign Affairs* 96:2 (March/April 2017).

Johnson, James Turner. Quoted in Simeon Ilesanmi, "Just War Theory in Comparative Perspective: A Review Essay." *Journal of Religious Ethics* 28:1 (2000), 139–155.

Johnson, Jenna. "Trump Calls for 'Total and Complete Shutdown of Muslims Entering the United States.'" *Washington Post*, December 7, 2015.

Johnston, Douglas. "The Churches and Apartheid in South Africa," in Douglas Johnston and Cynthia Sampson, eds., *Religion, the Missing Dimension of Statecraft*. New York: Oxford University Press, 1994.

Johnston, Douglas, ed. *Faith-Based Diplomacy: Trumping Realpolitik*. New York: Oxford University Press, 2003.

Johnston, Douglas. "We Neglect Religion at Our Peril." *U.S. Naval Institute Proceedings* 128:1 (January 2002).

Johnston, Douglas, and Brian Cox. "Faith-Based Diplomacy and Preventive Engagement," in Douglas Johnston, ed., *Faith-Based Diplomacy: Trumping Realpolitik*. New York: Oxford University Press, 2003.

Johnston, Douglas, and Cynthia Sampson, eds. *Religion, the Missing Dimension of Statecraft*. New York: Oxford University Press, 1994.

Jordan, Patrick. "A Man in Dark Times." *Commonweal* 127:18 (October 20, 2000).

Joseph, A. L. R. "Unfettered Religious Freedom Hangs by the Thread of Minority Dissent in Malaysia: A Review of the Dissenting Judgment of the Federal Court in the Lina Joy Case." *Review of Constitutional Studies* 14:2 (2009).

Juergensmeyer, Mark. *Global Rebellion: Religious Challenges to the Secular State, from Christian Militias to al Qaeda*. Berkeley: University of California Press, 2008.

Juergensmeyer, Mark. "The Global Rise of Religious Nationalism." *Australian Journal of International Affairs* 64:3 (June 2010), 262–273.

Juergensmeyer, Mark. "Martyrdom and Sacrifice in a Time of Terror." *Social Research* 75:2 (Summer 2008), 417–434.

Juergensmeyer, Mark. *The New Cold War? Religious Nationalism Confronts the Secular State*. Berkeley: University of California Press, 1993.

Juergensmeyer, Mark. "The New Religious State." *Comparative Politics* 27: 4 (July 1995), 379–391.

Juergensmeyer, Mark. *Terror in the Mind of God: The Global Rise of Religious Violence*, 4th ed. Berkeley: University of California Press, 2017.

Juergensmeyer, Mark. "The Worldwide Rise of Religious Nationalism." *Journal of International Affairs* 50:1 (Summer 1996).

Juergensmeyer, Mark, Dinah Griego, and John Sobslai. *God in the Tumult of the Global Square: Religion in Global Civil Society*. Berkeley: University of California Press, 2015.

Kaplan, Robert D. *Balkan Ghosts: A Journey Through History*. New York: St. Martin's Press, 1993.

Kaplan, Robert D. "The Post-Imperial Moment." *The National Interest* 143 (May/June 2016).

Karasipahi, Sena. "Comparing Islamic Resurgence Movements in Turkey and Iran." *Middle East Journal* 63:1 (Winter 2009), 87–107.

Karčić, Hamza. "In Support of a Non-Member State: The Organization of Islamic Conference and the War in Bosnia, 1992–1995." *Journal of Muslim Minority Affairs* 33:3 (September 2013).

Karcic, Harun. "Globalization and Islam in Bosnia: Foreign Influences and Their Effects." *Totalitarian Movements and Political Religions* 11:2 (June 2010).

Katzenstein, Peter J., and Timothy A. Byrnes. "Transnational Religion in an Expanding Europe." *Perspectives on Politics* 4:4 (December 1, 2006).

Kavakçı, Merve. "Headscarf Heresy." *Foreign Policy* 142 (May/June 2004).

Kazemzadeh, Firuz. "Reflections on Church and State in Russian History," in John Witte Jr. and Michael Bourdeaux, eds., *Proselytism and Orthodoxy in Russia: The New War for Souls*. Maryknoll, NY: Orbis Books, 1999.

Kegley, Charles W., and Shannon L. Blanton. *World Politics: Trend and Transformation, 2014–2015*, 15th ed. Boston: Wadsworth, 2015.

Kegley, Charles W., Jr., and Gregory A. Raymond. *The Global Future: A Brief Introduction to World Politics*. Belmont, CA: Thomson Wadsworth, 2005.

Kegley, Charles W., Jr., and Gregory A. Raymond. *The Global Future: A Brief Introduction to World Politics*, 3rd ed. Boston: Wadsworth, 2010.

Kegley, Charles W., Jr., and Gregory A. Raymond. *The Global Future: A Brief Introduction to World Politics*, 5th ed. Boston: Wadsworth, 2014.

Kegley, Charles W., Jr., and Eugene R. Wittkopf. *World Politics: Trend and Transformations*, 9th ed. Belmont, CA: Thomson Wadsworth, 2004.

Kelly, Michael. "Surrender and Blame." *The New Yorker*, December 19, 1994.

Kendhanmer, Brandon. *Muslims Talking Politics: Framing Islam, Democracy, and Law in Northern Nigeria*. Chicago: University of Chicago Press, 2016.

Kershaw, Roger. "The Penalties of Apostasy in Malaysia." *Contemporary Review* 290:1691 (2008).

Kettell, Steven. "The Militant Strain: An Analysis of Anti-Secular Discourse in Britain." *Political Studies* 63:3 (August 2015), 517.

Khatchadourian, Raffi. "Behind Enemy Lines." *Nation* 282:19 (May 15, 2006), 23–24, 27–28.

Kimball, Charles. *When Religion Becomes Lethal: The Explosive Mix of Politics and Religion in Judaism, Christianity, and Islam*. San Francisco: John Wiley, 2011.

Kingston, Jeff. *The Politics of Religion, Nationalism, and Identity in Asia*. Lanham, MD: Rowman & Littlefield, 2019.

Kinzer, Stephen. "Catholic Bishops and Sandinistas Meeting Again." *New York Times*, August 29, 1985.

Kissane, Bill. *Nations Torn Asunder: The Challenge of Civil War*. New York: Oxford University Press, 2016.

Klarevas, Louis. "Political Realism." *Harvard International Review* 26:3 (Fall 2004), 20.

Klausen, Jytte. "Why Religion Has Become More Salient in Europe: Four Working Hypotheses About Secularization and Religiosity in Contemporary Politics." *European Political Science* 8:3 (September 2009), 289–300.

Kollander, Patricia. "The Civil War in Former Yugoslavia and the International Intervention," in Jeffrey S. Morton, Stefano Bianchini, and Craig Nation, eds., *Reflections on the Balkan Wars: Ten Years After the Break-up of Yugoslavia.* New York: Palgrave Macmillan, 2004.

Kortteinen, Timo. "Islamic Resurgence and the Ethnicization of the Malaysian State: The Case of Lina Joy." *Sojourn: Journal of Social Issues in Southeast Asia* 23:2 (October 2008), 218.

Kubálková, Vendulka. "A 'Turn to Religion' in International Relations?" *Perspectives: Review of Central European Affairs* 17:2 (2009), 19.

Kurth, James. "Religion and Ethnic Conflict – In Theory." *Orbis* 45:2 (Spring 2001), 281–294.

Kurth, James. "The Vatican's Foreign Policy." *The National Interest* 32 (July 1, 1993).

Kurzman, Charles and Didem Türko¢glu. "Do Muslims Vote Islamic Now?" *Journal of Democracy* 26:4 (October 2015).

Lake, Anthony. "Confronting Backlash States." *Foreign Affairs*, March/April 1994.

Lamy, Steven L., et al. *Introduction to Global Politics, Brief Edition.* New York: Oxford University Press, 2012.

Lancaster, Roger N. *Thanks to God and the Revolution: Popular Religion and Class Consciousness in the New Nicaragua.* New York: Columbia University Press, 1988.

Landow, Charles, and Mohammed Aly Sergie. "The Northern Ireland Peace Process." Council on Foreign Relations, March 5, 2020. https://www.cfr.org/backgrounder /northern-ireland-peace-process.

Larsen, Timothy. "Bonhoeffer: Pastor, Martyr, Prophet, Spy: A Righteous Gentile vs. the Third Reich." *Fides et Historia* 43:2 (Summer 2011), 138–141.

Law Library of Congress, Global Legal Research Center. "China: Religion and Chinese Law." Report for the Department of Justice, June 2018. www.justice.gov.

Lean, Nathan. *Understanding Islam and the West: Critical Skills for Students.* Lanham, MD: Rowman & Littlefield, 2018.

Lee, Robert D. *Religion and Politics in the Middle East: Identity, Ideology, Institutions, and Attitudes.* Boulder: Westview Press, 2010.

Lefebvre, Solange. "Disestablishment of the Church: Discussion with Jose Casanova from a Canadian Point of View." *International Journal of Practical Theology* 11:2 (2007), 300.

Leftwich, Adrian. *States of Development: On the Primacy of Politics in Development.* Malden, MA: Polity, 2000.

Lerner, Hanna. "Permissive Constitutions, Democracy, and Religious Freedom in India, Indonesia, Israel, and Turkey." *World Politics* 65:4 (October 2013).

Leustean, Lucian N., and John T. S. Madeley. "Religion, Politics and Law in the European Union: An Introduction." *Religion, State and Society* 37:1/2 (March/June 2009).

Lind, William S. "Defending Western Culture." *Foreign Policy* 84 (Autumn 1991).

Little, David. "Introduction," in David R. Smock, *Religious Perspectives on War: Christian, Muslim, and Jewish Attitudes Toward Force*, rev. ed. Washington: United States Institute of Peace Press, 2002.

Little, David, ed. *Peacemakers in Action: Profiles of Religion in Conflict Resolution.* New York: Cambridge University Press, 2007.

Lister, Charles R. *The Islamic State: A Brief Introduction.* Washington DC: Brookings Institution Press, 2015.

Lodberg, Peter. "Apartheid as a Church-Dividing Ethical Issue." *Ecumenical Review* 48:2 (April 1996).

Lounsbery, Marie Olson, and Frederic Pearson. *Civil Wars: Internal Struggles, Global Consequences.* Toronto: University of Toronto Press, 2009.

Love, Maryann Cusimano. "Taking on Turkmenistan." Case 324. Washington DC: Institute for the Study of Diplomacy, 2011.

Lunkin, Roman. "The Status of and Challenges to Religious Freedom in Russia," in Allen D. Hertzke, ed., *The Future of Religious Freedom: Global Challenges.* New York: Oxford University Press, 2013.

Lust, Ellen, Gamal Solton, and Jakob Wichmann. "After the Arab Spring: Islamism, Secularism, and Democracy." *Current History* 111:749 (December 2012), 362–364.

Luttwak, Edward. "The Missing Dimension," in Douglas Johnston and Cynthia Sampson, eds., *Religion, the Missing Dimension of Statecraft.* New York: Oxford University Press, 1994.

Luxmoore, Jonathan. "From Solidarity to Freedom: The Mixed Fortunes of Churches in Postcommunist Eastern Europe," in Allen D. Hertzke, ed., *The Future of Religious Freedom: Global Challenges.* New York: Oxford University Press, 2013.

Lynch, Edward A. "Catholic Social Thought in Latin America." *Orbis* 42:1 (Winter 1998).

Lynch, Marc. "Veiled Truths." *Foreign Affairs* 89:4 (July/August 2010).

MacDonald, David Bruce. *Balkan Holocausts? Serbian and Croatian Victim Centred Propaganda and the War in Yugoslavia.* Manchester: Manchester University Press, 2003.

Macqueen, Ian. "Ecumenism and the Global Anti-Apartheid Struggle: The World Council of Churches' Special Fund in South Africa and Botswana, 1970–75." *Historia* 62:2 (November 2017).

Madden, Thomas F. "Crusade Propaganda." *National Review*, November 2, 2001.

Madeley, John. "Religion and the State," in Jeffrey Haynes, ed., *Routledge Handbook of Religion and Politics.* New York: Routledge, 2009.

Maffettone, Sebastiano. "Enlightenment and the European Union Model" *Monist* 92:2 (April 2009).

Magaziner, Daniel. "Christ in Context: Developing a Political Faith in Apartheid South Africa." *Radical History Review* 99 (Fall 2007).

Magid, Shaul. "Sacred Real Estate." *Christian Century*, July 25, 2006.

Magstadt, Thomas M. *Nations and Governments: Comparative Politics in Regional Perspective*, 4th ed. New York: Bedford/St. Martins.

Mainwaring, Scott, and Alexander Wilde, eds. *The Progressive Church in Latin America.* Notre Dame: University of Notre Dame Press, 1989.

Malekian, Farhad. *Jurisprudence of International Criminal Justice.* Newcastle upon Tyne: Cambridge Scholars, 2014.

Malki, Riad. "Beyond Hamas and Fatah." *Journal of Democracy* 17:3 (2006).

Mandle, Joan D. "Identity Politics, Feminism and Social Change." http://www.research.umbc.edu/~korenman/wmst/identity_pol.html.

Mang, Pum Za. "Oscar Romero: Champion of the Oppressed." *Asia Journal of Theology* 27:2 (October 2013).

Mansbach, Richard W., and Kirsten L. Taylor. *Introduction to Global Politics*, 2nd ed. New York: Routledge, 2012.

Ma'oz, Moshe. "A National or Religious Conflict? The Dispute over the Temple Mount/Al-Haram Al-Sharif in Jerusalem." *Palestine-Israel Journal of Politics, Economics, and Culture* 20/21:4/1 (2015), 25–32.

Mapendere, Jeffrey. "Track One and a Half Diplomacy and the Complementarity of Tracks." *Culture of Peace Online Journal* 2:1 (2006), 66–81.

Marshall, Paul. "Keeping the Faith: Religion, Freedom, and International Affairs." *USA Today* 128:2656 (January 2000), 52.

Martin, David. *Religion and Power: No Logos Without Mythos* (Burlington, VT: Ashgate, 2014).

Mason, John Brown. "The Concordat with the Third Reich." *Catholic Historical Review* 20:1 (April 1934), 23–24.

Mason, T. David, and Sara McLaughlin Mitchell, eds. *What Do We Know About Civil Wars?* Lanham, MD: Rowman & Littlefield, 2016.

Mason, T. David, Sara McLaughlin Mitchell, and Alyssa K. Prorok. "What Do We Know About Civil Wars? Introduction and Overview," in T. David Mason and Sara McLaughlin Mitchell, eds., *What Do We Know About Civil Wars?* Lanham, MD: Rowman & Littlefield, 2016.

Matsumoto, Futoshi. "The World Order and a New 'Behemoth.'" *Asia-Pacific Review* 22:1 (May 2015), 182.

Mazurczak, Filip. "Archbishop Romero and Liberation Theology." *National Catholic Register*, May 7, 2015.

McCants, William. "The Believer: How an Introvert with a Passion for Religion and Soccer Became Abu Bakr al-Baghdadi, Leader of the Islamic State." Brookings Essay, September 1, 2015. http://csweb.brookings.edu/content/research/essays/2015/thebeliever.html.

McDougall, Walter A. "Religion in World Affairs." *Orbis* 42:2 (Spring 1998), 159–170.

McGlinchey, Stephen. "How the Shah Entangled America." *The National Interest*, August 2, 2013.

McLean, Ian A. T. "The Fuzzy Picture of Hitler's Pope." *Political Science Reviewer* 32 (2003), 174–175.

Megheşan, Karin, and Teodora Dobre. "Political Psychology – New Challenges in Analyzing Foreign Policy." *Romanian Review of Social Sciences* 10 (2016), 57.

Menéndez, Agustín José. "A Christian or a Laïc Europe? Christian Values and European Identity." *Ratio Juris* 18:2 (June 2005).

Metraux, Daniel A. "Religious Terrorism in Japan: The Fatal Appeal of Aum Shinrikyo." *Asian Survey* 35:12 (December 1995), 152.

Mewes, Horst. "Religion and Politics in American Democracy," in William Safran, ed., *The Secular and the Sacred: Nation, Religion and Politics*. Portland, OR: Frank Cass, 2003.

Meyer, Steven E. "Religion and Security in the Post-Modern World." *Review of Faith and International Affairs* 6:3 (Fall 2008), 6.

Michalak, Stanley. *A Primer in Power Politics*. Wilmington, DE: Scholarly Resources, 2001.

Micklethwait, John, and Adrian Wooldridge. *God Is Back: How the Global Revival of Faith Is Changing the World*. New York: Penguin, 2009.

Miller, Judith. "War in the Gulf: Muslims, Saudis Decree Holy War on Hussein." *New York Times*, January 1, 1991.

Milton-Edwards, Beverly. "Political Islam and the Palestinian–Israeli Conflict." *Israel Affairs* 12:1 (Winter 2006), 68.

Mingst, Karen A. *Essentials of International Relations*, 4th ed. New York: Norton, 2008.

Mingst, Karen A., and Ivan M. Arreguín-Toft. *Essentials of International Relations*, 7th ed. New York: Norton, 2017.

Mingst, Karen A., and Margaret P. Karns. *The United Nations in the Post–Cold War Era*. Westview Press, 1995.

Minter, William. "South Africa: Straight Talk on Sanctions." *Foreign Policy* 65 (Winter 1986), 43–63.

Mohamad, Maznah. "The Ascendance of Bureaucratic Islam and the Secularization of the Sharia in Malaysia." *Pacific Affairs* 83:3 (2010).

Mohseni, Payam, and Clyde Wilcox. "Religion and Political Parties," in Jeffrey Haynes, ed., *Routledge Handbook of Religion and Politics*. New York: Routledge, 2009.

Mojzes, Paul. *Balkan Genocides: Holocaust and Ethnic Cleansing in the Twentieth Century*. Lanham, MD: Rowman & Littlefield, 2011.

Moll, Nicolas. "Fragmented Memories in a Fragmented Country: Memory Competition and Political Identity-Building in Today's Bosnia and Herzegovina." *Nationalities Papers* 41:6 (November 2013), 910–935.

Moll, Rob. "The Father of Faith-Based Diplomacy." *Christianity Today* 52:9 (September 2008).

Montalbano, William D. "Frail Pontiff Urges Croats to Forge Peace." *Los Angeles Times*, September 11, 1994.

Morgenthau, Hans J. "Enduring Realities and Foreign Policy." *American Foreign Policy Interests* 33 (2011), 14.

Morgenthau, Hans J. *Politics Among Nations: The Struggle for Power and Peace*, brief ed. New York: McGraw-Hill, 1993.

Morus, Christina M. "Slobo the Redeemer: The Rhetoric of Slobodan Milosevic and the Construction of the Serbian 'People.'" *Southern Communication Journal* 72:1 (January–March 2007), 1–19.

Moses, John A. "Dietrich Bonhoeffer's Repudiation of Protestant German War Theology," *Journal of Religious History* 30:3 (October 2006), 354–370.

Moustafa, Tamir. "Liberal Rights versus Islamic Law? The Construction of a Binary in Malaysian Politics." *Law and Society Review* 47:4 (December 2013).

Mueller, John. "War Has Almost Ceased to Exist: An Assessment." *Political Science Quarterly* 124:2 (2009), 320.

Mulligan, Joseph E. "On the Fifteenth Anniversary of the Sandinista Triumph: Interview with a Revolutionary Priest." *Monthly Review* 46:3 (July/August 1994).

Nafisi, Azar. "Shaping a Nation: Secular and Religious Intellectuals in Iran." *SAISPHERE*, 2009.

Nau, Henry R. *Perspectives on International Relations*, 2nd ed. Washington DC: CQ Press, 2009.

Neack, Laura. *The New Foreign Policy: Complex Interactions, Competing Interests*, 3rd ed. Lanham, MD: Rowman & Littlefield, 2014.

Neack, Laura. *The New Foreign Policy: U.S. and Comparative Foreign Policy in the 21st Century*. Lanham, MD: Rowman & Littlefield, 2003.

Nehorayoff, Andrea A., Benjamin Ash, and Daniel S. Smith. "Aum Shinrikyo's Nuclear and Chemical Weapons Development Efforts." *Journal of Strategic Security* 9:1 (Spring 2016).

Neo Ling-Chien, Jaclyn. "Malay Nationalism, Islamic Supremacy and the Constitutional Bargain in the Multi-Ethnic Composition of Malaysia." *International Journal On Minority and Group Rights* 13:1 (2006).

Nexon, Daniel H. "Religion and International Relations: No Leap of Faith Required," in Jack Snyder, ed., *Religion and International Relations Theory*. New York: Columbia University Press, 2011.

Norris, Pippa, and Ronald Inglehart. *Sacred and Secular: Religion and Politics Worldwide*. New York: Cambridge University Press, 2004.

Nye, Joseph S., Jr. "A Game of Three-Dimensional Chess with China." *Los Angeles Times*, June 13, 2013.

Nye, Joseph S., Jr. "The Information Revolution and Power." *Current History* 113:759 (January 2014).

Nye, Joseph S., Jr., and David A. Welch. *Understanding Global Conflict and Cooperation: An Introduction to Theory and History*, 9th ed. New York: Longman, 2013.

O'Brien, Conor Cruise. "Saddam Comes out Fighting as Champion of the Fanatics." *The Times*, August 4, 1990.

O'Leary, Brendan. "The Federalization of Iraq and the Break-up of Sudan." *Government and Opposition* 47:4 (2012), 481–516.

Omer-Cooper, J. D. *History of Southern Africa*, 2nd ed. Oxford: James Currey, 1994.

Onapajo, Hakeem, and Ufo Okeke Uzodike. "Boko Haram Terrorism in Nigeria: Man, the State, and the International System." *African Security Review* 21:3 (September 2012).

O'Neil, Patrick H., Karl Fields, and Don Share. *Cases in Comparative Politics*, 3rd ed. New York: Norton, 2010.

Öniş, Ziya. "Turkey's Two Elections: The AKP Comes Back." *Journal of Democracy* 27:2 (April 2016).

Opeloye, Muhib O. "The Socio-Political Factor in the Christian-Muslim Conflict in Nigeria." *Islam and Christian Muslim Relations* 9:2 (July 1998), 231–237.

O'Shaughnessy, Laura Nuzzi. "'God Speaks from Within History': The Challenging Witness of Liberation Theology." *Latin American Research Review* 51:3 (2016), 227–240.

Paldam, Ella, and Martin Paldam. "The Political Economy of Churches in Denmark, 1300–2015." *Public Choice* 172:3-4 (September 2017), 443–463.

Parachini, John. "Aum Shinrikyo," in Brian A. Jackson, John C. Baker, Kim Cragin, John Parachini, Horacio R. Trujillo, and Peter Chalk, eds., *Aptitude for Destruction: Case Studies of Organizational Learning in Five Terrorist Groups*, Vol. 2. Santa Monica: RAND Corporation, 2005.

Patterson, Eric. *Politics in a Religious World: Building a Religiously Informed U.S. Foreign Policy.* New York: Continuum, 2011.

Paul, T. V. "Assessing Change in World Politics." *International Studies Review* 20 (2018), 177–185.

Payne, James L. "What Do the Terrorists Want?" *Independent Review* 13:1 (Summer 2008), 31.

Pease, Kelly-Kate S. *International Organizations.* Upper Saddle River, NJ: Pearson Prentice-Hall, 2008.

Perko, F. Michael. "Toward a 'Sound and Lasting Basis': Relations between the Holy See, the Zionist Movement, and Israel, 1896–1996." *Israel Studies* 2.1 (1997), 1.

Perica, Vjekoslav. *Balkan Idols: Religion and Nationalism in Yugoslav States.* Oxford: Oxford University Press, 2002.

Perović, Latinka. "Why Did Yugoslavia Fall Apart?" *Kosovo Times*, June 28, 2009.

Petersen, Marie Juul. "International Religious NGOs at the United Nations: A Study of a Group of Religious Organizations." *Journal of Humanitarian Assistance*, November 17, 2010.

Peterson, Anna L., and Brandt G. Peterson. "Martyrdom, Sacrifice, and Political Memory in El Salvador." *Social Research* 75:2 (Summer 2008), 522.

Peus, Claudia, Susanne Braun, and Birgit Schyns. *Leadership Lessons from Compelling Contexts.* Bingley, UK: Emerald Group, 2016.

Pew Research Center. "The Age Gap in Religion Around the World." June 13, 2018. https://www.pewforum.org/2018/06/13/the-age-gap-in-religion-around-the-world.

Pew Research Center. "A Closer Look at How Religious Restrictions Have Risen Around the World." July 14, 2019. https://www.pewforum.org/2019/07/15/a-closer-look-at-how-religious-restrictions-have-risen-around-the-world.

Pew Research Center. "The Future of World Religions: Population Growth Projections, 2010–2050." April 2, 2015. http://www.pewforum.org/2015/04/02/religious-projections-2010-2050.

Pew Research Center. "Tolerance and Tension: Islam and Christianity in Sub-Saharan Africa." April 15, 2010. https://www.pewforum.org/2010/04/15/executive-summary-islam-and-christianity-in-sub-saharan-africa.

Philpott, Daniel. "The Catholic Wave." *Journal of Democracy* 15:2 (April 2004), 32–46.

Philpott, Daniel. "The Challenge of September 11 to Secularism in International Relations." *World Politics* 55:1 (October 2002), 66–95.

Philpott, Daniel. "Explaining the Political Ambivalence of Religion." *American Political Science Review* 101:3 (August 2007), 505–525.

Philpott, Daniel. "Has the Study of Global Politics Found Religion?" *Annual Review of Political Science* 12 (2009), 183–202.

Philpott, Daniel. "The Religious Roots of Modern International Relations." *World Politics* 52:2 (January 2000), 206–245.

Philpott, Daniel. "Why Politics Can't Be Freed from Religion." *Politics, Religion & Ideology* 13:1 (March 2012).

Pipes, Daniel. "Islam and Islamism: Faith and Ideology." *Policy* 18:1 (Autumn 2002), 22–26.

Podolnjak, Robert. "'The Assent of the People Is Not Necessary to the Formation of a Confederation': Notes on the Failure of the European Constitutional Referendums." *Politička Misao* 43:5 (2006), 99–120.

Pollis, Adamantia. "Greece: A Problematic Secular State," in William Safran, ed., *The Secular and the Sacred: Nation, Religion and Politics.* Portland, OR: Frank Cass, 2003.

Potter, Lawrence G., ed. *Sectarian Politics in the Persian Gulf.* New York: Oxford University Press, 2014.

Powers, Gerard F. "Religion, Conflict and Prospects for Reconciliation in Bosnia, Croatia and Yugoslavia." *Journal of International Affairs* 50:1 (Summer 1996).

Prendes, Jorge Cáceres. "Political Radicalization and Popular Pastoral Practices in El Salvador, 1969–1985," in Scott Mainwaring and Alexander Wilde, eds., *The Progressive Church in Latin America.* Notre Dame, IN: University of Notre Dame Press, 1989.

Preston, Julia. "Pope Returns in Jubilation and Triumph to Nicaragua." *New York Times,* February 8, 1996.

al-Rahim, Ahmed H. "Inside Iraq's Confessional Politics." *Journal of Democracy* 19:1 (January 2008).

Ramet, Sabrina Petra. "The Serbian Church and the Serbian Nation," in Sabrina Petra Ramet and Donald W. Treadgold, eds., *Render unto Caesar: The Religious Sphere in World Politics.* Lanham, MD: American University Press, 1995.

Ramet, Sabrina Petra. "Serbia's Slobodan Milosevic: A Profile." *Orbis* 35:1 (Winter 1991).

Ramet, Sabrina Petra, and Donald W. Treadgold, eds. *Render unto Caesar: The Religious Sphere in World Politics.* Lanham, MD: American University Press, 1995.

Al-Rasheed, Madawi, and Marat Shterin. *Dying for Faith: Religiously Motivated Violence in the Contemporary World.* London and New York: I.B. Tauris, 2014.

Ray, James Lee, and Juliet Kaarbo. *Global Politics.* New York: Houghton Mifflin, 2002.

Rees, John A. "'Really Existing' Scriptures: On the Use of Sacred Text in International Affairs." *Brandywine Review of Faith and International Affairs* 2:1 (Spring 2004), 17–26.

Reychler, Luc. "Religion and Conflict." *International Journal of Peace Studies* 2:1 (January 1997).

Ribuffo, Leo. "Religion and American Foreign Policy." *The National Interest,* Summer 1998.

Richardson, David B. "Pope's Challenge to the Communists" *U.S. News & World Report,* June 18, 1979.

Rieff, David. *Slaughterhouse: Bosnia and the Failure of the West.* New York: Simon and Schuster, 1995.

Ritner, Susan Rennie. "The Dutch Reformed Church and Apartheid." *Journal of Contemporary History* 2:4 (October 1967).

Rochester, J. Martin. *Fundamental Principles of International Relations.* Boulder: Westview Press, 2010.

Rodden, John, and John Rossi. "Not Hitler's Pope." *American Conservative* 12:4 (July/August 2013), 35.

Rompalske, Dorothy. "Rock Star to the Rescue." *Biography* 6:10 (October 2002), 56.

Ronen, Yehudit. "Radical Islam versus the Nation-State: Violent Conflict in Northeast Africa and the Nile Valley," in Jonathan Fox, ed., *Religion, Politics, Society, and the State.* New York: Oxford University Press, 2012.

Rouleau, Eric. "Khomeini's Iran." *Foreign Affairs* 59:1 (Fall 1980), 1–20.

Rourke, John T., and Mark A. Boyer. *International Politics on the World Stage: Brief,* 8th ed. Dubuque, IA: McGraw-Hill, 2010.

Roy, Olivier. "Breakthroughs in Faith." *World Policy Journal* 28:4 (Winter 2011), 7–13.

Roy, Olivier. *The Failure of Political Islam.* Cambridge, MA: Harvard University Press, 1994.

Roy, Olivier. *Globalized Islam: The Search for a New Ummah.* New York: Columbia University Press, 2004.

Royal, Robert. "What Has the Vatican Done Globally?" *World & I* 12:12 (December 1997).
Rubin, Aviad. "The Status of Religion in Emergent Political Regimes: Lessons from Turkey and Israel." *Nations and Nationalism* 19:3 (2013), 496.
Rubin, Barry. "Religion and International Affairs," in Douglas Johnston and Cynthia Sampson, eds., *Religion, the Missing Dimension of Statecraft*. New York: Oxford University Press, 1994.
Rubin, Lawrence. *Islam in the Balance: Ideational Threats in Arab Politics*. Stanford: Stanford University Press, 2014.
Rupert, James. "Once-Secularist Saddam Discovers Benefits of Moslem Piety." *Washington Post*, October 9, 1990.
Russell, Greg. "Hans J. Morgenthau and the National Interest." *Society* 31:2 (January/February 1994).
Ryan, Missy. "Imagining Iraq, Defining Its Future." *World Policy Journal* 27:1 (Spring 2010).
Rychlak, Ronald J. "The 1933 Concordat Between Germany and the Holy See: A Reflection of Tense Relations." *The Digest: National Italian American Bar Association Law Journal* 23 (2001), 23–47.
Ryngaert, Cedric. "The Legal Status of the Holy See." *Goettingen Journal of International Law* 3 (2011).
Sabbah, Michel. "Religion and the Palestinian-Israeli Conflict." *Palestine-Israel Journal of Politics, Economics, and Culture* 20/21:4/1 (2015).
Safran, William. "Religion and *Laïcité* in a Jacobin Republic: The Case of France," in William Safran, ed. *The Secular and the Sacred: Nation, Religion and Politics*. Portland, OR: Frank Cass, 2003.
Safran, William, ed. *The Secular and the Sacred: Nation, Religion and Politics*. Portland, OR: Frank Cass, 2003.
Saideman, Stephen. "Explaining the International Relations of Secessionist Conflicts: Vulnerability Versus Ethnic Ties." *International Organization* 51:4 (Autumn, 1997), 721–753.
Schäfer, Heinrich. "The Janus Face of Religion: On the Religious Factor in 'New Wars.'" *Numen: International Review for the History of Religions* 51:4 (2004).
Schenker, Hillel. "Religion and the Conflict." *Palestine-Israel Journal of Politics, Economics, and Culture* 20/21:4/1 (2015), 129–144.
Schlesinger, Philip, and François Foret. "Political Roof and Sacred Canopy? Religion and the EU Constitution." *European Journal of Social Theory* 9:1 (2006), 59–81.
Schmidt, Blake. "The 'Not So Cordial' Church-State Relations in Nicaragua." *National Catholic Reporter* 45:15 (May 15, 2009).
Schneider, Mark and Paul Teske. "Toward a Theory of the Political Entrepreneur: Evidence from Local Government." *American Political Science Review* 86:3 (September 1992), 737–747.
Scott, James M., Ralph G. Carter, and A. Cooper Drury. *IR*. Boston: Wadsworth, 2014.
Seay, Laura. "Review of *The Lord's Resistance Army: Myth and Reality*, by Tim Allen and Koen Vlassenroot." *African Studies Review* 56:1 (April 2013), 184–186
Sedgwick, Mark. "Salafism, the Social, and the Global Resurgence of Religion." *Comparative Islamic Studies* 8:1/2 (2012).
Segesten, Anamaria Dutceac. *Myth, Identity, and Conflict: A Comparative Analysis of Romanian and Serbian Textbooks*. Lanham, MD: Lexington, 2011.
Seiple, Robert A., and Dennis R. Hoover, eds. *Religion and Security: The New Nexus in International Relations*. Lanham, MD: Rowman & Littlefield, 2004.
Sellam, Amar, and Mohamed Dellal. *Moroccan Culture in the 21st Century: Globalization, Challenges and Prospects*. Hauppauge, NY: Nova Science, 2013.
Sells, Michael. "Crosses of Blood: Sacred Space, Religion, and Violence in Bosnia-Herzegovina." *Sociology of Religion* 64:3 (Fall 2003).

Sells, Michael. "Kosovo Mythology and the Bosnian Genocide," in Omer Bartov and Phyllis Mack, eds., *In God's Name: Genocide and Religion in the Twentieth Century*. NY: Berghahn Books, 2001.

Sells, Michael. "Religion, History, and Genocide in Bosnia-Herzegovina," in G. Scott Davis, ed., *Religion and Justice in the War over Bosnia*. New York: Routledge, 1996.

Seul, Jeffrey R. "'Ours is the Way of God': Religion, Identity, and Intergroup Conflict." *Journal of Peace Research* 36:5 (September 1999), 553–569.

Seymour, Lee J. M., and Kathleen Gallagher Cunningham. "Identity Issues and Civil War," in T. David Mason and Sara McLaughlin Mitchell, eds., *What Do We Know About Civil War?* Lanham, MD: Roman & Littlefield, 2016.

Shah, Timothy Samuel, and Daniel Philpott. "The Fall and Rise of Religion in International Relations: History and Theory," in Jack Snyder, ed., *Religion and International Relations Theory*. New York: Columbia University Press, 2011.

Shah, Timothy Samuel, and Monica Duffy Toft. "Why God Is Winning." *Foreign Policy* 155 (July/August 2006), 38–43.

Shaker, Sallama, and Colleen Bromberger. "Chess Game of Civilizations." *Comparative Civilizations Review* 76:76 (2017), 58–69.

Shamir, Yair. "Our Shared Islamist Enemy." *Foreign Policy*, May 1, 2013.

Shane, Scott, Matthew Rosenberg, and Eric Lipton, "Fringe, Sinister View of Islam Now Steers the White House." *New York Times*, February 2, 2017.

Shapiro, Faydra K. "Taming Tehran: Evangelical Christians and the Iranian Threat to Israel," in Jonathan Fox, ed., *Religion, Politics, Society, and the State*. New York: Oxford University Press, 2012.

Shea, Nina. "Barbarism 2014: On Religious Cleansing by Islamists." *World Affairs* 177:4 (November/December 2014), 34–46.

Sheikh, Mona Kanwal. "How Does Religion Matter? Pathways to Religion in International Relations." *Review of International Studies* 38:2 (April 2012), 365–392.

Shelledy, Robert. "The Vatican's Role in Global Politics." *SAIS Review* 24:2 (Summer-Fall 2004), 149–162.

Shimko, Keith L. *International Relations: Perspectives, Controversies and Readings*, 4th ed. Boston: Wadsworth, 2013.

Shiraev, Eric B., and Vladislave M. Zubok. *International Relations*. New York: Oxford University Press, 2014.

Shortell, Timothy. "Radicalization of Religious Discourse in El Salvador: The Case of Oscar A. Romero." *Sociology of Religion* 62:1 (April 1, 2001).

Sikka, Sonia, and Lori G. Beaman. *Multiculturalism and Religious Identity: Canada and India*. Montreal: McGill-Queen's University Press, 2014.

Silverman, Adam. "Just War, Jihad, and Terrorism: A Comparison of Western and Islamic Norms for the Use of Political Violence." *Journal of Church and State* 44:1 (Winter 2002), 73–92.

Singh, Ana. "Religion and Politics: The Limitations of Secularism and Liberal Discourse in the Non-West." *Berkeley Political Review*, May 29, 2016.

Sisk, Timothy D. *Between Terror and Tolerance: Religious Leaders, Conflict, and Peacemaking*. Washington: Georgetown University Press, 2011.

Skidmore, Thomas E., and Peter H. Smith. *Modern Latin America*, 5th ed. New York: Oxford University Press, 2001.

Skocpol, Theda. "Rentier State and Shi'a Islam in the Iranian Revolution." *Theory and Society* 11:3 (May 1982).

Smith, Calvin L. "Pentecostal Presence, Power and Politics in Latin America." *Journal of Beliefs and Values* 30:3 (December 2009), 219–229

Smock, David R. *Religious Contributions to Peacemaking*. New York: Nova Science, 2010.

Snow, Donald M. *Cases in International Relations: Portraits of the Future*, 3rd ed. New York: Pearson Longman, 2008.

Snow, Donald M. *Cases in International Relations: Portraits of the Future*, 4th ed. New York: Pearson Education, 2010.

Snow, Donald M. *Cases in International Relations*, 5th ed. New York: Pearson Education, 2012.

Snyder, Jack. "One World, Rival Theories." *Foreign Policy* 145 (November/December 2004).

Snyder, Jack, ed. *Religion and International Relations Theory*. New York: Columbia University Press, 2011.

Soage, Ana Belen. "Islam and Modernity: The Political Thought of Sayyid Qutb." *Totalitarian Movements and Political Religions* 10:2 (June 2009).

Soper, J. Christopher, and Joel Fetzer. "Religion and Politics in a Secular Europe: Cutting Against the Grain," in Ted G. Jelen and Clyde Wilcox, eds., *Religion and Politics in Comparative Perspective: The One, the Few, and the Many*. New York: Cambridge University Press, 2002.

Spanring, Paul. *Dietrich Bonhoeffer and Arnold Koster: Two Distinct Voices in the Midst of Germany's Third Reich Turmoil*. Cambridge: James Clarke, 2014.

Sparks, Allister. *The Mind of South Africa*. New York: Knopf, 1990.

Spiegel, Steven L., Elizabeth G. Matthews, Jennifer M. Taw, and Kristen P. William. *World Politics in a New Era*, 6th ed. New York: Oxford University Press, 2015.

Spiegel, Steven L., and Fred L. Wehling. *World Politics in a New Era*, 2nd ed. New York: Harcourt Brace, 1999.

Springer, Devin R., James L. Regens, and David N. Edger. *Islamic Radicalism and Global Jihad*. Washington DC: Georgetown University Press, 2009.

Squires, Josephine E. "The Significance of Religion in British Politics," in William Safran, ed., *The Secular and the Sacred: Nation, Religion and Politics*. Portland, OR: Frank Cass, 2003.

Stahl, A. E. "'Offensive Jihad' in Sayyid Qutb's Ideology." International Institute for Counter-Terrorism, IDC Herziliya, March 24, 2011.

Stanley, Tim. "Pope Francis Is a Man of Peace – and Immense Political Power." *The Telegraph*, January 19, 2015.

Steele, David. "Christianity in Bosnia-Herzegovina and Kosovo," in Douglas Johnston, ed., *Faith-Based Diplomacy: Trumping Realpolitik*. New York: Oxford University Press, 2003.

Steger, Manfred B. "Religion and Ideology in the Global Age: Analyzing al Qaeda's Islamist Globalism." *New Political Science* 31:4 (December 2009), 538–539.

Stein, Ewan. "Studying Islam After the Arab Spring." *Mediterranean Politics* 19:1 (March 2004).

Stein, Sabina A. "Competing Political Science Perspectives on the Role of Religion in Conflict." *Politorbis* 52:2 (2011), 21–26.

Stepan, Alfred. "Religion, Democracy, and the 'Twin Tolerations.'" *Journal of Democracy* 11 (October 2000).

Stephenson, Wen. Review of *Balkan Ghosts: A Journey Through History*, by Robert D. Kaplan. *Chicago Review* 40:4 (1994), 93–98.

Stern, Jessica, and J.M. Berger. *ISIS: The State of Terror*. New York: HarperCollins, 2015.

Stevanović, Vidosav, and Trude Johansson. *Milosevic: The People's Tyrant*. London: I.B. Tauris, 2004.

Stigen, Jo. *The Relationship Between the International Criminal Court and National Jurisdictions: The Principle of Complementarity*. Leiden: Brill, 2008.

Stilt, Kristen. "'Islam Is the Solution': Constitutional Visions of the Egyptian Muslim Brotherhood." *Texas International Law Journal* 46:1 (Fall 2010).

Stoessinger, John G. *Why Nations Go to War*, 11th ed. Belmont, CA: Wadsworth/ Thomson Learning, 2011.

Sturm, Tristan. "The Future of Religious Geopolitics: Towards a Research and Theory Agenda." *Area* 45:2 (June 2013).

Subotic, Jelena. "Europe Is a State of Mind: Identity and Europeanization in the Balkans." *International Studies Quarterly* 55:2 (June 2011), 309–330.

Svensson, Isak. "One God, Many Wars: Religious Dimensions of Armed Conflict in the Middle East and North Africa." *Civil Wars* 15:4 (December 2013).

Szmolka, Inmaculada. "Political Change in North Africa and the Arab Middle East: Constitutional Reforms and Electoral Processes." *Arab Studies Quarterly* 36:2 (Spring 2014).

Szulc, Tad. "Papal Secrets." *Newsweek* 125:15 (April 10, 1995).

Szyliowicz, Joseph S. "Religion, Politics and Democracy in Turkey," in William Safran, ed., *The Secular and the Sacred: Nation, Religion and Politics*. Portland, OR: Frank Cass, 2003.

Takeyh, Ray. "All the Ayatollah's Men." *The National Interest* 121 (September/ October 2012), 51–61.

Talisse, Robert B. "Religion in Politics: What's The Problem?" *Think* 12:33 (Spring 2013), 65–73.

Tamadonfar, Mehran. "Islamism in Contemporary Politics: Lessons in Authoritarianism and Democratization," in Ted G. Jelen and Clyde Wilcox, *Religion and Politics in Comparative Perspective: The One, the Few, and the Many*. New York: Cambridge University Press, 2002.

Tannenwald, Nina. "Using Religion to Restrain Iran's Nuclear Program." *Foreign Policy*, February 24, 2012.

Taras, Ray. "Poland's Transition to a Democratic Republic: The Taming of the Sacred?" in William Safran, ed., *The Secular and the Sacred: Nation, Religion and Politics*. Portland, OR: Frank Cass, 2003.

Tatari, Eren, and Renat Shaykhutdinov. "Muslims and Minority Politics in Great Britain." *Journal of Muslim Minority* Affairs 34:1 (2014).

Taylor, Frances Grandy. "Ex-Foes Unite in Pursuit of Peace." *Hartford Courant*, June 8, 2004.

Tehranian, Majid. "Globalization and Religious Resurgence: An Historical Perspective." *Muslim World* 97:3 (July 2007).

Tepe, Sultan. *Beyond Sacred and Secular: Politics of Religion in Israel and Turkey*. Stanford: Stanford University Press, 2008.

Thomas, Scott M. "A Globalized God." *Foreign Affairs* 89:6 (November/December 2010), 93–101.

Thomas, Scott M. *The Global Resurgence of Religion and the Transformation of International Relations: The Struggle for the Soul of the Twenty-first Century*. New York and London: Palgrave, 2005.

Thomas, Scott M. "Outwitting the Developed Countries? Existential Insecurity and the Global Resurgence of Religion." *Journal of International Affairs* 61:1 (Fall/Winter 2007), 21–45.

Thompson, Peter G. *Armed Groups: The 21st Century Threat*. Lanham, MD: Rowman & Littlefield, 2014.

Tibi, Bassam. "The Politicization of Islam in the Context of Global Religious Fundamentalism: Islam as Political Religion," in Vasile Boari and Natalia Vlas, eds., *Religion and Politics in the 21st Century: Global and Local Reflections*. Newcastle upon Tyne: Cambridge Scholars, 2013.

Tickner, J. Ann. "You Just Don't Understand: Troubled Engagements Between Feminists and IR Theorists." *International Studies Quarterly* 41:4 (December 1997), 611–632.

Titeca, Kristof. "The Spiritual Order of the LRA," in Tim Allen and Koen Vlassenroot, eds., *The Lord's Resistance Army: Myth and Reality*. London: Zed, 2010.

Toft, Monica Duffy. "Getting Religion? The Puzzling Case of Islam and Civil War." *International Security* 31:4 (Spring 2007), 97–131.

Toft, Monica Duffy. "Religion, Rationality, and Violence," in Jack Snyder, ed., *Religion and International Relations Theory*. New York: Columbia University Press, 2011.

Toft, Monica Duffy, Daniel Philpott, and Timothy Samuel Shah. *God's Century: Resurgent Religion and Global Politics*. New York: Norton, 2011.

Toft, Monica Duffy, Daniel Philpott, and Timothy Samuel Shah. "God's Partisans Are Back." *Chronicle of Higher Education* 57:33 (April 22, 2011).

Tomé, Luís. "The 'Islamic State': Trajectory and Reach a Year After Its Self Proclamation as a 'Caliphate.'" *JANUS.NET e-journal of International Relations* 6:1 (May–October 2015).

Trager, Eric. "The Unbreakable Muslim Brotherhood." *Foreign Affairs* 90:5 (September/October 2011), 114–126.

Turner, Bryan S., ed. *War and Peace: Essays on Religion and Violence*. London: Anthem, 2013.

Turshen, Meredeth. "Militarism and Islamism in Algeria." *Journal of Asian and African Studies* 39:1-2 (January–March 2004).

Tutu, Desmond. "The Struggle for Social Justice in Post-Apartheid South Africa." *Peace Research* 37:1 (May 2005).

Ullah, Haroon K. *Vying for Allah's Vote: Understanding Islamic Parties, Political Violence, and Extremism in Pakistan*. Washington DC: Georgetown University Press, 2013.

United States Commission on International Religious Freedom. "China," *Annual Report 2019*.

United States Commission on International Religious Freedom. "India." *Annual Report 2019*.

Ünver, Akin. "Schrödinger's Kurds: Transnational Kurdish Geopolitics in the Age of Shifting Borders." *Journal of International Affairs* 69:2 (Spring/Summer 2016), 88.

Uzer, Umut. *Identity and Turkish Foreign Policy: The Kemalist Influence in Cyprus and the Caucasus*. London: I.B. Tauris, 2011.

Van Slooten, Pippi. "Dispelling Myths About Islam and Jihad." *Peace Review* 17:2/3 (April–September 2005).

Van Wyk, Jo-Ansie. "Joseph Kony and the Lord's Resistance Army," in Caroline Varin and Dauda Abubakar, eds., *Violent Non-State Actors in Africa: Terrorists, Rebels and Warlords*. New York: Palgrave Macmillan, 2017.

van Wyk, Martha. "Sunset over Atomic Apartheid: United States–South African Nuclear Relations, 1981–93." *Cold War History* 10:1 (2010), 55.

Velikonja, Mitja. "In Hoc Signo Vinces: Religious Symbolism in the Balkan Wars 1991–1995." *International Journal of Politics, Culture, and Society* 17:1 (January 2003), 25–40.

Von Laue, Theodore H. *Why Lenin? Why Stalin? A Reappraisal of the Russian Revolution*. Philadelphia: Lippincott, Williams & Wilkins, 1971.

Wald, Kenneth D. "The Religious Dimension of Israeli Political Life," in Ted G. Jelen and Clyde Wilcox, eds., *Religion and Politics in Comparative Perspective: The One, the Few, and the Many*. New York: Cambridge University Press, 2002.

Wald, Kenneth D., and Allison Calhoun-Brown. *Religion and Politics in the United States*, 5th ed. Lanham, MD: Rowman & Littlefield, 2007.

Wald, Kenneth D., and Samuel Shye. "Interreligious Conflict in Israel: The Group Basis of Conflicting Visions." *Political Behavior* 16:1 (March 1994), 157–178.

Walsh, Declan. "Heads of Muslim Nations Not Targeted Are Conspicuously Silent." *New York Times*, January 30, 2017.

Walt, Stephen. "International Relations: One World, Many Theories." *Foreign Policy* 110 (Spring 1998).

Waltz, Kenneth N. "Explaining War," in Paul R. Viotti and Mark V. Kauppi, eds., *International Relations Theory: Realism, Pluralism, Globalism*, 2nd ed. New York: Macmillan, 1993.

Wang, Yaqiu. "Despite China-Vatican Agreement, Many Chinese Worry About Religious Freedom." Human Rights Watch, October 5, 2018.

Warhola, James W. "The Kremlin's Religion Temptation." *Current History* 106:702 (October 2007), 340–345.

Warr, Kevin. "The Normative Promise of Religious Organizations in Global Civil Society." *Journal of Church and State* 41:3 (Summer 1999), 499–523.

Warwick, Joby. *Black Flags: The Rise of ISIS.* New York: Doubleday, 2015.

Wass de Czege, Huba. "Defeating the Abu Bakr al Baghdadi Gang: A Realistic Strategy." *Small Wars Journal*, December 25, 2015.

Weigel, George. "Papacy and Power." *First Things: A Monthly Journal of Religion and Public Life*, February 2001.

Weigel, George. "Religion and Peace: An Argument Complexified," in Sheryl J. Brown and Kimber M. Schraub, eds., *Resolving Third World Conflict: Challenges for a New Era*. Washington: United States Institute of Peace, 1992.

Wiarda, Howard J. *Political Culture, Political Science, and Identity Politics: An Uneasy Alliance*. New York: Routledge, 2014.

Wilcox, Clyde, Lawrence C. Reardon, and Paul Christopher Manuel. *The Catholic Church and The Nation-State: Comparative Perspectives*. Washington: Georgetown University Press, 2006.

Wood, Graeme. "What Isis Really Wants." *Atlantic* 315:2 (March 2015).

Woodward, Kenneth L. "An Oxymoron: Europe without Christianity." *New York Times*, June 14, 2003.

Wooldridge, Adrian. "God Is Back." *Society* 53:2 (April 2016), 137–141.

Wright, Robin. *Rock the Casbah: Rage and Rebellion across the Islamic World*. New York: Simon and Schuster, 2011.

Yavuz, M. Hakan. "Political Islam and the Welfare (Refah) Party." *Comparative Politics* 30:1 (October 1997), 63–82.

Yilmaz, Ihsan. "Transnational Islam." *European Journal of Economic and Political Studies* 3 (2010), 1–5.

Youngs, Gillian. "Feminist International Relations." *International Affairs* 80:1 (2004), 75–87.

Zainiddinov, Hakim. "Religion and the State in Russia and China: Suppression, Survival, and Revival." *Europe-Asia Studies* 64:4 (June 2012), 799.

Zhang, Laney. "China: Revised Regulations on Religious Affairs." Library of Congress, November 9, 2017.

Zimmermann, Carol. "Religion Must Be Key Part of Foreign Policy, Says Madeleine Albright." April 11, 2016. https://catholicphilly.com/2016/04/news/national-news/religion-must-be-key-part-of-foreign-policy-says-madeleine-albright.

Zubaida, Sami. "Is Iran an Islamic State?" in Joel Beinin and Joe Stork, eds., *Political Islam: Essays from Middle East Report*. Berkeley: University of California Press, 1997.

Zuckerman, Phil. *Society Without God: What the Least Religious Nations Can Tell Us About Contentment*. New York: New York University Press, 2008.

Index

About the Book

The premise of this new text is straightforward: Religion matters in world politics. Therefore, to comprehend the world around us, we need to understand how and why religion matters, analyze the interaction in a systematic way, and have a framework in which to fit facts and events that we cannot yet anticipate. The goal of *Religion and Politics on the World Stage* is to provide the information and tools necessary to accomplish those tasks.

Designed with undergraduate students in mind, the book:
- Explains theories, trends, assumptions, and situations in an accessible way.
- Consistently applies an international relations framework.
- Presents individual, state, and global levels of analysis.

The vignettes that open each chapter, depicting key aspects of the nexus between religion and world politics, quickly engage readers and serve as compelling entryways into discussions of broader issues.

Lynda K. Barrow is professor of political science at Coe College.